Barren Ground

Books by Ellen Glasgow

Barren
Ground

by Ellen
Glasgow

WITH A PREFACE BY THE AUTHOR

SAGAMORE PRESS INC · NEW YORK · 1957

Preface

If I might select one of my books for the double-edged blessing of immortality, that book would be, I think, *Barren Ground*. Not only is this the kind of novel I like to read and had always wished to write, but it became for me, while I was working upon it, almost a vehicle of liberation. After years of tragedy and the sense of defeat that tragedy breeds in the mind, I had won my way to the other side of the wilderness, and had discovered, with astonishment, that I was another and a very different person. When I looked back, all my earlier work, except *Virginia*, the evocation of an ideal, appeared so thin that it seemed two-dimensional. All the forms in which I had thought and by which I had lived, even the substance of things and the very shape of my universe, had shifted and changed. The past was still there, but it was scarcely more solid than the range of clouds on the horizon. And while I realized this, I knew also that different and better work was ahead. Many other writers may have had this experience. I do not know. It is not a conversion of which one speaks often and naturally.

As a young girl, thinking over my first book, I had resolved that I would write of the South not sentimentally, as a conquered province, but dispassionately, as a part of the larger world. I had resolved that I would write not of Southern characteristics, but of human nature. Now, at this turning-point in my life, these early resolutions awoke again with a fresh impulse. It is true that I have portrayed the Southern landscape, with which I am familiar, that I have tried to be accurate in detail, to achieve external verisimilitude; but this outward fidelity, though important, is not essential to my interpretation of life. The significance of my work, the quickening spirit, would not have varied, I believe, had I been born anywhere else. For me, the novel is experience illumined by imagination, and the word "experience" conveys something more than an attitude or a gesture. In *Barren Ground*, as in *The Sheltered Life*, I felt that the scene, apart from the human figures, possessed an added dimension, a universal rhythm deeper and more fluid than any material texture. Beneath the lights and shadows there is the brooding spirit of place, but, deeper still, beneath the spirit of place there is the whole movement of life.

For the setting of this book, I went back into the past and gathered vivid recollections of my childhood. The country is as familiar to me as if the landscape unrolled both within and without. I had known every feature for years, and the saturation of my subject with the mood of sustained melancholy was effortless and complete. The houses, the roads, the woods, the endless fields of broomsedge and scrub pine, the low immeasurable horizon,—all these objects I had seen with the remembering eyes of a child. And time, like a mellow haze, had preserved the impressions unaltered. They were the lighter semblances folded over the heart of the book.

But Dorinda, though she had been close to me for ten years before I began her story, is universal. She exists wherever a human being has learned to live without joy, wherever the spirit of fortitude has triumphed over the sense of futility. The book is hers; and all minor themes, episodes, and impressions are blended with the one dominant meaning that character is fate. Blended by life, not imposed by the novel. Though I wrote always toward an end that I saw (I can imagine no other way of writing a book), Dorinda was free, while the theme was still undeveloped, to grow, to change, to work out her own destiny. From many parts of the world she has written to me; from Scotland, from Germany, from Australia, from South Africa, and at least once from China.

ELLEN GLASGOW

Richmond, Virginia, January, 1933.

Part First   Broomsedge

A girl in an orange-coloured shawl ...

1

A girl in an orange-coloured shawl stood at the window of Pedlar's store and looked, through the falling snow, at the deserted road. Though she watched there without moving, her attitude, in its stillness, gave an impression of arrested flight, as if she were running toward life.

Bare, starved, desolate, the country closed in about her. The last train of the day had gone by without stopping, and the station of Pedlar's Mill was as lonely as the abandoned fields by the track. From the bleak horizon, where the flatness created an illusion of immensity, the broomsedge was spreading in a smothered fire over the melancholy brown of the landscape. Under the falling snow, which melted as soon as it touched the earth, the colour was veiled and dim; but when the sky changed the broomsedge changed with it. On clear mornings the waste places were cinnamon-red in the sunshine. Beneath scudding clouds the plumes of the bent grasses faded to ivory. During the long spring rains, a film of yellow-green stole over the burned ground. At autumn sunsets, when the red light searched the country, the broomsedge caught fire from the afterglow and blazed out in a splendour of colour. Then the meeting of earth and sky dissolved in the flaming mist of the horizon.

At these quiet seasons, the dwellers near Pedlar's Mill felt scarcely more than a tremor on the surface of life. But on stormy days, when the wind plunged like a hawk from the swollen clouds, there was a quivering in the broomsedge, as if coveys of frightened partridges were flying from the pursuer. Then the quivering would become a ripple and the ripple would swell presently into rolling waves. The straw would darken as the gust swooped down, and brighten as it sped on to the shelter of scrub pine and sassafras. And while the

3

wind bewitched the solitude, a vague restlessness would stir in the hearts of living things on the farms, of men, women, and animals. "Broomsage ain't jest wild stuff. It's a kind of fate," old Matthew Fairlamb used to say.

Thirty years ago, modern methods of farming, even methods that were modern in the benighted eighteen-nineties, had not penetrated to this thinly settled part of Virginia. The soil, impoverished by the war and the tenant system which followed the war, was still drained of fertility for the sake of the poor crops it could yield. Spring after spring, the cultivated ground appeared to shrink into the "old fields," where scrub pine or oak succeeded broomsedge and sassafras as inevitably as autumn slipped into winter. Now and then a new start would be made. Some thrifty settler, a German Catholic, perhaps, who was trying his fortunes in a staunch Protestant community, would buy a mortgaged farm for a dollar an acre, and begin to experiment with suspicious, strange-smelling fertilizers. For a season or two his patch of ground would respond to the unusual treatment and grow green with promise. Then the forlorn roads, deep in mud, and the surrounding air of failure, which was as inescapable as a drought, combined with the cutworm, the locust, and the tobacco-fly, against the human invader; and where the brief harvest had been, the perpetual broomsedge would wave.

The tenant farmers, who had flocked after the ruin of war as buzzards after a carcass, had immediately picked the featureless landscape as clean as a skeleton. When the swarming was over only three of the larger farms at Pedlar's Mill remained undivided in the hands of their original owners. Though Queen Elizabeth County had never been one of the aristocratic regions of Virginia, it was settled by sturdy English yeomen, with a thin but lively sprinkling of the persecuted Protestants of other nations. Several of these superior pioneers brought blue blood in their veins, as well as the vigorous fear of God in their hearts; but the great number arrived, as they remained, "good people," a comprehensive term, which implies, to Virginians, the exact opposite of the phrase, "a good family." The good families of the state have preserved, among other things, custom, history, tradition, romantic fiction, and the Episcopal Church. The good people, according to the records of clergymen, which are the only surviving records, have preserved nothing except

4

themselves. Ignored alike by history and fiction, they have their inconspicuous place in the social strata midway between the lower gentility and the upper class of "poor white," a position which encourages the useful rather than the ornamental public virtues.

With the end of free labour and the beginning of the tenant system, authority passed from the country to the towns. The old men stayed by the farms, and their daughters withered dutifully beside them; but the sons of the good people drifted away to the city, where they assumed control of democracy as well as of the political machine which has made democracy safe for politics. An era changed, not rudely, but as eras do change so often, uncomfortably. Power, defying Jeffersonian theory and adopting Jeffersonian policy, stole again from the few to the many. For the good people, conforming to the logic of history, proceeded immediately to enact their preferences, prejudices, habits, and inhibitions into the laws of the state.

At Pedlar's Mill, where the old wooden mill, built a hundred years before by the first miller Pedlar, was now a picturesque ruin, a few stalwart farmers of Scotch-Irish descent rose above the improvident crowd of white and black tenants, like native pines above the shallow wash of the broomsedge. These surviving landowners were obscure branches of the great Scotch-Irish families of the upper Valley of Virginia. Detached from the parent tree and driven by chance winds out of the highlands, they had rooted afresh in the warmer soil of the low country, where they had conquered the land not by force, but by virtue of the emphatic argument that lies in fortitude.

James Ellgood, whose mother was a McNab, owned Green Acres, the flourishing stock farm on the other side of the railroad. It is true that an uncle in the far West had left him a small fortune, and for five years he had put more into the soil than he had got out of it. But in the end Green Acres had repaid him many times, which proved, as old Matthew, who was a bit of a philosopher, pointed out, that "it wa'n't the land that was wrong, but the way you had treated it."

On the near side of the station, secluded behind a barricade of what people called the back roads, which were strangled in mud from November to June, stood Five Oaks, the ruined farm of the

Greylocks. Though the place was still held insecurely in the loose clutches of old Doctor Greylock, who resembled an inebriated Covenanter, the abandoned acres were rapidly growing up in sumach, sassafras, and life-everlasting. The doctor had been a man of parts and rural prominence in his day; but the land and scarcity of labour had worn on his nerves, and he was now slowly drinking himself to death, attended, beyond the social shadow-line, by an anonymous brood of mulatto offspring.

Adjoining Five Oaks, and running slightly in front of it on one side, with a long whitewashed house situated a stone's throw from the main road, there was Old Farm, which belonged to Joshua Oakley and Eudora Abernethy, his wife. The Oakleys, as the saying ran in the neighbourhood, were "land poor." They owned a thousand acres of scrub pine, scrub oak, and broomsedge, where a single cultivated corner was like a solitary island in some chaotic sea.

Early in the nineteenth century, John Calvin Abernethy, a retired missionary from India and Ceylon, came from the upper Valley into the region of the Shenandoah, with a neat Scotch-Irish inheritance in his pocket. His reputation, as historians remark, had preceded him; and his subsequent career proved that he was not only an eloquent preacher of the Gospel, but a true explorer of the spirit as well, the last of those great Presbyterian romantics whose faith ventured on perilous metaphysical seas in the ark of the Solemn League and Covenant. Since there was no canny bargain to be driven, at the moment, in the Shenandoah Valley, John Abernethy regretfully left the highlands for the flat country, where he picked up presently, at a Dutch auction, the thousand acres of land and fifty slaves which had belonged to one William Golden Penner. One may charitably infer that the fifty slaves constituted a nice point in theology; but with ingenious Presbyterian logic and circumscribed Presbyterian imagination, John Calvin reconciled divine grace with a peculiar institution. The fifty slaves he sold farther south, and the price of black flesh he devoted to the redemption of black souls in the Congo. Dramatic, yet not altogether lacking in delicate irony. For he had observed in foreign fields that divine grace has strange gestures; and life, as even Presbyterians know, is without logic. To a thrifty theologian, bent on redemption with economy, there are few points of ethics too fine-spun for splitting.

6

From which it must not be concluded that the first Virginian Abernethy was unworthy of his high calling. He was merely, like the rest of us, whether theologians or laymen, seasoned with the favourite fruit of his age. Though he might occasionally seek a compromise in simple matters of conduct, realizing the fall of man and the infirmity of human nature, where matters of doctrine were concerned his conscience was inflexible. His piety, running in a narrow groove, was deep and genuine; and he possessed sufficient integrity, firmness, and frugality to protect his descendants from decay for at least three generations. A few years after he had settled near Pedlar's Mill, a small Presbyterian church, built of brick and whitewashed within and without, rose on the far side of the railroad, where it stands now at the gate of Green Acres. Conversion, which had begun as a vocation with John Calvin Abernethy, became a habit; and with the gradual running to seed of the Methodists in the community, the Presbyterian faith sprang up and blossomed like a Scotch thistle in barren ground.

In his long white house, encircled by the few cultivated fields in the midst of his still-virgin acres, John Calvin Abernethy lived with learning, prudence, and piety until he was not far from a hundred. He had but one son, for unlike the Scotch-Irish of the Valley, his race did not multiply. The son died in middle age, struck down by an oak he was felling, and his only child, a daughter, was reared patiently but sternly by her grandfather. When, in after years, this granddaughter, whose name was Eudora, fell a victim of one of those natural instincts which Presbyterian theology has damned but never wholly exterminated, and married a member of the "poor white" class, who had nothing more to recommend him than the eyes of a dumb poet and the head of a youthful John the Baptist, old Abernethy blessed the marriage and avoided, as far as possible, the connection. Knowing the aptitude of the poor for futility, he employed his remaining years on earth in accumulating a comfortable inheritance for his great-grandchildren. When he was dead, his granddaughter's husband, young Joshua Oakley, worked hard, after the manner of his class, to lose everything that was left. He was a good man and a tireless labourer; but that destiny which dogs the footsteps of ineffectual spirits pursued him from the hour of his birth. His wife, Eudora, who resembled her grandfather, recovered

7

promptly from the natural instinct, and revealed shortly afterwards signs of suppressed religious mania.

Of this union of the positive and the negative virtues, three children survived. Two of these were sons, Josiah and Rufus; the other was a daughter, Dorinda, the girl who, having thrown the orange shawl over her head, had come out of the store, and stood now with the snow in her face and her eager gaze on the road.

2

She was a tall girl, not beautiful, scarcely pretty even according to the waxen type of the 'nineties; but there was a glow of expression, an April charm, in her face. Her eyes were her one memorable feature. Large, deep, radiant, they shone beneath her black lashes with a clear burning colour, as blue as the spring sky after rain. Above them her jutting eyebrows, very straight and thick, gave a brooding sombreness to her forehead, where her abundant hair was brushed back in a single dark wave. In repose her features were too stern, too decisive. Her nose, powdered with golden freckles, was a trifle square at the nostrils; her mouth, with its ripe, beestung lower lip, was wide and generous; the pointed curve of her chin revealed, perhaps, too much determination in its outward thrust. But the rich dark red in her cheeks lent vividness to her face, and when she smiled her eyes and mouth lighted up as if a lamp shone within. Against the sordid background of the store, her head in the brilliant shawl was like some exotic flower.

Straight, tranquil, thin and fugitive as mist, the snow was falling. Though the transparent flakes vanished as soon as they reached the earth, they diffused in their steady flight an impression of evanescence and unreality. Through this shifting medium the familiar scene appeared as insubstantial as a pattern of frost on the grass. It was as if the secret spirit of the land had traced an image on the flat surface, glimmering, remote, unapproachable, like the expression of an animal that man has forced into sullen submission. There were hours at twilight, or beneath the shredded clouds of the sunrise, when the winter landscape reminded Dorinda of the look in the faces of overworked farm horses. At such moments she would find herself asking, with the intellectual thrill of the heretic, "I wonder if everything has a soul?" The country had been like this, she knew, long before she was born. It would be like this, she sometimes thought, after she and all those who were living with her were dead. For the one thing that seemed to her immutable and everlasting was the poverty of the soil.

Without knowing that she looked at it, her gaze rested on the bare station; on the crude frame buildings, like houses that children make out of blocks; on the gleaming track which ran north and south; on the old freight car, which was the home of Butcher, the lame negro who pumped water into the engines; on the litter of chips and shavings and dried tobacco stems which strewed the ground between the telegraph poles and the hitching-rail by the store. Farther away, in the direction of Whippernock River, she could see the vague shape of the ruined mill, and beyond this, on the other side of the track, the sunken road winding in scallops through interminable acres of broomsedge. Though the snow had fallen continuously since noon, the air was not cold, and the white glaze on the earth was scarcely heavier than hoar-frost.

For almost a year now, ever since Mrs. Pedlar had fallen ill of consumption, and Dorinda had taken her place in the store, the girl had listened eagerly for the first rumble of the approaching trains. Until to-day the passing trains had been a part of that expected miracle, the something different in the future, to which she looked ahead over the tedious stretch of the present. There was glamour for her in the receding smoke. There was adventure in the silver-blue of the distance. The glimpse of a rapidly disappearing face; a glance from strange eyes that she remembered; the shadowy outline of a gesture; these tenuous impressions ran like vivid threads in her memory. Her nature, starved for emotional realities, and nourished on the gossamer substance of literature, found its only escape in the fabrication of dreams. Though she had never defined the sensation in words, there were moments when it seemed to her that her inner life was merely a hidden field in the landscape, neglected, monotonous, abandoned to solitude, and yet with a smothered fire, like the wild grass, running through it. At twenty, her imagination was enkindled by the ardour that makes a woman fall in love with a religion or an idea. Some day, so ran the bright thread of her dream, the moving train would stop, and the eyes that had flashed into hers and passed by would look at her again. Then the stranger who was not a stranger would say, "I knew your face among a thousand, and I came back to find you." And the train would rush on with them into the something different beyond the misty edge of the horizon. Adventure, happiness, even unhappiness, if it were only different!

That was yesterday. To-day the miracle had occurred, and the whole of life had blossomed out like a flower in the sun. She had found romance, not in imagination, not in the pallid fiction crushed among the tomes in her great-grandfather's library, but driving on one of the muddy roads through the broomsedge. To the casual observer there was merely a personable young man, the son of old Doctor Greylock, making the scattered rural calls of a profession which his father was too drunk to pursue. A pleasant young man, intelligent, amiable, still wearing with a difference the thin veneer of the city. Though he was, perhaps, a trifle too eager to please, this was a commendable fault, and readily overlooked in an irreproachable son who had relinquished his ambition in order to remain with his undeserving old father. Filial devotion was both esteemed and practised in that pre-Freudian age, before self-sacrifice had been dethroned from its precarious seat among the virtues; and to give up one's career for a few months, at most for a possible year, appeared dutiful rather than dangerous to a generation that knew not psychoanalysis.

And he was not only an admirable young man, he was, what admirable young men frequently are not, attractive as well. His dark red hair, burnished to a copper glow, grew in a natural wave; his sparkling eyes were brown-black like chinkapins in the autumn; his skin was tanned and slightly freckled, with a healthy glow under the surface; his short moustache, a shade lighter than his hair, lent mystery to a charming, if serious, mouth, and his smile, indiscriminating in its friendliness, was wholly delightful. To Dorinda, meeting him in the early morning as she was walking the two miles from Old Farm to the store, it was as if an April flush had passed over the waste places. She recognized love with the infallible certainty of intuition. It was happiness, and yet in some strange way it was shot through with a burning sensation which was less pleasure than pain. Though her perceptions were more vivid than they had

11

ever been, there was an unreality about her surroundings, as if she were walking in some delicious trance. Beautiful as it was, it seemed to be vanishing, like a beam of light, in the very moment when she felt it flooding her heart. Yet this sense of unreality, of elusiveness, made it more precious. Watching the empty roads, through the veil of snow, she asked herself every minute, "Will he come this way again? Shall I wait for him, or shall I let him pass me in the road? Suppose he goes back another way! Suppose he has forgotten——"

The door behind her opened, and old Matthew Fairlamb came hobbling out with the help of his stout hickory stick. Though he was approaching ninety, he was still vigorous, with a projecting thatch of hair as colourless as straw and the aquiline profile of a Roman senator. In his youth, and indeed until his old age, when his son William succeeded him, he had been the best carpenter at Pedlar's Mill. His eyes were bleared now, and his gums toothless; but he had never lost his shrewd Scotch-Irish understanding or his sense of humour, which broke out in flashes as swift and darting as dry-weather lightning.

"You'd better be startin' home, Dorinda," he remarked as he passed her. "The snow means to keep up, and yo' Ma will begin to worry about you." Turning, he peered at her with his cackling laugh. "Yo' face looks like a May mornin' to my old eyes," he added. "I ain't seen you about here fur a couple of weeks."

With her gaze still on the distance, Dorinda answered impatiently, "No, Ma had one of her bad spells, and I had to help out at home. But no matter how sick she is she never gives up, and she never worries about anything smaller than eternal damnation."

"Yes, she's a pious one," old Matthew conceded. "It's faith, I reckon, that's kept her goin', sence the Lord must know He ain't made it none too easy for her."

"Oh, it's hard work that she lives on," replied Dorinda. "She says if she were to stop working, she'd drop down dead like a horse that is winded. She never stops, not even on Sundays, except when she is in church."

Old Matthew's hilarity dwindled into a sigh. "Well, thar ain't much rest to be got out of that," he rejoined sympathetically. "I ain't contendin' against the doctrine of eternal damnation," he hastened to explain, "but as long as yo' Ma is obleeged to work so

12

hard, 'tis a pity she ain't got a mo' restful belief." Then, as he observed her intent gaze, he inquired suspiciously, "You don't see nary a turnout on the road, do you?"

The dark red in the girl's cheeks brightened to carnation. "Why, of course not. I was just watching the snow."

But his curiosity, once aroused, was as insatiable as avarice. "I don't reckon you've seen whether young Doctor Greylock has gone by or not?"

She shook her head, still blushing. "No, I haven't seen him. Is anybody sick at your place?"

"It ain't that," returned the old man. "I was just thinkin' he might give me a lift on the way. It ain't more'n half a mile to my place, but half a mile looks different to twenty and to eighty-odd years. He's a spry young chap, and would make a good match for you, Dorinda," he concluded in merciless accents.

Dorinda's head was turned away, but her voice sounded smothered. "You needn't worry about that." (Why did old age make people so hateful?) "I haven't seen him but once since he came home."

"Well, he'll look long befo' he finds a likelier gal than you. I ain't seen him more than a few times myself; but in these parts, whar young men are as skeerce as wild turkeys, he won't have to go beggin'. Geneva Ellgood would take him in a minute, I reckon, an' her Pa is rich enough to buy her a beau in the city, if she wants one, hee-hee!" His malicious cackle choked him. "They do say that young Jason was sweet on her in New York last summer," he concluded when he had recovered.

For the first time Dorinda turned her head and looked in his face. "If everybody believed your gossip, Mr. Fairlamb, nobody at Pedlar's Mill would be speaking to anybody else."

Old Matthew's mouth closed like a nut-cracker; but she saw from the twinkle in his bleared eyes that he had construed her reprimand into a compliment. "Thar's some of 'em that wouldn't lose much by that," he returned, after a pause. "But to come back to young Jason, he's got a job ahead of him if he's goin' to try farmin' at Five Oaks, an' he'll need either a pile of money or a hard-workin' wife."

"Oh, he doesn't mean to stay here. As soon as his father dies, he will go back to New York."

The detestable cackle broke out again. "The old man ain't dead yit. I've known some hard drinkers to have long lives, an' thar ain't nothin' more wearin' on the young than settin' down an' waitin' fur old folks to die. Young Jason is a pleasant-mannered boy, though he looks a bit too soft to stand the hard wear of these here roads. I ain't got nothin' to say aginst him, but if he'd listen to the warnin' of eighty-odd years, he'd git away before the broomsage ketches him. Thar's one thing sartain sure, you've got to conquer the land in the beginning, or it'll conquer you before you're through with it."

It was all true. She had heard it before, and yet, though she knew it was true, she refused to believe it. Whether it was true or not, she told herself passionately, it had no connection with Jason Greylock. The bright vision she had seen in the road that morning flickered and died against the sombre monochrome of the landscape.

"I must go in," she said, turning away. "I haven't time to stand talking." Old Matthew would never stop, she knew, of his own accord. When his cackle rose into a laugh the sound reminded her of the distant *who—who—whoee* of an owl.

"Well, I'll be gittin' along too," replied the old man. "My eyes ain't all they used to be, and my legs ain't fur behind 'em. Remember me to yo' Ma, honey, and tell her I'll be lookin' over jest as soon as the mud holes dry up."

"Yes, I'll tell her," answered the girl more gently. Old Matthew had known her great-grandfather; he had added the wings to the house at Old Farm and built the Presbyterian church on the other side of the track. In the prime of his life, forty years ago, he had been the last man at Pedlar's Mill to see Gordon Kane, her mother's missionary lover, who had died of fever in the Congo. It was old Matthew, Dorinda had heard, who had broken the news of Kane's death to the weeping Eudora, while she held her wedding dress in her hands. Disagreeable as he had become, it was impossible for the girl to forget that his long life was bound up with three generations of her family.

When she entered the store, she felt for a moment that she should suffocate in the heated air from the wood stove at the far end. The stuffy smell, a mingling of turpentine, varnish, bacon, coffee, and kerosene oil, was so different from the crystal breath of the falling snow that it rushed over her like warm ashes, smothering, envelop-

14

ing. Yet there was nothing strange to her in the scene or the atmosphere. She was accustomed to the close, dry heat and to the heavy odours of a place where everything that one could not raise on a farm was kept and sold. For eleven months she had worked here side by side with Nathan Pedlar, and she was familiar with the usual stock-in-trade of a country store. In a minute she could put her hand on any object from a plough-share to a darning-needle.

"You'd better be going home early," said Nathan Pedlar, looking round from the shelf he was putting in order. "The snow may get heavier toward sunset."

He was a tall, lank, scraggy man, with a face that reminded Dorinda of a clown that she had once seen in a circus. Only the clown's nose was large and red, and Nathan's looked as if it had been mashed in by a blow. Aunt Mehitable Green, the coloured midwife, insisted that his features had been born like other children's, but that his mother had rolled on him in her sleep when he was a baby, and had flattened his nose until it would never grow straight again. Though he possessed a reserve of prodigious strength, he failed to be impressive even as an example of muscular development. Dorinda had worked with him every day for eleven months, and yet she found that he had made as little impression upon her as a pine tree by the roadside. Looking at him, she saw clearly his gaunt round shoulders beneath the frayed alpaca coat, his hair and eyebrows and short moustache, all the colour of dingy rabbit fur, and his small grey eyes with blinking lids; but the moment after he had passed out of her sight, the memory of him would become as fluid as water and trickle out of her mind. A kind but absurd man, this was the way she thought of him, honest, plodding, unassuming, a man whose "word was as good as his bond," but whose personality was negligible. The truth about him, though Dorinda never suspected it, was that he had come into the world a quarter of a century too soon. He was so far in advance of his age that his position inspired ridicule instead of respect in his generation. When his lagging age had caught up with Nathan Pedlar, it had forgotten what its prophet had prophesied. Though he made a comfortable living out of the store, and had put by enough to enable him to face old age with equanimity, he was by nature a farmer, and his little farm near the mill yielded a good harvest. Unlike most Southern

15

farmers, he was not afraid of a theory, and he was beginning to realize the value of rotation in crops at a period when a corn-field at Pedlar's Mill was as permanent as a graveyard. Already he was experimenting with alfalfa, though even the prosperous James Ellgood made fun of "the weed with the highfalutin' name from the Middle West." For it was a part of Nathan's perverse destiny that people asked his advice with recklessness and accepted it with deliberation.

"I am going as soon as I speak to Rose Emily," Dorinda replied. "Did the doctor say she was better this morning?"

Nathan's hands, which were fumbling among the boxes on the long shelf, became suddenly still.

"No, he didn't say so," he answered, without turning.

Something in his tone made Dorinda catch her breath sharply. "He didn't say she was worse, did he?"

At this Nathan pushed the boxes away and leaned over the counter to meet her eyes. His face was bleak with despair, and Dorinda's heart was wrung as she looked at him. She had often wondered how Rose Emily could have married him. Poverty would have been happiness, she felt, compared with so prosaic a marriage; yet she knew that, according to the standards of Pedlar's Mill, Nathan was an exceptional husband.

"Perhaps she'll pick up when the spring comes," she added when he did not reply.

Nathan shook his head and swallowed as if a pebble had lodged in his throat. "That's what I'm hoping," he answered. "If she can just get on her feet again. There's nothing this side of heaven I wouldn't do to make her well."

For an instant she was afraid he would break down; but while she wondered what on earth she could say to comfort him, he turned back to the boxes. "I must get this place tidied up before night," he said in his usual tone, with the flat, dry cough which had become chronic.

While she watched him, Dorinda threw the shawl back on one arm and revealed her fine dark head. The heavy eyebrows and the clear stern line of her features stood out as if an edge of light had fallen over them, leaving the rest of her face in shadow. She was wearing an old tan ulster, faded and patched in places, and beneath

16

the hem her brown calico dress and mud-stained country shoes were visible. Even at Pedlar's Mill the changing fashions were followed respectfully, if tardily, and in the middle 'nineties women walked the muddy roads in skirts which either brushed the ground or were held up on one side. But shabbiness and a deplorable fashion could not conceal the slim, flowing lines of her figure, with its gallant and spirited carriage.

"I'm going to say a word or two to Rose Emily before I start," she said in a cheerful voice. "I don't mind being late." Walking to the end of the store, beyond the wood stove, which felt like a furnace, she pushed back a curtain of purple calico, and turned the knob of a door. Inside the room a woman was sitting up in bed, crocheting a baby's sacque of pink wool.

"I thought you'd gone, Dorinda," she said, looking up. "The snow is getting thicker."

Propped up among her pillows, winding the pink wool through her fragile hands, Mrs. Pedlar faced death with the courage of a heroic illusion. Before her marriage, as Rose Emily Milford, she had taught school in the little schoolhouse near Pedlar's Mill, and Dorinda had been her favourite pupil. She was a small, intelligent-looking woman, pitiably thin, with prominent grey eyes, hair of a peculiar shade of wheaten red, and a brilliant flush on her high cheek bones.

Ball after ball of pink wool unwound on the patchwork quilt, and was crocheted into babies' sacques which she sold in the city; but crocheting, as she sometimes said, "did not take your mind off things as well as moving about," and it seemed to her that only since she had been ill had she begun to learn anything about life. The nearer she came to death, the more, by some perversity of nature, did she enjoy living. If death ever entered her mind, it was as an abstraction, like the doctrine of salvation by faith, never as a reality. Every afternoon she said, "If it is fine, I shall get up to-morrow." Every morning she sighed happily, "I think I'll wait till the evening."

The room was a small one, divided off from the brick store, which adjoined the new frame house Nathan had built for his bride; and there was a confusion of colour, for Mrs. Pedlar's surroundings reflected the feverish optimism of her philosophy. The rag carpet

17

and the patchwork quilt were as gay as an autumn flower-bed; the kerosene lamp wore a ballet skirt of crimson crepe paper; earthen pots of begonias and geraniums filled the green wooden stands at the windows. On the hearthrug, before the open fire, three small children were playing with paper dolls, while the fourth, a baby of nine months, lay fast asleep in his crib, with the nipple of a bottle still held tight in his mouth.

"I'm glad I chose that orange colour for your shawl," said Mrs. Pedlar, in the excited manner that had come upon her with her rising temperature. "It goes so well with your black hair. You ought to be glad you're a big woman," she continued thoughtfully. "Somehow life seems to go easier with big women. I asked young Doctor Greylock if that wasn't true, and he said small women seemed to think so."

Dorinda laughed, and her laughter contained a thrill of joy. Some inward happiness had bubbled up and overflowed into her voice, her look, and her shy dreaming movements. There was sweetness for her in hearing of Jason Greylock; there was ecstasy in the thought that she might meet him again in the road. Yet the sweetness and the ecstasy were thin and far off, like music that comes from a distance. It seemed incredible that anything so wonderful should have happened at Pedlar's Mill.

In front of the fire, the three children (Minnie May, the eldest, was only ten) were busy with their paper dolls. They had made a doll's house out of a cracker box, with the frayed corners of the rug for a garden. "Now Mrs. Brown has lost her little girl, and she is going to Mrs. Smith's to look for her," Minnie May was saying impressively.

"You've got your hands full with those children," remarked Dorinda because she could think of nothing else that sounded natural. Her mind was not on the children; it was miles away in an enclosed garden of wonder and delight; but some casual part of her was still occupying her familiar place and living her old meaningless life.

"Yes, but they're good children. They can always amuse themselves. Minnie May cut those paper dolls out of an old fashion book, and the younger children are all crazy about them."

"Minnie May is a great help to you."

"Yes, she takes after her father. Nathan is the best man that ever lived. He never thinks of himself a minute."

"He gave me some sugar for Ma," Dorinda sighed as she answered, for the thought had stabbed through her like a knife that Rose Emily was dying. *Here we are talking about sugar and paper dolls when she won't live through the summer.*

"There's a pat of butter too," said Rose Emily. "I told Minnie May to put it in your basket. I don't see how your mother manages without butter."

"We've had to do without it since our cow died last fall. I'm saving up, after the taxes are paid, to buy one in the spring." Again the thought stabbed her. "As if cows made any difference when she has only a few months to live!" Were the trivial things, after all, the important ones?

"And Mrs. Brown found that her little girl had been run over and killed in the middle of the road," Minnie May whispered. "So she decided that all she could do for her was to have a handsome funeral and spend the ten dollars she'd saved from her chicken money. That's the graveyard, Bud, down there by the hole in the rug. Lena, stop twistin', or you'll pull it to pieces."

"Nathan says you can get a good cow from old Doctor Greylock for thirty dollars," said Mrs. Pedlar. "He's got one, that Blossom of his, that he wants to sell." Then an idea occurred to her and she concluded doubtfully, "Of course, everything may be changed now that Jason has come back."

"Yes, of course, everything may be changed," repeated Dorinda, and the words, though they were merely an echo, filled her with happiness. Life was burning within her. Even the thought of death, even the knowledge that her friend would not live through the summer, passed like a shadow over the flame that consumed her. Everything was a shadow except the luminous stillness, which was so much deeper than stillness, within her heart.

"He is just the same pleasant-mannered boy he used to be when I taught him," resumed Mrs. Pedlar. "You remember how mischievous he was at school."

Dorinda nodded. "I was only there a year with him before he went away."

"Yes, I'd forgotten. I asked him to-day if he remembered you, and he said he knew you as soon as he saw you in the road this morning." She paused for an instant while a vision flickered in her eyes. "It would be nice if he'd take a fancy to you, Dorinda, and I'm sure you're handsome enough, with your blue eyes and your high colour, for anybody to fall in love with, and you're better educated, too, than most city girls, with all the books you've read. I sent Minnie May to find you while he was here, but she brought Nathan instead; and the doctor had to hurry off to old Mrs. Flower, who is dying."

So they were all pushing them together! It was no wonder, thought Dorinda, since, as old Matthew said, young men were as scarce as wild turkeys, and everybody wanted to marry off everybody else. Almost unconsciously, the power of attraction was increased by an irresistible force. Since every one, even the intelligent Rose Emily, thought it so suitable!

"I've seen him only once since he came home," said the girl.

"Well, I told him about you, and he was very much interested. I believe he's a good young man, and he seems so friendly and kind-hearted. He asked after all the coloured people he used to know, and he was so pleased to hear how well they are getting on. His father couldn't remember anything about anybody, he told me. I reckon the truth is that the old doctor is befuddled with drink all the time." She laughed softly. "Jason has picked up a lot of new-fangled ideas," she added. "He even called broomsedge 'brome-grass' till he found that nobody knew what he was talking about."

"Is he going to stay on?"

"Just for a little while, he says, until he can get the place off his hands. What he meant but didn't like to say, I suppose, was that he would stay as long as his father lives. The old man has got Bright's disease, you know, and he's already had two strokes of paralysis. The doctor up at the Court-House says it can't be longer than six months, or a year at the most."

Six months or a year! Well, anything might happen, anything *did* happen in six months or a year!

On the floor the children were busily pretending that the oblong hole in the rug was a grave. "Mrs. Brown bought a crape veil that came all the way down to the bottom of her skirt," Minnie May was whispering, alert and animated. "That paper doll in the veil is Mrs. Brown on the way to the funeral."

"Well, I'd better be going," Dorinda said, throwing the orange shawl over her head, while she thought, "I ought to have worn my hat, only the snow would have ruined my Sunday hat, and the other isn't fit to be seen."

Picking up the basket by the door, she looked over her shoulder at Rose Emily. "If the snow isn't too heavy, I'll be over early to-morrow, and help you with the children. I hope you'll feel better."

"Oh, I'm planning to get up in the morning," responded Rose Emily in her eager voice, smiling happily over the pink wool.

3

Outside, there was a little yard enclosed in white palings to which farmers tied their horses when the hitching-rail was crowded. Everything was bare now under the thin coating of snow, and the dried stalks of summer flowers were protruding forlornly from heaps of straw. Beyond the small white gate the Old Stage Road, as it was still called, ran past the cleared ground by the station and dipped into the band of pine woods beyond the Haney place, which had been divided and let "on shares" to negro tenants. Within the shadow of the pines, the character of the soil changed from the red clay on the hills to a sandy loam strewn with pine needles.

As Dorinda walked on rapidly, the shawl she wore made a floating orange cloud against the dim background of earth and sky. The snow was falling in larger flakes, like a multitude of frozen moths, and beneath the fluttering white wings the country appeared obscure, solitary, vaguely menacing. Though the road was quite deserted, except for the scarecrow figure of Black Tom, the county idiot, who passed her on his way to beg supper and a night's lodging at the station, the girl was not afraid of the loneliness. She had two miles to walk, and twilight was already approaching; but she knew every turn of the road, and she could, as she sometimes said to herself, "feel her way in the dark of the moon."

To-night, even if there had been wild beasts in the pines, she would not have turned back. A winged joy had risen out of the encompassing poverty and desolation. Though the world was colourless around her, there was a clear golden light in her mind; and through this light her thoughts were flying like swallows in the afterglow. Her old dreams had come back again, but they were different now, since they were infused with the warm blood of reality. She had found, in her mother's religious phraseology, a "kingdom of the spirit" to which she could retreat. She had only to close her eyes and yield herself to this clear golden light of sensation. She had

22

only to murmur, "I wonder if I shall meet him again," and immediately the falling snow, the neglected fields, and the dark pines melted away. She was caught up, she was possessed, by that flying rapture which was like the swiftness of birds. With a phrase, with a thought, or by simply emptying her mind of impressions, she could bring back all the piercing sweetness of surrender.

And she had discovered the miracle for herself! No one, not even Rose Emily, had ever hinted to her of this secret ecstasy at the heart of experience. All around her people were pretending that insignificant things were the only important things. The eternal gestures of milking and cooking, of sowing and reaping! Existence, as far as she could see, was composed of these immemorial habits. Her mother, her father, her brother, Nathan and Rose Emily, all these persons whom she saw daily were engaged in this strange conspiracy of dissimulation. Not one of them had ever betrayed to her this hidden knowledge of life.

Beyond the old Haney place and the stretch of pines there were the pastures of Honeycomb Farm, where three old maids, Miss Texanna Snead, the postmistress, and her sisters Seena and Tabitha, who made dresses, lived on the ragged remnant of once fertile acres. Recently the younger brother William had returned from the West with a little property, and though the fortunes of the sisters were by no means affluent, the fields by the roadside were beginning to look less forlorn. A few bedraggled sheep, huddled together beyond the "worm" fence, stared at her through the hurrying snowflakes. Then, springing to their awkward legs, they wavered uncertainly for a minute, and at last scampered off, bleating foolishly. An old horse rested his head on the rails and gazed meditatively after her as she went by, and across the road several cows filed slowly on their way from the pasture to the cow-barn.

"That's a nice cow, that red one," thought Dorinda. "I wish she belonged to us," and then, with the inconsequence of emotion, "if I meet him, he will ask if he may drive me home."

There was the steady *clop-clop* of a horse's hoofs, and the rapid turning of wheels in the road behind her. Not for the world would she have slackened her pace or glanced over her shoulder, though her heart fluttered in her throat and she felt that she was choking. She longed with all her soul to stop and look back; she knew, through some magnetic current, that he was pursuing her, that in a minute or two he would overtake her; yet she kept on rapidly, driven by a blind impulse which was superior to her will. She was facing the moment, which comes to all women in love, when life, overflowing the artificial boundaries of reason, yields itself to the primitive direction of instinct.

The wheels were grinding on a rocky place in the road. Though she hurried on, the beating of her heart was so loud in her ears that it filled the universe.

"I am going your way," he said, just as she had imagined he would. "Won't you let me drive you home?"

She stopped and turned, while all the glimmering light of the snow gathered in her orange shawl and deepened its hue. Around them the steep horizon seemed to draw closer.

"I live at Old Farm," she answered.

He laughed, and the sound quickened her pulses. She had felt this way in church sometimes when they sang the hymns she liked best, "Jesus, Lover of My Soul" or "Nearer, My God, to Thee."

"Oh, I know you live at Old Farm. You are Dorinda Oakley. Did you think I'd forgotten you?"

For an instant a divine dizziness possessed her. Without looking at him, she saw his eyes, black in the pallid snowflakes, his red hair, just the colour of the clay in the road, his charming boyish smile, so kind, so eager, so incredibly pathetic when she remembered it afterwards. She saw these disturbing details with the sense of familiarity which events borrow from the dream they repeat.

"I can't get out," he said, "because the mare is hungry and wants to go on. But you might get in."

She shook her head, and just as in every imaginary encounter with him, she could think of nothing to reply. Though her mind worked clearly enough at other times, she stood now in a trance between the rail fence, where the old horse was still watching her, and the wheel-ruts in the road. By some accident, for which nothing in her past experience had prepared her, all the laws of her being, thought, will, memory, habit, were suspended. In their place a force which was stronger than all these things together, a force with which she had never reckoned before, dominated her being. The powers of life had seized her as an eagle seizes its prey.

24

"Come, get in," he urged, and dumb with happiness, she obeyed him.

"I remember you very well," he said, smiling into her eyes. "You were little Dorinda Oakley, and you once poured a bottle of ink on my head to turn it black."

"I know—" If she had been talking in her sleep, it could not have seemed more unreal. At this moment, when of all the occasions in her life she longed to be most brilliant and animated, she was tongue-tied by an immobility which was like the drowsiness, only far pleasanter, that she felt in church on hot August afternoons.

"You've grown so tall," he resumed presently, "that at first I wondered a bit. Were your eyes always as big as they are now?"

Though she was drowning in bliss, she could only gaze at him stupidly. Why did love, when it came, take away all your ability to enjoy it?

"I didn't know you were coming back so soon," she said after a struggle.

"Well, Father got in such a fix I had to," he answered, with a slight frown which made his face, she thought, more attractive. The haunting pathos, which she detected but could not explain, looked out of his eyes; the pathos of heroic weakness confronting insurmountable obstacles. "Of course it isn't for ever," he said in a surprisingly cheerful voice. "Father had a second stroke a few weeks ago, and they sent for me because there was nobody to see that he was taken care of. But as soon as he gets better, or if he dies," his tone was kind but impersonal, "I'll go back again and take up my work. I had just got my degree, and was starting in for a year's experience in a big hospital. Until I came I thought it was for a few days. The doctor telegraphed that Father wouldn't last out the week; but he's picked up, and may go on for a while yet. I can't leave him until he is out of danger, and in the meantime I'm trying to enlighten the natives. God! what a country! Nobody seems to ask any more of life than to plod from one bad harvest to another. They don't know the first principles of farming, except of course Mr. Ellgood, who has made a success of Green Acres, and that clownish-looking chap who owns the store. I wonder what the first Pedlar's were like. The family must have been in the same spot for a hundred and fifty years."

"Oh, they've been there always. But most of the other farmers are tenants. Pa says that's why the land has gone bad. No man will work himself to death over somebody else's land."

"That's the curse of the tenant system. Even the negroes become thrifty when they own a piece of land. And I've noticed, by the way, that they are the best farmers about here. The negro who owns his ten or twelve acres is a better manager than the poor white with twice the number."

"I know," Dorinda assented; but she was not interested in a discussion of farming. All her life she had heard men talk of farming and of nothing else. Surely there were other things he could tell her! "I should think it would be dreary for you," she added, with a woman's antipathy to the impersonal.

Turning to her suddenly, he brushed the snowflakes from the fur robe over her knees. His gestures, like his personality, were firm, energetic, and indescribably casual. Against the brooding loneliness of the country his figure, for all its youthful audacity, appeared trivial and fugitive. It was as if the landscape waited, plunged in melancholy, for the passing of a ray of sunshine. Though he had sprung from the soil, he had returned to it a stranger, and there could be no sympathetic communion between him and the solitude. Neither as a lover nor as a conqueror could he hope to possess it in spirit.

"If I thought it was for ever, I'd take to drink or worse," he replied carelessly. "One can stand anything for a few weeks or even months; but a lifetime of this would be—" He broke off and looked at her closely. "How have you stood it?" he asked. "How does any woman stand it without going out of her head?"

Dorinda smiled. "Oh, I'm used to it. I even like it. Hills would make me feel shut in."

"Haven't you ever wanted to get away?"

"I used to think of it all the time. When I first went to the store, I was listening so hard for the trains that I couldn't hear anything else."

"And you got over it?"

Her lashes fluttered over the burning blue of her eyes. If only he could know how recently she had got over it! "Yes, I don't feel that way now."

26

"You've even kept your health, and your colour. But, of course, you're young."

"I'm twenty. When I'm forty I may feel differently. By that time I shan't have any books left to read."

He laughed. "By that time you'll probably begin listening again, harder than ever." He thought for a moment, and then added, with the optimism of inexperience, "While I'm here I'll try to get a few modern ideas into the heads of the natives. That will be worth while, I suppose. I ought to be able to teach them something in a few weeks."

If she had been older or wiser, she might have smiled at his assurance. As it was she repeated gently, innocent of ironical intention, "Yes, that will be worth while."

It was enough just to sit near him in silence; to watch, through lowered lashes, the tremor of his smile, the blinking of his eyelids, the way the pale reddish hair grew on the back of his neck, the indolent grasp with which he was holding the reins. It was enough, she felt, just to breathe in the stimulating smell of his cigarettes, so different from the heavy odour of country tobacco. And outside this enchanted circle in which they moved, she was aware of the falling snow, of the vague brown of the fields, of the sharp freshness of the approaching evening, of the thick familiar scents of the winter twilight. Far away a dog barked. The mingled effluvia of rotting leaves and manure-heaps in barnyards drifted toward her. From beyond a fence the sound of voices floated. These things belonged, she knew, to the actual world; they had no place in the celestial sphere of enchantment. Yet both the actual and the ideal seemed to occur within her mind. She could not separate the scent of leaves or the sound of distant voices from the tumult of her thoughts.

They passed Honeycomb Farm, and sped lightly over a mile of rutted track to the fork of the Old Stage Road, where a blasted oak of tremendous height stood beside the ruins of a burned cabin. On the other side of the way there was the big red gate of Five Oaks, and beyond it a sandy branch road ran farther on to the old brick house. The snow hid the view now; but on clear days the red roof and chimneys of the house were visible above the willow branches of Gooseneck Creek. Usually, as the mare knew, the doctor's buggy turned in at the big gate; but to-day it passed by and followed the main road, which dipped and rose and dipped again on its way to Old Farm. First there was a thin border of woods, flung off sharply, like an iron fretwork, against the sky; then a strip of corduroy road and a bridge of logs over a marshy stream; and beyond the bridge, on the right, stood the open gate of Dorinda's home. The mare stumbled and the buggy swerved on the rocky grade to the lawn.

"That's a bad turn," remarked Jason.

"I know. Pa is always hoping that he will have time to fix it. We used to keep the gate shut, but it has sagged so that it has to stay open."

"They ought to mend the bridge first. Those holes are dangerous for horses."

Again she assented. Why, she wondered vaguely, did he emphasize the obvious?

Within its grove of trees, in the midst of last summer's weeds, which were never cut, the long whitewashed house wore a forlorn yet not inhospitable air. Through the snow the hooded roof looked close and secretive; but there was the glimmer of a lamp in one of the lower windows, enormous lilac bushes, which must lend gaiety in April, clustered about the porch, and the spreading frame wings, added by old John Calvin Abernethy, still gave an impression of comfort. It was the ordinary Virginian farm-house of the early nineteenth century, built for service rather than for beauty; and retaining, because of its simplicity, a charm which had long since departed from more ambitious pieces of architecture.

"So we're home again," said Jason, glancing about him.

The buggy had come to a stop by the front steps, and regardless of the mare's impatience, he sprang to the ground and helped the girl to alight.

"Yes, it looks bare, doesn't it?"

She lifted her face to his as she answered, and while he looked down into her eyes, a quiver passed over his mouth under the short red moustache.

"Do you go over every day?" he asked. "Why haven't I met you before?"

She looked down. "Oh, I had to help out at home. But I've worked in the store ever since Mrs. Pedlar was taken ill. I get there about eight usually and stay until just before sunset."

28

"For which, I suppose, you receive an extravagant salary?"

She blushed at his whimsical tone. "They pay me ten dollars a month."

"Ten dollars a month!" A low whistle escaped his lips. "And you walk four miles a day to earn it."

"I don't mind the walk. In good weather I'd rather be out of doors. Besides somebody usually picks me up."

"Exactly. As I did this evening. If I hadn't, it would have been after dark when you got home. Well, I can help you while I'm here," he added carelessly. "I go that way every day, and I'll look out for you."

Again the dumbness seized her, and she stood there rooted like a plant, while he looked at her. For a moment, so intent was his gaze, she felt that he had forgotten her presence. It was not in the least as if he were staring at her shawl or her mud-stained ulster, or her broken shoes; it was not even as if he were looking at her eyes and thinking how blue they were. No, it was just as if he were seeing something within his own mind.

"I've known so few girls," he said presently, as if he were talking to himself, "but, somehow, you seem different." Then with delightful irrelevance, he added playfully, "Don't forget me. I shall see you soon."

After he had driven away, she stood gazing after him. Again the mare hesitated, again the wheels crunched on the rocky place. Then the buggy rolled over the bridge; she heard the sound of his voice as he avoided a hole; and a minute later the vehicle had disappeared in the border of leafless woods.

"*Don't forget me. I shall see you soon.*"

Eight words, and the something different had at last happened to her! Everything around her appeared fresh and strange and wonderful, as if she were looking at it clearly for the first time. The snow wrapped her softly like a mist of happiness. She felt it caressing her cheek, and it seemed to her, when she moved, that her whole body had grown softer, lighter, more intensely alive. Her inner life, which had been as bare as a rock, was suddenly rich with bloom. Never again could she find the hours dull and empty. "*Don't forget me. I shall see you soon,*" sang her thoughts.

4

As she stepped on the porch, Rambler, an old black and yellow hound, with flapping ears and the expression of a pragmatic philosopher, stole out of the shadows and joined her.

"You'd better come in or Pa will begin to worry about you," she said, and her voice startled her because it did not sound as if it were her own. "I know you've been chasing rabbits again."

She wondered if the suppressed excitement showed also in her face, and if her mother, who noticed everything, would detect it. After she had entered the hall, which smelled of bacon and dried apples, she stopped and tried to rub the bloom of ecstasy off her cheeks. Then, followed sedately by Rambler, she passed the closed door of the parlour, which was opened only for funerals or when the circuit minister was visiting them, and went into the kitchen at the back of the house. The family must have heard the wheels, and it was a mercy, she told herself, that Rufus or Josiah had not come out to meet the buggy.

"Ma, Rose Emily sent you a pat of butter," she said, "and Nathan gave me two pounds of brown sugar."

Her eyes blinked in the light; but it was not the smoky flare of the lamp on the table that made the big kitchen, with its rough white-washed walls, its old-fashioned cooking-stove, its dilapidated pine table and chairs, its battered pots and pans suspended from nails, its unused churn standing in the accustomed place on the brick hearth—it was not the lamp that made the room appear as unfamiliar as if she had never seen it before. Nor was it the lamp that cast this peculiar haziness, like a distant perspective, over the members of her family.

Mrs. Oakley, a tall, lean, angular woman, who had been almost

30

beautiful for a little while forty years before, placed the coffee-pot on the table before she turned to look at her daughter. Under her sparse grey hair, which was strained tightly back and twisted in a small knot on her head, her face was so worn by suffering that a network of nerves quivered beneath the pallid veil of her flesh. Religious depression, from which she still suffered periodically, had refined her features to austerity. Her pale grey eyes, with their wide fixed stare, appeared to look out of caverns, and endowed her with the visionary gaze of a mystic, like the eyes of a saint in a primitive Italian painting. Years ago, while Dorinda was still a child, her mother had been for weeks at a stretch what people called "not quite right in her mind," and she had talked only in whispers because she thought the country was listening. As long as the spell lasted, it had seemed to the child that the farm-house crouched like a beaten hound, in the midst of the brown fields, beneath the menacing solitude. Since then she had never lost the feeling that the land contained a terrible force, whether for good or evil she could not tell, and there were hours when the loneliness seemed to rise in a crested wave and surge over her.

As she took the basket from her daughter, Mrs. Oakley's features softened slightly, but she did not smile. Only very young things, babies, puppies, chickens just out of the shell, made her smile, and then her smile was more plaintive than cheerful.

"Rufus can have his buckwheat cakes for breakfast," she said, without stopping in her movements from the table to the safe and from the safe to the stove.

She had worked so hard for so many years that the habit had degenerated into a disease, and thrift had become a tyrant instead of a slave in her life. From dawn until after dark she toiled, and then lay sleepless for hours because of the jerking of her nerves. She was, as she said of herself, "driven," and it was the tragedy of her lot that all her toil made so little impression. Though she spent every bit of her strength there was nothing to show for her struggle. Like the land, which took everything and gave back nothing, the farm had drained her vitality without altering its general aspect of decay.

"That's good!" exclaimed Rufus, a handsome boy of eighteen, with straight black hair, sparkling brown eyes, and the velvety dark red of Dorinda's lips and cheeks. He was the youngest child, and

31

after he had been nursed through a virulent attack of scarlet fever, he had become the idol of his mother, in spite of a temperamental wildness which she made the subject of constant prayer. There was ceaseless contention between him and his elder brother, Josiah, a silent, hardworking man of thirty, with overhanging eyebrows and a scrubby beard which he seldom trimmed. After the birth of her first child there had been a sterile period in Mrs. Oakley's life, when her mental trouble began, and Dorinda and Rufus both came while she was looking ahead, as she told herself, to a peaceful middle age unhampered by childbearing.

"Sit down, Ma," said Dorinda, throwing her shawl on a chair and slipping out of her ulster, while Flossie, the grey and white cat, rubbed against her. "You look worn out, and it won't take me a minute. Have you been helped, Pa?" she asked, turning to the hairy old man at the end of the table.

"I ain't had my coffee yet," replied Joshua, raising his head from his plate. He was a big, humble, slow-witted man, who ate and drank like a horse, with loud munching noises. As his hair was seldom cut and he never shaved, he still kept his resemblance to the pictures of John the Baptist in the family Bible. In place of his youthful comeliness, however, he wore now an air of having just emerged from the wilderness. His shoulders were bent and slightly crooked from lifting heavy burdens, and his face, the little that one could see of it, was weather-beaten and wrinkled in deep furrows, like the fissures in a red clay road after rain. From beneath his shaggy hair his large brown eyes were bright and wistful with the melancholy that lurks in the eyes of cripples or of suffering animals. He was a dumb plodding creature who had as little share in the family life as had the horses, Dan and Beersheba; but, like the horses, he was always patient and willing to do whatever was required of him. There were times when Dorinda asked herself if indeed he had any personal life apart from the seasons and the crops. Though he was not yet sixty-five, his features, browned and reddened and seamed by sun and wind, appeared as old as a rock embedded in earth. All his life he had been a slave to the land, harnessed to the elemental forces, struggling inarticulately against the blight of poverty and the barrenness of the soil. Yet Dorinda had never heard him rebel. His resignation was the earth's passive acceptance of sun

32

or rain. When his crop failed, or his tobacco was destroyed by frost, he would drive his plough into the field and begin all over again. "That tobacco wanted another touch of sun," he would say quietly, or "I'll make out to cut it a day earlier next year." The earth clung to him; to his clothes, to the anxious creases in his face, to his finger-nails, and to his heavy boots, which were caked with manure from the stables. The first time Dorinda remembered his taking her on his knee, the strong smell of his blue jeans overalls had frightened her to tears, and she had struggled and screamed. "I reckon my hands are too rough," he had said timidly, and after that he had never tried to lift her again. But whenever she thought of him now, his hands, gnarled, twisted, and earth-stained like the vigorous roots of a tree, and that penetrating briny smell, were the first things she remembered. His image was embalmed in that stale odour of the farm as in a preserving fluid.

"It's snowing faster," Dorinda said, "but it doesn't stay on the ground." Bending over her father, she covered the corn-pone on his plate with brown gravy. "Maybe it will be clear again by to-morrow," she went on smoothly. "It's time spring was beginning."

Joshua's hand, which no amount of scrubbing could free from stain, closed with a heavy grip on the handle of his knife. "This brown gravy cert'n'y does taste good, honey," he said. "Yo' Ma's made out mighty well with no milk or butter."

A deep tenderness pervaded Dorinda's heart, and this tenderness was but a single wave of the emotion that flooded her being. "Poor Pa," she thought, "he has never known anything but work." Oh, how spendid life was and how hard! Aloud, she said, "I've saved up enough money to buy a cow in May. After I help you with the taxes and the interest on the mortgage, I'll still have enough left for the cow. Rose Emily says old Doctor Greylock will sell us his Blossom."

"Then we can have butter and buttermilk with the ash cake!" exclaimed Rufus.

"I ain't so sure I'd want to buy that red cow of Doctor Greylock's," observed Josiah in a surly tone. That was his way, to make an objection to everything. He had, as his mother sometimes said of him, a good character but a mean disposition. At twenty he had married a pretty, light woman, who died with her first child; and now, after a widowerhood of ten years, he was falling in love with

Elvira Snead, a silly young thing, the daughter of thriftless Adam Snead, a man with scarcely a shirt to his back or an acre to his name. Though Josiah was hardworking, painstaking, and frugal, he preferred comeliness to character in a woman. If it had been Rufus, Dorinda would have found an infatuation for Elvira easier to understand. Nobody expected Rufus to be anything but wild, and it was natural for young men to seek pleasures. The boy was different from his father and his elder brother, who required as little as cattle; and yet there was nothing for him to do in the long winter evenings, except sort potatoes or work over his hare-traps. The neighbours were all too far away, and the horses too tired after the day's work to drag the buggy over the mud-strangled roads. Dorinda could browse happily among the yellowed pages in old Abernethy's library, returning again and again to the Waverley Novels, or the exciting Lives of the Missionaries; but Rufus cared nothing for books and had inherited his mother's dread of the silence. He was a high-spirited boy, and he liked pleasure; yet every evening after supper he would tinker with a farm implement or some new kind of trap until he was sleepy enough for bed. Then he would march upstairs to the fireless room under the eaves, where the only warmth came up the chimney from the kitchen beneath. That was all the life Rufus had ever had, though he looked exactly, Dorinda thought, like Thaddeus of Warsaw or one of the Scottish Chiefs.

In the daytime the kitchen was a cheerful room, bright with sunshine which fell through the mammoth scuppernong grapevine on the back porch. Then the battered pots and pans grew bright again, the old wood stove gave out a pleasant song; and the blossomless geraniums, in wooden boxes, decorated the window-sill. Much of her mother's life was spent in this room, and as a child Dorinda had played here happily with her corn-cob or hickory-nut dolls. Poor as they were, there was never a speck of dust anywhere. Mrs. Oakley looked down on the "poor white" class, though she had married into it; and her recoil from her husband's inefficiency was in the direction of a scrupulous neatness. She knew that she had thrown herself away, in youth, on a handsome face; yet she was just enough to admit that her marriage, as marriages go, had not been unhappy. Her unhappiness, terrible as it had been, went deeper than any human relation, for she was still fond of Joshua with the maternal part of her nature while she despised him with her intelligence. He had made her a good husband; it was not his fault that he could never get on; everything from the start had been against him; and he had always done the best that he could. She realized this clearly; but all the romance in her life, after the death of the young missionary in the Congo, had turned toward her religion. She could have lived without Joshua; she could have lived even without Rufus, who was the apple of her eye; but without her religion, as she had once confessed to Dorinda, she would have been "lost." Like her daughter, she was subject to dreams, but her dreams differed from Dorinda's since they came only in sleep. There were winter nights, after the days of whispering in the past, when the child Dorinda, startled by the flare of a lantern out in the darkness, had seen her mother flitting barefooted over the frozen ground. Shivering with cold and terror, the little girl had crept down to rouse her father, who had thrown some garments over his nightshirt, and picking up the big raccoon-skin coat, had rushed out in pursuit of his demented wife. A little later Josiah had followed, and then Dorinda and Rufus had brought sticks and paper from the kitchen and started a fire, with shaking hands, in their mother's fireplace. When at last the two men had led Mrs. Oakley into the house, she had appeared so bewildered and benumbed that she seemed scarcely to know where she had been. Once Dorinda had overheard Joshua whisper hoarsely to Josiah, "If I hadn't come up with her in the nick of time, she would have done it"; but what the thing was they whispered about the child did not understand till long afterwards. All she knew at the time was that her mother's "missionary dream" had come back again; a dream of blue skies and golden sands, of palm trees on a river's bank, and of black babies thrown to crocodiles. "I am lost, lost, lost," Mrs. Oakley had murmured over and over, while she stared straight before her, with a prophetic gleam in her wide eyes, as if she were seeing unearthly visions.

They ate to-night, after Joshua had asked grace, in a heavy silence, which was broken only by the gurgling sounds Joshua and Josiah made over their coffee-cups. Mrs. Oakley, who was decently if not delicately bred, had become inured to the depressing table manners of her husband and her elder son. After the first disillusionment of her marriage, she had confined her efforts at improvement to the two younger children. They had both, she felt with secret satisfaction, sprung from the finer strain of the Abernethys; it was as if they had inherited from her that rarer intellectual medium in which her forbears had attained their spiritual being. There were hours when it seemed to her that the gulf between the dominant Scotch-Irish stock of the Valley and the mongrel breed of "poor white" which produced Joshua was as wide as the abyss between alien races. Then the image of Joshua as she had first known him would appear to her, and she would think, in the terms of theology which were natural to her mind, "It must have been intended, or it wouldn't have happened."

While the others were still eating, Mrs. Oakley rose from the food she had barely tasted, and began to clear the table. The nervous affection from which she suffered made it impossible for her to sit in one spot for more than a few minutes. Her nerves jerked her up and started her on again independently of her will or even of any physical effort. Only constant movement quieted the twitching which ran like electric wires through her muscles.

"Go and lie down, Ma. I'll clear off and wash up," Dorinda said. Her pity for her mother was stronger to-night than it had ever been, for it had become a part of the craving for happiness which was overflowing her soul. Often this starved craving had made her bitter and self-centred because of the ceaseless gnawing in her breast; but now it was wholly kind and beneficent. "If you would only stop and rest," she added tenderly, "your neuralgia would be better."

"I can't stop," replied Mrs. Oakley, with wintry calm. "I can't see things going to rack and ruin and not try to prevent it." After a minute, still moving about, she continued hopelessly, "It rests me to work."

"I brought the butter for you," returned Dorinda, in hurt tones, "and you didn't even touch it."

Mrs. Oakley shook her head. "I don't mind going without," she responded. "You must keep it for the boys."

It was always like that. The girl had sometimes felt that the greatest cross in her life was her mother's morbid unselfishness. Even her nagging—and she nagged at them continually—was easier to bear.

"I've got the water all ready," Mrs. Oakley said, piling dishes on the tin tray. "I'll get right through the washing up, and then we can have prayers."

Family prayers in the evening provided the solitary emotional outlet in her existence. Only then, while she read aloud one of the more belligerent Psalms, and bent her rheumatic knees to the rag carpet in her "chamber," were the frustrated instincts of her being etherealized into spiritual passion. When the boys rebelled, as they sometimes did, or Dorinda protested that she was "too busy for prayers," Mrs. Oakley contended with the earnestness of a Covenanter: "If it wasn't for the help of my religion, I could never keep going."

Now, having finished their meal in silence, they gathered in the chamber, as the big bedroom was called, and waited for evening prayers. It was the only comfortable room in the house, except the kitchen, and the family life after working hours was lived in front of the big fireplace, in which chips, lightwood knots, and hickory logs were burned from dawn until midnight. Before the flames there was a crooked brass footman, and the big iron kettle it supported kept up an uninterrupted hissing noise. In one corner of the room stood a tall rosewood bookcase, which contained the romantic fiction Dorinda had gleaned from the heavy theological library in the parlour across the hall. Between the front windows, which looked out on a cluster of old lilac bushes, there was the huge walnut bed, with four stout posts and no curtains, and facing it between the windows, in the opposite walls, a small cabinet of lacquer-ware which her great-grandfather had brought from the East. In the morning and afternoon the sunlight fell in splinters over the variegated design of the rag carpet and the patchwork quilt on the bed, and picked out the yellow specks in the engravings of John Knox admonishing Mary Stuart and Martyrs for the Covenant.

"*The heavens declare the glory of God; and the firmament sheweth his handywork,*" read Mrs. Oakley in her high thin voice, with her mystic gaze passing over the open Bible to the whitewashed wall where the shadows of the flames wavered.

Motionless, in her broken splint-seated chair, scarcely daring to breathe, Dorinda felt as if she were floating out of the scene into some world of intenser reality. The faces about her in the shifting firelight were the faces in a dream, and a dream that was without vividness. She saw Joshua bending forward, his pipe fallen from his mouth, his hands clasped between his knees, and his eyes fixed in a pathetic groping stare, as if he were trying to follow the words. The look was familiar to her; she had seen it in the wistful expressions of Rambler and of Dan and Beersheba, the horses; yet it still moved her more deeply than she had ever been moved by anything except the patient look of her father's hands. On opposite sides of the fireplace, Josiah and Rufus were dozing, Josiah sucking his empty pipe as a child sucks a stick of candy, Rufus playing with the knife he had used to whittle a piece of wood. At the first words of the Psalm he had stopped work and closed his eyes, while a pious vacancy washed like a tide over his handsome features. Curled on the rag carpet, Rambler and Flossie watched each other with wary intentness, Rambler contemplative and tolerant, Flossie suspicious and superior. The glow and stillness of the room enclosed the group in a circle that was like the shadow of a magic lantern. The flames whispered; the kettle hummed on the brass footman; the sound of Joshua's heavy breathing went on like a human undercurrent to the cadences of the Psalm. Outside, in the fields, a dog barked, and Rambler raised his long, serious head from the rug and listened. A log of wood, charred in the middle, broke in two and scattered a shower of sparks.

Prayers were over. Mrs. Oakley rose from her knees; Joshua prodded the ashes in his pipe; Josiah drew a twist of home-cured tobacco from his pocket, and cutting off a chew from the end of it, thrust it into his cheek, where it bulged for the rest of the evening; Rufus picked up a fishing-pole and resumed his whittling. Until bedtime the three men would sprawl there in the agreeable warmth between the fireplace and the lamp on the table. Nobody talked; conversation was as alien to them as music. Drugged with fatigue, they nodded in a vegetable somnolence. Even in their hours of freedom they could not escape the relentless tyranny of the soil.

After putting away the Bible, Mrs. Oakley took out a dozen damask towels, with Turkey-red borders and fringed ends, from her top bureau drawer and began to look over them. These towels were the possession she prized most, after the furniture of her grandfather, and they were never used except when the minister or a visiting elder came to spend the night.

"They're turning a little yellow," she remarked presently, when she had straightened the long fringe and mended a few places. "I reckon I might as well put them in soak to-night."

Rufus yawned and laid down his fishing-rod. "There ain't anything for me to do but go to bed."

"We all might as well go, I reckon," Joshua agreed drowsily. "It's gittin' on past eight o'clock, an' if the snow's off the ground, we've got a hard day ahead of us."

"I'll put these towels in soak first," his wife responded, "and I've got a little ironing I want to get through with before I can rest."

"Not to-night, Ma," Dorinda pleaded. While she spoke she began to yawn like the others. It was queer the way it kept up as soon as one of them started. Youth struggled for a time, but in the end it succumbed inevitably to the narcotic of dullness.

"I ain't sleepy," replied Mrs. Oakley, "and I like to have something to do with my hands. I never was one to want to lie in bed unless I was sleepy. The very minute my head touches the pillow, my eyes pop right open."

"But you get up so early."

"Well, the first crack of light wakes your father, and after he begins stirring, I am never able to get a wink more of sleep. He was out at the barn feeding the horses before day this morning."

Dorinda sighed. Was this life?

"I don't see how you keep it up, Ma," she said, with weary compassion.

"Oh, I can get along without much sleep. It's different with the rest of you. Your father is out in the air all day, and you and the boys are young."

She went back to the kitchen, with the towels in her hand, while Dorinda took down one of the lamps from a shelf in the back hall, removed the cracked chimney, and lighted the wick, which was too short to burn more than an hour or two.

The evening was over. It was like every one Dorinda had known in the past. It was like every one she would know in the future unless —she caught her breath sharply—unless the miracle happened!

5

The faint grey light crept through the dormer-window and glimmered with a diffused wanness over the small three-cornered room. Turning restlessly, Dorinda listened, half awake, to the sound of her mother moving about in the kitchen below. A cock in the henhouse crowed and was answered by another. "It isn't day," she thought, and opening her eyes, she gazed through the window at the big pine on the hill. The sun rose over the pine; every morning she watched the twisted black boughs, shaped like a harp, emerge from obscurity. First the vague ripple of dawn, spreading in circles as if a stone had been cast into the darkness; then a pearly glimmer in which objects borrowed exaggerated dimensions; then a blade of light cutting sharply through the pine to the old pear orchard, where the trees still blossomed profusely in spring, though they bore only small green pears out of season. After the edge of brightness, the round red sun would ride up into the heavens and the day would begin. It was seldom that she saw the sunrise from her window. Usually, unless she overslept herself and her mother got breakfast without waking her, the men were in the fields and the two women were attending to the chickens or cleaning the house before the branches of the big pine were gilded with light.

"Poor Ma," Dorinda said, "she wouldn't wake me." But she was not thinking of her mother. Deep down in her being some blissful memory was struggling into consciousness. She felt that it was floating there, just beyond her reach, dim, elusive, enchantingly lovely. Almost she seized it; then it slipped from her grasp and escaped her, only to return, still veiled, a little farther off, while she groped after it. A new happiness. Some precious possession which she had clasped to her heart while she was falling asleep. Then suddenly the thing that she had half forgotten came drifting, through unclouded light, into her mind. *"Don't forget me. I shall see you soon."*

The sounds in the kitchen grew louder, and the whole house was saturated with the aroma of coffee and frying bacon. Beyond these familiar scents and sounds, it seemed to her that she smelt and heard the stirring of spring in the fields and the woods, that the movement and rumour of life were sweeping past her in waves of colour, fragrance, and music.

Springing out of bed, she dressed hurriedly, and decided, while she shivered at the splash of cold water, that she would clean her shoes before she went back to the store. The day was just breaking, and the corner where her pine dressing-table stood was so dark that she was obliged to light the lamp, which burned with a dying flicker, while she brushed and coiled her hair. Beneath the dark waving line on her forehead, where her hair grew in a widow's peak, her eyes were starry with happiness. Though she was not beautiful, she had her moments of beauty, and looking at herself in the greenish mirror, which reminded her of the water in the old mill pond, she realized that this was one of her moments. Never again would she be twenty and in love for the first time.

"If only I had something pretty to wear," she thought, picking up her skirt of purple calico and slipping it over her head. The longing for lovely things, the decorative instinct of youth, became as sharp as a pang. Parting the faded curtains over a row of shelves in one corner, she took down a pasteboard box, and selected a collar of fine needlework which had belonged to Eudora Abernethy when she was a girl. For a minute Dorinda looked at it, strongly tempted. Then the character that showed in her mouth and chin asserted itself, and she shook her head. "It would be foolish to wear it to-day," she murmured, and putting it back among the others, she closed the box and replaced it on the shelf.

"I'll black my shoes, anyway," she thought, as she hurried downstairs to breakfast. "Even if they do get muddy again as soon as I step in the road."

That was with the surface of her mind. In the depths beneath she was thinking without words, "Now that he has come, life will never again be what it was yesterday."

In the kitchen the lamp had just been put out, and the room was

41

flooded with the ashen stream of daybreak. Mrs. Oakley was on her knees, putting a stick of wood into the stove, and the scarlet glare of the flames tinged her flesh with the colour of rusty iron. After a sleepless night her neuralgia was worse, and there was a look of agony in the face she lifted to her daughter.

"Why didn't you wake me, Ma?" Dorinda asked a little impatiently. "You aren't fit to get breakfast."

"I thought you might as well have your sleep out," her mother replied in a lifeless voice. "I'll have some cakes ready in a minute. I'm just making a fresh batch for Rufus."

"You oughtn't have made cakes, as bad as you feel," Dorinda protested. "Rufus could have gone without just as well as the rest of us."

Mrs. Oakley struggled to her feet, and picking up the cake lifter, turned back to the stove. While she stood there against the dull glow, she appeared scarcely more substantial than a spiral of smoke.

"Well, we don't have butter every day," she said. "And I can't lie in bed as long as I've got the strength to be up and doing. Wherever I turn, I see dirt gathering."

"No matter how hard you work, the dirt will always be there," Dorinda persisted. It was useless, she knew, to try to reason with her mother. One could not reason with either a nervous malady or a moral principle; but, even though experience had taught her the futility of remonstrance, there were times when she found it impossible not to scold at a martyrdom that seemed to her unnecessary. They might as well be living in the house, she sometimes thought, with the doctrine of predestination; and like the doctrine of predestination, there was nothing to be done about it.

With a sigh of resignation, she turned to her father, who stood at the window, looking out over the old geraniums that had stopped blooming years ago. Against the murky dawn his figure appeared as rudimentary as some prehistoric image of man.

"Do you think it is going to clear off, Pa?" she asked.

He looked round at her, prodding the tobacco into his pipe with his large blunt thumb. "I ain't thinkin', honey," he replied in his thick, earthy drawl. "The wind's settin' right, but thar's a good-size bank of clouds over toward the west."

"You'd better make Rufus take a look at those planting beds

42

up by Hoot Owl Woods," said Josiah, pushing back his chair and rising from the table. "One of Doctor Greylock's steers broke loose yesterday and was tramplin' round up there on our side of the fence."

Rufus looked up quickly. "Why can't you attend to it yourself?" he demanded in the truculent tone he always used to his elder brother.

Josiah, who had reached the door on his way out, stopped and looked back with a surly expression. With his unshaven face, where the stubby growth of a beard was just visible, and his short crooked legs, he bore still some grotesque resemblance to his younger brother, as if the family pattern had been tried first in caricature.

"I've got as much as I can do over yonder in the east meadow," he growled. "You or Pa will have to look after those planting beds."

Rufus frowned while he reached for the last scrap of butter. There would be none for his mother and Dorinda; but if this fact had occurred to him, and it probably had not, he would have dismissed it as an unpleasant reflection. Since he was a small child he had never lacked the courage of his appetite.

"What's the use of my trying to do anything when you and Pa are so set you won't let me have my way about it?" he asked. "I'd have moved those tobacco beds long ago, if you'd let me."

"Well, they've always been thar, son," Joshua observed in a peaceable manner. He stood in the doorway, blowing clouds of smoke over his pipe, while he scraped the caked mud from his boots. His humble, friendly eyes looked up timidly, like the eyes of a dog that is uncertain whether he is about to receive a pat or a blow.

"Besides, we ain't got the manure to waste on new ground," Josiah added, with his churlish frown. "We need all the stable trash we can rake and scrape for the fields."

Mrs. Oakley, bringing a plate of fresh cakes as a peace offering, came over to the table. "Don't you boys begin to fuss again," she pleaded wearily. "It's just as much as I can do to keep going anyway, and when you start quarrelling it makes me feel as if I'd be obliged to give up. You'd just as well take all these cakes, Rufus. I can make some more for Dorinda by the time she is ready."

Dorinda, who was eating dry bread with her coffee, made a gesture of exasperated sympathy. "I don't want any cakes, Ma. I'm going to start washing up just as soon as you sit down and eat your breakfast. If you'd try to swallow something, whether you want it or not, your neuralgia would be better."

Mrs. Oakley shook her head, while she dragged her body like an empty garment back to the stove. From the way she moved she seemed to have neither bone nor muscle, yet her physical flabbiness was sustained, Dorinda knew, by a force that was indomitable.

"I don't feel as if I could touch a morsel," she answered, pressing her fingers over her drawn brow and eyes.

"Oh, Rufus can eat his head off, but he'll never work to earn his keep," Josiah grumbled under his breath.

"Well, I'm not a slave, anyway, like you and Pa," Rufus flared up. "I'd let the farm rot before it would be my master."

Josiah had pushed past his father in the doorway. A chill draught blew in, and out of the draught his slow, growling voice floated back. "Somebody's got to be a slave. If Ma didn't slave for you, you'd have to, I reckon, or starve."

He went out after his father, slamming the door behind him, and Dorinda, hurriedly finishing her breakfast, rose and began to clear the table. The sallow light at the window was growing stronger. Outside, there was the sound of tramping as the horses were led by to the trough at the well, and the crowing in the henhouse was loud and insistent. The day had begun. It was like every other day in the past. It would be like every other day in the future. Suddenly the feeling came over her that she was caught like a mouse in the trap of life. No matter how desperately she struggled, she could never escape; she could never be free. She was held fast by circumstances as by invisible wires of steel.

Several hours later, when she started to the store, the trapped sensation vanished, and the gallant youth within her lifted its head. There was moisture that did not fall in the air. A chain of sullen clouds in the west soared like peaks through a fog. Straight before her the red road dipped and rose and dipped again in the monotonous brown of the landscape. A few ragged crows flapped by over the naked fields.

Turning at the gate, which was never closed, she looked back at the house huddled beneath its sloping shingled roof under the boughs of the old locust trees. The narrow dormer-windows stared like small blinking eyes, shy and furtive, down on the square Georgian porch, on the flagged walk bordered by stunted boxwood, on the giant lilac bushes which had thriven upon neglect, and on the ruined lawn with its dead branches and its thicket of unmown weeds. In recent years the white-washed walls had turned yellow and dingy; the eaves were rotting away where birds nested; and in June the empty chimneys became so alive with swallows that the whole place was faintly murmurous, as if summer stirred in the dead wood as well as in the living boughs.

Whenever she looked back upon it from a distance, she was visited again by the image of the house as a frightened thing that waited, shrinking closer to the earth, for an inevitable disaster. It was as if the place had preserved unaltered a mood from which she herself had escaped, and occasionally this mood awoke in her blood and nerves and flowed through her again. Recollection. Association. It was morbid, she told herself sternly, to cherish such fancies; and yet she had never been able entirely to rid her memory of the fears and dreads of her childhood. Worse than this even was the haunting thought that the solitude was alive, that it skulked there in the distance, like a beast that is waiting for the right moment to spring and devour.

Bleak, raw, wind-swept, the morning had begun with a wintry chill. The snow of yesterday was gone; only an iridescent vapour, as delicate as a cobweb, was spun over the ground. Already, as she turned and went on again, the light was changing, and more slowly, as if a veil fluttered before it was lifted, the expression of the country changed with it. In the east, an arrow of sunshine, too pallid to be called golden, shot through the clouds and flashed over the big pine on the hill at the back of the house. The landscape, which had worn a discouraged aspect, appeared suddenly to glow under the surface. Veins of green and gold, like tiny rivulets of spring, glistened in the winter woods and in the mauve and brown of the fields. The world was familiar, and yet, in some indescribable way, it was different, shot through with romance as with the glimmer of phosphorescence. Life, which had drooped, flared up again, burning clear and strong in Dorinda's heart. It had come back, that luminous expectancy, that golden mist of sensation. *"Don't forget me. I shall see you soon,"* repeated an inner voice; and immediately she was lost in an ecstasy

45

without words and without form like the mystic communion of religion. Love! That was the end of all striving for her healthy nerves, her vigorous youth, the crown and the fulfilment of life! At twenty, a future without love appeared to her as intolerable as the slow martyrdom of her mother.

Beyond the gate there was the Old Stage Road, and across the road, in front of the house, ran the pasture, with its winding creek fringed by willows. Though this stream was smaller than Gooseneck Creek on the Greylocks' farm, the water never dried even in the severest drought, and a multitude of silver minnows flashed in ripples over the deep places. For a quarter of a mile the road divided the pasture from the wide band of woods on the left, and farther on, though the woods continued, the rich grass land was fenced off from several abandoned acres, which had been once planted in corn, but were now overgrown with broomsedge as high as Dorinda's waist. Sprinkled over the fields, a crop of scrub pine, grown already to a fair height, stood immovable in the ceaseless rise and fall of the straw. Though her eyes wandered over the waste ground as she passed, Dorinda was blind to-day to the colour and the beauty. What a pity you could never get rid of the broomsedge, she thought. The more you burned it off and cut it down, the thicker it came up again next year.

For a quarter of a mile the road was deserted. Then she came up with a covered wagon, which had stopped on the edge of the woods, while the mules munched the few early weeds in the underbrush. She had seen these vehicles before, for they were known in the neighbourhood as Gospel wagons. Usually there was a solitary "Gospel rider," an aged man, travelling alone, and wearing the dilapidated look of a retired missionary; but to-day there were two of them, an elderly husband and wife, and though they appeared meagre, chilled and famished, they were proceeding briskly with their work of nailing texts to the trees by the wayside. As Dorinda approached, the warning, "Prepare to Meet Thy God," sprang out at her in thick charcoal. The road to the station was already covered, she knew, and she wondered if the wagon had passed Jason at the gate by the fork.

Hearing her footsteps, one of the missionaries, a woman in a black poke bonnet, turned and stared at her.

46

"Good morning, sister. You are wearing a gay shawl."

Dorinda laughed. "Well, it is the only gay thing you will find about here."

With the hammer still in her hand, the woman, a lank, bedraggled figure in a trailing skirt of dingy alpaca, scrambled over the ditch to the road. "Yes, it's a solemn country," she replied. "Is there a place near by where we can rest and water the mules?"

"Old Farm is a little way on. I live there, and Ma will be glad to have you stop."

Such visitors, she knew, though they made extra work, were the only diversion in her mother's existence. They came seldom now; only once or twice in the last few years had the Gospel wagon driven along the Old Stage Road; but the larger trees still bore a few of the almost obliterated signs.

"Then we'll stop and speak a word to her. We'd better be going on, Brother Tyburn," observed the woman to her companion, who was crawling over the underbrush. "This don't look as if it was a much-travelled road. Brother Tyburn is my husband," she explained an instant later. "We met when we were both doing the Lord's work in foreign fields."

Golden sands. Ancient rivers. Black babies thrown to crocodiles. Her mother's missionary dream had come to life.

"Were you ever in Africa?" asked Dorinda.

"Yes, in the Congo. But we were younger then. After Brother Tyburn lost his health, we had to give up foreign work. Did you say your house was just a piece up the road?"

"A quarter of a mile. After that you won't find anything but a few negro cabins till you come to the Garlicks' place, three miles farther on."

The man had already climbed into the wagon and was gathering up the reins; the mules reluctantly raised their heads from the weeds; and the woman lifted her skirt and stepped nimbly up on the wheel. After she had seated herself under the canvas, she leaned down, gesticulating with the hammer which she still held.

"Thank you, sister. Have you given a thought to your soul?"

Wrapped in her orange shawl, Dorinda lifted her head with a spirited gesture.

"I joined the church when I was fifteen," she answered.

47

While she spoke she remembered vividly the way grace had come to her, a softly glowing ecstasy, which flooded her soul and made her feel that she had entered into the permanent blessedness of the redeemed. It was like the love she felt now, only more peaceful and far less subject to pangs of doubt. For a few months this had lasted, while the prosaic duties of life were infused with a beauty, a light. Then, suddenly, as mysteriously as it had come, the illumination in her soul had waned and flickered out like a lamp. Religion had not satisfied.

The wagon joggled on its way, and floating back, above the rumble of the wheels, there came presently the words of a hymn, at first clear and loud, and then growing fainter and thinner as the distance widened. Often Dorinda had sung the verses in Sunday School. The hymn was a favourite one of her mother's, and the girl hummed it now under her breath:

> "*Res-cue the per-ish-ing, care for the dy-ing,*
> *Snatch them in pit-y from sin and the grave;*
> *Weep o'er the err-ing one, lift up the fall-en,*
> *Tell them of Je-sus, the migh-ty to save.*
> *Res-cue the per-ish-ing, care for the dy-ing,*
> *Je-sus is mer-ci-ful, Je-sus will save.*"

No, religion had not satisfied.

She was still humming when she reached the fork of the road. Then, glancing at the red gate of Five Oaks, she saw that Jason Greylock stood there, with his hand on the bar.

"I'd just got down to open the gate, when I looked up the road and saw you coming," he said. "I knew there wasn't another woman about who was wearing an orange shawl, and if there were, I'd wait for her just out of curiosity."

Though he spoke gaily, she felt, without knowing why, that the gaiety was assumed. He looked as if he had not slept. His fresh colour had faded; his clothes were rumpled as if he had lain down in them; and while she walked toward him, she imagined fancifully that his face was like a drowned thing in the solitude. If she had been older it might have occurred to her that a nature so impressionable must be lacking in stability; but, at the moment, joy in his presence drove every sober reflection from her mind.

48

"Is there anything the matter?" she asked, eager to help.

He looked down while the gate swung back, and she saw a quiver of disgust cross his mouth under the short moustache. Before replying, he led his horse into the road and turned back to lower the bar. Then he held out his hand to help her into the buggy.

"Do I look as if I'd had no sleep?" he inquired. "Father had a bad night, and I was up with him till day-break."

Then she understood. She had heard tales from Aunt Mehitable, whose daughter worked at Five Oaks, of the old man's drunken frenzies, and the way his mulatto brood ran shrieking about the place when he turned on them with a horsewhip. Would Jason be able to rid the house of this half-breed swarm and their mother, a handsome, slatternly yellow woman, with a figure that had grown heavy and shapeless, and a smouldering resentful gaze? Well, she was sorry for him if he had to put up with things like that.

"I am sorry," she responded, and could think of nothing to add to the words, which sounded flat and empty. In front of her on the blasted oak she saw the staring black letters of the Gospel riders, "After Death Comes the Judgment." Depression crept like a fog into her mind. If only she could think of something to say! While they drove on in silence she became aware of her body, as if it were a weight which had been fastened to her and over which she had no control. Her hands and feet felt like logs. She was in the clutch, she knew, of forces which she did not understand, which she could not even discern. And these forces had deprived her of her will at the very moment when they were sweeping her to a place she could not see by a road that was strange to her.

"I suppose my nerves aren't what they ought to be," he said presently, and she knew that he was miles away from her in his thoughts. "They've always been jumpy ever since I was a child, and a night like that puts them on edge. Then everything is discouraging around here. I thought when I first came back that I might be able to wake up the farmers, but it is uphill ploughing to try to get them out of their rut. Last night I had planned a meeting in the school-house. For a week I had had notices up at the store, and I'd got at least a dozen men to promise to come and listen to what I had to tell them about improved methods of farming. I intended to begin with crops and sanitation, you know, and to lead off gradually, as

49

they caught on, to political conditions;—but when I went over," he laughed bitterly, "there was nobody but Nathan Pedlar and that idiot boy of John Appleseed's waiting to hear me."

"I know." She was sympathetic but uncomprehending. "They are in a rut, but they're satisfied; they don't want to change."

He turned to look at her and his face cleared. "You are the only cheerful sight I've seen since I got here," he said.

The light had changed again and her inner mood was changing with the landscape. A feeling of intimate kinship with the country returned, and it seemed to her that the colour of the broomsedge was overrunning the desolate hidden field of her life. Something wild and strong and vivid was covering the waste places.

"I am glad," she answered softly.

"It does me good just to look at you. I ought to be able to do without companionship, but I can't, not for long. I am dependent upon some human association, and I haven't had any, nothing that counts, since I came here. In New York I lived with several men (I've never been much of a woman's man), and I miss them like the devil. I was getting on well with my work, too, though I never wanted to study medicine—that was Father's idea. At first I hoped that I could distract myself by doing some good while I was here," he concluded moodily; "but last night taught me the folly of that."

Though he seemed to her unreasonable, and his efforts at philanthropy as futile as the usual unsettling processes of reform, she felt passionately eager to comfort him in his failure. That she might turn his disappointment to her own advantage had not occurred to her, and would never occur to her. The instinct that directed her was an unconscious one and innocent of design.

"Well, you've just begun," she replied cheerfully. "You can't expect to do everything in the beginning."

He laughed. "I knew you'd say that. Even in New York they tell me I try to hurry nature. I'm easily discouraged, and I take things too hard, I suppose. Coming back here was a bitter pill, but I had to swallow it. If I'd been a different sort of chap I might have gone on with my work in New York, and let Father die alone there at Five Oaks. But when he sent for me I hadn't the heart or the courage to refuse to come. The truth is, I've never been able to go ahead. It seems to me, when I look back, that I've always been

50

balked or bullied out of having what I wanted in life. I remember once, when I was a little child, I went out with Mother to gather dewberries, and just as I found the finest brier, all heavy with fruit, and reached down to pick it, a moccasin snake struck out at my hand. I got a fit, hysterics or something, and ever since then the sight of a snake has made me physically sick. Worse than that, whenever I reach out for anything I particularly want, I have a jumping of the nerves, just as if I expected a snake to strike. Queer, isn't it? I wonder how much influence that snake has had on my life?"

Though he laughed, his laugh was not a natural one and she asked herself if he could be in earnest. She was still young enough to find it difficult to distinguish between the ironically wise and the incredibly foolish.

"I wish I could help you. I'll do anything in the world I can to help you," she murmured in a voice as soft as her glance.

Their eyes met, and she watched the bitterness, the mingling of disappointment and mortification, fade in the glow of pleasure—or was it merely excitement?—that flamed in his face.

"Then wear a blue dress the colour of your eyes," he rejoined with the light-hearted audacity of the day before.

The difference in his tone was so startling that she blushed and averted her gaze.

"I haven't a blue dress," she replied stiffly, while her troubled look swept the old Haney place as they went past. In a little while they would reach the station. Even now they were spinning up the long slope, white as bone dust, that led to the store.

The change in his tone sent the blood in quivering rushes to her cheeks. She felt the sound beating in her ears as if it were music.

"Then beg, borrow, or steal one," he said gaily, "before I see you again."

His smile died quickly, as if he were unable to sustain the high note of merriment, and the inexplicable sadness stole into his look. Was it substance or shadow, she wondered. Well, whatever it was, it stirred a profound tenderness in her heart.

6

When they parted at the station there was a dreaming smile on her lips; and though she tried to drive it away as she entered the store, she felt that the smile was still there, hovering about her mouth. A physical warmth, soft and penetrating, enveloped her like sunshine. And the miracle (for it was a miracle) had changed her so utterly that she was a stranger to the Dorinda of yesterday. Where that practical girl had been, there was now a tremulous creature who felt that she was capable of unimaginable adventures. How could she reflect upon the virtues of the red cow she would buy from old Doctor Greylock when she could not detach her mind from the disturbing image of Doctor Greylock's son? Over and over, she repeated mechanically, "Thirty dollars for the red cow"; yet the words might have been spoken by John Appleseed or his idiot boy, who was lounging near the track, so remote were they from her consciousness. Thirty dollars! She had saved the money for months. There would be just that much after the interest on the mortgage was paid. She had it put away safely in the best pickle-dish in the china press. Ten dollars a month didn't go far, even if it was "ready money." *Then wear a blue dress the colour of your eyes. Beg, borrow, or steal one before I see you again.* From whom or where had the words come? Something within herself, over which she had no control, was thinking aloud. And as if her imagination had escaped from darkness into light, a crowd of impressions revolved in her mind like the swiftly changing colours of a kaleidoscope. His eyes, black at a distance, brown when you looked into them. The healthy reddish tan of his skin. The white streak on his neck under his collar. The way his hair grew in short close waves like a cap. His straight red lips, with their look of vital and urgent youth. The fascinating curve of his eyebrows, which bent down when he smiled or frowned over his deep-set eyes. The way he smiled. The way he laughed. The way he looked at her.

Nathan had opened the store and was already sweeping the tracks of mud from the platform. Somebody was in the store behind him. He talked while he swept, jerking his scraggy shoulders with an awkward movement. Poor Nathan, he had as many gestures as a puppet, and they all looked as if they were worked by strings.

Then, as she hastened up the steps of the store, there occurred one of those trivial accidents which make history. Miss Seena Snead, attired for travelling in her best navy blue lady's cloth and her small lace bonnet with velvet strings, came out of the door.

"I'm runnin' down to Richmond to buy some goods and notions," she said. "Is there any errand I can do for you or yo' Ma?"

Out of that golden mist, the strange Dorinda who had taken the place of the real Dorinda, spoke eagerly:

"I wonder—oh, I wonder, Miss Seena, if you could get me a blue dress?"

"A blue dress? Why, of course I can, honey. Do you want gingham or calico? I reckon Nathan has got as good blue and white check as you can find anywhere. I picked it out for him myself."

Dorinda shook her head. Her eyes were shining and her voice trembled; but she went on recklessly, driven by this force which she obeyed but could not understand. "No, not gingham or calico. I don't want anything useful, Miss Seena. I want cashmere—or nun's veiling. And I don't want dark blue. I want it exactly the colour of my eyes."

"Well, I declar!" Miss Seena looked as if she could not believe her ears. "Who-ever heard of matchin' material by yo' eyes?" Then turning the girl round, she examined her intently. "I ain't never paid much attention to yo' eyes," she continued, "though I always thought they had a kind, pleasant look in 'em. But when I come to notice 'em, they're jest exactly the shade of a blue jay's wing. That won't be hard to match. I can carry a blue jay's wing in my mind without a particle of trouble. You want a new dress for spring, I s'pose? It don't matter whether a girl's a Methodist or an Episcopalian, she's mighty sure to begin wantin' a new dress when Easter is comin'. Geneva Ellgood ordered her figured challis yestiddy from

53

one of them big stores in New York. She picked the pattern out of a fashion paper, and when the goods come, I'm goin' to spend a week at Green Acres an' make it up for her. It is a real pretty pattern, and it calls for yards and yards of stuff. They say young Doctor Greylock was a beau of hers when she was in New York last summer, an' I reckon that's why she's buyin' so much finery. Courtin' is good for milliners, my Ma used to say, even if marriage is bad for wives. She had a lot of dry fun in her, my Ma had. Geneva is gettin' a mighty pretty hat too. She's bought a wreath of wheat and poppies, an' I'm takin' it down to Richmond to put on one of them stylish new hats with a high bandeau."

For an instant Dorinda held her breath while a wave of dull sickness swept over her. At that moment she realized that the innocence of her girlhood, the ingenuous belief that love brought happiness, had departed for ever. She was in the thick of life, and the thick of life meant not peace but a sword in the heart. Though she scarcely knew Geneva Ellgood, she felt that they were enemies. It was not fair, she told herself passionately, that one girl should have everything and one nothing! A primitive impulse struggled like some fierce invader in her mind, among the orderly instincts and inherited habits of thought. She was startled; she was frightened; but she was defiant. In a flash the knowledge came to her that habit and duty and respectability are not the whole of life. Beyond the beaten road in which her ideas and inclinations had moved, she had discovered a virgin wilderness of mystery and terror. While she stood there, listening to the gossip of the dressmaker, the passion that abides at the heart of all desperation inflamed her mind. She had learned that love casts its inevitable shadow of pain.

"I want a hat too, Miss Seena," she said quickly. "A white straw hat with a wreath of blue flowers round the crown."

Miss Seena lifted her spectacles to her forehead, and gazed at the girl inquiringly with her small far-sighted eyes. "I always thought you had too much character to care about clothes, Dorinda," she said, "but that jest proves, I reckon, that you never can tell. I s'pose youth is obleeged to break out sooner or later. But it will cost a good deal, I'm afraid. Wreaths are right expensive, now that they're so much worn. Yo' Ma told me the last time I was over thar that you were savin' all you made to help yo' Pa with the farm."

Her glance was mild, for she was not unsympathetic (when was a dressmaker, especially a dressmaker who was at the same time a sentimental spinster, unsympathetic about clothes?) but she wished to feel sure that Dorinda would not regret her extravagance after it was too late.

"You mustn't think that you can keep up with Geneva, honey," she added kindly but indiscreetly. "You're prettier than she is, but her Pa's the richest man anywhar about here, an' I reckon thar ain't much ugliness that money ain't able to cure."

The advice was wholesome, but Dorinda frowned and shook her head stubbornly. The shawl had slipped to her shoulders, and the sunlight, which was struggling through the clouds, brought out a bluish lustre on her black hair. Miss Seena, watching her closely, reflected that hair and eyes like those did not often go together. With this vivid contrast and the high colour in her lips and cheeks the girl appeared almost too conspicuous, the dressmaker decided. "It always seemed to me mo' refined when yo' eyes and hair matched better," she thought, "but I s'pose most men would call her handsome, even if her features ain't so small as they ought to be."

"I'm going to have one nice dress, I don't care what happens," Dorinda was saying. "I don't care what happens," she repeated obstinately. "I've got thirty dollars put away, and I want you to buy that dress and hat if it takes every cent of it. I'm tired of doing without things."

"Well, I don't reckon they will cost that much," returned Miss Seena, after a quick sum in mental arithmetic. "You can buy right nice, double-width nun's veiling for seventy-five cents a yard, and I can get you a dress, I reckon, by real careful cuttin', out of nine yards. The fashion books call for ten, but them New York folks don't need to cut careful. To be sure, these here bell skirts and balloon sleeves take a heap of goods, but I s'pose you'll want yours jest as stylish as Geneva's?" Since the girl was determined to waste her money, it would be a pity, Miss Seena reflected gently, to spoil the pleasure of her improvidence. After all, you weren't young and good-looking but such a little while!

"I'll do the best I can, honey," she said briskly. "And they'll charge it to me at Brandywine and Plummer's store, so you don't need to bring the money till the first of the month. Thar's the train whistlin' now, and Sister Texanna is waitin' at the track with my basket and things. Don't you worry, I'll get you jest the very prettiest material I can find."

Turning away, the dressmaker hurried with birdlike fluttering steps to the track, where Dorinda saw the stately figure of Miss Texanna standing guard beside an indiscriminate collection of parcels. Miss Texanna, unlike her sisters, had been pretty in her youth, and a dull glamour of forgotten romance still surrounded her. Though she had never married, she had had a lover killed in the war, which, as Miss Tabitha had once remarked, was "almost as good." But Dorinda, while she watched the approaching train, did not think of the three sisters. "I oughtn't to have done it," she said to herself, with a feeling of panic, and then desperately, "Well, I'm going to have one good dress, I don't care what happens!"

A few farmers were taking the early train to town, and Dorinda saw that Geneva Ellgood had driven her father to the station in her little dog-cart with red wheels. She was a plain girl, with a long nose, eyes the colour of Malaga grapes, and a sallow skin which had the greenish tinge of anæmia. Her flaxen hair, which she arranged elaborately, was profuse and beautiful, and her smile, though it lacked brightness, was singularly sweet and appealing.

As the two girls looked at each other, they nodded carelessly; then Geneva leaned forward and held out a slip of paper.

"I wonder if you would mind fixing up this list for me?" she asked in a friendly tone. "I don't like to leave Neddy, and Bob has gone in to see if there are any letters."

Running down the steps, Dorinda took the list from her and glanced over it. "We haven't got the kind of coffee you want," she said. "It was ordered two weeks ago, but it hasn't come yet."

"Well, we'll have to make out with what you have. If you'll wrap up the things, Bob will bring them out to me."

She was a shy girl, gentle and amiable, yet there was a barely perceptible note of condescension in her manner. "Just because she's rich and I'm poor, she thinks she is better than I am," Dorinda thought disdainfully, as she went up the steps.

While she was weighing and measuring the groceries, Bob Ellgood came from the post office (which consisted of a partition, with a window, in one corner of the store) and stopped by the counter to speak to her. He was a heavy, slow-witted young man, kind, temperate, and good-looking in a robust, beefy fashion. Because he was the eldest son of James Ellgood, he was regarded as desirable by the girls in the neighbourhood, and Dorinda remembered that, only a few Sundays ago, she had looked at him in church and asked herself, with a start of expectancy, "What if he should be the right one after all?" She laughed softly over the pure absurdity of the recollection, and a gleam of admiration flickered in the round, marble-like eyes of the young man.

"I hope the Greylocks' steer didn't harm your father's plant beds," he said abruptly.

"No," she shook her head. "I haven't heard that they suffered."

Having weighed the sugar, she was pouring it into a paper bag, and his eyes lingered on the competent way in which her fingers turned down the opening, secured it firmly, and snipped off the end of the string with an expert gesture. Only a week ago his attention would have flattered her, but to-day she had other things to think of, and his admiring oxlike stare made her impatient. Was that the way things always came, after you had stopped wanting them?

"Well, he ought to have a good crop after the work he's put on those fields," he continued, as she placed the packages in a cracker box and handed them to him over the counter.

She shook her head. "No matter how hard you work it always comes back to the elements in the end. You can't be sure of anything when you have to depend upon the elements for a living."

"That's what Father says." He accepted the fatalistic philosophy without dispute. "After all, the rain and frost and drought, not the farmer, do most of the farming." He had had a good education, and though his speech was more provincial than Jason's, it lacked entirely the racy flavour of Pedlar's Mill.

With the box under one arm, he was still gazing at her, when the impatient voice of Geneva rang out from the doorway, and the girl came hurrying into the store.

"What are you waiting for, Bob? I thought you were never coming." Then, as her eyes fell on Dorinda, she added apolo-

57

getically, "Of course I know the things were ready, but Bob is always so slow. I've got to hurry back because Neddy won't stand alone."

She turned away and went out, while Bob followed with a crest-fallen air.

"As if I cared!" thought Dorinda proudly. "As if I wanted to talk to him!"

The train to the north had gone by at five o'clock, and the next one, which Miss Seena had just taken to Richmond, was the last that would stop before afternoon. The few farmers who had lounged about the track were now waiting in the store, while Nathan weighed and measured or counted small change into callous palms. Here and there a negro in blue jeans overalls stood patiently, with an expression of wistful resignation which was characteristic less of an individual than of a race. There was little talk among the white farmers, and that little was confined to the crops or the weather. Rugged, gnarled, earth-stained, these men were as impersonal as trees or as transcendental philosophers. In their rustic pride they accepted silence as they accepted poverty or bad weather, without embarrassment and without humility. If they had nothing to say, they were capable of sitting for hours, dumb and unabashed, over their pipes or their "plugs" of tobacco. They could tell a tale, pro-vided there was one worth the telling, with caustic wit and robust realism; but the broad jest or the vulgar implication of the small town was an alien product among them. Not a man of them would have dared recite an anecdote in Pedlar's store that Dorinda should not have heard. The transcendental point of view, the habit of thought bred by communion with earth and sky, had refined the grain while it had roughened the husk.

"Do you want me to wait on Mr. Appleseed?" asked Dorinda, glancing past Nathan to the genial, ruddy old farmer, who was standing near her, with his idiot son close at his side. As she spoke she lifted the top from one of the tall jars on the counter, and held out a stick of striped peppermint candy. "Here's a stick of candy for you, Billy."

The boy grinned at her with his sagging mouth, and made a snatch at the candy.

58

"Say thanky, son," prompted John Appleseed, who had chosen his own name.

"Thanky," muttered Billy obediently, slobbering over the candy.

"No, I'll look after John as soon as I've fixed up this brown sugar," said Nathan. "I wish you'd take those ducks from Aunt Mehitable Green. She's been waitin' a long time, and she ain't so young as she used to be. Tell her I'll allow her seventy-five cents for the pair, if they're good size. She wants the money's worth in coffee and Jamaica ginger."

"Why, I didn't know Aunt Mehitable was here!" Glancing quickly about, she discovered the old woman sitting on a box at the far end of the room, with the pair of ducks in her lap. "I didn't see you come in, or I'd have spoken to you before," added the girl, hurrying to her.

Aunt Mehitable Green had assisted at Dorinda's birth, which had been unusually difficult, and there was a bond of affection, as well as a sentimental association, between them. Mrs. Oakley, with her superior point of view, had always been friendly with the negroes around her. During Dorinda's childhood both mother and daughter had visited Aunt Mehitable in her cabin at Whistling Spring, and the old midwife had invariably returned their simple gifts of food or wine made from scuppernong grapes, with slips of old-fashioned flowers or "physic" brewed from the mysterious herbs in her garden. She still bore the reputation, bestowed half in fear, half in derision, of "a conjure woman," and not a negro in the county would have offended her. Though there was a growing scepticism concerning her ability to "throw spells" or work love charms, even Mrs. Oakley admitted her success in removing moles and warts and in making cows go dry at the wrong season. She was a tall, straight negress, with a dark wrinkled face, in which a brooding look rippled like moonlight on still water, and hair as scant and grey as lichen on an old stump. Her dress of purple calico was stiffly starched, and she wore a decent bonnet of black straw which had once belonged to Mrs. Oakley. The stock she came of was a good one, for, as a slave, she had belonged to the Cumberlands, who had owned Honeycomb Farm before it was divided. Though that prosperous family had "run to seed" and finally disappeared, the slaves belonging to it

59

had sprung up thriftily, in freedom, on innumerable patches of rented ground. The Greens, with the Moodys and Plumtrees, represented the coloured aristocracy of Pedlar's Mill; and Micajah Green, Aunt Mehitable's eldest son, had recently bought from Nathan Pedlar the farm he had worked, with intelligence and industry, as a tenant.

"I hope you didn't walk over here," said Dorinda, for Whistling Spring was five miles away, on the other side of the Greylocks' farm, beyond Whippernock River.

The old woman shook her head, while she began unwrapping the strips of red flannel on the legs of the ducks. "Naw'm, Micajah brung me over wid de load er pine in de oxcyart. I ain' seen you en yo' Ma fur a mont' er Sundays, honey," she added.

"I've wanted to get down all winter," answered Dorinda, "but the back roads are so bad I thought I'd better wait until the mud dried. Are any of your children living at home with you now?"

Aunt Mehitable sighed. "De las oner dem is done lef' me, but I ain't never seed de way yit dat de ole hen kin keep de fledglin's in de chicken coop. Dey's all done moughty well, en dat's sump'n de Lawd's erbleeged ter be praised fur. Caze He knows," she added fervently, "de way I use'n ter torment de Th'one wid pray'r when dey wuz all little."

"Pa says Micajah is one of the best farmers about here."

"Dat's so. He sholy is," assented the old midwife. "En Micar he's steddyin' 'bout horse sickness along wid Marse Kettledrum, de horse doctah," she continued, "en Moses, he's gwineter wuck on de railroad ontwel winter, en Abraham, he's helpin' Micajah, en Eliphalet, he's leasin' a patch er ground f'om Marse Garlick over yonder by Whippernock, en Jemima, de one I done name arter ole Miss, she's wuckin' at Five Oaks fur ole Doctah Greylock——"

"I thought she'd left there long ago," Dorinda broke in.

"Naw'm, she ain' lef' dar yit. She wuz fixin' ter git away, caze hit's been kinder skeery over dar sence de ole doctah's been gittin' so rambunctious; en Jemima, she ain' gwineter teck er bit er sass f'om dat ar yaller huzzy, needer. Yas'm, she wuz all fixin' ter leave twel de young doctah come back, an he axed 'er ter stay on dar en wait on him. Huh!" she exclaimed abruptly, after a pause, "I 'low dar's gwineter be some loud bellowin's w'en de young en de ole steer is done lock dere horns tergedder." With a gesture of supreme disdain, she thrust the two ducks away from her into Dorinda's hands. "Dar, honey, you teck dese yer ducks," she said. "I'se moughty glad to lay eyes on you agin, but I'se erbleeged ter be gittin' erlong back wid Micajah. You tell yo' Ma I'se comin' ter see 'er jes' ez soon ez de cole spell is done let up. I sholy is gwineter do hit."

When the old woman had gone, with the coffee and Jamaica ginger in her basket, Dorinda hurried into the room at the back of the store, where Rose Emily and the children were waiting for her.

"I couldn't get here any sooner," she explained as she entered. "First Miss Seena Snead and then Aunt Mehitable stopped me. Are you feeling easier to-day, Rose Emily?"

Mrs. Pedlar, wrapped in a pink crocheted shawl, with her hectic colour and her gleaming hair, reminded Dorinda of the big wax doll they had had in the window of the store last Christmas. She was so brilliant that she did not look real.

"Oh, I feel like a different person this morning," she answered. It was what she always said at the beginning of the day. "I'm sure I shall be able to get up by evening."

"I'm so glad," Dorinda responded, as she did every morning. "Wait and see what the doctor says."

"Yes, I thought I'd better stay in bed until he comes." She closed her eyes from weakness, but a moment later, when she opened them, they shone more brightly than ever. "He said he would stop by."

For an instant Dorinda hesitated; then she answered in a hushed voice. "I met him in the road, and he drove me over."

Rose Emily's face was glowing. "Oh, did he? I'm so glad," she breathed.

"I'm afraid things aren't going well at Five Oaks," Dorinda pursued in a troubled voice. "He looked dreadfully worried. It's the old man, I suppose. Everybody says he's drinking himself to death, and there's that coloured girl with all those children."

"Well, he can't live much longer," Rose Emily said hopefully, "and then, of course, Jason will send them all packing." She reflected, as if she were trying to recall something that had slipped her memory. "Somebody was telling me the other day," she continued, "it must have been either Miss Texanna or Miss Tabitha.

61

Whoever it was thought Jason had made a mistake to come back. Oh, I remember now! It was Miss Tabitha, and she called Jason a fool to let his father manage his life. She said he had a sweet nature, but that he was as light as a feather and a strong wind could blow him away. Of course she didn't know him."

"Of course not," Dorinda assented emphatically.

"Well, I haven't seen him often, but he didn't seem to me to lack backbone. Anyhow, I'd rather be married to a sweet nature than to a strong will," she added. Ever since Jason's return, she had hoped so ardently that he might fall in love with Dorinda that already, according to her optimistic habit of mind, she regarded the match as assured.

They were still discussing young Doctor Greylock when Minnie May ran in to say that Bud "would not mind what she told him," and Mrs. Pedlar shifted her feverish animation in the direction of her daughter.

"Tell him if he doesn't do what you say, I'll make his Pa whip him as soon as the store is closed," she said sternly, for she was a disciplinarian; and the capable little girl ran out again, wiping her red and shrivelled hands on the towel she had pinned over her short dress.

"I declare that child's a born little mother," Rose Emily continued. "I don't see how I could ever have pulled through without her."

Trivial as the incident was, Dorinda never forgot it. Years afterwards the scene would return to her memory, and she would see again the sturdy, energetic little figure, with the two thick wheaten-red braids and the towel pinned about her waist, hurrying out of the room. A born little mother, that was the way Minnie May always appeared to her.

"Nathan needs me to help. I'd better go back," she said. "I'll look in every now and then to see how you are." Smoothing her hair with her hand, she hastened into the store.

As the morning advanced a line of white and coloured farmers, assembled by the counter, with the chickens, eggs, and pats of butter which they had brought to exchange for coffee, molasses, sugar, or simple household remedies such as Jamaica ginger and

62

Sloan's liniment. Tea was used only in case of illness, and the brown tin canister on the shelf sometimes remained empty for weeks.

Until yesterday Dorinda had regarded the monotonous routine of the store as one of the dreary, though doubtless beneficial, designs of an inscrutable Providence. A deep-rooted religious instinct persuaded her, in spite of secret recoils, that dullness, not pleasure, was the fundamental law of morality. The truth of the matter, she would probably have said, was that one did the best one could in a world where duty was invariably along the line of utmost resistance. But this morning, even while she performed the empty mechanical gestures, she felt that her mind had become detached from her body, and was whirling like a butterfly in some ecstatic dream. Flightiness. That was how it would have appeared to her mother. Yet, if this were flightiness, she thought, who would ever choose to be sober? Beauty, colour, sweetness, all the vital and radiant energy of the spring, vibrated through her. Her ears were ringing as if she moved in a high wind. Sounds floated to her in thin strains, from so great a distance that she was obliged to have questions repeated before they reached her ears. And all the time, while she weighed chickens and counted eggs and tasted butter, she was aware that the faint, slow smile clung like an edge of light to her lips.

7

The morning was well over when Minnie May came running into the store to ask Dorinda to come to her mother.

"The doctor is with her," said the child, "and he wants to leave some directions."

"Hadn't your father better see him?" Dorinda inquired, longing yet hesitating.

"No, you go," answered Nathan before the child could reply. "You're so much quicker at understanding," he explained, "and you can tell me what he says after he's gone."

He looked, for all his immense frame, more bent and colourless and ineffectual, she thought, than she had ever seen him. What a mean life he had had! And he was good. There wasn't a better husband and father in the world than Nathan Pedlar, and for the matter of that, there wasn't a more honest tradesman. Yet everybody, even his own children, pushed him aside as if he were of no consequence.

A few minutes later she was in Rose Emily's room, and her bright gaze was on the clean-cut youthful figure leaning over her friend. Though she had known that he would be there, her swift impression of him startled her by its vividness. It was like this every time that she saw him. There was an animation, a living quality in his face and smile which made everything appear lifeless around him. Long afterwards, when she had both remembered and forgotten, she decided that it was simply the glamour of the unknown that she had felt in him. In those first months after his return to Pedlar's Mill, he possessed for her the charm of distant countries and picturesque enterprises. It was the flavour of personality, she realized, even then, not of experience. He had travelled little, yet his presence diffused the perilous thrill of adventure.

"This is Dorinda," Rose Emily said; and he looked up and nodded as casually as if he had never seen her before, or had just parted from her. Which impression, Dorinda wondered, did he mean to convey?

"I suppose you haven't got such a thing as a hammock?" he inquired. "What we need is to get her out on the porch. I've told her that every time I've seen her."

"There are several hammocks in the store." As she answered his question, Dorinda glanced at him doubtfully. In the sick-room he appeared to have shed his youth as a snake sheds its skin. He might have been any age. He was brisk, firm, efficient, and as sexless as a machine.

"Wouldn't it be safer to wait until the weather is milder?" Rose Emily asked, with an anxious smile. "Cold is so bad for me."

"Nonsense!" He shook his head with a laugh. "That's the whole trouble with you. Your lungs are starving for air. If you'd kept out of doors instead of shutting the windows, you wouldn't be where you are now."

At this his patient made a timid protest. "Your father always said——"

He interrupted her brusquely. "My father was good in his generation, but he belongs to the old school."

After this he talked on cheerfully, flattering her, chaffing her, while he made fun of her old-fashioned hygiene and asked innumerable questions, in a careless manner, about her diet, her medicine, her diversions, and the deformity of the baby, John Abner, who was born with a clubfoot. Though it seemed a long time to Dorinda, it was in fact not more than a quarter of an hour before he said good-bye and nodded to the girl to follow him out on the porch.

"I'll show you the very place to hang that hammock," he remarked as he led the way out of doors.

Rose Emily stretched out her thin arm to detain him. "Don't you think I'm getting better every day, Doctor?"

"Better? Of course you're better." He looked down at her with a smile. "We'll have you up and out before summer."

Then he opened the door, and Dorinda obediently followed him outside.

"How on earth does she breathe in that oven?" he demanded

65

moodily, while he walked to the far end of the porch. "She'll be dead in three months, if she doesn't get some fresh air into her lungs. And the children. It's as bad as murder to keep them in that room."

He frowned slightly, and with his troubled frown, Dorinda felt that he receded from her and became a stranger. His face was graver, firmer, harassed by perplexity. It seemed to her incredible that he had looked at her that morning with the romantic pathos and the imperative needs of youth in his eyes.

"Will she really be up by summer?" she asked, breathless with hope and surprise.

"Up?" He lowered his voice and glanced apprehensively over his shoulder. "Why, she's dying. Don't you know she is dying?"

"I thought so," her voice broke. "But you told her——"

"You didn't expect me to tell her the truth, did you? What kind of brute do you take me for?"

This new morality, for which neither religious doctrine nor experimental philosophy had prepared her, stunned her into silence; and in that silence he repeated, with a gesture of irritation, as if the admission annoyed him excessively: "She'll be in her grave in six months, but you couldn't expect me to tell her so."

"You mean there is no hope?"

"Not of a cure. Her lungs are too far gone. Of course, if she gets out of doors, she may linger a little longer than we expect. Air and proper nourishment work wonders sometimes."

"But don't you think she ought to have time to prepare?" It was the question her mother would have asked, and she uttered it regretfully but firmly.

"Prepare? You mean for her funeral?"

"No, I mean for eternity."

If she had presented some prehistoric fossil for his inspection, he might have examined it with the same curious interest.

"For eternity?" he repeated.

Dorinda wavered. Though honest doubt was not unknown at Pedlar's Mill, it had seldom resisted successfully the onslaught of orthodox dogma. To the girl, with her intelligence and independence, many of her mother's convictions had become merely habits of speech; yet, after all, was not habit rather than belief the ruling principle of conduct?

66

"Will you let her die without time for repentance?" something moved her to ask.

"Repentance! Good Lord! What opportunity has she ever had to commit a pleasure?"

Then, as if the discussion irritated him, he picked up his medicine case which he had laid on the railing of the porch. "I'll be passing again about sundown," he remarked lightly, "and if you're ready to start home, I'll pick you up as I go by."

As casually as that! "I'll pick you up as I go by!" Just as if she were a bag of flour, she told herself in resentful despair. As he went from her down the path to the gate, she resolved that she would not let him drive her home if it killed her.

"I shan't be here at sundown," she called after him in the voice of a Covenanter.

He was almost at the gate. Her heart sank like a wounded bird, and then, recovering its lightness, soared up into the clouds. "Well, I'll manage to come a little earlier," he responded, with tender gaiety. "Don't disappoint me."

The small white gate between the two bare apple trees opened and closed behind him. He untied the reins from the paling fence, and springing into his buggy, drove off with a wave of his free hand. "God! What a life!" he said, looking round while the buggy rolled down the slope in the direction of the railway track. Standing there, she watched the wheels rock slightly as they passed over the rails, and then spin on easily along the road toward Green Acres. After the moving speck had disappeared in the powder blue of the distance, it seemed to her that it had left its vivid trail through the waste of the broomsedge. Her face glowed; her bosom rose and fell quickly; her pulses were beating a riotous tumult which shut out all other sounds. Suspense, heartache, disappointment, all were forgotten. Why had no one told her that love was such happiness?

Then, suddenly, her mind reproached her for the tumultuous joy. Rose Emily was dying; yet she could not attune her thoughts to the solemn fact of mortality. Walking the length of the porch, she opened the door and went back into the close room.

"The doctor insists that you must open the windows," she said gravely, subduing with an effort the blissful note in her voice.

So far had she been from the actual scene that she was not prepared for the eagerness in Rose Emily's look.

"Oh, Dorinda," cried the dying woman, "the doctor was so encouraging!"

The girl turned her face to the window. "Yes, he was very encouraging."

"What did he say to you on the porch?"

"Only that he wanted to have you up before summer." After all, the big lie was easier than the little one.

Mrs. Pedlar sighed happily. "I do wish summer would come!"

Dorinda bent down and straightened the pillow under the brilliant head. It was hard to die, she thought, when the world was so beautiful. There could be no drearier lot, she imagined, than marriage with Nathan for a husband; better by far the drab freedom of the Snead sisters. Yet even to Rose Emily, married to Nathan, life was not without sweetness. A warm pity for her friend pervaded Dorinda's heart; pity for all that she had missed and for the love that she had never known.

"It won't be long now." What more could she say?

"Dorinda!" Rose Emily's voice was quivering like the string of a harp. "Miss Texanna came in for a minute, and she was so excited about the dress Miss Seena is getting for you in town. Why didn't you tell me?"

"I wanted to, dear, only I didn't have time."

"I am so glad you are going to have a new dress. We can perfectly well make it here, after Miss Seena has cut it out. Sometimes I get tired crocheting."

Dorinda's eyes filled with tears. How kind Rose Emily was, how unselfish, how generous! Always she was thinking of others; always she was planning or working for the good of her children or Dorinda. Even as a school teacher she had been like that, sweet, patient, generous to a fault; and now, when she was dying, she grew nobler instead of peevish and miserable like other hopelessly ill women.

"I'd love it," she said, as soon as she could trust herself to reply, and she added hastily, "I wonder if you could eat a piece of duck to-morrow. Aunt Mehitable brought a pair of nice fat ones."

Rose Emily nodded. "Yes, to-morrow. I'd like to see Aunt Mehitable the next time she comes. She told me once she could conjure this mole off the back of my neck."

"Well, you might let her try when you're out again." Tears were beading Dorinda's lashes, and making some trivial excuse, she ran out of the room. To be worrying about a little mole when Rose Emily would be dead before summer was over!

A little before sunset, when the whistle of the train blew, Dorinda picked up her shawl and hastened down to the track. Miss Texanna, having nothing to do but knit in her box of a post office, had caught the whistle as far away as Turkey Station, and was already waiting between the big pump and the stranded freight car. "I reckon that's Sister Seena on the platform," she remarked; and a few minutes later the train stopped and the dressmaker was swung gallantly to the ground by the conductor and the brakeman.

"I've got everything," she said, after the swift descent. "I looked everywhere, and I bought the prettiest nun's veiling I could find. It's as near the colour of a blue jay's wing as I ever saw, and I've got some passementerie that's a perfect match." She was puffing while she walked up the short slope to the store, but they were the puffs of a victorious general. "Let's take it right straight into Rose Emily's room," she added. "She will be just crazy about it."

When the three of them gathered about Rose Emily's bed, and the yards of bright, clear blue unrolled on the counterpane, it seemed to Dorinda that they banished the menacing thought of death. Though she pitied her friend, she could not be unhappy. Her whole being was vibrating with some secret, irrepressible hope. A blue dress, nothing more. The merest trifle in the sum of experience; yet, when she looked back in later years, it seemed to her that the future was packed into that single moment as the kernel is packed into the nut.

"May I leave it here?" she asked, glancing eagerly out of the window. "The sun has gone down, and I must hurry." Would he wait for her or had he already gone on without her?

"We'll start cuttin' the first thing in the mornin'," said Miss Seena, gloating over the nun's veiling. "Jest try the hat on, Dorinda, before you go. I declar her own Ma wouldn't know her," she exclaimed, with the pride of creation. "Nobody would ever have dreamed she was so good-lookin', would they, Rose Emily? Ain't it jest wonderful what clothes can do?"

69

With that "wonderful" tingling in her blood, Dorinda threw the orange shawl over her head, and hastened out of the house. She felt as if the blue waves were bearing her up and sweeping her onward. In all her life it was the only thing she had ever had that she wanted. Yesterday there had been nothing, and to-day the world was so rich and full of beauty that she was dizzy with happiness. It was like a first draught of wine; it enraptured while it bewildered.

"I was a little late, and I was afraid you would have gone," Jason said.

What did he mean by that, she asked herself. Ought she not to have waited? She had no experience, no training, to guide her. Nothing but this blind instinct, and how could she tell whether instinct was right or wrong?

"Something kept me. I couldn't get away earlier," she answered.

"Have you worked all day?"

"Yes, but it isn't steady work. For hours at a time the store is empty. Then they all come together. Of course we have to tidy up in the off hours," she added, "and when there's nothing else to do I read aloud to Rose Emily."

"Are you content? You look happy."

He was gazing straight ahead of him, and it seemed to her that he was as impersonal as the Shorter Catechism. She suffered under it, yet she was powerless, in her innocence, to change it.

"I don't know. There isn't any use thinking." Were there always these fluctuations of hope and disappointment? Did nothing last? Was there no stability in experience?

"Well, I got caught too," he said presently, as if he had not heard her. "That's the rotten part of a doctor's life, everything and everybody catches him. Good Lord! Is there never any end to it? I'd give my head to get away. I'm not made for the country. It depresses me and lets me down too easily. I suppose I'm born lazy at bottom, and I need the contact with other minds to prod me into energy. This is the critical time too. If I can't get away, I'm doomed for good. Yet what can I do? I'm tied hand and foot as long as Father is alive."

"Couldn't you sell the farm?" Her voice sounded thin and colourless in her ears.

"How can I? Who would buy? And it isn't only the farm. I

wouldn't let that stand in my way. Father has got into a panic about dying, and he is afraid to be left alone with the negroes. He made me promise, when I thought he was on his death-bed, that I wouldn't leave him as long as he lived. He's got a will of iron—that's the only thing that keeps him alive—and he's always had his way with me. He broke my spirit, I suppose, when I was little. And it was the same way with Mother. She taught me to be afraid of him, and to dodge and parry before I was old enough to know what I was doing. When a fear like that gets into the nerves, it's like a disease." He broke off moodily, and then went on again without waiting for her response. "There's medicine now. I never wanted to study medicine. I knew I wasn't cut out for it. What I wanted to do was something entirely different,—but Father had made up his mind, and in the end he had his way with me. He always gets his way with me. He's thwarted everything I ever wanted to do as far back as I can remember. For my good of course. I understand that. But you can ruin people's lives—especially young people's lives—from the best motives."

His bitterness welled out in a torrent. It seemed to Dorinda that he had forgotten her; yet, even though he was unaware of her sympathy, she felt that she longed to reach out her hand and comfort him.

"I'm sorry," she said softly, "I'm sorry."

He looked at her with a laugh. "I oughtn't to have let that out," he returned. "Something happened to upset me. I'm easy-going enough generally, but there are some things I can't stand."

She was curious to know what had happened, what sort of things they were that he couldn't stand; but after his brief outburst, he did not confide in her. He was engrossed, she saw, in a recollection he did not divulge; and, manlike, he made no effort to assume a cheerfulness he did not feel. The drive was a disappointment to her; yet, in some inexplicable way, the disappointment increased rather than diminished his power over her. While she sat there, with her lips closed, she was shedding her allurement as prodigally as a flower sheds its fragrance. Gradually, the afterglow thinned into dusk; the road darkened, and the broomsedge, subdued by twilight, became impenetrable.

8

It was Easter Sunday, and Dorinda, wearing her new clothes with outward confidence but a perturbed mind, stood on the front porch while she waited for the horses to be harnessed to the spring wagon.

Though she was far less handsome in her blue dress and her straw hat with the wreath of cornflowers than she was in her old tan ulster and orange shawl, neither she nor Almira Pryde, her father's niece, who was going to church with them, was aware of the fact. Easter would not be acknowledged in the austere service of the church at Pedlar's Mill; but both women knew that spring would blossom on the head of every girl who could afford a new hat. Joshua had gone to harness the horses; and while Mrs. Oakley put on her bonnet and her broadcloth mantle trimmed with bugles, which she had worn to church ever since Dorinda could remember, Almira babbled on in a rapture of admiration.

She was a pink, flabby, irresponsible person, adjusting comfortably the physical burden of too much flesh to the spiritual repose of too little mind. All the virtues and the vices of the "poor white" had come to flower in her. Married at fifteen to a member of a family known as "the low-down Prydes," she had been perfectly contented with her lot in a two-room log cabin and with her husband, a common labourer, having a taste for whiskey and a disinclination for work, who was looked upon by his neighbours as "not all there." As the mother of children so numerous that their father could not be trusted to remember their names, she still welcomed the yearly addition to her family with the moral serenity of a rabbit.

"I declar, Dorrie, I don't see how you got such a stylish flare," she exclaimed now, without envy and without ambition. "That bell skirt sets jest perfect!"

"I hope we got it right," said Dorinda, anxiously, as she turned slowly round under Almira's gaze. "Is Ike staying with the children?"

"Yes, we couldn't both leave 'em the same day. Is Uncle Josh hitching up?"

"He's coming round right now," said Mrs. Oakley, wafting a pungent odour of camphor before her as she appeared. "I'm glad you came over, Almira. There's plenty of room in the wagon since we've put in the back seat. Ain't you coming to church with us, Josiah?"

"No, I ain't," Josiah replied, stubbornly. "When I get a day's rest, I'm goin' to take it. It don't rest me to be preached to."

"Well, it ought to," rejoined his mother, with an air of exhausted piety. "If going to church ain't a rest, I don't know what you call one."

But Josiah was in a stubborn and rebellious mood. He was suffering with toothache, and though he was of the breed, he was not of the temper of which martyrs are made. "I don't see that yo' religion has done so much for you," he added irascibly, "or for Pa either."

In her Sunday clothes, with her buckram-lined skirt spreading about her, Mrs. Oakley stopped, as she was descending the steps of the porch, and looked back at her son. "It is the only thing that has kept me going, Josiah," she answered, and her lip trembled as she repeated the solitary formula with which experience had provided her.

"Poor Ma," Dorinda thought while she watched her. "He might at least leave her the comfort of her religion."

"There's Uncle Josh now!" exclaimed Almira, who was by instinct a peacemaker. "Have you got yo' hymn book, Aunt Eudora? I forgot to bring mine along."

"It's in my reticule," Mrs. Oakley replied, producing a bag of beaded black silk, which she had used every Sunday for twenty years. "You'll get all muddied up, Dorinda, so I brought this old bedquilt for you to spread over your lap. It's chilly enough, anyway, for your ulster, and you can leave it with the quilt in the wagon. I can see you shivering now in that thin nun's veiling."

"I'm not cold," Dorinda answered valiantly; but she slipped her arms into the sleeves of the ulster, and accepted obediently the bedquilt her mother held out. Something, either Josiah's surliness or the slight chill in the early April air, had dampened her spirits, and she was realizing that the possession of a new dress does not confer happiness. Going down the steps, she glanced up doubtfully at the changeable blue of the sky. "I do hope it is going to stay clear," she murmured.

Round the corner of the house, she could see Joshua harnessing the horses, Dan and Beersheba. Dan, the leader, was still champing fodder as he backed up to the ramshackle vehicle, and while he raised his heavy hoofs, he turned his gentle, humid gaze on his master. He was a tall, raw-boned animal, slow but sure, as Joshua said proudly, with a flowing tail, plaited now and tied up with red calico, and the doleful face of a Presbyterian gone wrong. Beside him, Beersheba, his match in colour but not in character, moved with a mincing step, and surveyed the Sabbath prospect with a sportive epicurean eye. Unlike the Southern farmers around him, and the unimaginative everywhere, who are without feeling for animals, the better part of Joshua's life was spent with his two horses; and Dorinda sometimes thought that they were nearer to him than even his wife and his children. Certainly he was less humble and more at home in their company. In the midst of his family he seldom spoke, never unless a question was put to him; but coming upon him unawares in the fields or by the watering-trough, Dorinda had heard him talking to Dan and Beersheba in the tone a man uses only to the creatures who speak and understand the intimate language of his heart.

Always at a disadvantage in his Sunday clothes, which obscured the patriarchal dignity of his appearance, he looked more hairy and earth-bound than ever this morning. Though he had scrubbed his face until it shone, the colour of clay and the smell of manure still clung to him. Only his brown eyes, with their dumb wistfulness, were bright and living.

Wrapped in the old bedquilt, Dorinda jogged sleepily over the familiar road, which had become so recently the road of happiness. In a dream she felt the jolting of the wagon; in a dream she heard the creaking of the wheels, the trotting of the horses, the murmur of

74

wind in the tree-tops, the piping of birds in the meadows. In a dream she smelt the rich, vital scents of the ploughed ground, the sharp tang of manure on the tobacco-fields, the stimulating whiff of camphor from her mother's handkerchief. The trees were still bare in the deep band of woods, except for the flaming points of the maple and the white and rosy foam of the dogwood and redbud; but beside the road patches of grass and weeds were as vivid as emerald, and where the distance was webbed with light and shadow, the landscape unrolled like a black and silver brocade. While she drove on the vague depression drifted away from her spirits, and she felt that joy mounted in her veins as the sap flowed upward around her. In this dream, as in a remembered one of her childhood, she was for ever approaching some magical occasion, and yet never quite reaching it. She was for ever about to be satisfied, and yet never satisfied in the end. The dream, like all her dreams, carried her so far and no farther. At the very point where she needed it most, it broke off and left her suspended in a world of gossamer unrealities.

The mud spattered over the quilt in her lap, and she heard her mother say in her habitual tone of nervous nagging, "Drive carefully over that bad place, Joshua. If Elder Pursley stays with us during the missionary meetings, I'll have to ask Miss Texanna Snead to let us have some of her milk and butter. They have some fresh cows coming on, and I don't reckon she would miss it. Anyway, I'll try to pay her back with scuppernong grapes next September."

Again the prick in Dorinda's conscience! Though her mind rebelled, her conscience was incurably Presbyterian, and while she wore the blue dress gaily enough, she did not doubt that it was the symbol of selfishness. Between the blue dress and the red cow, she knew, the choice was, in its essence, one of abstract morality. Neither her father nor her mother had reproached her; but their magnanimity had served only to sharpen the sting of reflection. "Well, I reckon you won't be young but once, daughter," her mother had observed with the dry tolerance of disillusionment, "and the sooner you get over with it the better," while her father had stretched out his toil-worn hand and fingered one of the balloon sleeves. "That looks mighty pretty, honey, an' don't you worry about not gittin' the red cow. It'll save yo' Ma the trouble of churnin', an' you kind of lose the taste fur butter when you ain't had it fur some while."

"If Elder Pursley can't come, maybe one of the foreign missionaries will," Dorinda remarked, hoping to cheer her mother and to distract her mind from the mud holes.

"Of course we ain't got much to offer them," replied Mrs. Oakley in a tone of pious humility. "Though I don't reckon things of the flesh count much with a missionary, and, anyway, I'm going to have a parcel of young chickens to fry. Well, if we ain't most there! I declare Dan and Beersheba are getting real sprightly again!"

In the afternoon, sitting at the window of the spare chamber, to which she had been driven by the sultry calm of the Sabbath at Old Farm, Dorinda asked herself, and could find no answer, why the day had been a disappointment? She had expected nothing, and yet because nothing had come, she was dissatisfied and unhappy. Was there no rest anywhere? she asked without knowing that she asked it. Was love, like life, merely a passing from shock to shock, with no permanent peace?

Returning from church, the family had sat down, ill-humoured from emptiness, to dinner at four o'clock. It was the custom to have dinner in the middle of the afternoon, and no supper on Sunday; and the men were expected to gorge themselves into a state of somnolence which would, as Mrs. Oakley said, "tide them over until breakfast." When the heavy meal had been dispatched but not digested by the others, Dorinda (who had scarcely touched the apple dumplings her mother had solicitously pressed on her) came into the unused bedroom to put away her hat and dress in the big closet. The spare room, which was kept scrupulously cleaned and whitewashed, was situated at the back of the house adjoining Mrs. Oakley's chamber. All the possessions the family regarded as sacred were preserved here in a faint greenish light and a stale odour of sanctity. The windows were seldom opened; but Dorinda had just flung back the shutters, and the view she gazed out upon was like the coming of spring in an old tapestry. Though the land was not beautiful, that also had its moments of beauty.

Immediately in front of her, the pear orchard had flowered a little late and scattered its frail bloom on the grass. As the sunlight streamed through the trees, they appeared to float between earth and sky in some ineffable medium, while the petals on the ground

76

shone and quivered with a fugitive loveliness, as if a stir or a breath would dissolve the white fire to dew. Above the orchard, where a twisted path ran up to it, there was the family graveyard, enclosed by a crumbling fence which had once been of white palings, and in the centre of the graveyard the big harp-shaped pine stood out, clear and black, on the low crest of the hill. It was the tallest pine, people said, in the whole of Queen Elizabeth County; its rocky base had protected it in its youth; and later on no one had taken the trouble to uproot it from the primitive graveyard. In spring the boughs were musical with the songs of birds; on stormy days the tree rocked back and forth until Mrs. Oakley imagined, in her bad spells, that she heard the creaking of a gallows; and on hot summer evenings, when the moon rose round and orange-red above the hill, the branches reminded Dorinda of the dark flying shape of a witch.

While she sat there she lived over again the incidents of the morning; but the vision in her mind was as different from the actual occurrences as the image of her lover was different from the real Jason Greylock. Nothing had happened to disappoint her. Absolutely nothing. There was no reason why she should have been happy yesterday and miserable to-day; there was no reason except the eternal unreasonableness of love! She had tried to fix her mind on the sermon, which was a little shorter and no duller than usual. Sitting on the hard bench which she called a pew, bending her head over the bare back of the seat in front of her, she had sought to win spiritual peace by driving a bargain with God. "Give me happiness, and I will——"

Then before her prayer was completed, the congregation had stood up to sing, and she had met the eyes of Jason Greylock over the row of humble heads and proud voices. He was sitting in the Ellgood pew, and of course it was natural that he should have gone home with the Ellgoods to dinner. It was, she repeated sternly, perfectly natural. It was perfectly natural also that he should have forgotten that he had told her to beg, borrow, or steal a blue dress. In the few minutes when he had stopped to shake hands with her father and mother in the porch of the church, he had turned to her and asked, "How did you know that you ought to wear blue?" Yes, that, like everything else that had happened, was perfectly natural. For the last few weeks he had driven her to the store and back every day; he had appeared to have no happiness except in the hours that he spent with her; he had spoken to her, he had looked at her, as if he loved her; yet, she repeated obstinately, it was natural that he should be different on Sunday. Everything had always been different on Sunday. Since her childhood it had seemed to her that the movement of all laws, even natural ones, was either suspended or accelerated on the Sabbath.

She was thinking of this when the door opened, and Mrs. Oakley, who had resumed her ordinary clothes without disturbing her consecrated expression, thrust her head into the room.

"I've looked everywhere for you, Dorinda. Are you sick?"

"No, I'm not sick."

"Has Rufus been teasing you?"

"No."

"Has anybody said anything to hurt your feelings? Josiah is grouchy; but you mustn't mind what he says."

"Oh, no. He hasn't been any worse than usual. There isn't anything the matter, Ma."

"I noticed you didn't half eat your dinner, and your father kind of thought somebody had hurt your feelings."

Closing the door behind her, Mrs. Oakley crossed the room and sat down near her daughter in the best mahogany rocking-chair. Then, observing that she had disarranged the fall of the purple calico flounce, she rose and adjusted the slip-cover. While she was still on her feet, she went over to the bed and shook the large feather pillows into shape. After that, before sitting down again, she stood for a few moments with her stern gaze wandering about the room, as if she were seeking more dirt to conquer. But such things did not worry her. They drifted like straws on the surface of her mind, while her immortal spirit was preoccupied with a profound and incurable melancholy.

"I hope you ain't upset in your mind, daughter," she said abruptly.

Dorinda turned her lucid gaze on her mother. "Ma, whatever made you marry Pa?" she asked bluntly.

For an instant the frankness of the question stunned Mrs. Oakley. She had inherited the impenetrable Scotch reserve on the subject of sentiment, and it seemed to her, while she pondered the question, that there were no words in which she could answer her daughter. Both her vocabulary and her imagination were as innocent of terms of sex as if she were still an infant learning her alphabet.

"Well, your father's a mighty good man, Dorinda," she replied evasively.

"I know he is, but what made you marry him?"

"He's never given me a cross word in his life," Mrs. Oakley pursued, working herself up, as she went on, until she sounded as if she were reciting a Gospel hymn. "I've never heard a complaint from him. There never was a better worker, and it isn't his fault if things have always gone against him."

"I know all that," said Dorinda, as implacable as truth, "but what made you marry him? Were you ever in love with him?"

Mrs. Oakley's eyes lost suddenly their look of mystic vision and became opaque with memories. "I reckon I sort of took a fancy to him," she responded.

"Is there ever any reason why people marry?"

A mild regret flickered into the face of the older woman. "I s'pose they think they've got one."

She must have been pretty once, Dorinda thought while she watched her. She must have been educated to refinements of taste and niceties of manner; yet marriage had been too strong for her, and had conquered her.

"I don't see how you've stood it!" she exclaimed, with the indignant pity of youth.

Mrs. Oakley's bleak eyes, from which all inner glory had departed, rested pensively on her daughter. "There ain't but one way to stand things," she returned slowly. "There ain't but one thing that keeps you going and keeps a farm going, and that is religion. If you ain't got religion to lean back on, you'd just as well give up trying to live in the country."

"I don't feel that way about religion," Dorinda said obstinately. "I want to be happy."

"You're too young yet. Your great-grandfather used to say that most people never came to God as long as there was anywhere else for them to go."

"Was that true of great-grandfather?"

"It must have been. He told me once that he didn't come to Christ until he had thirsted for blood."

To Dorinda this seemed an indirect way to divine grace; but it made her great-grandfather appear human to her for the only time in her life.

"But he must have had something else first," she observed logically. "People always seem to have had something else first, or they wouldn't have found out how worthless it is. You must have been in love once, even if you have forgotten it."

Mrs. Oakley shook her head. "I haven't forgotten it, daughter," she answered. "It's time you were knowing things, I reckon, or you wouldn't be asking."

"Yes, it's time I was knowing things," repeated Dorinda. "You told me once that great-grandfather tried to keep you from marrying. Then why did you do it?"

For a minute or two before she replied the muscles in Mrs. Oakley's face and throat worked convulsively. "I was so set on your father that I moped myself into a decline," she said in a voice that was half strangled. "Those feelings have always gone hard in our family. There was your great-aunt Dorinda, the one you were named after," she continued, passing with obvious relief from her personal history. "When she couldn't get the man she'd set her heart on, she threw herself into the mill-race; but after they fished her out and dried her off, she sobered down and married somebody else and was as sensible as anybody until the day of her death. She lived to be upwards of ninety, and your great-grandfather used to say he prized her advice more than that of any man he knew. Then there was another sister, Abigail, who went deranged about some man she hadn't seen but a few times, and they had to put her away in a room with barred windows. They didn't have good asylums then to send anybody to. But she got over it too, and went as a missionary overseas. That all happened in Ireland before your great-grandfather came to this country. I never saw your great-aunt Dorinda, but she corresponded regularly, till the day of her death, with your great-grandfather. I remember his telling me that she used to say anybody could be a fool once, but only a born fool was ever a fool twice."

"I wonder what it was?" said Dorinda wearily.

Mrs. Oakley sighed. "It's nature, I reckon," she replied, without reproach but without sympathy. "Grandfather used to say that when a woman got ready to fall in love the man didn't matter, because she could drape her feeling over a scarecrow and pretend he was handsome. But, being a man, I s'pose he had his own way of looking at it; and if it's woman's nature to take it too hard, it's just as much the nature of man to take it too easy. The way I've worked it out is that with most women, when it seems pure foolishness, it ain't really that. It's just the struggle to get away from things as they are."

To get away from things as they are! Was this all there was in her feeling for Jason; the struggle to escape from the endless captivity of things as they are? In the bleak dawn of reason her dreams withered like flowers that are blighted by frost.

"Whatever it is, you haven't a good word for it," she said, vaguely resentful.

Mrs. Oakley considered the question impartially. "Well, it ain't catching and it ain't chronic," she remarked at last, with the temperate judgment of one who has finished with love. "I've got nothing to say against marriage, of course," she explained. "Marriage is the Lord's own institution, and I s'pose it's a good thing as far as it goes. Only," she added wisely, "it ain't ever going as far as most women try to make it. You'll be all right married, daughter, if you just make up your mind that whatever happens, you ain't going to let any man spoil your life."

The brave words, striking deep under the surface, rang against the vein of iron in Dorinda's nature. Clear and strong as a bell, she heard the reverberations of character beneath the wild bloom of emotion. Yes, whatever happened, she resolved passionately, no man was going to spoil her life! She could live without Jason; she could live without any man. The shadows of her great-aunts, Dorinda and Abigail, demented victims of love, stretched, black and sinister, across the generations. In her recoil from an inherited frailty, she revolted, with characteristic energy, to the opposite extreme of frigid disdain.

"Were all great-grandfather's sisters like that?" she asked hopefully, remembering that he had had six.

"Oh, no." Her mother was vague but encouraging. "I don't

81

recollect ever hearing anything foolish about Rebekah and Priscilla, and even the others were sensible enough when they had stopped running after men."

Running after men! The phrase was burned with acid into her memory. Was that what her mother, who did not know, would think of her? Was that what Jason, who did know, thought of her now? Her love, which had been as careless in its freedom as the flight of a bird, became suddenly shy and self-conscious. She had promised that she would meet him at Gooseneck Creek after sunset; but she knew now that she could not go, that something stronger than her desire to be with him was holding her back.

After her mother had gone she sat there for hours, with her eyes on the lengthening shadows over the pear orchard. This something stronger than her desire was hardening into resolution within her. She would avoid him in the future wherever she could; she would not look for him at the fork of the road; she would go to work an hour earlier and return an hour later in order that she might not appear to throw herself in his way. Already the inevitable battle between the racial temperament and the individual will was beginning, and before the evening was over she told herself that she was victorious. Though her longing drew her like a cord to Gooseneck Creek, and the quiver of her nerves was as sharp as the pain of an aching tooth, she stayed in her mother's chamber until bedtime, and tried unsuccessfully to fix her mind on her great-grandfather's dry sermon on temperance. When the evening was over at last, and she went upstairs to her room, she felt as if the blood had turned back in her veins. In the first fight she had conquered, but it was one of those victories, she knew without admitting the knowledge, which are defeats.

9

In May and June, for a brief season between winter desolation and summer drought, the starved land flushed into loveliness. Honey-coloured sunlight. The notes of a hundred birds. A roving sweetness of wild grape in the air. To Dorinda, whose happiness had come so suddenly that her imagination was still spinning from the surprise of it, the flowerlike blue of the sky, the songs of birds, and the elusive scent of the wild grape, all seemed to be a part of that rich inner world, with its passionate expectancy and its sense of life burning upward.

They were to be married in the autumn. Even now, when she repeated the words, they sounded so unreal that she could scarcely believe them; but her prudent Scotch mind, which still distrusted ecstasy, had ceased long ago to distrust Jason's love. The thing she wanted had come at last, and it had come, she realized, after she had deliberately turned her back upon it. She had found happiness, not by seeking it, but by running away from it. For two weeks she had persisted in her resolution; she had drawn desperately upon the tough fibre of inherited strength. For two weeks she had avoided Jason when it was possible, and in avoiding him, she could not fail to perceive, she had won him. To her direct, forward-springing nature there was a shock in the discovery that, where the matter is one of love, honesty is at best a questionable policy. Was truth, after all, in spite of the exhortations of preachers, a weaker power than duplicity? Would evasion win in life where frankness would fail? Then, as passion burned through her like the sunrise, doubt was extinguished. Since her heart told her that he was securely hers, what did it matter to her how she had won him?

For the first time in her life she had ceased longing, ceased striving. She was as satisfied as Almira to drift with the days toward some definite haven of the future. Detached, passive, still as a golden lily in a lily-pond, she surrendered herself to the light and the softness. Her soul was asleep, and beyond this inner stillness, men and women were as impersonal as trees walking. There was no vividness, no reality even, except in this shining place where her mind brooded with folded leaves. She was no longer afraid of life. The shadows of her great-aunts, Dorinda and Abigail, were as harmless as witches that have been robbed of their terror.

In those months, while her eyes were full of dreams, her immature beauty bloomed and ripened into its summer splendour. There was a richer gloss on her hair, which was blue black in the shadow, a velvet softness to her body, a warmer flush, like the colour of fruit, in her cheeks and lips. Her artless look wavered and became shy and pensive. Some subtle magic had transformed her; and if the natural Dorinda still survived beneath this unreal Dorinda, she was visible only in momentary sparkles of energy. When she was with Jason she talked little. Expression had never been easy for her, and now, since silence was so much softer and sweeter than speech, she sat in an ecstatic dumbness while she drank in the sound of his voice. Feeling, which had drugged her until only half of her being was awake, had excited him into an unusual mental activity. He was animated, eager, weaving endless impracticable schemes, like a man who is intoxicated but still in command of his faculties.

"Are you happy?" she asked one August afternoon, while they sat in the shade of the thin pines which edged the woods beyond Joshua's tobacco-field. It was the question she asked every day, and his answers, though satisfying to her emotion, were unconvincing to her intelligence. He loved her as ardently as she loved him; yet she was beginning to realize that only to a woman are love and happiness interchangeable terms. Some obscure anxiety working in his mind was stronger than all her love, all her tenderness. She gave way before it, but never, except in rare moments of ecstasy, did it yield place to her.

He smiled. "Of course; but I'll be happier when we can get away. I can't stand this country. My nerves begin to creep as soon as twilight comes on."

The woods behind them, known to the negroes in slavery days as

"Hoot Owl Woods," divided the front of Old Farm from the fallow meadows of Five Oaks, and stretched westward to the Old Stage Road and the gate at the fork. In front of the lovers, looking east, a web of blue air hung over the tobacco-field, where the huge plants were turning yellow in the intense heat. Back and forth in the furrows Joshua and Josiah were moving slowly, like giant insects, while they searched for the hidden "suckers" along the thick juicy stalks. Beyond the tobacco-field there was a ragged vegetable garden, where the tomatoes were rotting to pulp in the sun, and even the leaves of the corn looked wilted. The air was so breathless that a few languid crows appeared to float like dead things over the parched country.

"You don't feel that when you are with me," she said.

"The trouble is that I can't be with you but a part of the time. There's this worthless practice. I can't give it up, if I'm to keep on in medicine, and yet it means that I must spend half my life jogging over these God-forsaken roads. Then the night!" He shivered with disgust. "If you only knew, and I'm thankful you don't, what it means to be shut up in that house. Some nights my father doesn't sleep at all unless he is drugged into stupor. He wanders about with a horsewhip, looking in every room and closet for something to flog."

While he spoke she had a vision of the house, with its dust and cobwebs, and of the drunken old man, in his nightshirt and bare feet, roaming up and down the darkened staircase. She could see his bleared eyes, his purple face, his skinny legs, like the legs of a turkey gobbler, and his hands, as sharp as claws, lashing out with the horsewhip. The picture was so vivid that, coming in the midst of her dreamy happiness, it sickened her. Why did Jason have to stand horrors like that?

"It can't last much longer," she said. Was it the right thing, she wondered, or ought she to have kept up the pretence of loving the old man and dreading his death? Life would be so much simpler, she reflected, if people would only build on facts, not on shams.

He shook his head. "Nobody can say. Sometimes I think he can't last but a few weeks. Then he improves, without apparent reason, and his strength is amazing. According to everything we know about his condition, he ought to have died months ago; yet he appears to be getting better now instead of worse. I believe it is

85

simply a question of will. He is kept alive by his terror of dying. It's brutal, I know," he added, "to look forward to anybody's death, especially your own father's; but if you only knew how my life is eaten away hour by hour."

"You couldn't make some arrangement?" she asked. "Engage somebody to stay with him, or—or send him away?"

"I've thought of that. God knows I've thought of everything. But he isn't mad, you see. He is as sane as I am except when his craving for whiskey overcomes his fear of death, and he drinks himself into a frenzy. He won't have anybody else with him. I am the only human being who can do anything with him, and strange as it seems, I believe he has some kind of crazy affection for me in his heart. That's why I've put up with him so long. Several times I've been ready to leave, with my bags packed and the buggy at the door, and then he's broken down and wept like a child and begged me not to desert him. He reminds me then that he is dying, and that I promised to stick by him until the end. It's weakness in me to give in, but he broke my will when I was a child, he and my mother between them, and I can't get over the habit of yielding. I may be all wrong. Sometimes I know that I am. But, after all, it was a good impulse that made me promise to stick to him." For an instant he hesitated, and then added bitterly, "I can't tell you how often in life I've seen men betrayed by their good impulses."

"After it is over, you will be glad that you didn't leave him."

"I don't know. The truth is I'm in an infernal muddle. After all my medical training, there's a streak of darkey superstition somewhere inside of me. You'd think science would have knocked it out, but it hasn't. The fact is that I never really cared a hang about science. I was pushed into medicine, but the only aptitude I have for the profession is one of personality, and the only interest I feel in it is a sentimental pleasure in relieving pain. However, I've kept the superstition all right, and I have a sneaking feeling that if I break my word and desert the old man, it will come back at me in the end."

"But you're a wonderful doctor," she murmured, with her face against his shoulder. "Look at the people you've helped since you've been here."

He laughed without merriment. "That reminds me of the way

I used to think I'd bring civilization to the natives. I imagined, when I first came back, that all I had to do was to get people together and tell them how benighted they were, and that they'd immediately want to see wisdom. Do you remember the time I put up notices and opened the schoolhouse, and got only Nathan Pedlar and an idiot boy for an audience? The hardest thing to believe when you're young is that people will fight to stay in a rut, but not to get out of it. Well, that was almost six months ago, and those six months have taught me that any prejudice, even the prejudice in favour of the one-crop system, is a sacred institution. Look at the land!" He waved his hand vaguely in the direction of the sunbleached soil. "Even generations of failure can't teach the farmers about here that it is impossible to make bread out of straw."

"Do you think it is really the way they have treated the land?" she asked. "That's what Nathan is always saying, you know."

"Oh, the curse started with the tenant system, I'll admit. The tenants used the land as a stingy man uses a horse he has hired by the month. But the other farmers, even those who own their farms, are no better now than the tenants. They've worked and starved the land to a skeleton. Yet it's still alive, and it could be brought back to health, if they'd have the sense to treat it as a doctor treats an undernourished human body. Take Nathan Pedlar and James Ellgood. James Ellgood has made one of the best stock farms in the state; and that, by the way, is what this country is best suited for—stock or dairy farms. If I had a little money I could make a first rate dairy farm out of Five Oaks or Old Farm. You've got rich pasture land over the other side, and so have we, down by Whippernock River. It could be made a fine place for cattle, with the long grazing season and the months when cows could live in the open. Yet to suggest anything but the antiquated crop system is pure heresy. The same fields of tobacco that get eaten by worms or killed by frost. The same fields of corn year in and year out—" he broke off impatiently and bent his lips down to hers. "I'm talking you to sleep, Dorrie."

"I like to listen to you," she said, when she had kissed him. "If you tell them over and over, in time they may believe you."

"After I'm dead, perhaps. Hasn't Nathan Pedlar told them again and again? Hasn't he even proved it to them? He's been experimenting with alfalfa, and he's getting four cuttings now off those fields of his; but they think he's a fool because he isn't satisfied with one poor crop of corn."

"I know. Pa doesn't think anything of alfalfa," she answered. "He says Nathan is wasting his time raising a weed that cattle won't touch when it is dry."

"They all talk that way. Half daft, that's what they call anybody who wants to step out of the mud or try a new method. Ezra Flower told me yesterday that Nathan was half daft. No, I want to get away, not to spend my life as a missionary to the broomsedge. I feel already as if it were growing over me and strangling the little energy I ever had. That's the worst of it. If you stay here long enough, the broomsedge claims you, and you get so lazy you cease to care what becomes of you. There's failure in the air."

She remembered what old Matthew had said to her that March afternoon. "If he'd take the advice of eighty-odd years, he'd git away befo' the broomsage ketches him."

Was it true, what the old man believed, that the broomsedge was not only wild stuff, but a kind of fate? Fear, not for herself, but for Jason, stabbed through her.

"You're so easily discouraged," she said tenderly. To her, whose inner life was a part of the country, poverty had been an inevitable condition of living, and to fight had seemed as natural as to suffer or to endure.

"I suppose I am, but I'm made that way. I can't change my temperament," he replied, with a touch of the fatalism he condemned but could not resist.

"Well, I'll help you," she responded cheerfully. "After we are married, everything will be different. I am not afraid of Five Oaks or of anything else as long as I have you."

He was gazing over her head into the bleached distance, and she felt the tightened pressure of his arms about her. "I'd be all right here, even at Five Oaks, if you were with me," he answered. "You put something in me that I need. I don't know what it is—fibre, I suppose, the courage of living." Suddenly his eyes left the landscape and looked down into hers. "What I ought to do," he added impulsively, "is to marry you to-day. We could get the last train to
88

Washington, and be married to-morrow morning before any one knew of it. Would you come if I asked you?"

Her look did not waver. "I'll go anywhere that you ask me to. I'll do anything that will help you," she answered. Her body straightened as if its soft curves were moulded by the vein of iron in her soul.

But his impulse had spent its force in an imaginary flight. "That's what I'd like to do," he said slowly, while his rosy visions were obliterated by the first impact with reality. "But there are so many damned things to consider. There are always so many damned things to consider. First of all there's the money. I haven't got enough to take us away and keep us a week. After Father stopped helping me, I started out on my own hook in New York, and I was just making enough from the hospital to give me a living. I didn't put by a cent, and, of course, since I've been here I've made nothing. Down here the doctor gets paid after the undertaker, or not at all."

"I've got fifty dollars put away," she returned crisply, determined not to be discouraged. "And I don't need money. I've never had any." (How foolish she had been to buy the blue dress when clothes made so little difference!) "After we're married, I can keep on in the store just the same."

He laughed. "Ten dollars a month will hardly keep the fox from the henhouse."

Bending his head he began to kiss her in quick light kisses; then, as his ardour increased, in deeper and longer ones; and at last with a hungry violence. Though her love was the only thing that was vivid to her, she had even now, while she felt his arms about her and his lips seeking hers, the old haunting sense of impermanence, as if the moment, like the perfect hour of the afternoon, were too bright to endure. However much she loved him, she could not sink the whole of herself into emotion; something was left over, and this something watched as a spectator. Ecstasy streamed through her with the swiftness of light; yet she never lost completely the feeling that at any instant the glory might vanish and she might drop back again into the dull grey of existence.

10

When they parted, and she went home along the edge of the tobacco-field, the sun was beginning to go down, and from the meadows, veiled in quivering heat, there rose the humming of innumerable insects. The long drought had scorched the leaves of the trees, and even the needles on the pines looked rusty against the metallic blue of the sky. In the fields the summer flowers were dry and brittle, and over the moist places near the spring, clusters of pale blue butterflies, as fragile as flower petals, hung motionless. Only the broomsedge thrived in the furnace of the earth, and sprang up in a running fire over the waste places.

As she went by the tobacco-field, her father stopped work for a moment, and stooped to take a drink of water from the wooden bucket which stood at the end of the furrow. Before she reached him the steaming odour of his body, like that of an overheated ox, floated to her. His face, the colour of red clay, was dripping with sweat, and his shirt of blue jeans, which was open on his broad, hairy chest, was as wet as if he had been swimming. There was nothing human about him, except his fine prophet's head and the humble dignity of one who has kept in close communion with earth and sky. He had known nothing but toil; he had no language but the language of toil.

"Has the drought done much harm, Pa?" she asked.

With the gourd raised to his lips, Joshua looked round at her. "Middlin'," he replied hoarsely because of his parched throat. He had removed his hat while he worked, for fear that the wide brim might bruise the tender leaves of the tobacco; but resting now for a minute, he covered his head again from the bladelike rays of the sun.

"You'll get sunstroke if you go bareheaded," she said anxiously.

"The minister was in the store this morning, and he told me that, if the drought doesn't break by the end of the week, he's going to put up prayers for rain in church next Sunday. I wonder if prayer ever brought rain?"

Joshua rolled his eyes toward the implacable sky. "Don't it say so in the Bible, daughter?"

Dorinda nodded, without pursuing the inquiry. "And what the dry weather doesn't spoil, the tobacco-worms will. They were as thick as hops yesterday. It's this way every year unless we have a cool summer; then the tobacco ripens so late that the frost kills it. Why don't you give up tobacco next year and sow this field in peas or corn? Jason says the best method of farming is to change the crop whenever you can."

Having drained the last drop of tepid water, Joshua tilted the gourd bottom upward on the rim of the bucket. "I ain't one fur new-fangled ways, honey," he rejoined stubbornly.

He turned back to his work, and Dorinda went on slowly along the dusty path that skirted the field. "If I had my way," she was thinking, "I would do everything differently. I'd try all the crops, one after another, until I found out which was best."

As she approached the house, the mingled scents of drying apples and boiling tomatoes enveloped her; for her mother was working desperately in an effort to save the ripening fruit and vegetables before the sun spoiled them. Boards covered with sliced apples were spread on crude props and decrepit tables, which had been brought out of doors. Above them a crowd of wasps, hornets, flies, and gnats were whirling madly, and every now and then Mrs. Oakley darted out from beneath the scuppernong grapevine and dispersed the delirious swarms with the branch of a locust tree. Though she insisted that the dry weather had "helped her neuralgia," she was suffering now from a sun headache, and could hope for no relief until evening. Her face, with its look of blended physical pain and spiritual ecstasy, was as parched and ravaged as the drought-stricken landscape.

"You got home early to-day, daughter."

"Yes, it was too hot to walk, and Jason came by sooner than usual."

"How does Rose Emily stand the heat?"

"I'm afraid she isn't getting any better," Dorinda's voice trembled. "Jason says she can't last through another bad hæmorrhage."

"And all those children," sighed Mrs. Oakley, pressing one hand over her throbbing eyes and waving the locust branch energetically with the other. "Well, the Lord's ways are past understanding. I wonder if they will ever be able to do anything for that baby's clubfoot."

"I don't know. Jason would like to operate, but Nathan and Rose Emily won't let him. They are afraid it may make it worse. Poor Rose Emily. I don't see how she can be so cheerful."

"It's her faith," said Mrs. Oakley. "She feels she's saved, and she's nothing more to worry about. I'm sorry for Nathan too," she concluded, with the compassion of the redeemed for the heathen. "He's a good man, but he hasn't seen the light like Rose Emily."

"Yes, he's a good man," Dorinda assented, "but I never understood how she could marry him."

Mrs. Oakley dropped the branch, and then picking it up began a more vigorous attack on the cloud of insects. "I declare, it seems to me sometimes that the bugs are going to eat up this place. Did you see your father as you came by?"

"Yes. He was working bareheaded. I told him he would have sunstroke. I wish he would try a different crop next year, but he's so set in his ways."

"Well, it's being set in a rut, I reckon, that keeps him going. If he weren't set, he'd have stopped long ago. You've a mighty high colour, Dorinda. Have you been much in the sun?"

"I walked across from the woods. When we turned in at the red gate I saw Miss Tabitha Snead going up the road in her buggy. Did she stop by to see you?"

"Yes, she brought me a bucket of fresh buttermilk. I've got it in the ice-house with the watermelons, so it will be cold for supper. She told me Geneva Ellgood had gone away for the summer."

"Oh, she went the first of July. I saw her at the station."

Mrs. Oakley's gaze was riveted upon an enterprising hornet that had started out from the crowd and was pursuing a separate investigation of the tomato juice on her hands. While she watched it, she swallowed hard as if her throat were too dry. "Miss Tabitha told me that her brother William went up as far as Washington on the train with Geneva. He's just back last week, and what do you reckon he said Geneva told him on the way up?" She broke off and aimed a fatal blow at the hornet. "What with wasps and bees and hornets and all the thousand and one things that bite and sting," she observed philosophically, "it's hard to understand how the Lord ever had time to think of a pest so small as a seed tick. Yet I believe I'd rather have all the other biting things together. I got some seed ticks on me when I went down to the old spring in the pasture yesterday, and they've been eating me up ever since."

"They are always worse in a drought," Dorinda said, and she asked curiously: "What was it Geneva told Mr. William?"

Mrs. Oakley swallowed again. "Of course I know there ain't a bit of truth in it," she said slowly, as if the words hurt her as she uttered them. "But William says Geneva told him she was engaged to marry Jason Greylock. She said he courted her in New York a year ago."

Dorinda laughed. "Why, how absurd!" she exclaimed. "Miss Tabitha knows we are to be married in October. Hasn't she watched Miss Seena helping me with my sewing? I was spending the evening over there last week and we talked about my marriage. She knows there isn't a word of truth in it."

"Oh, she knows. She said she reckoned Geneva must be crazy. There ain't any harm in it, but I thought maybe I'd better tell you."

"I don't mind," replied Dorinda, and she laughed again, the exultant laugh of youth undefeated. "Ma," she asked suddenly, "did you ever want anything very much in your life?"

Startled out of her stony resignation, Mrs. Oakley let fall the branch, and the spinning swarms descended like a veil over the apples. "I'll have to hang a piece of mosquito-netting over these apples," she said. "There's some we used for curtains in the spare room. Well, I told you I'd kind of set my heart on your father," she added in a lifeless tone. "But there's one thing I can tell you, daughter, mighty few folks in this world ever get what they want."

"Oh, I mean before you knew Pa, when you were a girl. Didn't you ever feel that there was only one thing in the world that could make you happy?"

Mrs. Oakley pondered the question. "I reckon like most other

93

people I was afraid of the word happiness," she replied. "But when I was just a girl, not more than sixteen or seventeen, I felt the call to be a missionary, and I wanted it, I s'pose, more than I've ever wanted anything in my life. I reckon it started with my favourite hymn, the missionary one. Even as a little child I used to think and dream about India's coral strand and Afric's sunny fountains. That was why I got engaged to Gordon Kane. I wasn't what you'd call in love with him; but I believed the Lord had intended me for work in foreign fields, and it seemed, when Gordon asked me to marry him, that an opportunity had been put in my way. I had my trunk all packed to go to the Congo to join him. I was just folding up my wedding-dress of white organdie when they broke the news to me of his death." She gasped and choked for a moment. "After that I put the thought of the heathen out of my mind," she continued when she had recovered her breath. "Your great-grandfather said I was too young to decide whether I had a special vocation or not, and then before I came out of mourning, I met your father, and we were married. For a while I seemed to forget all about the missionary call; but it came back just before Josiah was born, and I've had it ever since whenever I'm worried and feel that I'll have to get away from things, or go clean out of my mind. Then I begin to have that dream about coral strands and palm trees and ancient rivers and naked black babies thrown to crocodiles. When it first came I tried to drive it away by hard work, and that was the way I got in the habit of working to rest my mind. I was so afraid folks would begin to say I was unhinged."

"Does it still come back?" asked the girl.

"Sometimes in my sleep. When I'm awake I never think of it now, except on missionary Sunday when we sing that hymn."

"That's why you enjoy sermons about the Holy Land and far-off places."

"I used to know all those pictures by heart in your great-grandfather's books about Asia and Africa. It was a wild streak in me, I reckon," she conceded humbly, "but with the Lord's help, I've managed to stamp it out."

A missionary, her mother! For more than forty years this dark and secret river of her dream had flowed silently beneath the com-

94

monplace crust of experience. "I wonder if there is any of that wildness in me?" thought the girl, with a sensation of fear, as if the invisible flood were rushing over her.

"Did you ever tell Pa?" she asked.

Mrs. Oakley shook her head. "I never told anybody when I was in my right mind. I don't believe in telling men more than you're obliged to. After all, it was nobody's fault the way things turned out," she added, with scrupulous justice. "I'm going in now to get that mosquito-netting. There's your father coming. I reckon he'd like a drink of fresh water from the well."

Following her mother's glance, Dorinda saw her father's bowed figure toiling along the path on the edge of the vegetable garden. Far beyond him, where a field had been abandoned because it contained a gall, where nothing would grow, she could just discern the scalloped reaches of the broomsedge, rippling, in the lilac-coloured distance, like still water at sunset. Yes, old Matthew was right. What the broomsedge caught, it never relinquished.

Lifting the wooden bucket from the shelf on the back porch, she poured the stale water over a thin border of portulaca by the steps, and started at a run for the well. By the time Joshua had reached the house, she had brought the bucket of sparkling water, and had a gourd ready for him.

"You must be worn out, Pa. Don't you want a drink?"

"That I do, honey." He took the gourd from her, and raised it to his bearded lips where the sweat hung in drops. "Powerful hot, ain't it?"

"It's scorching. And you've been up since before day. I'll hunt worms for you to-morrow." She was thinking, while she spoke, that her father was no longer young, and that he should try to spare himself. But she knew that it was futile to remind him of this. He had never spared himself in her memory, and he would not begin now just because he was old. The pity of it was that, even if he wore himself out in the effort to save his crop from the drought or the worms, there was still the possibility that the first killing frost would come too soon and inflict as heavy a damage.

He shook his head with a chuckle of pride. "Thar's no use yo' spilin' yo' hands. I've hired a parcel of Uncle Toby Moody's little niggers to hunt 'em in the mornin'. If they kill worms every day till Sunday, I've promised 'em the biggest watermelon I've got in the ice-house."

Before going on to feed the horses, he stopped to wash his face in the tin basin on the back porch. "I declar' I must be gittin' on," he remarked cheerfully. "I've got shootin' pains through all my j'ints."

This was nearer a complaint than any speech she had ever heard from him, and she looked at him anxiously while he dried his face on the roller towel. "You ought to take things more easily, Pa. The way you work is enough to kill anybody."

"Wall, I'll take my ease when the first snow falls," he responded jocosely.

"But you won't. You work just as hard in winter."

"Is that so?" He appeared genuinely surprised. "I never calculated! The truth is I've got the land on my back, an' it's drivin' me. Land is a hard driver."

"And a good steed, they say," she answered. "If you could only get the better of it."

He smiled wistfully, and she watched the clay-coloured skin above his thick beard break into diverging fissures. "We've got to wait for that, I reckon, till my ship comes in. It takes money to get money, daughter."

While he trudged away to the stable, Dorinda went up to her room and changed into a pink gingham dress which Rose Emily had given her a year ago. The flower-like colour tinged her face when she came downstairs and found her mother, who had dropped from exhaustion, in a rocking-chair on the front porch.

"I felt as if I couldn't stand the kitchen a minute longer." Mrs. Oakley glanced wearily at her daughter over the palm-leaf fan she was waving. "You ain't going out before supper, Dorinda?" Her damp hair looked as if it had been plastered over her skull, and in the diminishing light her pallid features resembled a waxen mask.

"I can't wait for supper," the girl replied. "I've promised to meet Jason over by Gooseneck Creek."

"Well, don't stay out too long after dark. The night air ain't healthy."

Dorinda laughed. "Jason says that's as much a superstition as the belief that Aunt Mehitable can make cows go dry. But I shan't be late. Jason can't stay out long at night, unless somebody is dying, and then he gets one of the field hands to sleep in the house. It must be terrible over at Five Oaks."

"I ain't easy in my mind about your living there with that old man, daughter. He's been a notorious sinner as far back as I can recollect, though he was a good enough doctor till he went half crazy from drink. But even before his wife died, he kept that bright yellow girl, Idabella, living over there in the old wing of the house. And he's not only as hard as nails," she concluded, with final condemnation, "he's close-fisted as well."

"Poor Jason can't help his father's sins," Dorinda rejoined loyally. "After all, it's worse on him than it is on anybody else." As she turned away from the flagged walk, she resolved that the dissolute old man should not spoil her happiness.

Her path led by the pear orchard, past the vegetable garden, which was fenced off from the tobacco-field, and continued in an almost obliterated track through the feathery plumes of the broomsedge. At the end of the barren acres the thin edge of Hoot Owl Woods began, and after she had passed this, there would be only a stretch of sandy road between her and the creek. By the willows she knew the air would be fresh and moist, and she knew also that Jason was waiting for her in the tall blue-eyed grasses.

She went slowly along the path, in a mood so pensive that it might have been merely a reflection of the summer trance. The vagrant breeze, which had roamed for a few minutes at sunset, had died down again with the afterglow. Heat melted like colour into the distance. Not a blade of grass trembled; the curled leaves on the pear trees were limp and heavy; even the white turkeys, roosting in a solitary oak near the orchard, were as motionless as if they were under a spell. As far as she could see there was not a stir or quiver in the landscape, and the only sounds that jarred the leaden silence were the monotonous chirping of the locusts, the discordant croak of a tree-frog, and the staccato shrieks of the little negroes hunting tobacco-flies.

The sun had gone down long ago, and the western sky was suffused with the transparent yellow-green of August evenings. All the light on the earth had vanished, except the faint glow that was still cast upwards by the broomsedge. Wave by wave, that symbol of desolation encroached in a glimmering tide on the darkened boundaries of Old Farm. It was the one growth in the landscape that thrived on barrenness; the solitary life that possessed an inexhaustible vitality. To fight it was like fighting the wild, free principle of nature. Yet they had always fought it. They had spent their force for generations in the futile endeavour to uproot it from the soil, as they had striven to uproot all that was wild and free in the spirit of man.

At the edge of the woods she paused and looked back. There would be light enough later, for the golden rim of a moon, paling as it ascended, was visible through the topmost branches of the big pine in the graveyard. While she stood there she was visited by a swift perception, which was less a thought than a feeling, and less a feeling than an intuitive recognition, that she and her parents were products of the soil as surely as were the scant crops and the exuberant broomsedge. Had not the land entered into their souls and shaped their moods into permanent or impermanent forms? Less a thought than a feeling; but she went on more rapidly toward the complete joy of the moment in which she lived.

11

On the first Sunday in October, Dorinda came out on the porch, with old Rambler at her side, and looked over the road and the pasture to the frowning sky. The range of clouds, which had huddled all the afternoon above the western horizon, was growing darker, and there was a slow pulsation, like the quiver of invisible wings, in the air. While she stood there, she wondered if the storm would overtake her before she reached Whistling Spring.

"I think I'll risk it," she decided at last. "It's looked this way for hours, and it won't hurt me to get wet."

For days she had felt disturbed, and she told herself that her anxiety had sprung from a definite cause, or, if not from a definite cause,—well, at least from a plausible reason. Jason had been away for two weeks, and she had had only one letter. He had promised to write every day, and she had heard from him once. More than this, when he left, against his father's wish, he had expected to stay only a week, and the added days had dragged on without explanation. Of course there were a dozen reasons why he should not have written. He had gone to select surgical instruments, and it was probable that he had been kept busy by professional matters. Her heart made excuses. She repeated emphatically that there was no need for her to worry; but, in spite of this insistence, it was useless, she found, to try to argue herself out of a condition of mind. The only thing was to wait as patiently as she could for his return. They were to be married in a week; and the hours before and after her work at the store were spent happily over her sewing. Mrs. Oakley had neglected her other work in order to help her daughter with her wedding clothes, and the drawers in Dorinda's walnut bureau were filled with white, lace-edged garments, made daintily, with fine, even stitches, by her mother's rheumatic fingers.

"I shouldn't be satisfied if you didn't have things to start with like other girls," Mrs. Oakley had remarked, while she pinned a paper pattern to a width of checked muslin. "I don't want that old doctor to say his son is marrying a beggar."

"Well, Jason won't say that," Dorinda had protested. "It would cost less if I were married in my blue nun's veiling; but Miss Seena thinks a figured challis would be more suitable."

"Well, I reckon Miss Seena knows," Mrs. Oakley had agreed. "It ain't lucky not to have a new dress to be married in, and though I don't set a bit of store by superstition, it won't do any harm not to run right up against it." Glancing round at her daughter, she had continued in a tone of anxiety: "Ain't you feeling well, daughter? You've been looking right peaked the last day or two, and I noticed you didn't touch any breakfast."

"Oh, I'm all right," Dorinda had responded. "I've been worrying about not hearing from Jason, that's all." As she answered, she had turned away and dropped into a chair. "I've been bending over all day," she had explained, "and the weather has been so sultry. It makes me feel kind of faint."

"Take a whiff of camphor," Mrs. Oakley had advised. "There's the bottle right there on the bureau. I get a sinking every now and then myself, so I like to have it handy. But there ain't a bit of use worrying yourself sick about Jason. It ain't much more than two weeks since he went away."

"Two weeks to-morrow, but I haven't heard since the day after he left. I am worried for fear something has happened."

"Your father could ask the old doctor?"

Frowning over the bottle of camphor, Dorinda had pondered the suggestion. "No, he doesn't like us," she had replied at last. "I doubt if he'd tell us anything. Jason told me once he wanted him to marry Geneva Ellgood."

"You might send a telegram," Mrs. Oakley had offered as the final resource of desperation.

Dorinda had flushed through her pallor. "I did yesterday, but there hasn't been any answer." After a minute's reflection, she had added, "If it's a good day to-morrow, I think I'll walk down to

Whistling Spring in the evening and see Aunt Mehitable Green. Her daughter Jemima works over at Five Oaks, and she may have heard something."

"Then you'd better start right after dinner, and you can get back before dark," Mrs. Oakley had returned. The word "afternoon" was never used at Pedlar's Mill, and any hour between twelve o'clock and night was known as "evening."

That was yesterday, and standing now on the front porch, Dorinda considered the prospect. Scorched and blackened by the long summer, the country was as bare as a conquered province after the march of an invader. "I'll start anyway," she repeated, and turning, she called out, "Ma, is there anything I can take Aunt Mehitable?"

"Doesn't it look as if it were getting ready to rain, Dorinda?"

"I don't care. If it does, I'll stop somewhere until it is over."

Entering the hall, the girl paused on the threshold of the room where her mother sat reading her Bible.

"Where would you stop?" Mrs. Oakley was nothing if not definite. "There ain't anybody living on that back road between Five Oaks and Whistling Spring. It makes me sort of nervous for you to walk down there by yourself, Dorinda. Can't you get Rufus to go with you?"

"No, he's gone over to see the Garlick girls, and I don't want him anyway. I'd rather walk down by myself. Anybody I'd meet on the road would know who I am. I see them all at the store. May I take a piece of the molasses pudding we had for dinner?"

"Yes, there's some left in the cupboard. I was saving it for Rufus, but you might as well take it. Then there are the last scuppernong grapes on the shelf. Aunt Mehitable was always mighty fond of scuppernong grapes."

Going into the kitchen, Dorinda put the molasses pudding into the little willow basket, and then, covering it with cool grape leaves, laid the loose grapes on top. A slip of the vine had been given to her great-grandfather by a missionary from Mexico, and had grown luxuriantly at Old Farm, clambering over the back porch to the roof of the house. It was a peculiarity of the scuppernong that the large, pale grapes were not gathered in a bunch, but dropped grape by grape, as they ripened. "Is there any message you want to send Aunt Mehitable?" she asked, returning through the hall.

On a rag carpet in the centre of her spotless floor, Mrs. Oakley rocked slowly back and forth while she read aloud one of the Psalms. It was the only time during the week that she let her body relax; and now that the whip of nervous energy was suspended, her face looked old, grey, and hopeless. The dreary afternoon light crept through the half-closed shutters, and a large blue fly buzzed ceaselessly, with a droning sound, against the ceiling.

"Tell her my leg still keeps poorly," she said, "and if she's got any more of that black liniment, I'd be glad of a bottle. You ain't so spry to-day yourself, daughter."

"I got tired sitting in church," the girl answered, "but the walk will make me feel better."

"Be sure you come back if you hear thunder. I don't like your setting out in the face of a storm. Can you take Rambler?"

"No, he's old and rheumatic, and it's too far. But I'm all right." Without waiting for more advice or remonstrance, Dorinda hastened through the hall and out of the house.

For the first quarter of a mile, before she reached the red gate at the fork and turned into the sandy road leading to Five Oaks, her naturally level spirits drooped under an unusual weight of depression. Then, as she lifted the bar and passed through the gate, she felt that the solitude, which had always possessed a mysterious sympathy with her moods, reached out and received her into itself. Like a beneficent tide, the loneliness washed over her, smoothing out, as it receded, the vague apprehensions that had ruffled her thoughts. The austere horizon, flat and impenetrable beneath the threatening look of the sky; the brown and yellow splashes of woods in the October landscape; the furtive windings and recoils of the sunken road; the perturbed murmur and movement of the broomsedge, so like the restless inlets of an invisible sea,—all these external objects lost their inanimate character and became as personal, reserved, and inscrutable as her own mind. So sensitive were her perceptions, while she walked there alone, that the wall dividing her individual consciousness from the consciousness of nature vanished with the thin drift of woodsmoke over the fields.

The road sank gradually to Gooseneck Creek and then ascended as evenly to the grounds of Five Oaks. To reach the back road by the short cut, which saved her a good mile and a half, she was obliged to pass between the house and the barn, where she caught a glimpse of the old doctor and heard the sound of a gun fired at intervals. He was shooting, she surmised, at a chicken hawk, which was hovering low over the barnyard. Why, she wondered, with all the heavens and the earth around him, had he placed the stoop-shouldered rustic barn within call of the dwelling house? The ice-house, three-cornered and red, like all the buildings on the place, was so near the front porch that one might almost have tossed the lumps of ice into the hall. Though the red roof, chimneys, and outbuildings produced, at a distance, an effect of gaiety, she felt that the colour would become oppressive on hot summer afternoons. Dirt, mildew, decay everywhere! White turkeys that were discoloured by mould. Chips, trash, broken bottles littering the yard and the back steps, which were rotting to pieces. Windows so darkened by dust and cobwebs that they were like eyes blurred by cataract. Several mulatto babies crawling, like small, sly animals, over the logs at the woodpile. "Poor Jason," she thought. "No wonder his nerves are giving way under the strain."

She followed the path between the house and the barn, and then, crossing an old corn-field, turned into the back road, which led, through thick woods, to Whistling Spring and Whippernock River. After she had lost sight of the house, she came up with old Matthew Fairlamb, who was trudging sturdily along, with his hickory stick in his hand and a small bundle, tied up in a bandanna handkerchief, swinging from his right arm.

"Are you on your way to see William?" she inquired as she joined him, for she knew that his son William lived a mile away, on one of the branch roads that led through to the station. "You must have come quite a distance out of your way."

Old Matthew wagged his knowing head. "That's right, gal, I'm gittin' along to William's now," he replied. "I took dinner over to John Appleseed's, that's why you find me trampin' through Five Oaks. Ain't you goin' too fur from home, honey? Thar's a storm brewin' over yonder in the west, and it'll most likely ketch you."

"I'm going down to Whistling Spring," Dorinda replied, falling into step at his side.

He smacked his old lips. "Then you'll sholy be caught," he rejoined, with sour pleasure. "It's a matter of five miles or so, ain't it?"

103

"That's by the long road. It isn't over four by the short cut through Five Oaks."

"Thar ain't nobody but the niggers livin' down by Whistling Spring."

"I'm going down to see Aunt Mehitable Green. She nursed Ma when she was sick."

"I recollect her." Old Matthew wagged again. "She conjured some liver spots off the face of my son's wife. They used to say she was the best conjure woman anywhar round here."

"I know the darkeys are still afraid of her," Dorinda returned. "But she was good to me when I was little, and I don't believe anything bad about her."

"Mebbe not, mebbe not," old Matthew assented. "Anyhow, if she's got a gift with moles an' warts, thar can't nobody blame her fur practisin' it. How's yo' weddin' gittin' on, honey? By this time next week you'll be an old married woman, won't you?"

Dorinda blushed. "It's hard for me to realize it."

"Jason's gone away, ain't he?"

"Yes, he went to New York to buy some instruments."

"It's a mortal wonder his Pa let him. I hear he keeps as tight a rein on him as if he'd never growed up. Wall, wall, he didn't ax the advice of eighty-odd years. But, mark my words, he'll live to regret the day he come back to Five Oaks."

"But what else could he do?" the girl protested loyally. "His father needed him."

Old Matthew broke into a sly cackle. "Oh, he'll larn, he'll larn. I ain't contendin'. He's a pleasant-mannered youngster, an' I wish you all the joy of him you desarve. You ain't heerd from Geneva Ellgood sence she went away, have you?"

"Oh, no. She never writes to me."

"I kind of thought she might have. But to come back to Jason, he's got everything you want in a man except the one quality that counts with the land."

"You speak as if Jason lacked character," she said resentfully.

"Wall, if he's got it, you'll know it soon," rejoined the disagreeable old man, "and if he ain't got it, you'll know it sooner. I ain't contendin'. It don't pay to contend when you're upwards of eighty." He rolled the words of ill omen like a delicate morsel on his tongue.

"This here is my turnout, honey. Look sharp that you don't git a drenchin'."

They nodded in the curt fashion of country people, and the old man tramped off, spitting tobacco juice in the road, while Dorinda hurried on into the deepening gloom of the woods. She was glad to be free of old Matthew. He was more like an owl than ever, she thought, with his ominous *who-who-whoee*.

Here alone in the woods, with the perpetually moist clay near the stream underfoot, the thick tent of arching boughs overhead, the aromatic smell of dampness and rotting leaves in her nostrils, she felt refreshed and invigorated. After all, why was she anxious? She was securely happy. She was to be married in a week. She knew beyond question, beyond distrust, that Jason loved her. For three months she had lived in a state of bliss so supreme that, like love, it had created the illusion of its own immortality. Yes, for three months she had been perfectly happy.

Above, the leaves rustled. Through the interlacing boughs she could see the grey sky growing darker. The warm scents of the wood were as heavy as perfumed smoke.

Presently the trees ended as abruptly as they had begun, and she came out into the broomsedge which surrounded the negro settlement of Whistling Spring. A narrow path led between rows of log cabins, each with its patchwork square of garden, and its clump of gaudy prince's feather or cockscomb by the doorstep. Aunt Mehitable's cabin stood withdrawn a little; and when Dorinda reached the door, there was a mutter of thunder in the clouds, though the storm was still distant and a silver light edged the horizon. On the stone step a tortoise-shell cat lay dozing, and a little to one side of the cabin the smouldering embers of a fire blinked like red eyes under an iron pot, which hung suspended from a rustic crane made by crossing three sticks.

In response to the girl's knock on the open door, the cat arched its back in welcome, and the old negress came hurriedly out of the darkness inside, wiping her hands on her blue gingham apron. She took Dorinda in her arms, explaining, while she embraced her, that she had just heated some water to make a brew of herbs from her garden.

"Dar ain' no use kindlin' a fire inside er de cabin twell you're obleeged ter," she remarked. "You ain' lookin' so peart, honey. I've got a bottle of my brown bitters put away fur yo' Ma, en you ax 'er ter gin you a dose de fust thing ev'y mawnin'. Yo' Ma knows about'n my brown bitters caze she's done tuck hit, erlong wid my black liniment. Hit'll take erway de blue rings unner yo' eyes jes' ez sho', en hit'll fill yo' cheeks right full er roses agin."

"I've been worrying," said the girl, sitting down in the chair the old woman brought. "It's taken my appetite, and made me feel as if I dragged myself to the store and back every day. Isn't it funny what worry can do to you, Aunt Mehitable?"

"Dat 'tis, honey, dat 'tis."

"I get dizzy too, when I bend over. You haven't got any camphor about, have you?"

Aunt Mehitable hastened into the cabin, and brought out a bottle of camphor. "Yo' Ma gun me dat de ve'y las' time I wuz at Ole Farm," she said, removing the stopper, and handing the bottle to Dorinda. "Hit's a long walk on dis heah peevish sort of er day. You jes' set en res' wile I git you a swallow uv my blackberry cord'al. Dar ain't nuttin' dat'll pick you up quicker'n blackberry cord'al w'en it's made right."

Going indoors again, she came out with the blackberry cordial in a ruby wineglass which had once belonged to the Cumberlands. "Drink it down quick, en you'll feel better right befo' you know hit. Huccome you been worryin', chile, w'en yo is gwineter be mah'ed dis time nex' week?" she inquired abruptly.

"I'm afraid something has happened," Dorinda said. "Jason has been away two weeks, and I haven't had a word since the day after he left. I thought you might have heard something from Jemima."

The old woman mumbled through toothless gums. She was wearing a bandanna handkerchief wrapped tightly about her head, and beneath it a few grey-green wisps of hair straggled down to meet the dried grass of her eyebrows. Her face was so old that it looked as if the flesh had been polished away, and her features shone like black lacquer where the light struck them.

"Naw'm, I ain't heerd nuttin'," she replied, "but I'se done been lookin' fur you all de evelin'. Dar's a lil' bird done tole me you wuz comin'," she muttered mysteriously.

"I wasn't sure of it myself till just before I started."

"I knowed, honey, I knowed," rejoined Aunt Mehitable, leaning against the smoke-blackened pine by her doorstep, while she fixed her bleared, witchlike gaze on the girl. There was the dignity in her demeanour that is inherent in all simple, profound, and elemental forces. The pipe she had taken out of the pocket of her apron was in her mouth, but the stem was cold and she mumbled over it without smoking. With her psychic powers, which were a natural endowment, she combined a dramatic gift that was not uncommon among the earlier generations of negroes. In another century Aunt Mehitable would have been either a mystic philosopher or a religious healer.

"Can you really see things, Aunt Mehitable?" Dorinda inquired, impressed but not convinced.

Aunt Mehitable grunted over her smokeless pipe. "Mebbe I kin en mebbe I cyan't."

"They say you can tell about the future?"

"Hi!" the old negress exclaimed, and continued with assumed indifference. "Dey sez I kin do a heap mo'n I kin do. But I ain' steddyin' about'n dat, honey. I knows w'at I knows. I kin teck moles en warts en liver spots off'n you twell you is jes' ez smooth ez de pa'm er my han', en ef'n ennybody's done put a conjure ball ovah yo' do' er th'owed a ring on de grass fur you to walk in, I kin tell you whar you mus' go ter jump ovah runnin' water. Ef'n you is in enny trubble, honey, hit's mos' likely I kin teck hit erway. Is you stuck full er pins an' needles in yo' legs an' arms, jes' lak somebody done th'owed a spell on you?"

"No, it isn't that," answered Dorinda. "I came because I thought you might have heard something from Jemima. I'd better be starting back now. I want to get home, if I can, before the storm breaks——"

She had risen to her feet, and was turning to look at the clouds in the west, when the broomsedge plunged forward, like a raging sea, and engulfed her. She felt the pain and dizziness of the blow; she heard the thunder of the waves as they crashed together; and she saw the billows, capped with spraylike plumes, submerging the cabin, the fields, the woods, and the silver crescent of the horizon.

When she came to herself, it was an hour, a day, or a year afterwards. She was still on the bare ground, beneath the blackened pine, in front of Aunt Mehitable's cabin. The tortoise-shell cat still dozed on the step. The dying embers still blinked under the hanging pot. There was a pungent smell in her nostrils, as the old woman splashed camphor over her forehead. Her consciousness was struggling through the fumes which saturated her brain.

"Dar now, honey. Don't you worry. Hit's all right," crooned Aunt Mehitable, bending above her.

Dorinda sat up slowly, and looked round her. "I believe I fainted," she said. "I never fainted before." The roar of far-off waters was still in her ears.

The old woman held out the ruby wineglass, which she had refilled. "Hit's all right, honey, hit's all right."

"It came on so suddenly." Dorinda pushed the glass away after she had obediently swallowed a few sips. "It was exactly like dying; but I'm well now. The walk must have been too long on a sultry day."

"Don't you worry, caze hit's gwineter be all right," crooned Aunt Mehitable. "I'se done axed de embers en hit's gwineter be all right." The magnetic force emanating from the old negress enveloped the girl, and she abandoned herself to it as to a mysterious and terrible current of wisdom. How did Aunt Mehitable know things before other people? she wondered. She shivered in the warm air, and laid her head on the wizened shoulder. Of course no one believed in witches any longer; but there was something queer in the way she could look ahead and tell fortunes.

"Befo' de week's up you is gwineter be mah'ed," muttered the old woman, "en dar ain't a livin' soul but Aunt Mehitable gwineter know dat de chile wuz on de way sooner——"

"I——" Dorinda began sharply. Rising quickly to her feet, she stood looking about her like a person who has been dazzled by a flash of lightning. She was bewildered, but she was less bewildered than she had been for the last three months. In the illumination of that instant a hundred mysteries were made plain; but her dominant feeling was one of sharp awakening from a trance. Swift and savage, animal terror clutched at her heart. Where was Jason? Suppose he was dead! Suppose he was lost to her! The longing to see him, the urgent need of his look, of his touch, of his voice, shuddered through her like a convulsion. It seemed to her that she could not live unless she could feel the reassuring pressure of his arms and hear the healing sound of her name on his lips.

"I must go back," she said. "I'll come again, Aunt Mehitable, but I must hurry before the storm."

Breaking away from the old woman's arms, she walked rapidly, as if she were flying before the approaching storm, through the acres of broomsedge to the road by which she had come.

12

On both sides of the road the trees grew straight and tall, and overhead the grey arch of sky looked as if it were hewn out of rock. The pines were dark as night, but the oaks, the sweet gums, the beeches, and hickories were turning slowly, and here and there the boughs were brushed with wine-colour or crimson. Far away, she could hear the rumble of the storm, and it seemed to her that the noise and burden of living marched on there at an immeasurable distance. Within the woods there was the profound silence of sleep. Nothing but the occasional flutter of a bird or stir of a small animal in the underbrush disturbed the serenity. The oppressive air stifled her, and she felt that her breath, like the movement of the wind, was suspended.

"If I don't hurry, I shall never get out of the woods," she thought. "I ought not to have come."

Forgetting the attack of faintness, she quickened her steps into a run, and stumbled on over the wheel ruts in the road, which was scarcely wider than a cart track. For a while this stillness was so intense that she felt as if it were palpitating in smothered throbs like her heart. The storm was gathering on another planet. So remote it was that the slow reverberations were echoed across an immensity of silence. The first mile was past. Then the second. With the ending of the third, she knew that she should come out into the pasture and the old corn-field at Five Oaks.

Presently a few withered leaves fluttered past her, flying through the narrow tunnel of the woods toward the clearer vista ahead. Immediately round her the atmosphere was still motionless. Like an alley in a dream the road stretched, brown, dim, monotonous, between the tall trees; and this alley seemed to her unutterably sad, strewn with dead leaves and haunted by an autumnal taint of decay. The fear in her own mind had fallen like a blight on her surroundings, as if the external world were merely a shadow thrown by the subjective processes within her soul.

Suddenly, without nearer warning, the storm broke. A streak of white fire split the sky, and the tattered clouds darkened to an angry purple. The wind, which had been chained at a distance, tore itself free with a hurtling noise and crashed in gusts through the tree-tops. Overhead, she heard the snapping of branches, and when she glanced back, it seemed to her that the withered leaves had gathered violence in pursuit, and were whirling after her like a bevy of witches. As she came out of the shelter of the trees, the stream of wind and leaves swept her across the corn-field, with the patter of rain on her shoulders. Where the road turned, she saw the red barn and the brick dwelling of Five Oaks, and in obedience to the wind rather than by the exercise of her own will, she was driven over the field and the yard to the steps of the back porch. Her first impression was that the place was deserted; and running up the steps, she sank into one of the broken chairs on the porch, and shook the water from her hat while she struggled for breath. On the roof of the house the rain was beating in drops as hard as pebbles. She heard it thundering on the shingles; she saw it scattering the chips and straws by the woodpile, and churning the puddles in the walk until they foamed with a yeasty scum. The sky was shrouded now in a crapelike pall, and where the lightning ripped open the blackness, the only colour was that jagged stain of dull purple. "I'm wet already," she thought. "In another minute I'd have been soaked through to the skin." Turning her head, she looked curiously at the home of her lover.

The thought in her mind was, "You could tell no woman lived here. When I get the chance, it won't take me long to make things look different." With the certainty that this "chance" would one day be hers, she forgot her anxiety and fatigue, and a thrill of joy eased her heart. Yes, things would be different when she and Jason lived here together and little children played under the great oaks in the grove. Her fingers "itched," as she said to herself, to clean up the place and make it tidy without and within. A rivulet of muddy water was pouring round the corner of the house, wearing a channel

111

in the gravelled walk, which was littered with rubbish. Beside the porch there was a giant box-bush, beneath which several bedraggled white turkeys had taken shelter. She could see them through the damp twilight of the boughs, shaking drenched feathers or scratching industriously in the rank mould among the roots.

Leaning back in her wet clothes, against the splints of the chair, which sagged on one rocker, she glanced about her at the refuse that overflowed from the hall. The porch looked as if it had not been swept for years. There was a pile of dusty bagging in one corner, and, scattered over the floor, she saw a medley of oil-cans, empty cracker-boxes and whiskey-bottles, loose spokes of cartwheels, rolls of barbed wire, and stray remnants of leather harness. "How can any one live in such confusion?" she thought. Through the doorway, she could distinguish merely a glimmer of light on the ceiling, from which the plaster was dropping, and the vague shape of a staircase, which climbed, steep and slender, to the upper story. It was a fairly good house of its period, the brick dwelling, with ivy-encrusted wings, which was preferred by the more prosperous class of Virginia farmers. The foundation of stone had been well laid; the brick walls were stout and solid, and though neglect and decay had overtaken it, the house still preserved, beneath its general air of deterioration, an underlying character of honesty and thrift. Turning away, she gazed through the silver mesh of rain, past the barn and the stable, to the drenched pasture, where a few trees rocked back and forth, and a flock of frightened sheep huddled together. Where were the farm labourers, she wondered? What had become of Jemima, who, Aunt Mehitable had said, was still working here? Two men living alone must keep at least one woman servant. Had the storm thrown a curse of stagnation over the place, and made it incapable of movement or sound? She could barely see the sky for the slanting rain, which drove faster every minute. Was she the only living thing left, except the cowering sheep in the pasture and the dripping white turkeys under the box-bush?

While she was still asking the question, she heard a shuffling step in the hall behind her, and looking hastily over her shoulder, saw the figure of the old man blocking the doorway. For an instant his squat outline, blurred between the dark hall and the sheets of rain, was all that she distinguished. Then he lurched toward her, peering out of the gloom. Yesterday, she would have run from him in terror. Before her visit to Whistling Spring she would have faced the storm rather than the brooding horror at Five Oaks. But the great fear had absorbed the small fears as the night absorbs shadows. Nothing mattered to her if she could only reach Jason.

"Come in, come in," the old doctor was mumbling, with a deary effort at hospitality.

He held out his palsied hand, and all the evil rumours she had heard since he had given up his practice and buried himself at Five Oaks rushed into her mind. It must be true that he had always been a secret drinker, and that the habit had taken possession now of his faculties. Though she had known him all her life, the change in him was so startling that she would scarcely have recognized him. His once robust figure was wasted and flabby, except for his bloated paunch, which hung down like a sack of flour; his scraggy throat protruding from the bristles of his beard reminded the girl of the neck of a buzzard; his little fiery eyes, above inflamed pouches of skin, flickered and shone, just as the smouldering embers had flickered and shone under Aunt Mehitable's pot. And from these small bloodshot eyes something sly and secretive and malignant looked out at her. Was this, she wondered, what whiskey and his own evil nature could do to a man?

"I am on my way back from Whistling Spring," she explained, while she struggled against the repulsion he aroused in her. "The storm caught me just as I reached here."

He smirked with his bloodless old lips, which cracked under the strain. "Eh? Eh?" he chuckled, cupping his ear in his hand. Then catching hold of her sleeve, he pulled her persuasively toward the door. "Come in, come in," he urged. "You're wet through. I've kindled a bit of fire to dry my boots, and it's still burning. Come in, and dry yourself before you take cold from the wetting."

Still clutching her, he stumbled into the hall, glancing uneasily back, as if he feared that she might slip out of his grasp. On the right a door stood ajar, and a few knots of resinous pine blazed, with a thin blue light, in the cavernous fireplace. As he led her over the threshold, she noticed that the windows were all down, and that the only shutters left open were those at the back window, against which the giant box-bush had grown into the shape of a hunchback.

There was a film of dust or woodashes over the floor and the furniture, and cobwebs were spun in lacy patterns on the discoloured walls. A demijohn, still half full of whiskey, stood on the crippled mahogany desk, and a pitcher of water and several dirty glasses were on a tin tray beside it. Near the sparkling blaze a leather chair, from which the stuffing protruded, faced a shabby footstool upholstered in crewel-work, and a pile of hickory logs, chips, and pine knots, over which spiders were crawling. While Dorinda sat down in the chair he pointed out, and looked nervously over the dust and dirt that surrounded her, she thought that she had never seen a room from which the spirit of hope was so irrevocably banished. How cheerful the room at Pedlar's Mill, where Rose Emily lay dying, appeared by contrast with this one! What a life Jason's mother must have led in this place! How had Jason, with his charm, his fastidiousness, his sensitive nerves, been able to stay here? Her gaze wandered to the one unshuttered window, where the sheets of rain were blown back and forth like a curtain. She saw the hunched shoulder of the box-bush, crouching under the torrent of water which poured down from the roof. Yet she longed to be out in the storm. Any weather was better than this close, dark place, so musty in spite of its fire, and this suffocating stench of whiskey and of things that were never aired.

"Just a thimbleful of toddy to ward off a chill?" the old man urged, with his doddering gestures.

She shook her head, trying to smile. A drop of the stuff in one of those fly-specked glasses would have sickened her.

Darkness swept over her with the ebb and flow of the sea. She felt a gnawing sensation within; there was a quivering in her elbows; and it seemed to her that she was dissolving into emptiness. The thin blue light wavered and vanished and wavered again. When she opened her eyes the room came out of the shadows in fragments, obscure, glimmering, remote. On the shingled roof the rain was pattering like a multitude of tiny feet, the restless bare feet of babies. Terror seized her. She longed with all her will to escape; but how could she go back into the storm without an excuse; and what excuse could she find? After all, repulsive as he appeared, he was still Jason's father.

"No, thank you," she answered, when he poured a measure of

whiskey into a glass and pushed it toward her. "Aunt Mehitable gave me some blackberry cordial." After a silence she asked abruptly: "Where is Jemima?"

Lifting the glass she had refused, he added a stronger dash to the weak mixture, and sipped it slowly. "There's nothing better when you're wet than a little toddy," he muttered. "Jemima is off for the evening, but she'll be back in time to get supper. I heard her say she was going over to Plumtree."

A peal of thunder broke so near that she started to her feet, expecting to see the window-panes shattered.

"There, there, don't be afraid," he said, nodding at her over his glass. "The worst is over now. The rain will have held up before you're dry and ready to go home."

It was like a nightmare, the dark, glimmering room, with its dust and cobwebs, the sinister old man before the blue flames of the pine knots, the slanting rain over the box-bush, the pattering sound on the roof, and the thunderbolts which crashed near by and died away in the distance. Even her body felt numbed, as if she were asleep, and her feet, when she rose and took a step forward, seemed to be walking on nothing. It was just as if she knew it was not real, that it was all visionary and incredible, and as if she stood there waiting until she should awake. The dampness, too, was not a genuine dampness, but the sodden atmosphere of a nightmare.

"Why, it has stopped now!" she exclaimed suddenly. "The storm is over." Then, because she did not wish to show fear of him, she came nearer and held her wet dress to the flames. "You won't need a fire much longer," she said. "It is warmer out of doors than it is inside."

"That's why I keep the windows down." He looked so dry and brittle, in spite of the dampness about him, that she thought he would break in pieces if he moved too quickly. There was no life, no sap, left in his veins.

"I'm by myself now," he winked at her. "But it won't be for long. Jason comes back to-night."

"To-night!" Joy sang in her voice. But why hadn't he written? Was there anything wrong? Or was he merely trying to surprise her by his return?

"You hadn't heard? Well, that proves, I reckon, that I can keep a secret." He lurched to his feet, balanced himself unsteadily for an instant, and then stumbled to the window. Beyond him she saw the black shape of the box-bush, with a flutter of white turkeys among its boughs, and overhead a triangle of sky, where the grey was washed into a delicate blue. Yes, the storm was over.

"They ought to reach the station about now," he said. "When the windows are open and the wind is in the right direction, you can hear the whistle of the train." There was malignant pleasure in his tone. "You didn't know, I s'pose, that he'd gone off to get married?"

"Married?" She laughed feebly, imagining that he intended a joke. How dreadful old men were when they tried to be funny! His pointed beard jerked up and down when he talked, and his little red blinking eyes stared between his puffed eyelids like a rat's eyes out of a hole. Then something as black and cold as stale soot floated out from the chimney and enveloped her. She could scarcely get her breath. If only he would open the windows.

"Hasn't he told you that we are to be married next week?" she asked.

"No, he hasn't told me." He gloated over the words as if they were whiskey, and she wondered what he was like when he was not drinking, if that ever happened. He could be open-handed, she had heard, when the humour struck him. Once, she knew, he had helped Miss Texanna Snead raise the money for her taxes, and when Aunt Mehitable's cow died he had given her another. "I had a notion that you and he were sweethearts," he resumed presently, "and he'd have to look far, I reckon, before he could pick out a finer girl. He's a pleasant-tempered boy, is Jason, but he ain't dependable, even if he is my son, so I hope you haven't set too much store by him. I never heard of him mixing up with girls, except you and Geneva. That ain't his weakness. The trouble with him is that he was born white-livered. Even as a child he would go into fits if you showed him a snake or left him by himself in the dark——"

"He loves me," she said stoutly, closing her ears and her mind to his words.

He nodded. "I don't doubt it, I don't doubt it. He loved you well enough, I reckon, to want to jilt Geneva; but he found out, when he tried, that she wasn't as easy to jilt as he thought. He'd courted her way back yonder last year, when they were in New York to-gether. Later on he'd have been glad to wriggle out of it; but when Jim and Bob Ellgood came after him, he turned white-livered again. They took him off and married him while he was still shaking from fright. A good boy, a pleasant boy," continued the old man, smack-ing his dry lips, "but he ain't of my kidney."

When he had finished, she gazed at him in a dumbness which had attacked her like paralysis. She tried to cry out, to tell him that she knew he lied; but her lips would not move in obedience to her will, and her throat felt as if it were petrified. Was this the way people felt when they had a stroke, she found herself thinking. On the surface she was inanimate; but beneath, in the buried jungle of her consciousness, there was the stirring of primitive impulses, and this stirring was agony. All individual differences, all the acquired at-tributes of civilization, had turned to wood or stone; yet the racial structure, the savage fibre of instinct, remained alive in her.

The room had grown darker. Only the hearth and the evil features of the old man were picked out by the wavering blue light. She saw his face, with its short wagging beard and its fiery points of eyes, as one sees objects under running water. Everything was swimming round her, and outside, where a cloud had drifted over the triangle of clear sky, the box-bush and the white turkeys were swimming too.

"You'll meet 'em on the road if you go by the fork," piped a voice beneath that shifting surface. "They will be well on the way by the time you have started."

Stung awake at last, she thrust out her arm, warding him off. The one thought in her mind now was to escape, to get out of the room before he could stop her, to put the house and its terrors behind her. It couldn't be true. He was drunk. He was lying. He was out of his head. She was foolish even to listen, foolish to let the lie worry her for an instant.

Turning quickly, she ran from him out of the room, out of the house, out of the stagnant air of the place.

At the beginning of the sandy road, where the water had hollowed a basin, she met the coloured woman, Idabella, who said "good evening," after the custom of the country, as she went by. She was a handsome mulatto, tall, deep-bosomed, superb, and unscrupulous, with the regal features that occasionally defy ethnology in the women of mixed blood. Her glossy black hair was worn in a coronet, and she moved with the slow and arrogant grace which springs from a profound immobility.

"The dreadful old man," thought Dorinda, as she hurried in the direction of Gooseneck Creek. "The dreadful, lying old man!"

13

The sun had riddled the clouds, and a watery light drenched the trees, the shrubs, and the bruised weeds. This light, which bathed the external world in a medium as fluid as rain, penetrated into her thoughts, and enveloped the images in her mind with a transparent brilliance.

"It isn't true," she repeated over and over, as she went down the sandy slope to Gooseneck Creek, and over the bridge of logs in the willows. When she reached the meadows, rain was still dripping from the golden-rod and life-everlasting. A rabbit popped up from the briers and scuttled ahead of her, with his little white tail bobbing jauntily.

"How funny it looks," she thought, "just as if it were beckoning me to come on and play. The rain is over, but I am soaked through. Even my skin is wet. I'll have to dry all my clothes by the kitchen fire, if it hasn't gone out. What a terrible old man!" Out of nowhere there flashed into her mind the recollection of a day when she had gone to a dentist at Queen Elizabeth Court-House to have an aching tooth drawn. All the way, sitting beside her father, behind Dan and Beersheba, she had kept repeating, "It won't hurt very much." Strange that she should have thought of that now! She could see the way Dan and Beersheba had turned, flopping their ears, and looked round, as if they were trying to show sympathy; and how the bunches of indigo, fastened on their heads to keep flies away, had danced fantastically like uprooted bushes. "It isn't true," she said now, seeking to fortify her courage as she had tried so passionately on the drive to the dentist. "When Jason comes back, we will laugh over it together. He will tell me that I was foolish to be worried, that it proved I did not trust him. But, of course, I trust him. When we are married, I will stand between him and the old man as much as I can. I am not afraid of him. No, I am not afraid," she said aloud, stopping suddenly in the road as if she had seen a snake in her path. "When Jason comes back, everything will be right. Yes, everything will be right," she repeated. "Perhaps the old man suspected something, and was trying to frighten me. Doctors always know things sooner than other people. . . . What a dirty place it is! Ma would call it a pig-sty. Well, I can clean it up, bit by bit. Even if the old man doesn't let anybody touch his den, I can clean the rest of the house. I'll begin with the porch, and some day, when he is out, I can make Jemima wash that dreadful floor and the window-panes. The outside is almost as bad too. The walk looks as if it had never been swept." In order to deaden this fear, which was gnawing at her heart like a rat, she began to plan how she would begin cleaning the place and gradually bring system out of confusion. "A little at a time," she said aloud, as if she were reciting a phrase in a foreign language. "A little at a time will not upset him."

At the fork of the road, approaching the red gate, where the thick belt of woods began, her legs gave way under her, and she knew that she could go no farther. "I'll have to stop," she thought, "even if the ground is so wet, I'll have to sit down." Then the unconscious motive, which had guided her ever since she left Five Oaks, assumed a definite form. "If he came on that train, he ought to be here in a few minutes," she said. "The whistle blew a long time ago. Even if he waited for the mail, he ought to be here in a little while."

Stepping over the briers into the woods, she looked about for a place to sit down. An old stump, sodden with water, pushed its way up from the maze of creepers, and she dropped beside it, while she relapsed into the suspense that oozed out of the ground and the trees. As long as her response to this secret fear was merely physical, she was able to keep her thoughts fixed on empty mechanical movements; but the instant she admitted the obscure impulse into her mind, the power of determination seemed to go out of her. She felt weak, unstrung, incapable of rational effort.

A thicket of dogwood and redbud trees made a close screen in front of her, and through the dripping branches, she could see the red gate, and beyond it the blasted oak and the burned cabin on the other side of the road. Farther on, within range of her vision, there were the abandoned acres of broomsedge, and opposite to them she imagined the Sneads' pasture, with the white and red splotches of cows and the blurred patches of huddled sheep.

While she sat there the trembling passed out of her limbs, and the strength that had forsaken her returned slowly. Removing her hat, she let the branches play over her face, like the delicate touch of cool, moist fingers. She felt drenched without and within. The very thoughts that came and went in her mind were as limp as wet leaves, and blown like leaves in the capricious stir of the breeze. For a few minutes she sat there surrounded by a vacancy in which nothing moved but the leaves and the wind. Without knowing what she thought, without knowing even what she felt, she abandoned herself to the encompassing darkness. Then, suddenly, without warning from her mind, this vacancy was flooded with light and crowded with a multitude of impressions.

Their first meeting in the road. The way he looked at her. His eyes when he smiled. The red of his hair. His hand when he touched her. The feeling of his arms, of his mouth on hers, of the rough surface of his coat brushing her face. The first time he had kissed her. The last time he had kissed her. No. It isn't true. It isn't true. Deep down in her being some isolated point of consciousness, slow, rhythmic, monotonous, like a swinging pendulum, was ticking over and over: *It isn't true. It isn't true. True. True. It isn't true.* On the surface other thoughts came and went. That horrible old man. A fire in summer. The stench of drunkenness. Tobacco stains on his white beard. A rat watching her from a hole. How she hated rats! Did he suspect something, and was he trying to frighten her? Trying to frighten her. But she would let him see that she was too strong for him. She was not afraid. . . . The thoughts went on, coming and going like leaves blown in the wind, now rising, now fluttering down again. But far away, in a blacker vacancy, the pendulum still swung to and fro, and she heard the thin, faint ticking of the solitary point of consciousness: *True. True. It isn't true. It isn't true—true—true—*

No, he couldn't frighten her. She was too sure of herself. Too sure of Jason, too sure of her happiness. "Too sure of Jason," she repeated aloud.

The little sad, watery sun sputtered out like a lantern, and after a few minutes of wan greyness, shone more clearly, as if it had been relighted and hung up again in the sky. Colour flowed back into the landscape, trickling in shallow streams of blue and violet through the nearer fields and evaporating into dark fire where the broom-sedge enkindled the horizon. She started up quickly, and fell back. When she put her hand on the slimy moss it felt like a toad.

Far down the road, somewhere in the vague blur of the distance, there was the approaching rumble of wheels. She heard the even rise and fall of the hoofs, the metallic clink of horseshoes striking together, the jolting over the rock by the Sneads' pasture, the splash of mud in the bad hole near the burned cabin, and the slip and scramble of the mare as she stumbled and then, recovering herself, broke into a trot.

It isn't true. It isn't true, ticked the pin point of consciousness. Her mind was still firm; but her limbs trembled so violently that she slipped from the stump to the carpet of moss and soaked creepers. Shutting her eyes, she held fast to the slimy branch of a tree. "When he turns at the fork, I will look. I will not look until he turns at the fork."

The rumble was louder, was nearer. An instant of silence. The buggy was approaching the fork. It was at the fork. She heard close at hand the familiar clink of the steel shoes and the sharper squeak of a loosened screw in the wheel. Rising on the sodden mould, she opened her eyes, pushed aside the curtain of branches, and looked out through the leaves. She saw Jason sitting erect, with the reins in his hands. She saw his burnished red hair, his pale profile, his slightly stooping shoulders, his mouth which was closed in a hard straight line. Clear and sharp, she saw him with the vividness of a flash of lightning, and beside him, she saw the prim, girlish figure and the flaxen head of Geneva Ellgood.

It isn't true. It isn't true. The pendulum was swinging more slowly; and suddenly the ticking stopped, and then went on in jerks like a clock that is running down. *It isn't true. It isn't true—true—true.*

She felt cold and wet. Though she had not lost the faculty of recollection, she was outside time and space, suspended in ultimate darkness. There was an abyss around her, and through this abyss wind was blowing, black wind, which made no sound because it was sweeping through nothingness. She lay flat in this vacancy, yet she did not fall through it because she also was nothing. Only her hands, which clutched wood-mould, were alive. There was mould under her finger-nails, and the smell of wet earth filled her nostrils. Everything within her had stopped. The clock no longer ticked; it had run down. She could not think, or, if she thought, her thoughts were beyond her consciousness, skimming like shadows over a frozen lake. Only the surface of her could feel, only her skin, and this felt as if it would never be warm again.

"So it is true," she said aloud, and the words, spoken without a thought behind them, startled her. The instant afterwards she began to come back to existence; she could feel life passing through her by degrees, first in her hands and feet, where needles were pricking, then in her limbs, and at last in her mind and heart. And while life fought its way into her, something else went out of her for ever—youth, hope, love—and the going was agony. Her pain became so intolerable that she sprang to her feet and started running through the woods, like a person who is running away from a forest fire. Only she knew, while she ran faster and faster, that the fire was within her breast, and she could not escape it. No matter how far she ran and how fast, she could not escape it.

Presently the running shook her senses awake, and her thoughts became conscious ones. In the silence the shuddering beats of her heart were like the unsteady blows of a hammer—one, two, one, one, two, two. Her breath came with a whistling sound, and for a minute she confused it with the wind in the tree-tops.

"So this is the end," she said aloud, and then very slowly, "I didn't know I could feel like this. I didn't know anybody could feel like this." A phrase of her mother's, coloured with the barbaric imagery of a Hebrew prophet, was driven, as aimlessly as a wisp of straw, into her mind: "Your great-grandfather said he never came to Christ till he had thirsted for blood." Thirsted for blood! She had never known what that meant. It had seemed to her a strange way to come to Christ, but now she understood.

The wet briers tore her legs through her stockings. Branches whipped her face and bruised its delicate flesh. Once, when she came out of the woods, she slipped and fell on her hands and knees. The splinters of the fence pierced her skin when she climbed over the rails. But still she ran on, trying to escape from the fire within her breast.

14

On the front porch, with her hand shielding her eyes from the sunset, her mother stood and looked out for her.

"I was watching for you, Dorinda. You must have got caught in the storm."

"Just at the beginning. I stopped at Five Oaks."

"Was anybody there?"

"Nobody but the old doctor. Jemima was off."

"Did he say when he expected Jason?"

"Yes, he told me he might come back this evening."

Once, long ago, she had heard a ventriloquist at a circus, and her voice was like the voice that had come out of the chair, the table, or the wax doll. As she stepped on the porch, her mother examined her closely. "Well, you're as white as a sheet. Go up and take off your wet things as quick as you can, and bring 'em down to the fire. Supper'll be ready in a minute."

Dorinda tried to smile when she hurried by, but her muscles, she found, eluded the control of her will, and the smile was twisted into a smirking grimace. Without trusting herself to meet her mother's eyes, she went upstairs to her room and took off her rain-soaked clothes, hanging her skirt and shirtwaist in the closet, and putting her muddy shoes side by side, as if they were standing at attention on the edge of the rug. Pushing back the curtain over the row of hooks, she selected an old blue gingham dress which she had discarded, and put it on, carefully adjusting the belt, from which the hooks and eyes were missing, with the help of a safety-pin. All the time, while she performed these trivial acts, she felt that her intimate personal self had stepped outside her body, and was watching her from a distance. When she went downstairs, it was only a marionette, like one of the figures she had seen as a child in a Punch and Judy show, that descended the stairs and sat down at the table. She looked at her father and mother, her father eating so noisily, her mother pouring buttermilk, without spilling a drop, into the row of glasses, and wondered what she had to do with these people? Why had she been born in this family and not in another? Could she have been a changeling that they had picked up?

"Dorinda stopped at Five Oaks until the storm was over," she heard her mother say to the others; and suddenly, as if the sound had touched some secret spring in her mind, she became alive again, and everything was bathed in the thin blue light of that room at Five Oaks. The pain was more than she could bear. It was more than anybody could be expected to bear. In a flash of time it became so violent that she jumped up from her chair, and began walking up and down as if she were in mortal agony.

"What's the matter, daughter? Did you come down on your tooth?" inquired Mrs. Oakley solicitously.

"No, it isn't that. I don't want any supper," replied the girl, hurrying out of the room and walking the length of the hall to the front door. "I must do something," she thought. "If I don't do something, this pain will go on for ever."

She had crossed the threshold to the porch, when, wheeling abruptly, she went back into the hall and from the hall into her mother's chamber, where the family Bible lap open on the table and the big fly was still knocking against the ceiling. She had not known that flies lived so long! It seemed an eternity, not a few hours ago, when her mother had sat there reading the Psalms and the fly had buzzed in the stillness. The peaceful room, pervaded by the Sabbath lethargy, with the open Bible waiting for family prayers, and the battered old furniture arranged in changeless order, seemed to close over her like a trap. "I must do something, or this misery will never end," she thought again. But there was nothing that she could do. There would never be anything that she could do in her life. It was over. Everything was over, and she might live to be ninety. "And the child coming too." There also she could find no escape. "No matter what I do, I can change nothing." Something had caught her. Life had caught her. She could not get away, no matter how hard she struggled. A drop of blood fell on her fingers, and glancing into the mirror, she saw that she had bitten her lip until it bled, yet she had not felt it. Nothing like that, nothing on the outside of herself, could ever hurt her again. "If I could only do something," she said in a whisper, and walked from the chamber to the spare room, and from the spare room, which looked as if it were hiding something, out into the hall. Suddenly, like a person moving in delirium, she walked out of the house, and along the path between the pear orchard and the vegetable garden. The green afterglow had faded; but a sallow moon was riding high over the big pine, and gave light enough for her to see her way. Like a wet sheet the twilight folded about her, clinging to her arms and legs when she tried to shake herself free from it. She would have moonlight in the woods, and besides she had nothing to fear. A dry sob broke from her, hurting her throat. You had reached the worst, she realized, when you had nothing to fear.

She followed the path rapidly. By the pear orchard, by the big pine on the hill, by the tobacco-field, through the pasture, and into the dark belt of woods. Here the smell of wet earth stifled her, and she lived over again the moment when she had waited there, listening, in the suspense which was more terrible than any certainty. "I didn't know what it was when I went through with it," she thought. "I didn't know what it was until afterwards." Memory, she felt, was gathering like an ulcer in her mind. If she could not let out the pain, the sore would burst from its own swelling. "If I don't do something, I shall die," she said aloud, standing there, on the edge of the woods, among the wet leaves and rotting mould. Then, swift as an inspiration, there came to her the knowledge of what she must do. She must find Jason. Yes, she must find Jason. This knowledge, which was as infallible as instinct, went no further than the imperative necessity of seeing him. Beyond this, the impulse gave way, like a bridge that breaks in the middle of a stream. It left her there, without prop, without direction, hanging over the black current of emptiness.

As she hurried on, a bough struck her so sharply that it bruised her cheek, but she did not feel it. With the act of decision her body had become so airy and transparent that she was no longer conscious of it as a drag on her spirit. Though she ought to have been tired, she felt instead amazingly strong and fresh, amazingly full of vitality. Only now and then, as she walked rapidly through the willows and over the log bridge, lights flickered and vanished and flickered again before her eyes. At first she thought that a million sparks glittered out there in the moist purple twilight; then she realized that they were not there at all but within her brain. And these lights, which flitted round her as she went on, illumined the blind impulse that directed her movements. It was as if she were harnessed to this impulse and driven by it toward some end of which she was ignorant, but which she would presently discern in the fog.

She moved quickly, with her gaze fixed straight in front of her. The dusk was gilded with fireflies, but she could not distinguish these vagrant insects from the roving lights in her brain. The earth underfoot gave out, when it was crushed, a strong, warm, vital odour. Very near and loud, there was the hoot of an owl, followed presently by another; but the cries seemed to be a part of the inner voice which was urging her on. Her feet slipped on the logs. She recovered herself and went on more quickly, more lightly, as if her body did not exist, or existed merely as a cloud. Now she could see the lamps glimmering in the lower windows of the house. There were lights in the hall, in the dining-room, in the old doctor's retreat; but all the upstairs windows were dark except for the reflected rays of the moonbeams. Was the old man still crouching over his fire, she wondered, with his rat eyes watching out of a hole?

Around the house there were puddles of water and the piles of trash that she had seen in the afternoon. Like a fawn, she sped over them and stopped, unaware of her panting breath, with her eyes on the back door, which was open. She could see within the hall, where a kerosene lamp was fastened in a bracket near the staircase. The same heaps of bagging and boxes and empty bottles were scattered about; the same collection of rusty guns and broken fishing-rods. For the first time she thought clearly, while her gaze travelled over these ordinary objects, "Why did I come? What is the meaning of it? Why am I waiting out here in the night?" But there was no answer to her question. She could not remember why she had come, why she was standing there alone, with her eyes on the open door, watching. Vacancy was around her, was within her; she was drowning in vacancy. Looking away from the house, she saw that there was a light in the barn, and that the big musty place was deserted. The buggy, from which the horse had been taken, was standing near the door, and one of those formless thoughts which she could not distinguish from feeling told her that Jason would come out to put it under the shed. "If I wait here long enough, I shall see him." Though the words were spoken outside her brain, she knew that she must wait there all night if he did not come.

Stepping over the loosened boards of the threshold of the barn, she glanced about at the disorder, which was like the disorder of the house, only it seemed to her cleaner because it was less human. Wheat, corn, fodder. Farming implements. A reaping machine. Medicine for stock. A jumble of odds and ends that had been thrown out of a tool-house. Against a barrel by the door there was the gun with which the old doctor had shot the hawk in the afternoon. Her hands moved over it caressingly, wonderingly. A good gun, not rusty, like everything else on the place. Jason's probably. Far away over the fields a voice was speaking, and the sound floated to her, thin and clear as distant chimes. "*He never came to Christ till he had thirsted for blood*." A strange way—but she knew now, she understood.

There was a noise at the house. A figure darkened the lamplight on the porch; she heard a familiar step; she saw a shadow approaching. It was Jason, she knew, and as he came toward her, she left the barn and went out into the moonlight to meet him. She felt calm now, fresh, strong, relentless; but the ulcer in her mind throbbed as if it were bursting. Yes, it was Jason. He was coming down the steps. He was coming along the path to the barn. In a minute he would see her standing there, another shadow in the moonlight. In a minute he would speak to her.

Suddenly, while she stood there in silence, the gun went off in her hands. She saw the flash; she heard the sound, as if the discharge were miles away; she smelt the powder. The next instant she felt the tremor of the shock as the weapon recoiled in her hands; and she thought quietly and steadily, "I tried to do it. I wanted to do it."

"Dorinda," he called out, while the smoke drifted past him, and she saw his face go as white as paper in the dimness.

Then, as swiftly as it had come, her resolution went out of her. The gun slipped from her hands to the ground, and lay there in the mud at her feet. Her will, with all its throbbing violence, urged her to shoot him and end the pain in her mind. But something stronger than her conscious will, stronger than her agony, stronger than her hate, held her motionless. Every nerve in her body, every drop of her blood, hated him; yet because of this nameless force within the chaos of her being, she could not compel her muscles to stoop and pick up the gun at her feet. Like a dream, like a fantasy of delirium, her resolution vanished, and she knew that it would not return. "Why am I here? What is the meaning of it all?" she asked wildly of the emptiness within her soul.

"Dorinda!" he said again. He had seen her; he had called her name. They were alone together in the moonlight as they had been when she loved him. If only she had the power to stoop and pick up the gun! If only she had the power to make her muscles obey the wish in her heart! If only she had the power to thrust him out of her life! It was not love, it was not tenderness, it was not pity even, that held her back. Nothing but this physical inability to bring her muscles beneath the control of her will.

"Dorinda!" he said again incoherently, as if he had been drinking. "So you know. But you can't know all. Not what I've been through. Not what I've suffered. Nobody could. It is hell. I tell you I've been through hell since I left you. I never wanted to do it. You are the one I care for. I never wanted to marry her. It was something I couldn't help. They brought pressure on me that I couldn't bear. They made me do it. I was engaged to her before I came back. It was in New York last summer. She showed she liked me and it seemed a good thing. Then I met you. I didn't want to marry her. Before God, Dorinda, I never meant to do it. But I did it. You will never understand. I told you that I funked things. I have ever since I can remember. It's the way my mother funked things with my father. Well, I'm like that, so you oughtn't to blame me so much. God knows I'd help it if I could. I never meant to throw you over. It was their fault. They oughtn't to have brought that pressure to bear on me. They oughtn't to have threatened me. They ought to have let me do the best I could. Speak to me. Say something, Dorinda——"

He went on endlessly, overcome by the facile volubility of a weak nature. Was it in time or in eternity that he was speaking? She thought that he would never stop; but his words made as little impression on her as the *drip, drip* of rain from the eaves. Nothing that he said made any difference to her. Nothing that he could ever say in the future would make any difference. In that instant, with a piercing flash of insight, she saw him as he was, false, vain, contemptible, a coward in bone and marrow. He had wronged her; he had betrayed her; he had trampled her pride in the dust; and he had done these things not from brutality, but from weakness. If there had been strength in his violence, if there had been one atom of genuine passion in his duplicity, she might have despised him less even while she hated him more. But weak, vain, wholly contemptible as she knew him to be, she had given him power over her. She had placed her life in his hands, and he had ruined it. With the fury of a strong nature toward a weak one that has triumphed over it, she longed to destroy him and she knew that she was helpless. Nothing that she could do would alter a single fact in his future. Even now he excused himself. Even now he blamed others.

"I swear I never meant to do it, Dorinda," he repeated more vehemently, encouraged by her silence. "You won't give me up, will you?"

Thoughts wheeled like a flight of bats in her mind, swift, vague, dark, revolving in circles. They were pressing upon her from every side, but she could distinguish nothing clearly in the thick palpitating darkness. Impressions skimmed so swiftly over her consciousness that they left no visible outline. Before she was aware of them they had wheeled away from her into ultimate chaos. Bats, nothing more. And outside, against the lighted door of the barn, other bats were revolving.

While she stood there without thinking, her perceptions of external objects became acutely alive. She saw Jason's face, chalk-white in the moonlight; she saw the jerking of his muscles while he talked; she saw his arm waving with a theatrical gesture, like the arm of an evangelist. *Drip, drip,* like water from the eaves, she heard the fall of his words, though the syllables were as meaningless as the rain or the wind.

She had not spoken since he approached her; and she realized, standing there in the mud, that she was silent because she could find no words to utter. There was no vehicle strong enough to endure the storm of pain and bitterness in her mind. Dumbness had seized her, and though she struggled to pour out all that she suffered, when she opened her lips to speak, she could make no audible sound. No, there was nothing that she could say, there was nothing that she could do.

"You won't give me up, will you, Dorinda?" he pleaded.

Turning away, she started back again as rapidly as she had come. Though he called after her in a whisper, though he followed her as far as the end of the yard, she did not slacken her pace or look back at him. Swiftly and steadily, like a woman walking in her sleep, she went down the narrow sandy road to the creek and over the bridge of logs. There was a stern beauty in her face and in her tall, straight figure, which passed, swiftly and unearthly as a phantom, through the moonlight. An impulse was driving her again, but it was the impulse to escape from his presence. She was flying now from the vision she had seen of his naked soul.

She walked in the moonlight without seeing it; past the frogs in the bulrushes without hearing them; through the moist woods without smelling them. Time had stood still for her, space had vanished; there was no beginning and no end to this solitary aching nerve of experience. She was aware of nothing outside herself until she entered the house and saw her mother's chamber, with the open Bible and the big blue fly, which still buzzed against the ceiling.

"We're waiting prayers for you, Dorinda. Ain't you coming?"

"No, I'm not coming. I've got a headache."

"Why did you go out again?"

"I thought I heard a coon or something in the henhouse."

"It might make your head better to hear a chapter of the Bible."

"No, it won't. I'm not coming. I'm never coming to prayers again."

15

In the morning she awoke with the feeling that she was lying under a stone. Something was pressing on her, holding her down when she struggled to rise, and while she came slowly back to herself, she realized that this weight was the confused memory of all that had happened. Yes, it was life. She was caught under it and she couldn't escape.

So far only her muscles had awakened. Sensation was returning by slow degrees to her limbs; she could feel the quiver of despair in her knees and elbows; but her mind was still drugged by the stupor of exhaustion. Recollection was working its way upward to her brain. Deadened as she was, it astonished her that her muscles should remember more accurately than her mind, that they should record a separate impression. "Something dreadful has happened," she found herself saying mechanically. "It will all come back in a minute."

While she dragged herself out of bed, she tried to fix her thoughts on insignificant details. Her shoes were still damp, and she changed them for a pair her mother had given her a few weeks ago because they drew her ankles. There was a broken lace. She must remember to buy a new one at the store. Beyond the window she could see the orchard and the graveyard, with the big pine on the hill, and farther away the shallow ripples of the broomsedge. All these things seemed to her fantastic and meaningless, as if they were painted on air. She recalled now what had happened last evening; but this also appeared meaningless and unreal, and she felt that the whole flimsy situation would evaporate at the first touch of an actual event. She could remember now; but it was a recollection without accompanying sensation, as inanimate as the flitting picture cast by a lantern.

Some terrible mistake seemed to have occurred to her. Just as if she had stepped, for a few dreadful moments, into a life that was not her own. And all the past, when she looked back upon it, wore this aspect of unreality. The world in which she had surrendered her being to love—that world of spring meadows and pure skies— had receded from her so utterly that she could barely remember its outlines. By no effort of the imagination could she recapture the ecstasy. Colours, sounds, scents, she could recall; the pattern of the horizon; evening skies the colour of mignonette; the spangled twi-light over the bulrushes; but she could not revive a single wave, a single faint quiver, of emotion. Never would it come back again. The area of feeling within her soul was parched and blackened, like an abandoned field after the broomsedge is destroyed. Other things might put forth; but never again that wild beauty. Around this barren region, within the dim border of consciousness, there were innumerable surface impressions, like the tiny tracks that birds make in the snow. She could still think, she could even remember; but her thoughts, her memories, were no deeper than the light tracks of birds.

"Why did it happen? What was the meaning of it?" she asked dully, sitting on the side of her bed, with her shoe in her hand. A few hours ago she had loved Jason; now she loved him no longer. All that had drawn her to him seemed now to drive her away; all that had been desire had turned into loathing; all that was glowing with flame was now burned out to cinders. There were women, she knew, who could love even when they hated; but she was not one of these. The vein of iron in her nature would never bend, would never break, would never melt completely in any furnace. "He is weak and a coward," she thought. "How could I love a coward?" Yes, how could she love a coward? And, strangely enough, when she despised him most bitterly, she thought not of the wrong he had done her, not of his treachery and his betrayal of her love, but of the way he had looked in the moonlight, with his chalk-white face, his jerking muscles, and his arm waving with the gestures of an evangelist.

Well, it was all over now. Everything was over but the immediate trouble that she must face. Memories, impressions, undeveloped sensations that led to nothing, swarmed upon her from the hidden

crevices of her being. The Old Stage Road. The way it branched at
the burned cabin. The blasted oak with the Gospel sign on it.
The clink of the mare's shoes. The benign faces of Dan and Beersheba as they looked back at her under bunches of indigo. Work.
Never anything but work. Her mother's voice nagging, always
nagging. Coral strands and palm trees and naked black babies.
What was the meaning of it? Jason as he looked last night. Weak,
whining, apologetic, blaming everything and everybody except himself. His hair plastered in damp streaks on his forehead. His eyes,
red and blinking, as if he had wept. His hands that were never still;
nervous hands, without a firm grip on anything. How she hated him.
What had she ever seen in him to love? Cinders. Nothing left of it
but cinders. Not so much as a spark. Life. That was what it meant.
Then, suddenly, the way he used to look. His eyes when he smiled,
crinkling at the corners. His straight eyebrows brooding like a storm
over his brown-black eyes. The feeling of his hand on her arm. His
charm. Yes, his charm that she had forgotten. Like a breath of air,
or a subtle fragrance, she felt his charm stealing back through her
senses, as if minute waves of aromatic incense were blowing over her
nerves. Though she hated him, could so slight a thing as the memory
of his smile awake the familiar vibrations? Though her mind had
broken away from him, was her body still held a prisoner? And
would his power come back always, without warning of its approach, like the aching of a tooth that one has touched in a sensitive
spot? A few minutes ago she was deadened into the emotional stupor
she called peace. Now, because of a single external image, because
of so trivial a recollection as the way his eyebrows drew down over
his eyes, all the agony of life was beginning again.

She thrust her foot into the shoe and stood up, flinging back her
head as she went to the mirror to shake out her hair. The stubborn
resolution, which was the controlling motive in her character, shot
through her like a bolt. "Well, there's no use thinking," she said
aloud. "I've got to go through with it." While she combed her hair
back from her forehead, and twisted it into its usual compact knot
on her head, she gazed wonderingly at her face in the mirror. After
all she had suffered it seemed strange to her that her face had not
withered and her hair turned white in a night. But there was
scarcely a perceptible change in her appearance. The line of her

hair was still dark and waving; her eyes were still clear and blue; the velvety colour still flowed beneath the few golden freckles on her cheeks. Only there was something in her eyes that had not been there until yesterday. She knew life now, she reflected, and that showed in her eyes.

Fastening her dress as she left the room, she hurried downstairs and into the kitchen where her mother was already busy about breakfast.

"What do you want me to do, Ma?"

"Everything's 'most ready. You can call your father and the boys and then pour out the coffee."

"Why didn't you wake me?"

"You're always tired Monday morning, so I thought I'd let you sleep. I don't see how it is. Sermons rest me. Why didn't you bring your wet things down to the kitchen last night?"

"I was so tired I forgot." Would her mother never stop nagging? Would there never be any quiet?

She called the men to breakfast, poured out their coffee, and helped her mother serve the cornbread and bacon. Then she sat down and ate slowly and deliberately, forcing herself to swallow, as she had forced herself to take gruel when she had had measles. The agony had died down; she felt bruised and sore as if she had been beaten; but the intensity of the pain had settled into a hard substance like lead in her breast. There was not a ripple of emotion surrounding this island of bitterness into which her love had resolved; there was only a vast sea of indifference. The torture would return, she supposed. She was accustomed now to the fact that it came and went, without reason, like one of her mother's attacks of neuralgia; but, for the moment, at least, her nerves had ceased their intolerable vibration.

After breakfast, when she walked along the road to the store, it seemed to her that the landscape had lost colour, that the autumn glow had gone out of the broomsedge. When she came to the fork she found herself listening for the clink of the mare's shoes, and she resolved that she would run into the woods or cower down in the brushwood if she heard the buggy approaching. Never would she see him again, if she could prevent it. Her mind played with absurd fancies. She imagined him dying, and she saw herself looking on

135

without pity, refusing to save him, standing motionless while he drowned before her eyes, or was trampled to death by steers. No, she would never see him again.

There was no sound at the fork. She walked on past the burned cabin, past the Sneads' farm, where the cows looked at her pensively, past the second belt of woods, and up the bone-white slope to the station. Here she found the usual sprinkling of passengers for the early train, and in order to avoid them she went into the store and began arranging the shelves. In a minute Minnie May came to fetch her, and following the little girl into the bedroom, Dorinda found Mrs. Pedlar lying flat in bed, with the pink sacque, which she was too weak to slip on, spread over her breast. The summer had drained the last reserve of her strength. She was growing worse every hour, and she was so fragile that her flesh was like paper. Yet she still kept her vivacity and her eager interest in details.

"Oh, Dorinda," she breathed. "It isn't true, is it?"

Dorinda picked up the sacque and slipped it over the meagre shoulders. "If you aren't careful, you'll take cold," she said quietly, and then, after an imperceptible pause. "Yes, it is true."

"You don't mean he has married Geneva?"

"Yes, he has married Geneva."

"Oh, why? But, Dorinda——"

While Rose Emily was still talking, the girl turned away and went back into the store. If she didn't work and deaden thought, she couldn't possibly go through with it. All this numbness was on the surface of her being, like the insensibility that is produced by a narcotic. It didn't lessen a single pang underneath, nor alter a solitary fact of existence. At any minute, without premonition, the effects of the narcotic might wear off, and she might come back to life again. Coming back to life, with all that she had to face, would be terrible. Taking the broom from the corner behind the door, she began sweeping the floor in hard, long strokes, as if she were sweeping away a mountain of trash; and into these strokes she put as much as she could of her misery. When she had finished sweeping the store, she brushed the mud from the platform and the steps to the pile of refuse which had accumulated at the back of the house. Then she brought a basin of water and a cake of soap, and scrubbed the counter and the shelves where the dry goods were kept. She worked relentlessly, with rigid determination, as if to clean the store were the one absorbing purpose of her life.

"What's got into you, Dorinda?" asked Nathan, while he watched her. "You look as if you'd gone dirt crazy." Dirt crazy! That was what the boys said of her mother.

"I get so tired looking at dust," she replied.

"Dust? I didn't know there was a speck of dust anywhere around. Old Jubilee swept and dusted tihs morning."

With her dripping brush in her hand, Dorinda turned from the shelves she was washing and looked at him over the counter. She wondered why he had not spoken of Jason, and some dormant instinct, buried in the morass of her consciousness, was grateful to him because he had avoided the subject. He must know. Everybody knew by this time. Yet he had not alluded by word or look to the wreck of her happiness. Though she did not think of it at the moment, long afterwards she realized that this was one of the occasions when Nathan had shown a tactfulness which she had never imagined that he possessed.

She finished the shelves, going scrupulously into each crack and corner. Then, putting the basin and the cake of soap aside, she wiped the dampness off with a cloth, and arranged the bolts of figured calico and checked gingham in orderly rows. When this was over she attacked the pasteboard boxes on the adjoining shelf, cleaning, dusting, reassorting the contents of each separate box. It was amazing the way dust collected. Old Jubilee had cleaned the store. Yet here was dirt poked away in the corners.

She had made herself cheap, that was the trouble. If you are going to cheapen yourself, her mother had said, be sure first that the man is not cheap also. Then, even if you are sure, it pays to be prudent. Prudence builds no poorhouses—that was her mother again. Oh, if only she had known when knowledge could have been useful! If only you could live your life after experience and not before! She knew now how to face things. . . .

At that instant, with a stab of anguish, she became alive. Her pain, which had been merely a dull ache, was suddenly as keen as if a blade had been driven into her wound. She couldn't bear it. Nobody could bear it. In a kind of daze she picked up the cloth, the dust-pan, the cake of soap, and carried them to the end of the room. Then, taking down her hat from a peg behind the door, she put it on and went out of the store and across the yard to the gate and the road. It seemed to her that if only she could reach home quickly, she should find that it had all been a mistake, that something had happened to make the situation less terrible than it appeared from a distance. What this something was she tried to imagine. Perhaps the old man had lied. Perhaps Jason was not really married. Perhaps he hadn't meant her to understand that he was married. There were so many possibilities, she told herself, that she could not think of them all. A hundred accidents—anything might have occurred. Only at the store she felt smothered and shut away, as if she were left behind by the hours. A deep instinct, like the instinct that drives a wounded animal to flight, was urging her to go somewhere—anywhere—as long as it was to a different place. She had made a mistake, she saw now, to come to the store. At home it would be easier. At home she should be able to think of some way out of her misery.

She walked as fast as she could, panting for breath, hurrying over the bad places in the road, as if the thing she feared were pursuing her. Down the long slope; through the thin pines; over the mile of red clay road, broken with mud holes; past the Sneads' pasture, where the sourish smell of cattle hung perpetually in the air; by the burned cabin at the fork; and on into the edge of Hoot Owl Woods at the beginning of Old Farm. When, at last, she struggled over the sagging bridge and up the rocky grade to the porch, she was almost surprised to find that the house was not on fire. There was an unnatural aspect, she felt, in the familiar scene, as of a place that had suffered beneath a tornado and yet remained unchanged on the surface. And this smiling October serenity appeared to her to be unendurable. Trembling like a blade of grass, she stood hesitating on the threshold. "Why did I come?" she asked in amazement. "What did I expect to find?"

"Is that you, Dorinda?" called her mother from the kitchen, where she was washing clothes. A kettle of "sour pickle" was simmering on the stove, and the air was laden with the pungent aroma. "What on earth is the matter?"

"I forgot something."

138

"It must have been mighty important. What was it you forgot?"

The trembling had passed from Dorinda's limbs to her thoughts. She felt as if she should drop. "I—I can't remember," she answered.

"Well, I never!" Mrs. Oakley appeared in the doorway, her bare arms glazed with soapsuds and her face beaded with steam. "You ain't sick, are you?"

"No, I remember now. It was a piece of embroidery Rose Emily was doing. She asked me to bring it."

"Embroidery? I should think she might have managed to wait till to-morrow."

"I didn't mind the walk. It is better than being in the store."

"Anyway, you'd better rest a bit before you go back. You look real peaked. Have you got a headache?" So her mother hadn't heard! Who would be the first one to tell her?

"A little. It was getting wet yesterday, I reckon." She must say something. If she didn't, her mother would question her all day.

"If you'd listened to what I told you," said Mrs. Oakley, "you wouldn't have got caught in that storm. Before you go upstairs you'd better rub a little camphor on your forehead."

She lifted her arms, on which soapsuds had dried like seaweed, and went back into the kitchen, while Dorinda, without stopping to look for the camphor, toiled upstairs to her room. Here she flung herself on the bed and lay staring straight up at the stained ceiling, where wasps were crawling. One, two, three, she counted them idly. There was a pile of apples on her mantelpiece. That must have brought them. But she couldn't lie here. Springing up, she went over to the mirror and began nervously changing things on her dressing-table.

Yes, she was ashen about the eyes and her features were thin and drawn. Her warm colour still held firm, but she was mottled about the mouth like a person in a high fever. Even her full red lips looked parched and unnatural. "I am losing my looks," she thought. "I am only twenty and I look middle-aged."

Why had she come back? It was worse here than it was at the store. Her suffering was more intolerable, and she seemed farther away from relief than she had been while she was cleaning the shelves. Perhaps if she went back she should find that it was easier.

Something might have happened to change things. At least her mother wouldn't be at the store, and she dreaded her mother more than anything that she had to face. Yes, she had made a mistake to come home.

Going over to the curtain, she pushed it aside and looked at her dresses, taking them down from the hooks and hanging them back again, as if she could not remember which one she wanted. Then, in a single flash, just as it had returned at the store, all the horror rushed over her afresh, and she turned away and ran out of the room. Any spot, she realized, was more endurable than the place she was in.

"You ain't going back already, Dorinda?" called her mother from the kitchen.

"Yes, I'm going back. I feel better."

"It seems to me it wasn't worth your while walking all that way twice. I'd take my time going back. There ain't a bit of use hurrying like that. When you come home in the evening, I wish you'd remember to bring me that box of allspice. You forgot it on Saturday. It seems to me you're growing mighty forgetful."

But Dorinda was far down the walk on her way to the gate, and she did not stop to reply. She retraced her steps rapidly over the bridge and along the edge of the woods, where the shadows lay thick and cool. Behind her she heard the bumping of a wagon in the mud-holes; but she did not glance round, for she knew that it was only one of the farmers on the way to the station.

"Going to the store?" inquired the man, as he came up with her. "Can I give you a lift?"

She shook her head, smiling up at him. "I'm not going back yet awhile, thank you. I'm out looking for one of our turkeys."

Stepping out of the road, she waited until the wagon had bumped out of sight, and then went on, in a bewildered way, as if she could not see where she was walking. As she approached the fork, her legs refused to carry her farther, and scrambling on her knees up the bank by the roadside, she dropped to the ground and abandoned herself to despair. She couldn't go on and she couldn't sit still. All she could do was to cower there behind the thicket of brushwood, and let life have its way with her. She had reached the end of endurance. That was what it meant, she had reached the end of what she could bear. The trembling, which had begun in her hands and feet, ran now in threads all over her body. For a minute her mind was a blank; then fear leaped at her out of the stillness. Springing to her feet, she looked wildly about, and sank down again because her legs would not support her.

"I've got to do something," she thought. "I've got to do something, or I'll go out of my mind." Never once, in her fright and pain, did the idea of an appeal to Jason enter her thoughts. No, she had finished with him for ever. There was no help there, and if there were help in him, she would die before she would seek it.

Raising her head, she leaned against the bole of a tree and looked, with dimmed eyes, at the October morning. Around her she heard the murmurous rustle of leaves, the liquid notes of a wood robin, like the sprinkling of rain on the air, the distant shrill chanting of insects; all the natural country sounds which she would have called silence. Smooth as silk the shadows lay on the red clay road. Over the sky there was a thin haze, as if one looked at the sun through smoked glasses. "You've got to do something," repeated a derisive voice in her brain. "You've got to do something, or you'll go out of your mind." It seemed to her that the whole landscape waited, inarticulate but alive, for her decision.

Despair overwhelmed her; yet through all her misery there persisted a dim, half-conscious recognition that she was living with only a part of her being. Deep down in her, beneath the rough texture of experience, her essential self was still superior to her folly and ignorance, was superior even to the conspiracy of circumstances that hemmed her in. And she felt that in a little while this essential self would reassert its power and triumph over disaster. Vague, transitory, comforting, this premonition brooded above the wilderness of her thoughts. Yes, she was not broken. She could never be broken while the vein of iron held in her soul.

For a long while she sat there by the roadside, with her eyes on the pale sunshine and the transparent shadows. What would her mother say if she knew? When would she know? Who would have the courage to tell her? For twenty years they had lived in the house together, yet they were still strangers. For twenty years they had not spent a night apart, and all the time her mother had dreamed of coral strands and palm trees, while she herself had grown into a thing as strange and far away as Africa. Were people like this everywhere, all over the world, each one a universe in one's self, separate like the stars in a vast emptiness?

16

Far over the autumn fields, she heard the whistle of the train as it rounded the long curve at the station. Before the sound had floated past her she had come to one of those impetuous decisions which were characteristic of her temperament. "I'll go away in the morning," she resolved. "I'll go on the first train, the one that whistles at sunrise. If I take that, I can leave the house before light."

Immediately afterwards, as soon as the idea had taken possession of her, she felt the renewal of courage in her thoughts. Once that was settled, she told herself, and there was no turning back, everything would be easier. Just to go away somewhere. It made no difference where the train went. She would go to the very end, the farther the better, as long as her money held out. "I can scrape together almost seventy dollars," she thought. "Besides the fifty I made at the store, I've saved the twenty dollars Nathan and Rose Emily gave me for a wedding present. That much ought to take me somewhere and keep me until I can find something to do." Her father, she realized with a pang, would have to manage without her. Perhaps he would be obliged to mortgage the place again. She hoped he wouldn't have to sell Dan and Beersheba, and she was confident in her heart that he would never do this. He would sooner part with the roof over his head. It would be hard on him; but he had Josiah and Rufus, and after her marriage, it was doubtful if she could have continued to help him. "Josiah may marry too," she reflected, "and of course Rufus is always uncertain." Nobody could tell what Rufus might some day take it into his head to do. Then, because weakness lay in that direction, she turned her resolute gaze toward her own future. There was no help outside herself. She knew that the situation, bad as it was now, would be far worse before it was better. Romantic though she was, she was endowed mentally with a stubborn aptitude for facing facts, for looking at life fearlessly; and now that imagination had done its worst, she set herself to the task of rebuilding her ruined world. All her trouble, she felt, had come to her from trying to make life over into something it was not. Dreams, that was the danger. Like her mother she had tried to find a door in the wall, an escape from the tyranny of things as they are; and like her mother, she had floundered among visions. Even though she was miserable now, her misery was solid ground; her feet were firmly planted among the ancient rocks of experience. She had finished with romance, as she had finished with Jason, for ever.

Twisting about on the earth, she pushed aside the branches, and looked down on Old Farm, folded there so peacefully between the road and the orchard. Wreathed in sunlight as pale as cowslips, she saw the house under the yellowing locust trees. Over the roof a few swallows were curving; from a single chimney smoke rose in a column; there was a cascade of shadows down the rocky path to the gate. She saw these blended details, not as she had seen them yesterday or the moment before she had made her decision, but as one looks on a place which one has loved and from which one is parting for ever. A bloom of sentiment and regret coloured the stark outline; and so, she knew, it would remain indelibly softened in her memory.

Rising from the ground, she went back over the road to the bridge and up the rocky grade to the porch. As she drew nearer she saw her mother come out of the kitchen and go in the direction of the hog-pen, with a basin of vegetable parings in her hand. For a few minutes at least the house would be empty! Running indoors and up the two flights of stairs to the attic, Dorinda brought down an old carpet-bag which had belonged first to her grandfather and then to her mother. Once, when she was a child, her mother had used it when she had taken her to spend a night in Richmond, with a distant relative, an old maid, who had died the next year, and again Josiah and Rufus had carried the bag with them when they went to the State fair one autumn. Now, while she dusted it inside and out, and tossed the few papers it contained into a bureau drawer, she decided that it would hold all the clothes she could take with her. "It will be heavy, but I'll manage it," she thought, moving softly lest her mother should return without stopping to gather the eggs in the hen-house. "I'd just as well pack and get it over," she added. "Anything is better than sitting down and waiting for something to happen."

One by one, she smoothed and folded her wedding clothes. Six of everything; nightgowns, chemises, corset covers, with frills across the bosom, starched white petticoats, with wide tucked flounces. She looked at each garment with swimming eyes and a lump like a rock in her throat, before she laid it away in one of the bulging compartments of the carpet-bag. How fine the stitches were! It was a wonder what her mother could do with her rheumatic joints.

Stepping as lightly as she could, she brought her shoes from the closet and packed them away. Then the dresses, one after another. Two blue cotton dresses that she wore in the store. The pink gingham Rose Emily had given her. Would she ever need that again, she wondered. Last of all, the blue nun's veiling. "It would have been more sensible to have got it darker," she thought grimly. There wasn't room for the hat; but, after she had put in her stockings and handkerchiefs and collars, with the bits of ribbon she sometimes wore at her neck, she folded the orange shawl and spread it on top of everything else. "That may come in useful," she added. "You never can tell what the weather will be." It was October, and everybody said winter came earlier in the North. She had decided prudently that she would wear her old blue merino, with the tan ulster and the felt hat she had put away from moths in the spare room. She could easily steal in and get them out of the closet while her mother was looking after the pigs or the chickens.

Well, that was over. After she had closed and strapped the bag, she pushed it behind the curtain. There was no telling, she reminded herself, when her mother would poke her nose into places.

When she went downstairs it was twelve o'clock and the men had come in from the fields.

"Why, Dorinda, I didn't know you'd be here to dinner!" her mother exclaimed. "Is your head bad again?"

"Yes, I wasn't feeling so well, and there wasn't much to do at the store."

"I thought Monday was the busiest day." How like her mother

that was! She could never let a thing drop. Some demon of con-
tradiction impelled her to find a point of offense everywhere.

There was a glass pitcher of buttermilk on the table. A little boy,
the son of William Snead, had brought it over early in the morning,
as soon as Miss Tabitha had churned. Lifting the pitcher, Dorinda
filled the five glasses standing in a circle at the end of the table. As
she handed a glass to her father, she looked at him with a grave
impersonal sentiment, as if he were a part of the farm that she was
leaving. Nothing, not even her mother's nervous nagging, could
annoy her to-day. She felt only a despairing tenderness, like a mist
of tears, in her heart.

"I'm sorry you ain't well, daughter," Joshua said, as he took the
glass from her hand; and she felt that he had put an incalculable
affection into the words. It was the only remark he made during
the meal, and ordinary as it was, it seemed to bring her closer to him
than she had ever been in her life. Or was it only because she was
parting from him so soon? Everything was precious to her now,
precious and indescribably sad and lovely. If she were to speak a
word, she knew that she should burst into tears.

In the afternoon, when she had helped her mother hang out the
clothes at the back of the house, she came indoors and waited for an
opportunity to bring down the carpet-bag. "Perhaps I've always
tried too hard," she thought wearily. "If I'd just give up and let
things drift, it might be that something would go right." She
dropped on the bottom step of the staircase; but she had no sooner
decided to give up the struggle than she heard her mother's voice
telling her that she was going down into the garden.

"The last of those tomatoes will spoil if I don't pick them," she
said.

"Do you want me to help you?" Dorinda called back.

"No, the sun is kind of sickening. You'd better keep out of it.
There ain't much left after the storm, but I might as well use the
tomatoes."

She went out, with the big splint-basket on her arm; and she was
scarcely out of sight before Dorinda had dragged down the carpet-
bag and hidden it under the front porch behind one of the primitive
rock pillars of the foundation. It would be impossible, she knew, to
bring down the bag in the morning without waking her mother,

146

who was a light sleeper. Her father and the boys, drugged by toil in the open, could sleep through thunder; but her mother would start up and call out at the scratching of a mouse. After she had hidden the bag, she went back into the spare room and unwrapped her tan ulster and brown felt hat from the newspapers which protected them from moths. As she unpinned the parcels, a smell of mingled camphor and lavender was released on the air, and she hoped that her mother would not detect it. "If she says anything, I'll tell her it's time to be wearing my winter clothes," she decided, while she carried the ulster and hat upstairs to her room. Since she had clung desperately to the thought of going away, her suffering had been more endurable; the vehement pain had dulled into an apathetic despair which deadened every cell of her body. She dreaded the moment when the stupor would lift and she should think and feel clearly again.

All night she slept only in restless waves of unconsciousness. The darkness was broken up into false dawns, and at every deceptive glimmer she would steal softly to the window and watch for the first splinter of light. While it was still dark, she dressed herself in the clothes she had laid by her bed, and then sat waiting for the sound of a crow in the henhouse. In the early part of the night there was a vaporous moon; but as the hours wore on, the sky clouded over, and when the day began to break a fine, slow rain was falling. "I hate so terribly to go," she thought, while she smoothed her hair and then wrapped up her brush and comb and slipped them into the pocket of her ulster. "I don't believe I'll go after all." But she knew, even while she lingered over the idea, that there was no turning back.

When she remembered it afterwards it seemed to her that the longest journey of her life was the one down the dark staircase. In reality her descent occupied only a few minutes; but the tumult of her emotions, the startled vigilance of her nerves, crowded these vivid instants with excitement. She lived years, not moments, while she hung there in the darkness, expecting the sound of her mother's voice or the vision of a grey head thrust out of the chamber doorway. What would her mother say if she discovered her? What would she say when she went upstairs and found her room empty? At the foot of the staircase Rambler poked his nose into her hand, and padded after her to the front door. He would have followed her outside, but stooping over him, she kissed his long anxious face before she pushed him back into the hall. Her eyes were heavy with tears as she hurried noiselessly across the porch, down the steps, and round the angle of the house to the rock pillar where she had hidden her bag. Not until she had passed through the gate and into the shadow of the woods, did she rest the heavy bag on the ground and stop to draw breath. Now, at last, she was safe from discovery. "If nobody comes by, I'll have to take some of the things out of the bag and try to carry it," she said aloud, in a desperate effort to cling to practical details. But it was scarcely likely, she told herself presently, that nobody would come by. Even on a rainy morning there were always a few farmers who went out to the station at daybreak.

While she waited there by the bridge, she seemed to be alone on the earth. It was a solitude not of the body but of the spirit, vast, impersonal, and yet burdened, in some strange way, with an incommunicable regret. The night had released the wild scents of autumn, and these were mingled with the formless terrors that overshadowed her mind. She thought without words, enveloped in a despondency as shapeless as night.

Up the road there was the measured beat of a trot, followed by the light rattle of a vehicle beyond the big honey-locust at the pasture bars. While she watched, the rattle grew louder, accompanied by the jarring turn of a screw, and a minute later a queer two-wheeled gig, with a hood like a chicken coop, appeared on the slope by the gate. She knew the vehicle well; it belonged to Mr. Kettledrum, the veterinarian, and she had passed it frequently on the road to the station.

"He will talk me to death," she thought, with dogged patience, "but I can't help it."

Lifting the carpet-bag, which felt heavier than it had done at the start, she stepped out into the road and waited until the nodding gig drew up beside her. Mr. Kettledrum, a gaunt, grizzled man of middle age, with a beaked nose and a drooping moustache, which was dyed henna-colour from tobacco, looked down at her with his sharp twinkling eyes.

"Thanky, Dorinda, I'm as well as common," he replied to her greeting. "I declar', it looks for all the world as if you was settin' out on a journey."

148

"So I am." Dorinda smiled bravely. "I wonder if you'll give me a lift to the station?"

"To be sure, to be sure." In a minute he was out on the ground and had swung the bag into the gig beside a peculiar kind of medicine case made of sheepskin. "I'm on my way back from Sam Garlick's, and it'll be more than a pleasure," he added gallantly, "to have you ride part of the way with me. Sam sets a heap of store by that two-year-old bay of his, and he had me over in the night to ease him with colic. Wall, wall, it ain't an easy life to be either a horse or a horse doctor in this here oncertain world."

It was easier to laugh than to speak, and his little joke, which was as ancient and as trustworthy as his two-wheeled gig, started them well on their way. After all, he was a kind man; her father had had him once or twice to see Dan or Beersheba; and people said that, at a pinch, he had been known to treat human beings as successfully as horses. He had a large family of tow-headed children; and though she had heard recently that his wife was "pining away," nobody blamed him, for he had been a good provider, and wives were known occasionally to pine from other causes than husbands.

"It's a right good thing I came by when I did," he remarked genially. "As it happened, I was goin' to stop by anyway for that early train. I like to allow plenty of time, and I generally unhitch my mare befo' the train blows. She ain't skittish. Naw, I ain't had no trouble with her; but she's got what some folks might consider eccentric habits, an' I ain't takin' no chances. So you say you're goin' off on a journey?" he inquired, dropping his voice, and she knew by intuition that he was wondering if he had better allude to Jason's marriage. He would blame him of course; a man couldn't jilt a woman with impunity at Pedlar's Mill; but what good would that, or anything else, do her now?

"Yes, I'm going away." She tried to make her voice steady.

"On the up train or the down one?" he inquired, as he leaned out of the gig to squirt a jet of tobacco juice in the road. Upon reflection, he had abandoned his sympathetic manner and assumed one of facetious pleasantry.

"The earliest. The one that goes north. Shall we be in time for it?"

He pursed his lips beneath the sweeping moustache. "Don't you worry. We'll git you thar. Whar are you bound for?"

149

She spoke quickly. "I'm going to New York." That was the farthest place that came to her mind.

"You don't say so?" He appeared astonished. "Then you'll be on the train all day. You didn't neglect to bring along a snack, did you?"

A snack? No, she had not thought of one, and she had eaten no breakfast.

Mr. Kettledrum was regretful but reassuring. "It's always better to provide something when you set out," he remarked. "An empty stomach ain't a good travellin' companion; but it's likely enough that the conductor can git you a bite at one of the stops. Along up the road, at the junction, thar's generally some niggers with fried chicken legs; but all the same it's safer to take along a snack when you're goin' to travel far."

They were passing the fork of the road. Over the big gate she could see the ample sweep of the meadows, greenish-grey under the drizzle of rain; and beyond Gooseneck Creek, the roof and chimneys of Five Oaks made a red wound in the sky. Seen through the cleft of the trees, the whole place wore a furtive and hostile air. How miserable the fields looked on a wet day, miserable and yet as if they were trying to keep up an appearance. Some natural melancholy in the scene drifted through her mind and out again into the landscape. She felt anew her kinship with the desolation and with the rain that fell, fine and soft as mist, over it all. Even when she went away she would carry a part of it with her. "That's what life is for most people, I reckon," she thought drearily. "Just barren ground where they have to struggle to make anything grow."

"Now, I've never been as far as New York," Mr. Kettledrum was saying in a sprightly manner. "But from all accounts it must be a fine city. My brother John's son Harry has lived there for fifteen years. He's got a job with some wholesale grocers—Bartlett and Tribble. If you run across him while you're there, be sure to tell him who you are. He'll be glad of a word from his old uncle. Don't forget the name. Bartlett and Tribble. They've stores all over the town, Harry says. You can't possibly miss them."

They had reached the Sneads' pasture, deserted at this early hour except for a mare and her colt. A minute later they passed the square brick house, where the cows were trailing slowly across the

150

lawn in the direction of the bars which a small coloured boy was lowering. Then came the mile of bad road, broken by mud-holes. On they spun into the thin woods and out again to the long slope. At the farm her mother was calling her. There was the smell of frying bacon in the kitchen. Her father was coming in from the stable. Rufus was slouching into his chair with a yawn. Steam was pouring from the spout of the big tin coffee-pot on the table. The glint of light on the stove and the walls. Rambler. Flossie. . . . She remembered that she had eaten nothing. Hunger seized her, and worse than hunger, the longing to burst into tears.

"Wall, here we are. The train's blowing now down at the next station. You've plenty of time to take it easy while I unhitch the mare." He helped her to alight, and then, picking up her bag, carried it down to the track. "You jest stand here whar the train stops," he said. "I'll take the mare out and be back in a jiffy. You've got your ticket ready, I reckon?"

She shook her head. No, she hadn't her ticket; but it didn't matter; she would get one on the train. It occurred to her, while he stepped off nimbly on his long legs, which reminded her of stilts, that if she had not met him in the road, she would have missed the early train north and have taken the later one that went to Richmond. So small an incident, and yet the direction in which she was going, and perhaps her whole future, was changed by it. Well, she knew what was ahead of her, she thought miserably, while she stood there shivering in the wet. She was chilled; she was empty; she was heartbroken; yet, in spite of her wretchedness, hope could not be absent from her courageous heart. The excitement of her journey was already stirring in her veins, and waiting there beside the track, in the rain, she began presently to look, not without confidence, to the future. After all, things might have been worse. She was young; she was strong; she had seventy dollars pinned securely inside the bosom of her dress. Dimly she felt that she was meeting life, at this moment, on its own terms, stripped of illusion, stripped even of idealism, except the idealism she could wring from the solid facts of experience. The blow that had shattered her dreams had let in the cloudless flood of reality. "You can't change the past by thinking," she told herself stubbornly, "but there must be something ahead. There must be something in life besides love."

151

The train whistled by the mill; the smoke billowed upward and outward; and the engine rushed toward her. Her knees were trembling so that she could barely stand; but her eyes were bright with determination, and there was a smile on her lips. Then, just as the wheels slackened and stopped, she saw Nathan running down the gradual descent from the store. Reaching her as she was about to step on the train, he thrust a shoe box into her hand.

"You couldn't go so far without a bite of food. I fixed you a little snack." There was a queer look in his eyes. Absurd as it seemed, for a minute he reminded her of her father.

"So Mr. Kettledrum told you I was going away?"

He nodded. "Take care of yourself. If you want any money, write back for it. You know we're here, don't you?"

She smiled up at him with drenched eyes. A moment more and she would have broken down; but before she had time to reply she was pushed into the train; and when she looked out of the window, Nathan was waving cheerfully from the track. "I wonder how I could ever have thought him so ugly?" she asked herself through her tears.

The figures at the station wavered, receded, and melted at last into the transparent screen of the distance. Then the track vanished also, the deserted mill, the store, the old freight car, and the dim blue edge of the horizon. All that she could see, when she raised the window and looked out, was the dull glow of the broomsedge, smothered yet alive under the sad autumn rain.

Part Second **Pine**

The big pine was like greenish bronze ...

1

The big pine was like greenish bronze against the October sky. . . .

A statue in Central Park had brought it back to her, the pine and the ruined graveyard and the autumn sunlight raking the meadows. It was a fortnight since she had come to New York, and in that fortnight she felt that she had turned into stone. Her shoes were worn thin; her feet throbbed and ached from walking on hard pavements. There were times, especially toward evening, when the soles of her feet were edged with fire, and the pain brought stinging tears to her eyes. Yet she walked on grimly because it was easier to walk than to wait. Up Fifth Avenue; down one of the cross streets to the Park, which was, she thought, merely an imitation of the country; back again to Sixth Avenue; and up Sixth Avenue until she drifted again over the Park and into the prison-like streets that ran toward the river. Occasionally she glanced up to read the name of a street; but the signs told her nothing. Fifth Avenue she had learned by name, and Broadway, and the dirty street where she rented a hall room, for fifty cents a day, over a cheap restaurant. Yesterday, she had asked for work on the other side of the city; but nobody wanted help in a store, and her obstinate pride insisted that she would rather starve than take a place as a servant. Twice she had waited in the restaurant beneath her room; but the dirt and the close smells had nauseated her, and by the end of the second day she had been too sick to stand on her feet. After that the waitress whose place she had taken had returned, and the woman in charge had not wanted her any longer. "You'd better get used to smells before you try to make a living in the city," she had said disagreeably. The advice was sound, as Dorinda knew, and she had no just cause for resentment.

155

Yet there were moments when it seemed to her that New York would live in her recollection not as a place but as an odour.

All day she walked from one stony street to another, stopping to rest now and then on a bench in one of the squares, where she would sit motionless for hours, watching the sparrows. Her food, usually a tough roll and a sausage of dubious tenderness, she bought at the cheapest place she could find and carried, wrapped in newspaper, to the bench where she rested. Her only hope, she felt, lay in the dogged instinct which told her that when things got as bad as they could, they were obliged, if they changed at all, to change for the better. There was no self-pity in her thoughts. The unflinching Presbyterian in her blood steeled her against sentimentality. She would meet life standing and she would meet it with her eyes open; but she knew that the old buoyant courage, the flowing outward of the spirit, was over for ever.

What surprised her, when she was not too tired to think of it, was that the ever-present sense of sin, which made the female mind in mid-Victorian literature resemble a page of the more depressing theology, was entirely absent from her reflections. She was sorry about the blue dress; she felt remorse because of the cow her mother might have had; but everything else that had happened was embraced in the elastic doctrine of predestination. It had to be, she felt, and no matter how hard she had struggled she could not have prevented it.

At night, worn out with fatigue, she would go back to the room over the restaurant. The brakeman on the train had given her the address, and he had put her in the street car that brought her to the door in Sixth Avenue. Here also the smells of beer and of the cooking below stairs had attacked her like nausea. The paper on the walls was torn and stained; all the trash in the room had been swept under the bed; and when she started to wash her hands at the rickety washstand in one corner, she had found a dead cockroach in the pitcher. Turning to the narrow window, she had dropped into a chair and stared down on the crawling throng in the street. Disgust, which was more irksome than pain, had rushed over her. After all the fuss that had been made over it, she had asked in bitter derision, was this Life?

Walking up Sixth Avenue one afternoon, she asked this question again. Something was trying to break her. Life or the will of God, it made no difference, for one hurt as much as the other. She could not see any use in the process, but she went on as blindly as a machine that has been wound up and cannot stop until it has run down. Nothing was alive except the burning sore of her memory. All the blood of her body had been drawn into it. Every other emotion—affection, tenderness, sympathy, sentiment—all these natural approaches to experience had shrivelled up like nerves that are dead. She was consumed by a solitary anguish, and beyond this anguish there was nothing but ashes. The taste of ashes was in her mouth whenever she tried to look ahead or to pretend an interest in what the future might bring. Though her mind saw Jason as he was, weak, false, a coward and a hypocrite, he was so firmly knit into her being that, even when she tore him from her thoughts, she still suffered from the aching memory of him in her senses. Pedlar's Mill or New York, what did it matter? The city might have been built of straw, so little difference did it make to her inescapable pain.

At first the noises and the strange faces had confused her. Then it occurred to her that there might be temporary solace in the crowd, that she might lose herself in the street and drift on wherever the throng carried her. Her self-confidence returned when she found how easy it was to pursue her individual life, to retain her secret identity, in the midst of the city. She discovered presently that when nothing matters the problem of existence becomes amazingly simple. Fear, which had been perversely associated with happiness, faded from her mind when despair entered it. From several unpleasant episodes she had learned to be on the watch and to repulse advances that were disagreeable; but at such moments her courage proved to be as vast as her wretchedness. Once an elderly woman in deep mourning approached her while she sat on a bench in the Park, and inquired solicitously if she needed employment. In the beginning the stranger had appeared helpful; but a little conversation revealed that, in spite of her mourning garb, she was in search of a daughter of joy. After this several men had followed Dorinda on different occasions. "Do I look like that kind?" she had asked herself bitterly. But in each separate instance, when she glanced round at her pursuer, he had vanished. In a city where joy may be had for a price, there are few who turn and follow the footsteps of tragedy. Yes, she could take care of herself. Poverty might prove to be a match for her strength, but as far as men were concerned, she decided that she had taken their measure and was no longer afraid of them.

A surface car clanged threateningly in her ears, and stepping back on the corner, she looked uncertainly over the block in front of her. While she hesitated there, a man who had passed turned and stared at her, arrested by the fresh colour in the face under the old felt hat. Her cheeks were thinner; there were violet half-moons under her eyes; but her eyes appeared by contrast larger and more radiantly blue. The suffering of the last two weeks, fatigue, hunger, and unhappiness had refined her features and imparted a luminous delicacy to her skin.

Threading the traffic to the opposite pavement, she turned aimlessly, without purpose and without conjecture, into one of the gloomy streets. It was quieter here, and after the clamour and dirt of Sixth Avenue, the quiet was soothing. Longer shadows stretched over the grey pavement, and the rows of dingy houses, broken now and then by the battered front of an inconspicuous shop, reminded her fantastically of acres of broomsedge. When she had walked several blocks she found that the character of the street changed slightly, and it occurred to her, as she glanced indifferently round, that by an accident she had drifted into the only old-fashioned neighbourhood in New York. Or were there others and had she been unable to find them? She had stopped, without observing it, in front of what had once been a flower garden, and had become, in its forlorn and neglected condition, a refuge for friendless statues and outcast objects of stone. For a few minutes the strangeness of the scene attracted her. Then, as the pain in her feet mounted upward to her knees, she moved on again and paused to look at a collection of battered mahogany furniture, which had overflowed from a shop to the pavement. "I wonder what they'll do with that old stuff," she thought idly. "Some of it is good, too. There's a wardrobe exactly like the one great-grandfather left."

She was looking at the mahogany wardrobe, when the door of the shop widened into a crack, and a grey and white cat, with a pleasant face, squeezed herself through and came out to watch the sparrows in the street.

"She is the image of Flossie," thought Dorinda. Her eyes smarted

158

with tears, and stooping over, she stroked the cat's arching back, while she remembered that her mother would be busy at this hour getting supper.

"Anybody can see you like cats," said a voice behind her; and turning her head, she saw that a stout middle-aged woman, wearing a black knitted shawl over a white shirtwaist, was standing in the midst of the old furniture. Like her cat she had a friendly face and wide-awake eyes beneath sleek grey and white hair.

"She is just like one we had at home," Dorinda answered, with her ingenuous smile.

"You don't live in New York, then?" remarked the woman, while she glanced charitably at the girl's faded tan ulster.

"No, I came from the country two weeks ago. I want to find something to do."

The woman folded her shawl tightly over her bosom and shook her head. "Well, it's hard to get work these days. There are so many walking the streets in search of it. The city is a bad place to be when you are out of work."

Dorinda's heart trembled and sank. "I thought there was always plenty to do in the city."

"You did? Well, whoever told you that never tried it, I guess."

"There are so many stores. I hoped I could find something to do in one of them."

"Have you ever worked in a store?"

"Yes, at home. It was a country store where they kept everything."

"I know that kind. My father used to keep one up the State."

As she bent over the cat, Dorinda asked in a voice that she tried to keep steady. "You don't need any help, do you?"

The other shook her head sorrowfully. "I wish we did; but times are so hard that we've had to give up the assistant we had. I'm just out of the hospital, too, and that took up most of our savings for the last year." Her large, kind face showed genuine sympathy. "I'd help you if I could," she continued, "because you've got a look that reminds me of my sister who went into a convent. She's dead now, but she had those straight black eyebrows, jutting out just like yours over bright blue eyes. That sort of colouring ain't so common as it used to be. Anyhow, it made me think of her as soon as I looked at

159

you. It gave me a start at first. That's because I'm still weak after the operation, I guess."

"Was it a bad operation?"

"Gallstones. One of the worst, they say, when it has gone on as long as my trouble. Have you ever been in a hospital?"

Dorinda shook her head. "There wasn't any such thing where I lived. We always nursed the sick at home. Great-grandfather was bedridden for years before his death, and my mother nursed him and did all the work too."

The woman looked at her with interest. "Well, that's the way you do in the country, of course," she replied, adding after a moment's hesitation, "You look pretty tired out. Would you like to come in and rest a few minutes? I was getting so low in my spirits a little while ago that I looked out to see if I couldn't find somebody to speak a few words to. When this sinking feeling comes on me in the afternoon, I don't like to be by myself. I thought a cup of tea might help me. They haven't let me touch beer since I went to the hospital, so I'd just put the kettle on to boil. It ought to be ready about now, and a bite of something might pick you up as well as me. My mother came from England and she was always a great one for a cup of tea. 'Put the kettle on,' she used to say, 'I'm feeling low in my spirits.' Day or night it didn't make any difference. Whenever she felt herself getting low she used to have her tea."

She led the way, the cat following, through the shop to a corner at the back, where she could still watch the door and the pavement. Here a kettle was humming on a small gas-stove; and a quaint little table, with a red damask cloth over it, was laid for tea. There were cups and saucers, a tea-set, and a wooden caddy with a castle painted on the side. "It looks old-fashioned, I know, but we are old-fashioned folks, and my husband sometimes says that we haven't got any business in the progressive 'nineties. Everything's too advanced for us now, even religion. I guess it's living so much with old furniture and things that were made in the last century."

Dorinda smiled at her gratefully and sat down beside the little red cloth, with her smarting feet crossed under the table. If only she might take off her shoes, she thought, she could begin to be comfortable. At Pedlar's Mill tea was not used except in illness or bereavement, and she was not prepared for the immediate consola-

160

tion it afforded her. Strange that a single cup of tea and a buttered muffin from a bakery should revive her courage! After all, the city wasn't so stony and inhospitable as she had believed. People were friendly here, if you found the right ones, just as they were in the country. They liked cats too. She remembered that she had seen a number of cats in New York, and they all looked contented and prosperous. It was pleasant in the little room, with its restful air of another period; but at last tea was over, and she thanked the woman and rose to leave. "I can't tell you the good it's done me," she said, and added plaintively, "Do you know of any place where I might find work?"

The woman—her name, she said, was Garvey—bent her head in meditation over the tea-pot. "I do know a woman who wants a plain seamstress for a few weeks," she said at last a trifle dubiously, for, in spite of her kindness, she was a cautious body. "The girl she had went to the hospital the day I came out, and she has never been suited since then. Do you know how to sew?"

"I've helped make children's dresses, and of course my own clothes," Dorinda added apologetically. "You see, I never had much to make them out of."

"I see," Mrs. Garvey assented, without additional comment. After pondering a minute or two, she continued cheerfully, "Well, you might suit. I can't tell, but I'd like to help you. It's hard being without friends in a big city, and the more I talk to you, the more you remind me of my sister. I'll write down the address for you anyway. It's somewhere in West Twenty-third Street. You know your way about, don't you?"

"Oh, I'll find it. People are good about directing me, especially the policemen."

"Well, be sure you don't go until after six o'clock. Then the other girls will be gone, and she will have more time to attend to you. But you mustn't set your heart on this place. She may have taken on some one since I talked with her."

Dorinda smiled. No, she wouldn't set her heart on it. "I'll go and sit in a park while I'm waiting," she replied gratefully. "If I'm going to be a dressmaker, I ought to notice what women are wearing."

With the slip of paper in her purse, and her purse slipped into the bosom of her dress, she left the shop and followed the street back to Fifth Avenue. The hour spent with the stranger had restored her confidence and there was no shadow of discouragement in her mind. Something told her, she would have said, that her troubles were beginning to mend. "I can sew well enough when I try, even if I don't like it," she thought. "Ma taught me how to make neat buttonholes, and I can run up a seam as well as anybody."

As she approached Fifth Avenue she began to observe the way the women were dressed, and for the first time since she left Pedlar's Mill she felt old-fashioned and provincial. The younger women who passed her were all wearing enormous balloon sleeves and bell skirts, which were held up with the newest twist by tightly gloved hands. Now and then, she noticed, the sleeves were made of a different material from the dress, but the gloves were invariably of white kid, and the small coquettish hats were perched very high above crisply waved hair which was worn close at the temples.

In spite of her blistered feet, she walked on rapidly, lifting her face to the wind, which blew strong and fresh over the lengthening shadows. How high and smooth and round the sky looked over the steep brown houses! Presently, from a hotel of grey stone, as gloomy as a prison, a gaily dressed girl flitted out into a hansom cab which was waiting in front of the door. There was a vision of prune-coloured velvet sleeves in a dress of grey satin, of a skirt that rustled in eddying folds over the pavement, and of a jingling gold chatelaine attached to the front of a pointed basque. "How happy she must be," Dorinda thought, "dressed like that, and with everything on earth that she wants!"

She had turned to move on again, when a man carrying a basket of evergreens brushed against her, and she saw that he was engaged in replenishing the stone window-boxes on the ground floor of the hotel. As she passed, a whiff of wet earth penetrated her thoughts, and immediately, in a miracle of recollection, she was back at Five Oaks in the old doctor's retreat. Every detail of that stormy afternoon started awake as if it had been released from a spell of enchantment. She saw the darkened room, lighted by the thin blue flame from the resinous pine; she saw the one unshuttered window, with the hunched box-bush and the white turkeys beyond; she heard the melancholy patter of the rain on the shingled roof; and she watched the old man's face, every line and blotch distorted by the quivering light, while he wagged his drunken head at her. A shudder jerked through her limbs. Her memory, which was beginning to heal, was suddenly raw again. Would she never be free? Was she doomed to bear that moment of all the moments in her life wherever she went? Her courage faded now as if the sun had gone under a cloud. She had been dragged back by the wind, by an odour, into the suffocating atmosphere of the past. Though her body was walking the city street, in her memory she was rushing out of that old house at Five Oaks. She was running into the mist; she was hurrying down the sandy road through the bulrushes; she was crouching by the old stump, with the wet leaves in her face and that suspense more terrible than any certainty in her mind. She listened again for the turn of the wheels, the clink of the mare's shoes; the slip and scramble in the mud-holes; the hollow sound of hoofs striking on rock. . . .

Never in her life had she been so tired. In an effort to shake her thoughts free from despair, she quickened her pace, and looked about for a bench where she could rest. On the opposite side of Fifth Avenue a row of cab horses waited near a statue under some fine old trees. She had never seen the name of the square, but it appeared restful in the afternoon light; and crossing the street, she found a place in the shade on a deserted bench. It was five o'clock now, and Mrs. Garvey had told her not to go to see the dressmaker until six. Well, it was a relief to sit down. Slipping off her shoes, she pushed them under the bench and spread her wide skirt over her feet. The quiet was pleasant in the moving shadows of the trees. From where and how far, she wondered, did the people come who were lounging on the benches around her? So many people in New York were always resting, but she concluded that they must have money put by or they couldn't afford to spend so much time doing nothing.

Gradually, while she sat there, watching the sparrows fluttering round the nose-bags of the horses, hollow phrases, without meaning and without sequence, swarmed into her mind. Five o'clock. At home her mother would be getting ready for supper. That grey and white cat had made her think of Flossie. They were alike as two peas. Remembering the old man had upset her. She must put him out of her mind. You couldn't change things by thinking. How could horses feed in those nose-bags? What would Dan and Beersheba think of them? There was another woman with velvet sleeves in a silk dress. How Miss Seena would exclaim if you told her that so many women were wearing sleeves of different material from their dresses! That flaring collar of lace was pretty though. . . . The way the old man had leered at her over the whiskey-bottle. "He's coming back this evening. He went away to be married." No, she must stop thinking about it. If she could only blot it all out of her memory. The buildings in New York were so high. She wondered people weren't afraid to go to the top of them. There was a poor-looking old man on the bench by the fountain. In rags and with the soles dropping away from his shoes. People were rich in New York, but they were poor too. Nobody but Black Tom, the county idiot, wore rags like that at Pedlar's Mill. How her feet ached! Would they ever stop hurting? . . . "He went away to be married. He went away to be married." How dark the room was growing, and how black the box-bush looked in the slanting rain beyond the window. Feet were pattering on the shingled roof, or was it only the rain? . . . It was getting late. Almost time to go to the dressmaker's. Suppose the dressmaker were to take a fancy to her. Such things happened in books. "You are the very girl I am looking for. One who isn't afraid to work." There was a fortune, she had heard, in dressmaking in New York. Miss Seena knew of a dressmaker who kept her own carriage. . . . How funny those lights were coming out in the street! They were winking at her, one after another. It was time to be going; but she didn't feel as if she could stir a step. Her knees and elbows were full of pins and needles. It's resting that makes you know how tired you are, her mother used to say. . . .

Suddenly nausea washed over her like black water, rising from her body to her exhausted brain. She could scarcely sit there, holding tight to the bench, while this icy tide swept her out into an ocean of space. The noises of the city grew fainter, receding from her into the grey fog which muffled the sky, the lights, the tall buildings, the vehicles in the street. It would be dreadful if she were sick here in the square, with that ugly old man and all the cab drivers staring at her. . . . Then the sickness passed as quickly as it had come; and leaning back against the bench, she closed her eyes until she should be able to get up and start on again. After a minute or two, she felt so much better that she slipped her feet into her shoes, fastened the buttons with a hairpin, and rising slowly and awkwardly, walked across the square to the nearest corner.

The noises, which had almost died away, became gradually louder. There was a tumult of drums in the air, but she could not tell whether the beating was in her ears or a parade was marching by somewhere in the distance. Evidently it was a procession, though she could see nothing except the moving line of vehicles in the street, which had left the ground and were swimming in some opaque medium between earth and sky. "How queer everything looks," she thought. "It must be the lights that never stop winking."

She put her foot cautiously down from the curb, imagining, though she could not see it, that the street must be somewhere in front of her. As she made a step forward into the traffic, the sickness swept over her again, and an earthquake seemed to fling the pavement up against the back of her head. She saw the lights splinter like glass when it is smashed; she heard the drums of the invisible procession marching toward her; she tried to struggle up, to call out, to move her arms, and with the effort, she dropped into unconsciousness.

2

She opened her eyes and looked at the white walls, white beds, white screens, white sunlight through the windows, and women in white caps and dresses moving silently about with white vessels in their hands.

"Why, this must be a hospital," she thought. "How on earth did I come here?"

Her arm, lying outside the sheet, looked blue and cold and felt as if it did not belong to her. She could not turn her head because it was bandaged, and when, after an eternity of effort, she succeeded in lifting her hand, she discovered that her hair had been cut away on one side. Closing her eyes again, she lay without thinking, without stirring, without feeling, while she let life cover her slowly in a warm flood. The blessed relief was that nothing mattered; nothing that had happened or could ever happen mattered at all. After the months when she had cared so intensely, it was like the peace of the Sabbath not to care any longer, neither to worry nor to wonder about the future.

"I must have hurt myself when I fell," she said.

To her surprise a voice close by the bed answered, "Yes, you fainted in the street and a cab struck you. You have been ill, but you're getting all right now."

A man was standing beside her, a large, ruddy, genial-looking man, with a brown beard and the kindest eyes she had ever seen. He wore a red and black tie and there was a square gold medal hanging from his watch-chain.

"Have I been here long?" she asked, and her voice sounded so queer that she couldn't believe it had come out of her lips.

"A week to-day. It will be another week at least before you're strong enough to be out."

"Was I very ill?"

"At first. We had to operate. That's why your head is shaved on one side. But you came through splendidly," he added in his hearty manner. "You have a superb constitution."

For an instant she pondered this. "Are you the doctor?" she inquired presently.

"I am Doctor Faraday." His hand was on her wrist and he was smiling at her as if he hadn't a care or a qualm.

She wondered if he knew anything about her. He appeared so big and wise and strong that he might have known all there was to know about everybody.

"Is there anything that worries you?" he asked gently, with his air of taking the world and all it contained as an inexhaustible joke.

She shook her head as well as she could for the bandages, which made all her movements seem clumsy and unnatural. "I was just thinking——"

"Do you remember where you were going?"

She met his eyes candidly, yielding her will to the genial strength of his personality. "I was looking for work. There was a dressmaker in West Twenty-third Street. She will have filled the place by now."

"You mustn't worry about that." She liked the way the wrinkles gathered about his merry grey eyes. "Don't worry about anything. We'll see that you have something to do as soon as you're strong enough. Meanwhile, just lie still and get well. Keep a stiff upper lip," he concluded, with a subdued laugh which would have boomed out if he hadn't suppressed it. "That's the only way to meet life. Keep a stiff upper lip."

"I can't help thinking,"—she glanced weakly about the room, where the white iron beds—they were the smallest beds she had ever seen—stood in a row. "Is this a charity place?"

"Now, I told you not to worry. No, we don't call it charity, but there is no charge for those who need treatment and cannot afford to pay for it. We don't expect you to be one of the rich patients. Is there anything else?"

She tried again to shake her head. All at once she had forgotten what she wanted to know. She was too weak to remember things, even important things. There was a pain at the back of her head, and this pain was shooting in wires down her neck and through her shoulders to her spine. Nothing made any difference.

"Don't make an effort. Don't try to talk," he said, and turned away to one of the beds by the door.

Hours later, when one of the nurses brought her a cup of broth, she struggled to speak collectedly. "What did the doctor tell me his name is? I don't seem to remember things."

"That's because you're still weak. His name is Faraday. He is a celebrated surgeon, and he operated on you because he brought you to the hospital. He was driving by when you were struck. The operation saved your life."

"Does he come often?"

"Not as a rule. He hasn't time to visit the patients. But he is interested in your case. It is an unusual one, and he is very much interested."

"Does he know who I am?"

"Yes, the woman you rented a room from read about the accident in the papers, and came to identify you. Can you remember anything of this last week?"

"Only that my head hurt me. Yes, and figures passing to and fro against white walls."

"It was a wonder you weren't killed. But you're all right now. You'll be as well as you ever were in a little while."

"I feel so queer with my head shaved. I can feel it even with the bandages."

"That will soon be well, and the scar won't show at all under your hair. You've everything to be thankful for," the nurse concluded in a brisk professional tone.

Dorinda was gazing up at her with a strange, groping expression. Her eyes, large, blue, and wistful in the pallor of her face, appeared to have drained all the vitality from her body. "There was something I wanted to ask the doctor," she began. "I don't seem to be able to remember what it was. . . ."

"Don't remember," replied the nurse with authority. She hesitated an instant, and stared down into the empty cup. Then, after reflection, she continued clearly and firmly, "It won't hurt you to know that you have been very ill, now that you are getting well again?"

Dorinda's features, except for her appealing eyes, were without expression. Yes, she remembered now; she knew what she had wished to ask, "Oh, no, it won't hurt me," she answered.

"Well, I thought you'd take it sensibly." After waiting a moment to watch the effect of her words, the nurse turned away and walked briskly out of the ward.

Lying there in her narrow bed, Dorinda repeated slowly, "I thought you would feel that way about it." Words, like ideas, were dribbling back into her mind; but she seemed to be learning them all over again. Relief, in which there was a shade of inexplicable regret, tinged her thoughts. She would have liked a child if it had been all hers, with nothing to remind her of Jason. For a second she had a vision of it, round, fair and rosy. Then, "it might have had red hair," she reminded herself, "and I should have hated it."

Relief and regret faded together. She closed her eyes and lay helpless, while the stream of memory, now muddy, now clear, flowed through her into darkness. At first this stream was mere swirling blackness, swift, deep, torrential as a river in flood. Then gradually the rushing noise passed away, and the stream became lighter and clearer, and bore fragmentary, rapidly moving images on its surface. Some of these images floated through her in obscurity; others shone out brightly and steadily as long as they remained within range of her vision; but one and all, they came in fragments and floated on before she could grasp the complete outline. Nothing was whole. Nothing lasted. Nothing was related to anything else.

Thirst. Would they soon bring her something to drink? The old well bucket at home. The mossy brim; the cool slippery feeling of the sides; the turning of the rope as it went down; the dark greenish depths, when one looked over, with the gleaming ripple, like a drowned star, at the bottom. Cool places. Violets growing in hollows. A hollow at Whistling Spring, where she had stepped on a snake in the tall weeds. What was it she couldn't remember about snakes? Something important, but she had forgotten it. "I've always funked things." Who said that? Why was that woman moaning so behind the screen in the corner? . . . The snake had come back now. Jason had put his hand on a snake, and that was why everything else had happened. If Jason hadn't put his hand on a snake when he was a child, he would never have deserted her, she would never have been picked up in the street, she would not be lying now in a hospital with half of her hair shaved away. How ridiculous that sounded when one thought of it; yet it was true. What was it her mother said so often? The ways of Providence are past finding out. . . . The nurse again. Oh, yes, water. . . .

The morning when she sat up for the first time, Doctor Faraday stayed longer than usual and asked her a number of questions. She felt quite at home with him. "When any one has saved your life, I suppose he feels that you have a claim on him," she thought; and she replied as accurately as she could to whatever he asked. Naturally reticent, she found now that she suffered from a nervous inability to express any emotion. She could talk freely of external objects, of the hospital, the nurses, the other patients in the ward; but constraint sealed her lips when she endeavoured to put feeling into words.

"When you are discharged, I think we can find a place for you," said Doctor Faraday. "My wife is coming to talk to you. We've been looking for a girl to stay in my office in the morning and help with the children in the afternoon. Not a nurse, you know. The office nurse has other duties; but some one to receive the patients and make appointments."

She looked at him incredulously. "You aren't just making it up?"

With a laugh he ignored the question. "You haven't any plans?"

"Oh, no. It will be too late to go to the dressmaker, and besides she might not have wanted me."

"You are sure you don't wish to go home?"

She gazed at his firm fleshy face, over which the clean shining skin was drawn so smoothly that it looked as if it were stretched; the thick brown hair, just going grey and divided by a pink part in the centre; the crisp beard, clipped close on the cheeks and rounding to a point at the chin. Yes, she liked his face. It was a comfortable face to watch, and she had never seen hands like his before, large, strong, mysteriously beneficent hands.

"No," she answered in her reserved voice, "I can't go back yet."

If she went back, she should be obliged to face the red chimneys of Five Oaks, the burned cabin, and the place where she had sat and waited for Jason's return. These things were still there, perpetual and unchanged.

170

"I've talked to my wife about you," Doctor Faraday said. "I believe you are a good girl, and we both wish to help you to lead a good life."

"You've been so kind," she responded. "I can't tell you what I feel, but I do feel that. I want you to know."

"My dear girl." He bent over and touched her hand. "I know it. If you'd had as much experience with emotional women as I've had, you'd understand the blessedness of reserve. Wait till you see my wife. You'll find her easy to talk to. Every one does."

A few mornings afterwards, as she was preparing to get up, Mrs. Faraday came and sat by the little bed. She was a plump, maternal-looking woman, with an ample figure, which did not conform to the wasp-waist of the period, and a round pink face, to which her tightly crimped hair and small fashionable hat lent an air of astonishment, as if she were thinking continually, "I didn't know I looked like this." Her mantle was of claret-coloured broadcloth heavily garnished with passementerie, and she wore very short white kid gloves, above which her plump wrists bulged in infantile creases. While she sat there, panting a little from her tight stays and her unnatural elegance, Dorinda gazed at her sympathetically and thought it was a pity that she did her hair in a way that made her temples look skinned.

"Doctor Faraday is very much interested in your case," she began in a voice that was as fresh and sweet as her complexion.

"He has been so kind to me."

"We both wish to help you, and we think it might be good for you to take the place in his office for a little while—a few weeks," she added cautiously, "until you are able to find something else. In that way the doctor can keep an eye on you until you are well again. Of course the work will be light. He has a nurse and a secretary. However, you could help with the children after the office hours are over. The nurse and Miss Murray, the governess, take them to the Park every afternoon; but there are six of them, and we can't have too much help. That's a large family for New York," she finished gaily.

"We have much larger ones at Pedlar's Mill. The Garlicks were twelve until one died last year, and old Mrs. Flower, the mother of the auctioneer, had thirteen children."

"You like children?"

"Oh, yes, I like children." She couldn't put any enthusiasm into her voice, and she hated herself for the lack of it. She was dead, turned into stone or wood, and she didn't really care about anything. Did she or did she not like children? She couldn't have answered the question truthfully if her life had depended upon it. In her other existence she had liked them; but that was so long ago and far away that it had no connection with her now.

"Then that is settled." What a happy manner Mrs. Faraday had! "The nurse tells me you are leaving to-morrow. Will you come straight to us or would you like a day to yourself?"

"A day to myself, if you don't mind. I ought to get a dress, oughtn't I?"

"Oh, any plain simple dress will do. Navy blue poplin with white linen collar and cuffs would be nice. But don't tire yourself or spend any money you can't afford. We'll arrange all that later."

Mrs. Faraday had risen and was holding out one firmly gloved hand. As she grasped it, Dorinda could feel the soft flesh beneath the deeply embedded buttons. "Then I'll look for you day after to-morrow," said the older woman in her sprightly tone. "Navy blue will look well on you with your hair and eyes," she added encouragingly. "I always liked blue eyes and black hair."

Dorinda smiled up at her. "And now half my hair is gone. I must look a fright, and the scar isn't even hidden. I'll be marked all my life."

"Oh, but your hair will come back thicker than ever. Even now your scalp is covered, and in a little while no one will know that there is a scar." She beamed down on the bed. "Here is the address. Have you a place you can put the card, so it won't slip away?"

"I've got my purse under my pillow." As Dorinda drew out the little leather bag, and slipped the card into it, she thought wearily, "How funny it is that this should have happened to me."

Since her illness, the whole of life, all she had gone through, all she saw around her, all feeling everywhere, appeared less tragic than ludicrous. Though her capacity for emotion was dead, some diabolical sense of humour had sprung up like fireweed from the ruins. She could laugh at everything now, but it was ironic laughter.

3

Her first thought, when she opened her eyes the next morning, was that she was free to leave the hospital as soon as she pleased. If only she might have stayed there until she died, tranquil, indifferent, with nothing left but this sardonic humour. A little later, as she glanced at the other patients in the ward, at the woman who moaned incessantly and at the young girl, with flaming red hair, who had lost her leg in an accident, she told herself that there were people in the world who were worse off than she was. Through the high window she could see that the sky was clear, and that a strong breeze was blowing a flag on the top of a grey tower. She was glad it was not raining. It would have been a pity to go back into the world on a wet day.

After she had had her breakfast, and a glib young doctor had given her some directions, she got out of bed and a pupil nurse helped her to dress. They had arranged, she discovered presently, that a friend of one of the other patients—the moaning woman, it soon appeared—should go with her as far as her lodging-house. That was the stranger's way also, and she had promised to see that Dorinda reached her room safely.

"Do they know that you are coming?"

"Yes, the nurse telephoned for me. I can get the same room, and they've put my bag in it."

"Well, I'll be glad to go with you," said the woman, a depressed-looking person, in rusty mourning. "You must be careful about crossing the street while you're so weak."

"I don't feel as if I could walk a step," Dorinda answered, sinking into a chair while she dressed.

Her street clothes were so uncomfortable that she wondered how she could ever have worn them. Her stockings were too large, and the feet of them were drawn out of shape; her dress felt as if it weighed tons. But her hair troubled her most. No matter how hard she tried, she could not make it look neat. So much of it had been cut away on the right side that she was obliged to wind what was left into a thin twist and fasten it like a wreath round her head. Her face was thin and pallid, just the shape and colour of an egg, she thought despondently, and "I'm all eyes," she added, while she gazed at herself in the small mirror.

It was late afternoon when she left the hospital, leaning on the arm of the stranger, who remarked with every other step, "I hope you ain't beginning to feel faint," or, "You'd better take it more slowly." The bereaved woman was provided with a collection of gruesome anecdotes, which she related with relish while they crept along the cross street in the direction of Sixth Avenue. "There ain't much I don't know about operations," she concluded at the end of her recital.

As the air brushed her face, Dorinda's first sensation was a physical response to the invigorating frostiness. Then it seemed to her that whenever she took a step forward the pavement rose slightly and slid up to meet her. In so short a time she had forgotten the way to walk, and she felt troubled because in her case the law of gravitation appeared to be arbitrarily suspended. When she put her foot out, she did not know, she told herself, whether it would have the weight to come down or would go floating up into the air. "Could anything have happened to my brain," she wondered, "when I was struck on the head?" In a little while, however, the sensation of lightness gave place to the more familiar one of strained muscles. Though she could walk easily now, she was beginning to feel very tired, and she could barely do more than crawl over the long block.

A high wind was blowing from the west, billowing the sleeves and skirts of women's dresses, whipping the dust into waves, and tossing the gay streamers in Fifth Avenue. The sunlight appeared to splinter as it struck against the crystal blue of the sky and to scatter a shower of sparkling drops on the city. Though it was all bright, gay, beautiful, to Dorinda the scene might have been made of glass in the windy hollow of the universe. "I'm dried up at the core," she

174

thought, "and yet, I've got to go on pretending that I'm alive, that I'm like other people." She felt nothing; she expected nothing; she desired nothing; and this insensibility, which was worse than pain, had attacked her body as well as her heart and mind. "If somebody were to stick a pin in me, I shouldn't feel it," she told herself. "I'm no better than a dead tree walking."

At the corner of Sixth Avenue, a gust of wind struck her sharply, and still leaning on the arm of her companion, she drew back into the shelter of a shop.

"Let's stand here until the next car comes."

"Do you feel any worse?"

"No, not worse, only different."

"I've known 'em to faint dead away the first time they left the hospital."

"Well, I've no idea of fainting. Just tell me when you see the right car coming."

The thing that worried her most, and she had puzzled over this from the minute she came down the steps of the hospital, was the curious impression in her mind that she had seen everything and everybody before. Every face was familiar to her. She seemed to have known each person who passed her in some former time and place, which she dimly remembered; and each reminded her, in some vague resemblance of contour, feature, or shifting expression, of the way Jason had looked when she first loved him. "Just as I was trying to forget him," she thought, with irritation, "everybody begins to look like him."

When the car came, and she got on and found a seat beside a fat German, who was buried in his newspaper, this senseless irritation still persisted. "Maybe if I stop looking at their faces and keep my eyes fixed on their clothes, the resemblance will pass away," she told herself resolutely. "What a funny hat, just like a cabbage, that woman is wearing, and the man with her has on a tie like a little boy's. He must be an artist. I read in some book that artists wore velvet coats and flowing ties." Then, inadvertently, she raised her eyes to the face of the stranger, and discovered that he was gazing at her with a look that reminded her of Jason. Even the fat German wore a familiar expression when he turned to touch the bell and glanced down at her as he rose to go out of the car.

At the lodging-house, where she had to explain her case all over again, she was still haunted by this delusive resemblance. There might have been a general disintegration and reassembling of personalities since she had gone to the hospital, and she felt that she had seen them all before in other circumstances and other periods.

Alone, at last, in her little room, she dropped wearily on the hard bed, which, like the wife of the proprietor, bulged in the wrong places, and lay, without seeing or hearing, surrendered to the grey hollowness of existence. Sheer physical weakness kept her motionless for an hour; and when at the end of that time, she lifted her hands to take off her hat, she felt as if she were recovering from the effects of an anæsthetic. Gradually, as the stupor wore off, she became aware of the objects around her; of the hissing gas-jet, which burned in the daytime; of the dirty carpet, with an ink splotch in the centre; of the unsteady washstand that creaked under its own weight; of the stale ashes of a cigar in the top of the soap-dish; of the sharp ridge down the middle of the bed on which she was lying. And she thought clearly, "No matter how bad it is, I've got to go through with it."

The hardest thing, she knew, that she had to face was not the wreck of her happiness, but the loss of a vital interest in life. Even people who were unhappy retained sometimes sufficient interest in the mere husk of experience to make life not only endurable but even diverting. With her, however, she felt that she had nothing to expect and nothing to lose. One idea had possessed her so completely that now, when it had been torn out from the roots like a dying nerve, there was no substitute for happiness that she could put in its place. "I've finished with love," she repeated over and over. "I've finished with love, and until I find something else to fill my life, I shall be only an empty shell. . . ."

Rising from the bed, she opened her bag and unfolded her dresses. None of them would do for New York, she realized. All of them, she saw now, were absurd and countrified. As she shook out the blue nun's veiling, she said to herself, "If I hadn't bought this dress, perhaps he would never have fallen in love with me, and than I should still be living at Old Farm, and Ma would have her cow and nothing would have happened that has happened." She laughed with the perverse humour that she had brought back out of the depths of unconsciousness. If only one could get outside of it and stand a little way off, how ridiculous almost any situation in life would appear! Even those moments when she had waited in anguish at the fork of the road were tinged with irony when they revived now in her memory. "All the same I wouldn't go through them again for anything that life could offer," she thought.

4

Dorinda stood in Doctor Faraday's office and looked out into East Thirty-seventh Street. Beneath her there was a grey pavement swept by wind and a few pale bars of sunshine. She saw the curved iron railing of the porch and the steps of the area, where an ashcan, still unemptied, awaited the call of the ashcart. A four-wheeler, driven by a stout, red-faced driver, was passing in the street; at the corner an Italian youth with a hunchback was selling shoe-strings; on the pavement in front of the house, a maltese cat, wearing a bell on a red ribbon, sunned himself lazily while he licked the fur on his stomach. Overhead, the vault of the sky appeared remote, colourless, as impenetrable as stone.

When she turned into the house, she knew to weariness what she should find awaiting her. A narrow oval room, with sand-coloured walls, curtains of brown damask, and furniture of weathered oak, which was carved and twisted out of all resemblance to her mother's cherished pieces of mahogany. On the long tables piles of old magazines lay in orderly rows. In the fireplace three neat gas logs shed a yellow flame shot with blue sparkles. Very far apart, three patients were sitting, with strained expectant eyes turned in the direction of the folding doors which led into the inner office. In the last two years she had learned to know the office and the street outside as if they were books which she had studied at school.

Standing there, she thought idly of her new dress of navy blue poplin. She knew that she looked well in it, that the severe white linen collar and cuffs suited the grave oval of her face. Though she had lost her girlish softness and bloom, she had gained immeasurably in dignity and distinction, and people, she noticed, turned to look at her now when she went out alone in the street. The severe indifference of her expression emphasized the richness of her lips and the vivid contrast of her colouring. Her eyes had lost their springtime look, but they were still deeply blue beneath the black shadows of her lashes. Young as she was she had acquired the ripe wisdom and the serene self-confidence of maturity; she had attained the immunity from apprehension which comes to those only who can never endure the worst again. Yet she was not unhappy. In the security of her disenchantment there was the quiet that follows a storm.

While she waited there for the sound of the doctor's bell, she thought dispassionately of what the last two years had meant in her life. Everything and nothing! Her outward existence had been altered by them, but to her deeper self they had been scarcely more than dust blowing across her face. Dust blowing, that was all they had meant to her!

She lived the period over again in her recollection, as she might have lived over one of the plays she had seen. She thought of the Faradays; of her diffidence, of their kindness; of the English governess and the French teacher, neither of whose speech was intelligible to her. She recalled the morning breakfasts; the walks in the Park in the afternoon; her nervous dread of the office; her first mistakes; the patience of the doctor and Mrs. Faraday; the way she had gradually become one of the family circle; the six small children, and especially the little girl Penelope, who had taken a fancy to her from the beginning; the two summers when she had gone to Maine with the family; the bathing, and how strange she had felt coming out on the beach with no shoes on and skirts up to her knees. Then she thought of Penelope's illness; of the sudden attack of pneumonia while Mrs. Faraday was in bed with influenza; of the days and nights of nursing because Penelope cried for her and refused to take her medicine from the trained nurse; of the night when they thought the child was dying, and how she had sat by the bed until the crisis at dawn. Then of the crisis when it came. The quieter breathing; the way the tiny hand fluttered in hers; the band of steel that loosened about her heart; and Mrs. Faraday crying from her bed, "Dorinda, we can never forget what you have done! You must stay with us always!" After that she had grown closer to them. Where else could she go? Nowhere, unless she went back to Pedlar's Mill, and that, she felt, was still impossible. Some day she might go back again. Not yet, but some day, when her hate was as dead as her love. There were moments when she missed Old Farm, vivid moments when she smelt growing things in the Park, when she longed with all her heart for a sight of the April fields and the pear orchard in bloom and the big pine where birds were singing. But the broomsedge she tried to forget. The broomsedge was too much alive. She felt that she hated it because it would make her suffer again.

They missed her at home, she knew. Her father had not been well. He was getting old. Every month she sent him half of her salary. They would not have had that much if she had stayed at Pedlar's Mill; and then there was the extra money at Christmas. Last Christmas the doctor had given her a check for fifty dollars, and after Penelope's illness, they had wished to give her more, but she had refused to let them pay her for nursing the child. . . . There was a cow at home now, not the red one of Doctor Greylock's, but a Jersey her father had bought from James Ellgood. Her father's tobacco crop had done well last year, and he had mended some of the fences. When the mortgage came due, she hoped he would be able to meet it. She wondered if life had changed there at all. Rose Emily was dead—that would make a difference to her. And Jason's father, that horrible old man, was actually dying, her mother had written. . . .

The doctor's bell rang, and she turned, while the folding doors opened, to usher the next patient into the private office. Two women went in together, while the doctor's assistant, a young physician named Burch, led the remaining patient away for examination. She had grown to know the young doctor well, and since last summer, when he spent his vacation in Maine, she had suspected that he was on the verge of falling in love with her. Cautious, deliberate, methodical, he was in no danger, she felt, of plunging precipitately into marriage. Doctor Faraday approved, she was aware, and his wife had done all in her power to make the match; but Dorinda had felt nothing stronger than temperate liking. Richard Burch was not ugly; he was even attractive looking after you got used to his features. He had a short, rather stocky figure, and a square, not uninteresting face, a good face, Mrs. Faraday called it. Almost any girl who had the will to love might have argued herself into loving
180

him. That emotion was, in part at least, the result of a will to love, Dorinda had learned in the last two years, since she had picked up more or less of the patter of science; and the last thing she wished to do, she assured herself, was ever to live through the destructive process again. With a complete absence of self-deception, she could ask herself now if she had been in love with love when she met Jason Greylock, and if any other reasonably attractive man would have answered as well in his place. Was it the moment, after all, and not the man, that really mattered? If Bob Ellgood had shown that admiring interest in her the year before instead of the day after she met Jason, would her life have been different? Did the importunate necessity exist in the imagination, and were you compelled to work it out into experience before you could settle down to the serious business of life?

She looked round as the door opened, and saw Doctor Burch coming out with the two women patients.

"At ten to-morrow," the elder woman said, as she slipped on her fur coat.

"Ten to-morrow," Dorinda repeated mechanically, while she went over to the desk and wrote down the appointment in the office book. When she turned away, the woman had gone, and Doctor Burch was gazing at her with his twinkling, near-sighted eyes from behind rimless eyeglasses.

"There's one more to come," she observed in a brisk, professional tone.

"One more?"

"Patient, I mean."

"Oh, yes. That will finish them till we go out. You ought to thank your stars you don't have to make calls."

"Yes. I get tired listening to complaints."

He smiled. "You aren't sympathetic?"

She thought of Rose Emily. "Well, I've seen so much real misery."

"It's real enough everywhere."

"Yes, I know. I suppose the truth is that life doesn't seem to me to be worth all the fuss they make over it. The more they suffer, the harder they appear to cling to living. I believe in facing what you have to face and making as little fuss about it as possible."

"I've noticed that. You hate fussiness."

She assented gravely. "When you've been very poor, you realize that it is the greatest extravagance."

"You've been very poor, then?"

"Almost everybody is poor at Pedlar's Mill. The Ellgoods are the only people who have prospered. The rest of us have had to wring whatever we've had out of barren ground. It was a struggle to make anything grow."

"Well, your face gives you away," he said thoughtfully. "Any nerve specialist could tell you that you are made up of contradictions. You've got the most romantic eyes I ever saw—they are as deep as an autumn twilight—and the sternest mouth. Your eyes are gentle and your mouth is hard—too hard, if you don't mind my saying so."

"Oh, I don't mind. People say we make our mouths. I heard Doctor Faraday tell a woman that a few days ago. But it isn't true. Life makes us and breaks us. We don't make life. The best we can do is to bear it."

"And you do that jolly well."

She did not smile as she answered. "Oh, I'm satisfied. I'm not unhappy—except in spots," she corrected herself.

"Yet you have very little pleasure. You never go out."

"Yes, I do—sometimes. Every now and then Mrs. Faraday takes me to the theatre."

"Do you ever go to hear music?"

"No, Mrs. Faraday doesn't care for it." She laughed. "The best I've ever heard was a band in the street."

For an instant he hesitated, and she wondered what was coming. Then he said persuasively: "There's a good concert to-morrow. Would you care to come?"

She glanced at him inquiringly. "Sunday afternoon?"

"Yes, there's this new pianist, Krause. You aren't too pious, are you?"

"I'm not pious at all." A satirical memory sifted through her mind, and she heard her own voice saying, "Will you let her die without giving her time to prepare?"

"Then I'll come for you at half-past two. We'll hear the concert, and then have tea somewhere, or a stroll in the Park."

When he had gone, she put the office in order, and then waited until the last patient should leave. After all, why shouldn't she try to find some pleasure in life? Her hesitation had come, she felt, from a nervous avoidance of crowds, a shrinking from any change in her secluded manner of living. She hummed a line from one of the Gospel hymns. "Rescue the perishing, care for the dying." "How ignorant he will think me when he discovers I have never heard any music. I am ignorant, yet I am educated compared to what I was two years ago. I know life now, and that is a great deal."

The patient came out and left, and in a few minutes Doctor Faraday passed through the room on his way to put on his overcoat.

"Are you going out before lunch?" she asked, because she knew Mrs. Faraday hated to have him miss his meals.

"Yes, I can't wait, but I'll light a cigar."

He took out one of the long slender cigars he preferred, and stopped in front of her while she struck a match and held her hand by the flame.

"That's a suitable young man, Dorinda," he remarked irrelevantly, with his whimsical smile.

"Young man?" She glanced up inquiringly. Though her sense of humour had developed almost morbidly, she had discovered that it was of a wilder variety than Doctor Faraday's.

"I think, my dear girl," he explained, "that you could go farther and do worse than take Richard. If I'm not mistaken, he has a future before him."

She laughed. "There wouldn't be much for me in that sort of future."

"But there might be in the results." Then he grew serious. "He is interested in you, and I hope something will come of it."

A pricking sensation in her nerves made her start away from him. "Don't," she said sharply. "I've finished with all that sort of thing."

"Not for good. You are too young."

"Yes, for good. I can't explain what I mean, but the very thought of that makes me—well, sick all over."

Her face had gone white, and struck by the change, he looked at her closely. "Some women," he said, "are affected that way by a shock."

"You mean by a blow on the head?"

"No, I **don't mean** a physical blow. I mean an emotional shock. Such a thing may produce a nervous revulsion."

"Well, that has happened to me."

He laid his hand on her shoulder. "It will pass probably. You are handsomer than ever. It is natural that you should need love."

A wave of aversion swept over her face. "But I don't need it. I am through with all that."

He looked at her gravely. "And you will fill your life—with what?"

She laughed derisively. How little men knew! "With something better than broomsedge. That's the first thing that puts out on barren soil, just broomsedge. Then that goes and pines come to stay —pines and life-everlasting. You won't understand," she explained lightly. "I was talking to Doctor Burch about Pedlar's Mill just before you came in, and I told him we had to get our living from barren ground."

He patted her shoulder. "Well, I hope that, too, will pass," he answered as he turned to put on his overcoat.

She remembered his words the next day while she sat in the concert hall waiting for the music to begin. At first she had tried to make out the names on the programme, desisting presently because they confused her. Beethoven. Bach. Chopin. She went over the others again, stumbling because she could make nothing of the syllables. A-p-p-a-s-s-i-o-n-a-t-a. What did the strange word mean? P-a-t-h-é-tique—that she could dimly grasp.

Suddenly, while she struggled over the letters, the music floated toward her from the cool twilight of the distance. This was not music, she thought in surprise, but the sound of a storm coming up through the tall pines at Old Farm. She had heard this singing melody a thousand times, on autumn afternoons, in the woods. Then, as it drew nearer, the harmony changed from sound into sensation; and from pure sensation, rippling in wave after wave like a river, it was merged and lost in her consciousness.

In the beginning, while she sat there, rapt in startled apprehension, she thought of innumerable things she had forgotten; detached incidents, impressions which glittered sharply, edged with light, against the mosaic of her recollections. Mellow sunshine, sparkling like new cider, streamed over her. Music, which she had

184

imagined to be sound only, was changing into colour. She saw it first in delicate green and amber; then in violent clashes of red and purple; but she saw it always as vividly as if it reached her brain through her eyes. She thought first of the evening sky over the bulrushes; of the grass after rain in the pasture; of the pear trees breaking with the dawn from palest green into white. Then the colours changed, and she remembered sunsets over the broomsedge. The glow cast upward from the earth as if the wild grass were burning. The bough of a black-gum tree emblazoned in scarlet on the blue sky. The purple mist of autumn twilight, like the bloom on a grape. The road home through the abandoned fields. The solitary star in a sky which was stained the colour of ripe fruit. The white farmhouse. The shingled roof like a hood. Swallows flying. Swallows everywhere, a world of swallows spinning like curved blades in the afterglow.

With the flight of wings, ecstasy quivered over her, while sound and colour were transformed into rhythms of feeling. Pure sensation held and tortured her. She felt the music playing on her nerves as the wind plays on a harp; she felt it shatter her nerves like broken string, and sweep on crashing, ploughing through the labyrinth of her soul. Down there, in the deep below the depths of her being, she felt it tearing her vitals. Down there, in the buried jungle, where her thoughts had never penetrated, she felt it destroying the hidden roots of her life. In this darkness there was no colour; there was no glimmer of twilight; there was only the maze of inarticulate agony. . . .

Now it was dying away. Now it was returning. Something that she had thought dead was coming to life again. Something that she had buried out of sight under the earth was pushing upward in anguish. Something that she had defeated was marching as a conqueror over her life. Suddenly she was pierced by a thousand splinters of crystal sound. Little quivers of light ran over her. Beads of pain broke out on her forehead and her lips. She clenched her hands together, and forced her body back into her chair. "I've got to stand it. No matter what it does to me, I've got to stand it."

5

"I am afraid you found it difficult," Doctor Burch said, when it was over. "It wasn't an easy programme. I wish there had been more of Krause."

"I'm not sure I liked it," she answered wearily. "I feel as if I had ploughed a field. It made me savage, just the way moonlight used to when I was growing up."

"That is the pure essence of sensation. Now, I never get that response to music. To me it is little more than an intellectual exercise. The greatest musician I ever knew told me once that his knowledge of the theory of music had, in a way, spoiled his complete enjoyment of a concert."

She had refused tea, and they had strolled in the direction of the Park. As she left the concert hall, it had seemed to her that she was stifling for air, and now, when they entered the Park, she threw back her head and breathed quickly, with her gaze on the bright chain of sky threading the tree-tops.

"This smells like November at Old Farm," she said. "Whenever I smell the country, I want to go home."

"Yours is a large farm?"

She laughed. "A thousand acres and we couldn't afford to buy a cow. Do you know what it means to be land poor? After the war my father couldn't hire labour, so he had to let all the land go bad, as we say, except the little he could cultivate himself. The rest has run to old fields. Everything is eaten up by the taxes and the mortgage. There are pines, of course, and Nathan Pedlar tells us if we let the timber stand, it will one day be valuable. Now we can't get a good price because the roads are so bad it takes too many mules to haul it away. Once in a while, we sell some trees to pay the taxes, but they bring so little. My father cut down seven beautiful poplars at Poplar Spring; but when he sold them he couldn't get but a dollar and a half for each one where it fell. It doesn't seem worth while destroying trees for that."

"What do you do with the abandoned fields?"

"Nothing. Some people turn sheep into them, but my father says that doesn't pay. The fields run to broomsedge and life-everlasting, and in time pine and scrub oak get a good start."

"But they can be reclaimed. The land can be brought back, if it is well treated."

"I know, but that takes labour; and Father and Josiah have as much work as they can manage. There isn't any money to pay the wages of hands. We've got some good pastures too. If only there was something to begin with, we might have a dairy farm. Nathan Pedlar says, or a stock farm like James Ellgood's. I wish I knew the science of farming," she concluded earnestly. "Doctor Faraday says it is as much a science as medicine."

It was the first time he had seen her deeply interested. Strange, the hold the country could get over one!

"Is there any way I could learn farming from books?" Dorinda asked before he could reply. "I mean learn the modern ways of getting the best out of the soil?"

He smiled. "It all comes back to chemistry, doesn't it? That, I imagine, is what Doctor Faraday meant—the chemistry of agriculture. Yes, there are books you can study. I'll get you a list from a friend of mine who is a professor in the University of Wisconsin. By the way, he is to give a lecture on that very subject in New York next month. There is to be a series of lectures. I'll find out about it and take you if you'll go with me. You must remember, though, that practical experience is always the best teacher."

She shook her head. "We have the experience of generations, and it has taught us nothing except to do things the way we've always done them. Mother used to say that the only land she would ever cultivate, if she had to choose over again, is the land of Canaan where

> "*generous fruits that never fail,*
> *On trees immortal grow!*"

He laughed. "I think I'd like your mother."

The casual remark arrested her. Would he really like her mother, she wondered, with her caustic humour, her driven energy, her periodical neuralgia, and her perpetual melancholy? Had he ever known any one who resembled her? Had he ever known any woman whose life was so empty?

"Poor Ma!"—She corrected herself: "Poor Mother, the farm has eaten away her life. It caught her when she was young, and she was never able to get free."

"Doesn't she care for it?"

"I don't know. I sometimes think she hates it, but I know it would kill her to leave it. It is like a bad heart. You may suffer from it, but it is your life, and it would kill you to lose it." She broke off, pondered deeply for a few moments, and then added impulsively, "If I had the money, I'd go back and start a dairy farm there."

While she spoke a vision glimmered between the windy dusk in the Park and the orange light of the afterglow. She saw it with an intensity, an eagerness that was breathless;—the fields, the roads, the white gate, the long low house, the lamp shining in the front window. For the first time she could think of Old Farm without invoking the image of Jason. For the first time since she had left home, she felt that earlier and deeper associations were reaching out to her, that they were groping after her, like the tendrils of vines, through the darkness and violence of her later memories. Earlier and deeper associations, rooted there in the earth, were drawing her back across time and space and forgetfulness. Passion stirred again in her heart; but it was passion transfigured, recoiling from the personal to the impersonal object. It seemed to her, walking there in the blue twilight, that the music had released some imprisoned force in the depths of her being, and that this force was spreading out over the world, that it was growing wider and thinner until it covered all the desolate country at Old Farm. With a shock of joy, she realized that she was no longer benumbed, that she had come to life again. She had come to life again, but how differently!

"I feel as if the farm were calling to me to come back and help it," she said.

That night she dreamed of Pedlar's Mill. She dreamed that she was ploughing one of the abandoned fields, where the ghostly scent of the life-everlasting reminded her of the smell of her mother's flowered bandbox when she took it out of the closet on Sunday mornings—the aroma of countless dead and forgotten Sabbaths. Dan and Beersheba were harnessed to the plough, and when they had finished one furrow, they turned and looked back at her before they began another. "You'll never get this done if you plough a hundred years," they said, "because there is nothing here but thistles, and you can't plough thistles under." Then she looked round her and saw that they were right. As far as she could see, on every side, the field was filled with prickly purple thistles, and every thistle was wearing the face of Jason. A million thistles, and every thistle looked up at her with the eyes of Jason! She turned the plough where they grew thickest, trampling them down, uprooting them, ploughing them under with all her strength; but always when they went into the soil, they cropped up again. Millions of purple flaunting heads! Millions of faces! They sprang up everywhere; in the deep furrow that the plough had cut; in the dun-coloured clods of the upturned earth; under the feet of the horses; under her own feet, springing back, as if they were set on wire stems, as soon as she had crushed them into the ground. "I am going to plough them under, if it kills me," she said aloud; and then she awoke. A chill wind was blowing the white curtains at the window. Was it only her imagination, or did the wind, blowing over the city, bring the fragrance of pine and life-everlasting? For an instant, scarcely longer than a quick breath, she felt a sensation of physical nearness, as if some one had touched her. Then it vanished, leaving her in a shudder of memory. It was not love; of this she was positive. Was it hate which had assumed, in the moment between sleep and waking, the physical intensity of love? It was the first time she had dreamed of Jason. Long after she had ceased to think of him, she told herself resentfully.

The next morning, when office hours were over, she went to the library and asked for a list of books on dairy farming. She read with eagerness every one that was given to her, patiently making notes, keeping in her mind the peculiar situation at Old Farm. When Doctor Burch arranged for the course of lectures, she attended them regularly, adding, with diligence, whatever she could to her knowledge of methods; gleaning, winnowing, storing away in her memory

189

the facts which she thought might some day be useful. Before her always were the neglected fields. She saw the renewal of promise in the land; the sowing of the grain, the springing up, the ripening, the immemorial celebration of the harvest. She saw the yellowing waves of wheat, the poetic even swath falling after the mower. "All that land," she thought, "all that land wasted!" The possibility of the dairy farm haunted her mind. Enterprise, industry, and a little capital with which to begin! That was all that one needed. If she could start with a few cows, six perhaps, and do all the work of the dairy herself, it might be managed. But Old Farm must be made to pay, she decided emphatically. Old Farm with a thousand acres could supply sufficient pasture and fodder for as many cows as she would ever be likely to own. "If I could get the labour it wouldn't be so hard," she thought one day, while she was sitting by the window in the nursery. "If I could buy the cows and hire a little extra labour, it wouldn't be impossible to make a success." Then her spirit drooped. "You can't do anything without a little money," she thought, and laughed aloud. "Not much, but a little makes all the difference."

"What are you laughing at, Dorinda?" asked Mrs. Faraday, turning from the crib, where she was bending over the baby.

"I was thinking I'd give anything I've got for six—no, a dozen cows."

"Cows?"

"At Old Farm. It hurts me to think of all that land wasted."

"It is a pity. I suppose it was good land once?"

"In great-grandfather's day it was one of the best farms in that part of the country. Of course he never cultivated much of it. He let a lot of it stand in timber. That's what we paid the taxes with right after the war. Father and Josiah do the best they can," she added, "but everything is always against them. Some people are like that, you know."

"It's a bad way to be," commented Mrs. Faraday, and she asked presently, "What would you like to do with the farm?"

Dorinda's cheeks flushed as she answered. "First, if I had the money, I'd try to bring up the fields. I'd sow cow-peas and turn them under this year wherever I could. Then I'd add to the pasture. We can easily do that, and in a little while we could get a good stand of grass. Then I'd buy some cows from James Ellgood, some of his Jerseys, and try to set up a dairy farm, a very little one, but I wouldn't let anybody touch the milk and butter except Mother and myself. I wouldn't be satisfied with anything that wasn't better than the best," she concluded, with an energy that was characteristic of the earlier Dorinda.

"And you'd sell your butter—where?"

For an instant this dampened the girl's enthusiasm. How funny that she had never once thought of that!

"Oh, well, we're near enough to Richmond or Washington," she said. "The road to the station is bad, but it is only two miles. We could churn one day and send the butter out before sunrise the next morning."

Mrs. Faraday looked at her sympathetically. "I could help you in Washington," she said. "I've a friend there who owns one of the biggest hotels. The manager would take your butter, I know, and eggs too, if they are the very best that can be bought. And you'd ask a large price. People are always willing to pay for the best."

Dorinda sighed. "It's just like a fairy tale," she said, "but, of course, it is utterly out of the question."

"Well, I don't see why." Mrs. Faraday lifted the baby from the crib and sat down to nurse it. "We would lend you the money you needed to start with. After all you've done for Penelope, we'd be only too glad to do that in return. But it would be drudgery, even if you succeeded, and you ought not to look forward to that. You ought to marry, my dear."

Dorinda flinched. "Oh, I've finished with all that!"

"But you haven't. You're too young to give up that side of life."

"I don't care. I'm through with it," repeated Dorinda, and she meant it.

"Well, just remember that we are ready to help you at any time. It would mean nothing to us to invest a few thousand dollars in your farm. You could pay us back when you succeeded."

"And I could pay you interest all the time."

"Of course—if it would make you feel easier. Only don't let your foolish pride stand in the way of achieving something in the end."

Dorinda gazed thoughtfully out of the window. Her pride was

191

foolish, she supposed, but it was all that she had. With nothing else to fall back on, she had taken refuge in an exaggerated sense of independence.

"You are so capable," Mrs. Faraday was saying, "that I am sure you will never fail in anything that you undertake. The doctor was telling me only yesterday that, for a woman without special training, your efficiency is really remarkable. It isn't often the girls of your age are so practical."

A laugh without merriment broke from Dorinda's lips. "That would please my mother," she said. "They used to say at Old Farm that my head was full of notions."

"Most young girls' heads are. But you were fortunate to settle down as soon as you did."

Without replying, Dorinda stared at the baby in Mrs. Faraday's arms. It was a fat, pink baby, with a round face in which the features were like tiny flowers, and a bald head, as clear and smooth as an egg shell. When it laughed back at her, the pink face crumpled up and it gurgled with toothless gums.

"If you've ever been poor, you can't get over the dread of having to borrow," she answered after a pause.

For the next few months, while she read books and attended lectures without understanding them, the idea of the country worked like leaven in Dorinda's imagination. Gradually, though she was unprepared for the change in her attitude, some involuntary force was driving her back to Old Farm. Problems that had appeared inexplicable became as simple as arithmetic; obstacles that had looked like mountains evaporated into mist as she approached them. "I couldn't let them do it," she would declare, adding a minute later, with weakening obstinacy, "After all, it isn't as if they were giving me the money. I can always pay them in the end, even if I have to mortgage the farm."

As the winter passed, she saw more and more of Burch. She liked him; she enjoyed her walks with him; his friendship had become a substantial interest in her life; but she realized now and then, when he accidentally touched her hand, that every nerve in her body said, "So far and no farther" to human intercourse. Her revulsion from the physical aspect of love was a matter of the nerves, she knew, for more than two years under the roof of a great surgeon had taught her something deeper than the patter of science. Yet, though her shrinking was of the nerves only, it was none the less real. One side of her was still dead. The insensibility of the last two years, which had made her tell herself at moments that she could not feel the prick of a pin in her flesh, had worn off slowly from that area of her mind which was superior to the emotions. But the thought of love, the faintest reminder of its potency, filled her with aversion, with an inexpressible weariness. She simply could not bear, she told herself bluntly, to be touched.

"There must be something in life besides love," she thought, in revolt from the universal harping upon a single string. Watching the people in the street, she would find herself thinking, "That woman looks as if she lived without love, but she doesn't look unhappy. She must have found something else." Then, with the vision of Old Farm in her mind, she would reflect exultantly: "There is something else for me also. Love isn't everything."

"Do you know, I've almost decided to go home," she said to Doctor Burch one day in April, when they were sitting in the Park. "Did you see those lilacs in the florists' windows as we passed? It is lilac time at Old Farm now, and the big bushes in the corner of the west wing are all in bloom. They are so old that they reach to the roof, and the catbirds build in them every year." She lifted her head and looked at the delicate pattern of the elms against the pale sky. How cold and thin spring was in the North!

"You mean you'll go back and begin farming?"

"I mean I can't stay away any longer. I'm part of it. I belong to the abandoned fields."

"Will you let me come?" he asked abruptly.

Her hand lay, palm upward, in her lap, and as he asked the question, his fingers closed caressingly over hers. Instantly the alarm began in her nerves; she felt the warning quiver dart through them like the vibration in a wire. Her nerves, not her heart, repulsed him. She might even love him, she thought, if only he could keep at a distance; if he would never touch her; if he would remain contented and aloof, neither giving nor demanding the signs of emotion. But at the first gesture of approach every cell in her body sprang on the defensive.

"You wouldn't be comfortable," she said, while an expression that was almost hostile crept over her full red mouth. "It is so different from anything you have known."

His smile was winning. "I shouldn't mind that if you wanted me."

She looked over his head at the elm boughs arching against the sky. Yes, it was lilac time in Virginia. She saw the rich clusters drooping beside the whitewashed walls, under the grey eaves where wrens were building. The door was open, and the fragrance swept the clean, bare hall, with the open door at the other end, beyond which the green slope swelled upward to the pear orchard. Over all, there was the big pine on the hill, brushing the quiet sky like a bird's outstretched wing. How peaceful it seemed. After the storm through which she had passed, tranquillity meant happiness.

The silence had grown intimate, tender, provocative; and for a moment she had a feeling of relaxation from tension, as if the iron in her soul were dissolving. Then the pressure of his fingers tightened, and she shivered and drew away her hand.

"You don't like me to touch you?" he asked, and there was a hurt look in his eyes.

She shook her head. "I don't like anybody to touch me."

"Are you as hard as that?"

"I suppose I am hard, but I can't change."

"Not if I wait? I can wait as long as you make me."

"It wouldn't make any difference. Waiting wouldn't change me. I've finished with all that."

She rose because the thought of Jason had come to her out of the vision of Old Farm; and though she no longer loved him, though she hated him, this thought was so unexpected and yet so real that it was as if he had actually walked into her presence. He was nothing to her, but his influence still affected her life; he was buried somewhere in her consciousness, like a secret enemy who could spring out of the wilderness and strike when she was defenseless.

On the hall table, when she entered the house, she found a letter, addressed in the pale, repressed handwriting of her mother. As she went upstairs she tore it open, and dropping into a chair by the window of her room, she read the closely written sheets by the last gleam of daylight.

My dear Daughter:

I hate to have to send you bad news, but your father had a stroke last Saturday while he was ploughing the tobacco-field. He had not been well for several days, but you know he never complains, and he did not stop work till he dropped in the field. Josiah and Rufus had to pick him up between them and bring him into the house.

We sent straight for the doctor. Rufus saddled Beersheba and rode to Pedlar's Mill, and Nathan sent word to Doctor Stout up near the Court-House. It was more than two hours before the doctor got here, but your father had not come to himself. The doctor says he will never be up again, and if you want to see him alive, you had better come as soon as you can. We do everything that is possible, and Nathan has been the greatest help in the world. I don't know what I should do without him. Josiah spends the nights here. Since his marriage he has lived, as I wrote you, in that place over beyond Plumtree, but he is real good about helping, and so is Elvira. She has offered to help me nurse, but she is so flighty that I had rather have Aunt Mehitable's granddaughter, Fluvanna Moody. Fluvanna comes every day. She is a mighty good nurse and your father likes to have her around, even if she is one of the new order of darkeys. I believe she takes after Aunt Mehitable more than any of the other grandchildren. Your father does not give any trouble, and he has not spoken but twice since his fall. It is right hard to understand what he says—he speaks so thickly—but Fluvanna and I both think he was asking for you.

The farm is going on just the same. Rufus hates the work here, and wants to go to the city. A week before his stroke your father was offered a thousand dollars for the timber between Poplar Spring and the back gate. Nathan advised him to hold on a little longer, but I reckon we will have to sell it now to pay for your father's sickness. The cow is a great comfort. Your father cannot take any solid food. I give him a little milk and a few swallows of chicken broth. Mrs. Garlick sent him some chicken broth yesterday, and one of the Miss Sneads comes over with something every day.

> *Your affectionate mother,*
> EUDORA ABERNETHY OAKLEY.

So, after all, the decision had been taken out of her hands. Life was treating her still as if she were a straw in the wind, a leaf on a stream. The invisible processes which had swept her away were sweeping her back again. While she sat there with the letter in her hand, she had the feeling that she was caught in the whirlpool of universal anarchy, and that she could not by any effort of her will bring order out of chaos.

"Poor Pa." This was her first thought, and she used instinctively the name that had been on her lips as a child. So this was the end for him, and what had he ever had? He had known nothing except toil. Suddenly, as if the fact added an intolerable poignancy to her grief, she remembered that he had never learned even to read and write. He could sign his name, that was all. When he was a child the "poor white" was expected to remain unlettered, and in later years the knowledge her mother had taught him had not, as he used to say apologetically, "stuck by him."

Rising quickly, she put the letter aside and began folding her clothes.

6

As the train rushed through the familiar country, Dorinda counted the new patches of ploughed ground in the landscape. "James Ellgood must be trying to reclaim all his old fields," she thought.

The sun had not yet risen above the fretwork of trees on the horizon, but the broomsedge had felt the approach of day and was flying upward to meet it. Out of the east, she saw gradually emerge the serpentine curves of Whippernock River; then the clouds of blown smoke, the irregular pattern of the farms, and the buildings of the station, which wore a startled and half-awake air in the dawn.

After more than two years how strange it felt to be back again! To be back again just as if nothing had happened! How small the station looked, and how desolate, stranded like a wrecked ship in the broomsedge. What isolation! What barrenness! In her memory the horizon had been so much wider, the road so much longer, the band of woods so much deeper. It seemed to her that the landscape must have diminished in an incredible way since she had left it. Even the untidy look of the station; the litter of shavings and tobacco stems; the shabbiness and crudeness of the country people meeting the train; the disreputable rags of Butcher, the lame negro, who lived in the freight car; the very fowls scratching in the dust of the cleared space;—all these characteristic details were uglier and more trivial than she had remembered them. A sense of loneliness swept her thoughts, as if the solitude had blown over her like smoke. She realized that the Pedlar's Mill of her mind and the Pedlar's Mill of actuality were two different places. She was returning home, and she felt as strange as she had felt in New York. Well, at least she had not crawled back. She had returned with her head held high, as she had resolved that she would.

The whistle was sounding again, and the brakeman was hastily gathering her bags. She followed him to the platform, where the conductor stood waiting, the same conductor who had helped her into the train the morning she had gone away. He did not recognize her, and for some obscure reason, she felt flattered because he had forgotten her.

The train was stopping slowly. The faces of the assembled farmers started out so close to the track that they gave her a shock. There was Jim Ellgood ready to leave for Richmond; there was Mr. Garlick meeting somebody, his daughter probably; there was Mr. Kettledrum, looking as stringy and run to seed, as if he had not moved out of his wheel-rut since the morning he had picked her up in the rain. In the little group she saw Rufus, slender, handsome, sullen as ever. How black his eyes were, and how becoming the dark red was in his cheeks! Then, as the train reached the station, she saw Nathan Pedlar running down to the track with the mail bag in his hand. Just at the last minute, but always in time—how like Nathan that was!

The conductor, with one foot on the step, was swinging his free leg while he felt for the ground. She put up her hand, hurriedly arranging her small blue hat with the flowing chiffon veil. Then she lifted the folds of her skirt as the conductor, who was firmly planted now on the earth, helped her to alight. Her heart was sad for her father, but beneath the sadness her indomitable pride supported her. Yes, she had come back unashamed. She might not return as a conqueror, but she had returned undefeated. They were looking at her as she stepped to the ground, and she felt, with a thrill of satisfaction, that, in her navy blue poplin with the chiffon veil framing her face (hanging veils were much worn in New York that year) she was worthy of the surprised glances they cast at her. A little thinner, a little paler, less girlish but more striking, than she had been when she went away. Her height gave her dignity, and this dignity was reflected in her vivid blue eyes, with their unflinching and slightly arrogant gaze. Romantic eyes, Burch had called them, and she had wondered what he meant, for surely there was little romance left now in her mind. If experience had taught her nothing else, it had at least made her a realist. She had learned to take things as

198

they are, and that, as Burch had once remarked whimsically, "in the long run fustian wears better than velvet." She had learned, too, she told herself in the first moments of her home-coming, that so long as she could rule her own mind she was not afraid of the forces without.

They had gathered round her. She was smiling and shaking the outstretched hands. "Well, it looked as if we'd about lost you for good." "You've been gone two years, ain't you?" "Hardly know Pedlar's Mill, I reckon, since Nathan's painted the store red?" "I saw her off," Mr. Kettledrum was saying over and over. "I saw her off. A good long visit, warn't it?"

Moving out of the throng, she kissed Rufus, who looked dejected and resentful.

"How is Pa, Rufus?"

"There ain't any change. The doctor says he may drag on this way for several weeks, or he may go suddenly at any time."

"Well, we'd better start right on." Walking quickly up the slope to where the old buggy was standing, she put her arms round Dan's neck and laid her cheek against him. "He knows me," she said, "dear old Dan, he hasn't forgotten me. Is there anything you want for Ma at the store?"

"She gave me a list. I left it with Minnie May."

"Minnie May doesn't work in the store, does she? Who looks after the children?"

"She does. She does everything."

"Well, it's a shame. She oughtn't to, and only thirteen. I'll speak to Nathan about it."

At her commanding tone, Rufus grinned. "You've come back looking as if you could run the world, Dorinda," he observed, with envy. "I wish I could go away. I'd start to-morrow, if it wasn't for Pa."

"Yes, that's why I came back. We can't leave Pa and Ma now. But it's hard on you, Rufus."

"You bet it is! It's my turn to get away next."

She assented. "I know it. If the time comes when Pa can do without you, I'll help you to go. You'll never make much of a farmer."

He stared moodily at the road, but she could see that her promise had encouraged him. "There's nothing in it," he answered. "I believe it is the meanest work ever made. You may slave till you drop, and there's never anything to show for it. Look at Pa."

"Pa never had a chance. He grew up at the wrong time. But all farming isn't bad. Suppose we had a dairy farm?"

He grinned again. "O Lord! with one cow! You're out of your head!"

"Perhaps. Anyway, I've come back to see what I can do."

Her glance wavered as Nathan, having dashed into the store with the mail bag, came toward them with the kind of lope that he used when he was in a hurry. "I didn't get a chance to speak to you at the train, Dorinda," he said, "but all the same I'm glad you're home again. The children want to get a peek at you in your city clothes. Minnie May's gone crazy about your veil."

In two years he had altered as little as the landscape. Lank, sand-coloured, with his loping stride, his hands that were all knuckles, and his kindly clown's face under hair that was as short as rubbed-off fur, he appeared to her, just as he used to do, as both efficient and negligible. Poor Nathan, how unattractive he was, but how good and faithful! Clean, too, notwithstanding the fact that he never stopped working. His face and neck looked well scrubbed, and his blue cotton shirt was still smelling of starch and ironing. The memory of the lunch he had given her when she went away was in her mind as she held out her hand to him and then stooped to kiss the children, one after another. How they must miss their mother, these children! She must do something for Minnie May, who had the stunted look of overworked childhood. Nathan was well off for Pedlar's Mill, yet he let the little girl work like a servant. It was simply that he did not know, and she would make it her business, she told herself firmly, to instruct him. Minnie May was a nice, earnest child, with the look of her mother. She would be almost pretty, too, if she could get that driven expression out of her pinched little face. Her hair was really lovely, wheaten red like Rose Emily's, only it needed brushing, and she wore it dragged back from her forehead where, at thirteen, wrinkles were already forming. Yes, Dorinda decided, she would certainly speak to Nathan.

"You look fine, Dorinda," he was saying while he stared at her.

"She is like a paper doll in a book," Minnie May exclaimed. "One of those fashion books Miss Seena Snead has."

The three smaller children were staring with wide-open eyes and mouths, and John Abner, the baby, she remembered, with the club-foot, was holding a slice of bread and butter in both hands. He limped badly when he walked, she noticed. What a job it must be keeping these children washed and dressed.

"Are you the nurse too, Minnie May?" she inquired.

"Yes, I do everything," the little girl replied proudly, wrinkling her forehead. "We had a coloured girl, but the children didn't like her and wouldn't mind her."

Dorinda turned to Nathan. "It's too much, Nathan. You oughtn't to let her do it."

"I tell her not to slave so hard," he answered helplessly. "But it doesn't do any good. She promised her mother that she would take care of the children."

"But Rose Emily never meant this. It is making an old woman of the child before she grows up."

"I can't help it. She's as stubborn as a mule about it. Maybe you can do something."

Dorinda nodded with her capable air. "Well, I'll fix it." She looked cool, composed, and competent, the picture of dignified self-reliance, as she stepped between the muddy wheels of the dilapidated buggy.

"I hope you'll find your father better," Nathan said. "I'll come over later in the day and see if there is anything I can help about."

She smiled gratefully over her shoulder, and Rufus remarked, in his sullen, suppressed voice, as they drove off, "He's been over every single evening since Pa had his stroke."

"Nobody ever had a kinder heart," Dorinda responded absently, for she was not thinking of Nathan.

As the buggy jolted down the slope to the pine woods, a dogcart passed them on the way to the station, and she recognized Geneva Greylock. She was driving the dogcart with red wheels which she had used before her marriage; she was wearing the same jaunty clothes; but the change in her appearance made Dorinda turn to glance back at her. Though she was still in her early twenties, she

201

looked like a middle-aged woman. Her sallow cheeks had fallen in, her long nose was bony and reddened at the tip, and her abundant flaxen hair was lustreless and untidy.

"How soon blondes break," Dorinda said aloud, and she thought, "Two years of marriage have made an old woman of her."

"Yes, she's lost what looks she ever had," returned Rufus. "She was always delicate, they say, and now her health has gone entirely. It's the life she leads, I reckon. Folks say he is beginning to follow in his father's footsteps. That's why the new doctor up by the Court-House is getting all his practice." When he spoke of Jason he carefully refrained from calling his name.

"Are there any children?" Dorinda asked. Her spirits were drooping; but this depression, as far as she was aware, had no connection with Jason. Not her own regret, but the futility of things in general, oppressed her with a feeling of gloom.

"Not that I ever heard of," Rufus replied. "To tell the truth I never hear anybody mention his name. You can ask Nathan. He knows everything about everybody." He shut his sullen lips tight, and stared straight ahead of him.

"Oh, it doesn't matter. I was merely wondering why her health had failed."

They had come out of the woods, and the wheels were creaking over the dried mud-holes. The sun had risen through a drift of cloud, and beneath the violet rim an iridescent light rained over the abandoned fields. While they drove on, it seemed to Dorinda that it was like moving within the heart of an opal. Every young green leaf, every dew-drenched weed, every silken cobweb, every brilliant bird, or gauzy insect,—all these things were illuminated and bedizened with colour. Only the immense black shadow of the horse and buggy raced sombrely over the broomsedge by the road-side.

"Nothing has changed," Dorinda thought. "Nothing has changed but myself."

Yes, it was all familiar, but it was different, and this difference existed only within herself. All that she had suffered was still with her. It was not an episode that she had left behind in the distance; it was a living part of her nature. Even if she worked her unhappiness into the soil; even if she cut down and burned it off with the broom-sedge, it would still spring up again in the place where it had been. Already, before she had reached the house, the past was settling over her like grey dust.

They passed the Sneads' red brick house with white columns. The same flowers bloomed in the borders; the same shrubs grew on the lawn; the same clothes appeared to hang perpetually on the same clothes-line at the corner of the back porch. In the pasture, the friendly faces of cows looked at her over the rail-fence, and she remembered that two years ago, as she went by, she had seen them filing to the well-trough. In a few minutes she would pass the burned cabin and the oak with the fading Gospel sign fastened to its bark. Her heart trembled. The racing shadow by the road appeared to stretch over the sunrise. She felt again the chill of despair, the involuntary shudder of her pulses. Then she lifted her eyes with a resolute gesture and confronted remembrance.

The place was unchanged. The deep wheel-ruts where the road forked; the flat rock on which the mare slipped; the cluster of dog-wood which screened the spot where she had waited for Jason's return; the very branch she had pushed aside,—not one of these things had altered. Only the fire in her heart had gone out. The scene was different to her because the eyes with which she looked on it had grown clearer. The stone was merely a stone; the road was nothing more than a road to her now. Over the gate, she could see the willows of Gooseneck Creek. Beyond them the tall chimneys of Five Oaks lay like red smears on the changeable blue of the sky.

After they had left the fork, Dan quickened his pace.

"The fence has been mended, I see, Rufus."

"Yes, we had so much trouble with the cow straying. Pa was trying to get all the fences near the house patched before fall. We were using the rails that were left over from the timber he sold."

"Those weren't the woods Ma wrote me about?" She could never think of living trees as timber.

"No, he is holding on to that in hope of getting a better price."

They travelled the last quarter of a mile without speaking, and not until the buggy had turned in at the gate and driven up the rocky grade to the porch, did Dorinda ask if her father expected her.

203

"Yes, Ma told him, but she wasn't sure that he understood. He was awake before I left the place and Ma was seeing about breakfast."

"Haven't you had any yet?"

"Yes, I had a bite before I started. I'm no friend to an empty stomach, and I reckon I can manage a little something after I've turned Dan into the pasture. Pa was ploughing the tobacco-field when he had his stroke, but he had decided not to plant tobacco there this year. We're going to try corn."

"I'm glad he's given up tobacco."

"He hasn't. Not entirely. But it takes more manure than he can spare this year. Well, we're here at last. Is that you, Ma?" he shouted, as the wheel scraped against the "rockery" by the steps.

At his second call, the door opened and Mrs. Oakley ran out on the porch.

"So you've come, daughter," she said, and stood wiping her hands on her apron while she waited for Dorinda to alight. How old she had grown, thought the girl, with a clutch at her heart. Only the visionary eyes looked out of the ravaged face through a film of despair, as stars shine through a fog.

7

Jumping out of the buggy, Dorinda took her mother into her arms; but while she pressed her lips to the wrinkled cheek, it occurred to her that it was like kissing a withered leaf.

"How is Pa?" she asked in an effort to conceal the embarrassment they both felt.

"About the same. I don't see any change."

"May I speak to him now?"

"You'd better have your breakfast first. I've got breakfast ready for you."

"In a minute, but I'd like just to say a word to him. Oh, there's dear old Rambler." She stooped to caress the hound. "I don't see Flossie."

"I reckon she's up at the barn hunting mice. She had a new set of kittens, but we had to drown all but one. We couldn't feed so many cats."

Embarrassment was passing away. How much had her mother known, she wondered; how much had she suspected?

"Well, I shan't be a minute," the girl said. "Is he in the chamber?"

"Yes, he hasn't been out of bed since his stroke. Go right in. I don't know whether he'll recognize you or not."

Pushing the door open, Dorinda went in, followed by Rambler, walking stiffly. The room was flooded with morning sunlight, for the green outside shutters were open, and the window was raised that looked on the pear orchard and the crooked path to the grave-yard. It was all just as she remembered it, except that in her recol-lection the big bed was empty, and now her father lay supine on one side of it, with his head resting upon the two feather pillows.

There was a grotesque look in his face, as if it had been pulled out of shape by some sudden twist, but his inquiring brown eyes, with their wistful pathos, seemed to be asking, "Why has it happened? What is the meaning of it all?" When she bent over and touched his forehead with her lips, she saw that he could not move himself, not even his head, not even his hand. Fallen and helpless, he lay there like a pine tree that has been torn up by the roots.

"I've come back to help take care of you, Pa."

His lips quivered, and she apprehended rather than heard what he said.

"I'm glad to see you again, daughter."

Dropping into the chair by the bedside, she laid her arms gently about him. "You don't suffer, do you?"

How immeasurably far away he seemed! How futile was any endeavour to reach him! Then she remembered that he had always been far away, that he had always stood just outside the circle in which they lived, as if he were a member of some affectionate but inarticulate animal kingdom.

He tried to smile, but the effort only accentuated the crooked line of his mouth.

"No, I don't suffer." For a moment he was silent; then he added in an almost inaudible tone: "It's sort of restful."

A leaden weight of tears fell on her heart. Not his death, but his life seemed to her more than she could bear. What was her pain, her wretchedness, compared to his monotony of toil? What was any pain, any wretchedness, compared to the emptiness of his life?

For a little while she talked on cheerfully, telling him of the lectures she had heard and the books she had read, and of all the plans she had made to help him with the farm.

"I've borrowed some money to start with, and we'll make something of it yet, Pa," she said brightly.

His lips moved, but she could not understand what he said. Straining her ears, she bent over him. For an instant it seemed to her that his tone became clearer, and that he was on the point of speaking aloud; then the struggle ceased, and he lay looking at her with his expression of mute resignation.

After this, though she tried to interest him in her plans, she saw

206

that his attention was beginning to wander. Every now and then he made an effort to follow her, while a bewildered expression crept into his face; but it was only for a minute at a time that he could fix his mind on what she was saying, and when the strain became too great for him, his gaze wandered to the open window and the harp-shaped pine, which towered, dark as night, against the morning blue of the sky.

"Well, I'll go to breakfast now," she said, as carelessly as she could. "Ma has it ready for me."

Rising from her chair, she stood looking down on him with misty eyes. After all, the pathos of life was worse than the tragedy. "Is the light too strong?" she asked, as she turned away. "Shall I close one of the shutters?"

At first he did not follow her, his thoughts had roved so far away, and she repeated her question in another form. "Does the sun hurt your eyes?"

A smile wrung his lips. "No, I like to see the big pine," he answered; and stealing out noiselessly, she left him alone with the tree and the sky.

In the kitchen her mother stood over her while she ate, watching every mouthful with the eyes of repressed and hungry devotion.

"You ain't so plump as you were, Dorinda, but you've kept your high colour."

"Oh, I'm well enough, but you look worn out, Ma."

Mrs. Oakley hurried to the stove and back again. "Let me give you another slice of bacon. You must be empty after that long trip. Well, of course, I've had a good deal on me since your father got sick. Until Fluvanna came, I didn't have anybody but Elvira to help me, and though she was willing to do what she could, her fingers were all thumbs when it came to making up a bed or moving things in a sick-room."

"I can take most of the burden off you now. You know I learned a good deal about illness when I was with Doctor Faraday."

"Yes, you'll be a comfort, I know, but you're going back again as soon as your father begins to mend, ain't you?"

Dorinda shook her head with a smile, which, she told herself, looked braver than it felt. "No, I'm not going back. I'd sooner stay here and try to make something out of the farm. A thousand acres of land ought not to be allowed to run to broomsedge like an old field."

"Heaven knows we've tried, daughter. Nobody ever worked harder than your father, and whatever came of it?"

"Poor Pa. I know, but he came after the war when there wasn't any money or any labourers."

She told of the money Doctor Faraday would lend her, and of the hotel in Washington which would take all the butter she could make. "But it must be as good as the best," she explained, with a laugh. "I'm going over to Green Acres to buy seven Jersey cows. Seven is a lucky number for me, so I am going to start with it."

"You'll have to have some help, then."

"Not at first. Of course I'll need a boy for the barnyard, but I am going to do the milking and all the work of the dairy myself. You can help me with the skimming until we get a separator, and when Fluvanna isn't waiting on Pa, she can lend a hand at the churning."

Mrs. Oakley shook her head drearily. "You haven't tried it, Dorinda."

"I know I haven't, but I'm going to. I learned a lot in the hospital, and the chief thing was that it is slighting that has ruined us, white and black alike, in the South. Hasn't Fluvanna got a brother Nimrod that I could hire?" she asked more definitely.

"Yes, and he's a good boy too. Fluvanna had him over here one day last week chopping wood when Rufus was out in the field ploughing. That's a thrifty family, the Moodys. I never saw a darkey that had as much vim as Fluvanna. And she belongs to the new order too. I always thought it spoiled them to learn to read and write till I hired her. She's got all the sense Aunt Mehitable had, and she's picked up some education besides. I declare, she talks better than a lot of white people I know."

"I wonder if she'd stay on and help me with the farm?" Dorinda asked. "I mean," she added, while her face clouded, "after Pa is up again." Though she knew that her father would never be up again, she united with her mother in evading the fact.

"Oh, I'm sure she will," Mrs. Oakley responded, with eagerness. "She has been helping me with my white Leghorns. All the hens are laying well. I am setting Eva and Ida now."

208

"You didn't have them when I was here."

"No, Juliet hatched them. You remember Juliet? She was the first white Leghorn hen I ever had."

"Yes, I remember her. Have you got her still?"

Mrs. Oakley sighed. "No, a coon broke into the henhouse last winter and killed her. She was a good hen, if I ever had one."

It was amazing to Dorinda the way her mother knew every fowl on the place by name. To be sure, there were only a dozen or so; but these white Leghorns all looked exactly alike to the girl, though Mrs. Oakley could tell each one at a distance and was intimately acquainted with the peculiarities of every rooster and hen that she owned.

"I'd like to get a hundred and fifty white Leghorns, if we could look after them," Dorinda said thoughtfully. "That's one good way to make money."

A ray of light, which was less a flush than a warmer pallor, flickered across Mrs. Oakley's wan features. While her mother's interest was awakening, Dorinda felt that her own was slowly drugged by the poverty of her surroundings. The sunlight bathing the ragged lawn only intensified the aspect of destitution. Colour, diversity, animation, all these were a part of the world she had relinquished. Pushing her chair away from the table, she went to the back door and stood gazing out over the woodpile in the direction of the well-house. A few cultivated acres in the midst of an encroaching waste land! From the broomsedge and the flat horizon, loneliness rose and washed over her. Loneliness, nothing more! The same loneliness that she had feared and hated as a child; the same loneliness from which she had tried to escape in flights of emotion. Food, work, sleep, that was life as her father and mother had known it, and that life was to be hers in the future. For an instant it seemed to her that she must break down. Then, lifting her head with a characteristic gesture of defiance, she turned back into the room.

"I'd better start straight about it," she said aloud, smiling at Mrs. Oakley's startled look.

"Did you say anything, Dorinda? I believe I've got something wrong with my ears."

"I said I was going upstairs to change my dress. The same old room, I suppose?"

"Yes, I fixed the same room for you."

While she cleared off the table, Mrs. Oakley gazed after her daughter with a perplexed and anxious expression. Dorinda in her flowing veil, with her air of worldly knowledge and disillusioned experience, had awed and impressed her. Was it possible that she had created this superior intelligence, that she had actually brought this paragon of efficiency into the world? "Well, I hope it will turn out the way you want it," she remarked presently to her daughter's retreating back, "but, in my time, I've watched many a big bloom that brought forth mighty small fruit."

At sunset, when Nathan Pedlar came for his daily visit, Dorinda walked over a part of the farm with him. He was wearing his Sunday suit of clothes, and though this emphasized his grotesqueness, it increased also the air of having been well scrubbed and brushed which had distinguished him from the other farmers at the station. Since his wife's death he had prospered, as widowers were so frequently known to do, Dorinda reflected; and now that he was able to employ an assistant, he was not closely confined to the store. Though his neighing laugh still irritated the girl, she found herself regarding his deficiencies more leniently. After all, he was not to blame for the way he looked; he was not even to blame, she conceded less readily, for the things that he thought funny. Since that fantastic humour had taken root in her mind, she had been continually puzzled by the variety of obvious facts which people, and especially men, found amusing. She could not, to save her life, laugh at the spectacles they enjoyed, nor did the freakish destiny that provoked her to merriment appear to divert them at all. From the cool and detached point of view she had attained, life appeared to her to be essentially comic; but comic acts, whether presented in the theatre or in the waggish hilarity of Pedlar's Mill, seemed to her merely depressing. She was not amused by the classic jokes of the period, which were perpetually embodied in a married man who was too fat or an unmarried woman who was too thin. Flesh or the lack of it, hats or the pursuit of them, crockery or the breaking of it; none of these common impediments to happiness possessed, for her, the genuine qualities of mirth. But reprehensible though she knew it to be, she could not recall the misguided earnestness of her girlhood without the pricking of ridicule; and the image of mankind strutting with pompous solemnity into the inevitable abyss impressed her as the very spirit of comedy. Tragic but comic, too, as most tragedy was. Would it ever pass, she wondered, this capricious and lonely laughter?

"I can't help it," she thought, walking by Nathan's side, and listening soberly to his story of a coloured woman who had tried to make him pay an additional price for a chicken with three legs. "I can't help it if they, not the things they laugh at, seem funny to me."

It was a misty, lilac-scented afternoon in April. The sun shone softly when it began to go down, as if it were caught in a silver scarf, and the grass in the pear orchard was white with drifting blossoms. Those old trees always bloomed late, she remembered, and the ground was still snowy with fallen petals when the lilac bushes by the west wing were breaking into flower.

As she followed the beaten track by the orchard, her gaze swept the ploughed fields, where the upturned earth was changing from chocolate to purple as the light faded. Around her the farm spread out like an open fan, ploughed ground melting into waste land, fields sinking into neglected pasture, pasture rising gradually into the dark belt of the pines. She knew that the place was more to her than soil to be cultivated; that it was the birthplace and burial ground of hopes, desires, and disappointments. The old feeling that the land thought and felt, that it possessed a secret personal life of its own, brushed her mood as it sped lightly by.

"All this and just waste, waste, waste," she said slowly.

Nathan glanced up at the big pine on the hill. "Ever think of cutting that tree down for timber?" he inquired.

She shook her head. "It's the only thing Pa likes to watch now. He loves it."

Nathan neighed under his breath, with the sound Dan gave when he saw clover.

"Well, I kind of know how he feels. I like a big tree myself."

"Sometimes in stormy weather that pine is like a rocky crag with the sea beating against it," Dorinda said. "I used to remember it up in Maine. I suppose that is why Pa likes to look at it. All the meaning of his life has gone into it, and all the meaning of the country. Endurance, that's what it is."

"What a fancy you've got," Nathan answered admiringly, "and

always had even when you were a child. But you're right about endurance. This farm looks to me as if it had endured about as much as it can stand."

"Oh, I'm going to change all that."

"Then you'd better get busy."

"I'll begin to-morrow, if you'll send me some field-hands." She stopped and made a gesture, full of vital energy, in the direction of the road. "I want to make a new pasture out of that eighteen-acre field next to the old one."

"It has run to broomsedge now, hasn't it?"

"Yes, but it used to be a corn-field in great-grandfather's day. If you can get me the hands, I'll start them clearing it off the first thing in the morning."

He chuckled with enjoyment. "Oh, I'll get you anything you want, but the niggers won't work for nothing, you know."

"I've borrowed two thousand dollars. That ought to help, oughtn't it?" She wished he wouldn't say "niggers." That scornful label was already archaic, except among the poorest of the "poor white class" at Pedlar's Mill.

"Two thousand dollars!" he ejaculated. "Well, that ought to go some way."

"I'll have to spend a good deal for cows," she explained. "How much will they ask at Green Acres?"

For a minute he hesitated. "That's a fine Jersey herd," he replied presently. "I don't reckon they'll take less than a hundred dollars for a good cow. You can get scrub cows cheaper, but you want good ones."

"Oh, yes. I want good ones."

"Well, seeing it's you, Jim Ellgood may let you have them for less. I don't know; but he got a hundred and fifty for those he sold at the fair. One of his young bulls took the blue ribbon, you know."

She nodded. "I'm going over to see him to-morrow, if Pa doesn't get worse."

"Jim's a first-rate land doctor. He'll tell you what to do with that old field."

"Why, everybody says you're as good a farmer as James Ellgood."

"Oh, no, I'm not. Not by a long way. He spends a lot of money on phosphate and nitrate of soda; but in the end he gets it back again. He reclaimed some bad land several years ago and made it yield forty bushels an acre. For several years he kept sowing cowpeas and turning them under. Then he sowed sweet clover with lime, and when it was in full bloom, he turned that under too. Takes money, his method, but it pays in the long run. He has just begun using alfalfa; but you watch and he'll get five cuttings from it in no time. I get four, and Jim always goes me one better."

She was listening to him, for the first time in her life, with attention and interest. It was surprising, she reflected, what a bond of sympathy farming could make. He was as dull probably as he had ever been; but his dullness had ceased now to bore her. "I'll find him useful, anyhow," she thought; and usefulness, she was to discover presently, makes an even firmer bond than an interest in farming. Her mind was filled with her new vocation, and just as in that earlier period she had had ears for any one who would speak to her of Jason, so she listened now to whoever displayed the time and the inclination to talk of Old Farm. After all, how much mental tolerance, she wondered, was based upon the devouring egoism at the heart of all human nature? It was a question her great-grandfather might have asked, for though she had burst the cocoon of his theology, her mind was still entangled in the misty cobwebs of his dialectics. Yes, she had always deluded herself with the belief that the superior Rose Emily had made it possible for her to think tolerantly of Nathan. Yet, deprived of that advantage, and left to flounder on without intelligent guidance, he had become, Dorinda admitted thoughtfully, more likable than ever. For the first time it occurred to her that a marriage too much above one may become as great an obstacle as a marriage too much below one.

"How big is Green Acres?" she asked, keenly interested.

Nathan's gaze sought the horizon. Before he replied he spat a wad of tobacco from his mouth, while she looked vaguely over the fields.

"Counting the wasteland, it's near about fourteen hundred acres, I reckon," he answered. "If Old Farm and Five Oaks were thrown together, they'd more than balance Jim's land."

"Are they doing anything over at Five Oaks?"

"It don't look so, does it?" He waved his arm vaguely toward the blur of spring foliage in the southeast. "I ain't heard any talk of it lately." His tone had taken a sharper edge, and Dorinda knew he was thinking that Jason had jilted her. People would always remember that whenever they heard her name or Jason's. If they both lived to be old persons, and never spoke to each other again, they could never dissolve that intangible bond. In some subtle fashion, which she resented, she and Jason were eternally joined together.

"If they don't look sharp," Nathan concluded without glancing at her, "the place will slip through their fingers. The old man has a big mortgage on it. I took a share of it myself, and some day, if Jason keeps going downhill, there'll be a foreclosure right over his head."

A flame passed over Dorinda's face. So vivid was the sensation that she felt as if they were encircled by burning grass. Ambition, which had been formless and remote, became definite and immediate.

"I'd give ten years of my life to own Five Oaks," she said.

"You would?" The wish appeared to amuse him. "Looks as if you were beginning to count your chickens before they're hatched."

"Yes, it's absurd; but all the same I'd give ten years of my life to own Five Oaks."

The colour burned in her face and in her blue eyes which were looking straight at the sunset. She appeared suddenly taller, stronger, more imperious in her demands of life.

"If we ever foreclose the mortgage, I'll bid in the farm for you," he returned, with admiring facetiousness. A flush like the stain of pokeberry juice was spreading over his leathery skin.

She nodded gravely. "By that time I may be able to buy it. If hard work can get you anywhere on a farm, I am going to be one of the best farmers in this country."

"Is Rufus to have any hand in it? You won't get far with Rufus."

"No, he hates it. He is going to the city next winter. There won't be anybody but Pa and me to manage." Her voice faltered from its dominant note. Would there be her father?

"Well, I'll help you," he promised, "all I can. I've learned a little by failing. That's as much as most farmers can say." When he dropped the personal tone and began to talk of the things he knew, there was a rustic dignity in his ugliness. After all, she could depend on him, and that meant a good deal to her as a farmer. Rose Emily, she remembered, used to say that you never realized Nathan's value

214

until you tried depending upon other people. The vision of Rose Emily illuminated her thoughts like the last flare of the sunset. How brave she was, and how brilliant! Though Nathan had loved her and been faithful to her while she lived, after her death he had ceased to think of her with the mental alacrity which appeared to overtake the emotions of the faithful and the unfaithful alike. Already, she felt, Rose Emily was becoming nearer to her than to Nathan. Nathan had lost a wife; but as the years passed her friend would begin to live more vitally in her memory.

They followed the band of pines and crossed an old hayfield, where a flock of meadow-larks drifted up from the grass and scattered with a flutter of white tail feathers. It was the thrushes' hour, and the trees, reaching tall and straight up into the golden air, were as musical as harps. She had forgotten Nathan now, and while she walked on rapidly she was thinking that she would divide the farm into five separate parts, leaving the larger part still abandoned. "I must go slowly," she thought. "If I overdo it in the beginning, I'll spoil everything."

"You're up against something," Nathan was saying facetiously but firmly. "This used to be good land in your great-grandfather's day, and some of it ain't gone so bad but a thorough fertilizing would bring it back. Your father did all he could, but one man ain't a team. He had to work uphill with every darn thing, including the elements, against him."

"Yes, of course Pa did all he could." She had spoken the words so often that they sounded now as hollow as a refrain. Yet they were true. Her father had done all that one man could do on the farm. Yet the farm had conquered him in the end and eaten away his strength.

They were approaching Poplar Spring, where a silver vein of a stream trickled over the flat grey rocks. The smell of wet leaves floated toward her, and instantly the quiet moment snapped in two as if a blow had divided it. Half of her mind was here, watching the meadow-larks skimming over the fields, and the other half crouched under the dripping boughs by the fork of the road. Only the imaginary half seemed more real, more physical even, than the actual one. Not her mind, she felt with horror, but her senses, her nerves, and the very corpuscles of her blood, remembered the agony.

215

"I think I'll go back," she said, turning quickly. "Ma might want me to help her."

"You look tired," he returned, with the consideration which Rose Emily had disciplined into a habit. "Would you like to sit down and rest?"

"No, I'd better go back."

They walked to the house in silence, and she scarcely heard him when he said, "Good night," at the porch.

"I hope you'll find your father better."

"Yes, I hope I'll find him better."

"If there's anything I can do, let me know."

"If there is, I'll let you know."

As he stepped into his buggy, he turned and called out, "I'll try to get word to the hands to-night, and send them over the first thing in the morning."

What hands? What did they matter? What did anything matter? It seemed to her suddenly that, not only her love for Jason, but everything, the whole of life, was a mistake. Even her best endeavours, even her return to the farm—"It might have been better if I'd decided differently," she thought wearily; but when she tried to be definite, to imagine some other decision she might have made, nothing occurred to her. Something? But what? Where? She saw no other way, and she felt blindly that she should never see one.

"I'm tired," she thought, "and this makes me weak. Weakness doesn't help anything." For an instant this thought held her; then it occurred to her that, in the years to come, she would be continually tired; and that, tired or not, she must fight against weakness. "I've got to go straight ahead, no matter how I feel."

8

"Ebenezer Green?"
  "Dat's me."
  "Peter Plumtree?"
  "Dat's me."
  "Toby Jackson?"
  "Dat's me, Miss D'rindy."
  "Rapidan Finley?"
  "Dat's me."

She was calling the names of the field-hands, and while she went over the list, her mind was busily assorting and grouping the faces before her. Yes, she knew them all. Ever since she could remember they had been a part of the country; she had passed them in the road every week, or seen them in the vegetable patches in front of their cabins. Like her mother, she was endowed with an intuitive understanding of the negroes; she would always know how to keep on friendly terms with that immature but not ungenerous race. Slavery in Queen Elizabeth County had rested more lightly than elsewhere. The religion that made people hard to themselves, her mother had often pointed out, made them impartially just to their dependents; and like most generalizations, this one was elastic enough to cover the particular instance. It was true that the coloured people about Pedlar's Mill were as industrious and as prosperous as any in the South, and that, within what their white neighbours called reasonable bounds, there was, at the end of the nineteenth century, little prejudice against them. Here and there a thriftless farmer, such as Ike Pryde or Adam Snead, would display a fitful jealousy of Micajah Green, who had turned a few barren acres into a flourishing farm; but the better class of farmers preferred the intelligent coloured neighbour to the ignorant white one. Both were social inferiors; but where the matter was one solely of farming, the advantages would usually fall to the more diligent. As for the negroes themselves, they lived contentedly enough as inferiors though not dependents. In spite of the influence of Aunt Mehitable Green, they had not yet learned to think as a race, and the individual negro still attached himself instinctively to the superior powers.

"I remember you well, Ebenezer," she said; "you have a sister, Mary Joe. I want her to help look after my hen-house." She laughed as she spoke because she knew that the negroes would work twice as well for an employer who laughed easily; but she wondered if they detected the hollowness of the sound. It occurred to her, as she looked at the doomed broomsedge across the road, that farming, like love, might prove presently to be no laughing matter.

Turning back toward the house, she met her mother, who was coming out with a basin of cornmeal dough for the chickens. The sun had just risen, and there was a sparkling freshness over the earth and in the luminous globe of the sky. She had slept well, and with the morning weakness had vanished. The wild part of her had perished like burned grass; out of nothing, into nothing, that was the way of it. Now, armoured in reason, she was ready to meet life on its own terms.

"Do you know where Rufus is?" she asked. "I want him to see the hands start work in the eighteen-acre field."

Mrs. Oakley shook her head. "I don't know. I thought he was going to finish ploughing the tobacco-field, but I saw him start off right after breakfast with Ike Pryde. It seems they found honey in a big oak over by Hoot Owl Woods, and they've set off with an axe to cut down the tree."

"Oh, the fool, the fool!" Dorinda exclaimed, and determined that she would expect nothing more from Rufus.

"Well, you know how men are," returned her mother, with unpolemical wisdom. "They'll seize any excuse to stop work and cut down a tree."

"I do know. But to cut down a big oak, and for honey!"

The old woman scattered dough on the ground with an impartial hand. "Rufus has got a mighty sweet tooth," she remarked.

218

"So has Pa, but you never found him making an excuse to stop work."

"I know. Your Pa always put his wishes aside. There ain't many men you can say that of." Though she sighed over the fact, she accepted it as one of the natural or acquired privileges of the male; and she felt that these were too numerous to justify a special grievance against a particular one. Even acquiescence with a sigh is easier than argument when one is worn out with neuralgia and worse things. A frost had blighted her impulse of opposition, and this seemed to Dorinda one of the surest signs that her mother was failing. There were moments when it would have been a relief to be contradicted.

"Well, I'll have to do it myself. Because I am a woman the hands will expect me to shirk, and I must show them that I know what I am about."

"I'll help you all I can, daughter."

"I know you will." Dorinda's conscience reproached her for her impatience. "You will be wonderful with the hens, and I'll get Ebenezer's sister Mary Joe to help you. She must be fourteen or fifteen."

"Yes, she's a real bright girl," Mrs. Oakley remarked, without enthusiasm. She had scarcely closed her eyes all night, and bright coloured girls, even when they helped in the hen-house, left her indifferent. "I'm going down in the garden to see if I can find a mess of turnip salad," she added after a pause, in which she scooped the last remnant of dough out of the basin and flung it into the midst of the brood of chickens.

"Let me go while you sit with Pa. I was coming in to see about him before I went down to the field where they are working."

Mrs. Oakley shook her head. "No, I can't keep still in the daytime. It's hard enough having to do it at night. Fluvanna couldn't get over early to-day; but she sent her little sister Ruby, and she is keeping the flies off your father's face. That's all anybody can do for him now."

"Well, I'll speak to him anyway. Then I'll see after the hands."

Mrs. Oakley raised her eyes to her daughter's face. "You've brought back a heap of vim, Dorinda," she said dispassionately,

219

"but I reckon you've been away from the farm too long to know what it's like."

She put the basin down on a bench, picked up a blue gingham sunbonnet she had laid there when she came out, and started, with her nervous walk, to the garden at the end of the yard.

In her father's room, Dorinda found a small coloured girl, in a pink calico slip, perched on a high stool by the bedside. Her bare feet clutched the round of the stool; her eyes, like black beads, roved ceaselessly from the wall to the floor; and her thin monkey-like hand waved a palm-leaf fan to and fro over Joshua's immovable features.

"Good morning, Ruby. Has Pa moved since you've been here?"

"Gwamawnin'. Naw'm, he ain' don ez much ez bat 'is eyelids."

Dorinda caught the fan away from her. "Don't you go to school in the mornings?" she inquired, after a pause in which she tried to think of something to say.

"Dar ain' none."

"Aren't you learning to read and write?"

"Yes'm. Fluvanna she knows, en she's larnin' me."

"Well, run away now, and come back when I call you."

The little girl ran out gladly, and Dorinda took her place on the stool and brushed the flies away with slow, firm waves of the fan. Immediately, as soon as she had settled herself, something of her mother's restlessness rushed over her, and she felt a hysterical longing to get up and move about or to go out into the air. "If I feel this way," she thought, "what must it mean to poor Pa to lie there like that?"

Since the hour of her return he had not appeared to recognize her. He was beyond reach of any help, of any voice, of any hand, lost in some mental wilderness which was more impenetrable than the jungles of earth. Though he was apparently not unconscious, he was beyond all awareness. His eyes never left the great pine, and once when his wife had started to close the shutters, a frown had gathered on his forehead and lingered there until she had desisted and turned away from the window. Then his face had cleared and the look of hard-earned rest had returned to his features.

While she sat there, Dorinda began counting imaginary chickens, a method of collecting her thoughts which she had learned as a child from Aunt Mehitable. She was still counting the fictitious flock when Joshua opened his eyes and looked straight up at her with an expression of startled wonder and surprise, as if he were on the point of speaking.

"What is it?" she asked, bending nearer.

His lips moved, and for an instant she was visited by an indescribable sensation. He was so near to her that she seemed, in the same moment, never to have known him before and yet to know him completely. She felt that he was trying to speak some words that would make everything clear and simple between them, that would explain away all the mistakes and misunderstandings of life.

"What is it?" she repeated, breathless with hope.

Again his lips moved slightly; but no sound came, and the look of wonder and surprise faded slowly out of his face. His eyes closed, and a minute later his heavy breathing told her that he had relapsed into stupor.

"I must ask him when he wakes," she thought. "I must ask him what he wanted to tell me."

After dinner she hunted for Rufus again, but he had not, it appeared, returned to the farm.

"I reckon he went home with Ike Pryde," his mother said. "He's been seeing too much of Ike, and I'm afraid it ain't good for him. The last time Almira was over here she told me Ike was drinking again." She was worried and anxious, and the twitching was worse in her face. "I declare I don't see how Almira can put up with him," she said.

"Then I'll have to harness Dan myself," Dorinda replied. "I've got on my best dress, so I hoped Rufus would drag out the buggy. I'm going over to Green Acres."

"I was wondering what you'd put on your blue poplin for," Mrs. Oakley returned. "I'd think that hanging veil would get in your way; but if you're going over to the Ellgoods', I'm glad you dressed up. Fluvanna, I reckon, will hitch up the buggy for you."

Fluvanna, emerging from the kitchen, offered eagerly to look for Dan in the pasture. "He ain't got away," she said, "for I saw him at the bars jest a minute ago." She had gone to school whenever there was one for coloured children in the neighbourhood, and though her speech was still picturesque, she had discarded the pure

221

dialect of Aunt Mehitable and her generation. "Don't you worry, Miss Dorinda," she added, hurrying down the path to the pasture.

"I tell Fluvanna that her sunny disposition is worth a fortune," Mrs. Oakley remarked. "She never gets put out about anything."

"I believe she'll be a great comfort to us," Dorinda returned thoughtfully. She liked the girl's pleasant brown face, as glossy as a chestnut, her shining black eyes, and her perfect teeth, which showed always, for she never stopped smiling. "Just to have anybody look intelligent is a relief."

"Well, you'll find that Fluvanna has plenty of sense. Of course she slights things when she can, but she is always willing and good-humoured. You don't often find a hard worker, white or black, with a sunny temper."

They were still discussing her when Fluvanna drove up in the buggy and descended to offer the dilapidated reins to Dorinda.

"Thank you, Fluvanna. I declare this buggy looks as if it hadn't been washed off for a year."

Fluvanna, who had not observed the mud, turned her beaming eyes on the buggy and perceived that it was dirty.

"I'll come over the first thing in the mawnin' an' wash it for you," she promised. "There ain't a bit of use dependin' on Mr. Rufus. He won't do nothin'."

Dorinda gathered up the reins, settled herself on the bagging which covered the seat, and turned Dan's head kindly but firmly away from the pasture.

"I wonder if things used to look as dilapidated, only I didn't notice them so much," she thought.

9

Dan travelled slowly, and the Ellgoods lived three miles on the other side of Pedlar's Mill. Green Acres was the largest stock farm in the county; but what impressed Dorinda more than the size was the general air of thrift which hovered over the pastures, the deep green meadows, and the white buildings clustering about the red brick house.

"I couldn't have anything like this in a hundred years," she thought cheerlessly. Her scheme, which had appeared so promising when she surveyed it from Central Park, presented, at a closer view, innumerable obstacles. There was not one chance in a thousand, she told herself now, that the venture would lead anywhere except into a bog. "But I'm in it now, and I must see it through," she concluded, with less audacity than determination. "I'll not give up as long as there is breath left in my body." Rolling in mud-caked wheels up the neat drive to the house, she resolved stubbornly that no one, least of all James Ellgood, should suspect that she had lost heart in her enterprise.

James Ellgood was at Queen Elizabeth Court-House for the day; but Bob, his son, who had recently brought home a dissatisfied and delicate wife from a hospital in Baltimore, was on the front porch awaiting his visitor. When she appeared in sight, he threw away the match he was striking on his boot, and after thrusting his old brier pipe into his pocket, descended the steps and came across the drive to the buggy. Nathan would have smoked, or still worse have chewed, Dorinda knew, while he received her; but inconsistently enough, she did not like him the less for his boorishness. Utility, not punctilio, was what she required of men at this turning-point in her career.

While Bob Ellgood held out his hand, she could see her reflection in his large, placid eyes as clearly as if her features were mirrored in the old mill-pond. It gave her pleasure to feel that she was more distinguished, if less desirable, than she had been two years ago; but her pleasure was as impersonal as her errand. She had no wish to attract this heavy, masterful farmer, who reminded her of a sleek, mild-mannered Jersey bull; no wish, at least, to attract him beyond the point where his admiration might help her to drive a bargain in cows. Gazing critically at his handsome face, she remembered the Sunday mornings when she had watched him in church and had wished with all her heart that he would turn his eyes in her direction. Then he had not so much as glanced at her over his hymn-book, his slow mind was probably revolving round his engagement; but now she felt instinctively that he was ready to catch fire from a look or a word. The absurd twist of an idea jerked into her mind. "He would have suited me better than Jason, and I should have suited him better than the woman he married." Well, that was the way the eternal purpose worked, she supposed, but it seemed to her a cumbersome and blundering method.

"Nathan told me you wanted to buy some cows," he was saying, for he was as single-minded as other successful men, only more so. "I picked out seven fine ones this morning and had them brought up to the small pasture. They'll be at the bars now, and you can look them over. There isn't a better breed than the Jersey, that's what we think, and these young cows are as good as any you'll find."

At the bars of the pasture, where a weeping willow dipped over the watering trough, the Jerseys were standing in a row, satin-coated, fawn-eyed, with breath like new-mown hay. What beauties they were, thought Dorinda, swept away in spite of her determination to bargain. When Bob told her the names she repeated them in blissful accents. "Rose. Sweetbrier. Hollyhock. Pansy. Daisy. Violet. Verbena." To think that she, who had never owned anything, should actually possess these adorable creatures! Even the price, which seemed to her excessively high, could not spoil her delight. A hundred dollars for each cow, Bob explained, was a third less than they would bring at the fair next autumn.

"I am glad you are going into the dairy business," he proceeded. "I always said this country would do for dairy farming, though it takes more money, of course, to start a dairy farm than it does just to plant crops. The cows ain't all of it, you know. You ought to raise your own hay and the corn you need for silage. Borrow money, too, if you haven't got it, to drain and tile your fields. It will pay you back in the long run, for I doubt if you will get any good clover until you put ditches in your land. All that takes money, of course," he continued, with depressing accuracy, "but it is the only way to make anything out of a farm. Father says there ain't but one way to learn to do anything, and that's the right way."

"I know," Dorinda assented. Her tone was confident, but it seemed to her while she spoke that she was being buried under the impoverished acres of Old Farm.

"And there's machinery," he added. "Father borrowed money after the war to buy new machinery. When he came home after Appomattox, all the farm implements were either lost or good for nothing. He went in debt and bought the newest inventions, and that was the beginning of his success. The legacy from Uncle Mitchell came after he was well started, and he always says he could have got on without it, though perhaps not on so large a scale."

"Well, I'll borrow," said Dorinda defiantly. "We've always been afraid of debt; but I've already borrowed two thousand dollars, and if I need more, I'll try to get it. Nathan is going to pick up whatever machinery he can at auction. That will be less than half the actual cost, he says."

He was looking at her now with keen, impersonal admiration. Just as if she had been a man, she thought, with a glow of triumph. Though the sensation was without the excitement of sex vanity, she found that it was quite as gratifying, and, she suspected, more durable. Already he had forgotten the momentary physical appeal she had made to him in the beginning; and she felt that his respect for her was based upon what he believed to be her character. "It isn't what I am really that matters," she thought. "It is just the impression I make on his mind or senses. Men are all like that, I suppose. They don't know you. They don't even wish to know you. They are interested in nothing on earth but their own reactions." And she remembered suddenly that Jason had once generalized like this about women, and that she was merely copying what he had said. How stupid generalizations were, and how deceptive!

"I hope you'll make a success of it," Bob said. "I like women who take hold of things and aren't afraid of work when they have to do it. That's the right spirit." A moody frown contracted his forehead, and she knew that he was thinking of his wife, though he added after a moment's hesitation, "Look at my sister now. She's as young as you are and she lies round all day like an old woman."

"Perhaps it's her health," Dorinda suggested, moving away.

"Why shouldn't she be healthy? We're all healthy enough, Heaven knows! Not that I wonder at it," he continued thoughtlessly, "when I remember that she was such a fool as to fall in love with Jason Greylock." The next instant a purple flush dyed his face, and she could see his thoughts rising like fish to the fluid surface of his mind. "Not that he ill-treats her. He knows Father wouldn't stand for that," he added hurriedly, caught in the net he had unconsciously spread. "But his laziness is bred in the bone, and he's the sort that will let apples rot on the ground rather than pick them up."

"I know," Dorinda said, and she did. That was what her mother called the mental malaria of the country.

"Well, it's the blood, I reckon," he conceded more tolerantly. "There's enough to work against without having to struggle to get the better of your own blood. Come this way," he continued, leading her to a different pasture, "I want you to have a look at our prize bull. Five blue ribbons already; and we've a yearling that promises to be still finer. A beauty, isn't he?"

Dorinda gazed at the bull with admiration and envy, while he returned her look with royal, inscrutable eyes. "I wonder if I shall ever own a creature like that?" she thought. "He looks as if he owned everything and yet despised it," she said aloud.

Bob laughed. "Yes, he's got a high-and-mighty air, hasn't he? By the way, those Jerseys have never been milked by a woman. I don't know how they'll take to it. Will you hire a man?"

"Not at first. Until I get started well, I'm going to do my own milking. I can put on Rufus's overalls, and when I milk myself I can be sure of the way the cows are handled. With negroes you can never tell. Nathan says they let his cows go dry because they don't take the trouble to milk them thoroughly. And they won't be clean, no matter how much you talk to them. When I tell them I'm going to keep my cows washed and brushed and the stalls free from a speck of dirt, they think it's a joke."

"That's the trouble. Cleanliness is a joke with most of the farmers about here, but it's the first step to success in dairy farming. It keeps down disease, especially contagious abortion, better than anything else. Yes, you've got the right idea. It means hard work, of course, though you'll find it's worth while in the end."

"Oh, I don't mind work. What else is there in life?"

His eyes were shining as he looked at her. "Well, I wish my wife had a little of your spirit. It isn't only that she's delicate. I believe that she's afraid of everything in the country from a grasshopper to an ox."

"She didn't grow up on a farm. That makes a difference."

He sighed. "Yes, it does make a difference."

"Well, it's a pity. I'm glad I don't have to struggle with fear."

A little later, as she drove across the railway tracks and down the long slope in the direction of Old Farm, she reflected dispassionately upon the crookedness of human affairs. Why had that honest farmer, robust, handsome, without an idea above bulls and clover, mated with a woman who was afraid of a grasshopper? And why had she, in whom life burned so strong and bright, wasted her vital energy on the mere husk of a man? Why, above all, should Nature move so unintelligently in the matter of instinct? Did this circle of reasoning lead back inevitably, she wondered, to the steadfast doctrine of original sin? "The truth is we always want what is bad for us, I suppose," she concluded, and gave up the riddle.

Just beyond the station, in front of the "old Haney place," she met William Fairlamb, and stopped to ask him about repairing the cow-barn and the hen-house. He was a tall, stooped, old-looking young man, with shaggy flaxen hair and round grey eyes as opaque as pebbles. Though his expression was stupid, he had intelligence above the ordinary, and was the best carpenter at Pedlar's Mill.

"If you're going to keep cows, you'd better see that Doctor Greylock mends his fences," he said, after he had promised to begin on the cow-barn as soon as he had finished his contract with Ezra Flower. "That old black steer of his is a public nuisance. I've had him wandering over my wheat-fields all winter. It's a mortal shame the way the Greylocks are letting that farm peter out."

"Yes, it's a shame," she agreed, and drove on again. Wherever she turned, it appeared that she was to be met by a reminder that Jason was living so near her. "If only he were dead," she thought, as impersonally as if she were thinking of the black steer that trampled the ploughed fields. "I shall have to go on hearing about him now until the end of my days."

There was no regret, she told herself, left in her memory; yet whenever she heard his name, or recalled his existence, her spirits flagged beneath an overpowering sense of futility. At such moments, she was obliged to spur her body into action. "It will be like this always, until one of us is dead," she reflected. Though she neither loved nor hated him now, the thought of him, which still lived on in some obscure chamber of her mind, was sufficient to disturb and disarrange her whole inner life. The part of her consciousness that she could control she had released from his influence; but there were innate impulses which were independent of her will or her emotions; and in these blind instincts of her being there were even now occasional flashes of longing. While she was awake she could escape him; but at night, when she slept, she would live over again all the happiest hours she had spent with him. Never the pain, never the cruelty of the past; only the beauty and the unforgettable ecstasy came back to her in her dreams.

As she drove out of the woods the sun was sinking beyond the cleft of the road, and a slow procession of shadows was moving across the broomsedge, where little waves of light quivered and disappeared and quivered again like ripples in running water. While she passed on, the expression of the landscape faded from tranquil brightness to the look of unresisting fortitude which it had worn as far back as she could remember. In her heart also she felt that the brightness quivered and died. With her drooping energy, weariness had crept over her; but out of weariness, she passed presently, like the country, into a mood of endurance. She realized, without despair, that the general aspect of her life would be one of unbroken monotony. Enthusiasm would not last. Energy would not last. Cheerfulness, buoyancy, interest, not one of these qualities would last as long as she needed it. Nothing would last through to the end except courage.

Her gaze was on the horizon. The reins, tied together with a bit of rope, were held loosely in her hands. With every turn of the wheel, a shower of dried mud was scattered over her clothes. So completely lost was she in memory that at first she barely heard the noise of an approaching rider, and the hollow sound of horseshoes striking on rock. Even before her mind became aware of Jason's approach, her startled senses leaped toward him. Her body bent for an instant, and then sprang back like a steel wire. With an impassive face, and a torment of memory in her heart, she sat staring far ahead at the blur of road by the cabin. She was back again within the prison of that moment which was eternal; yet there was no sign of suffering in the blank look of her eyes. Her hand did not tremble; the loosened reins did not waver; and when a voice called her name, she did not reveal by the quiver of an eyelash that she listened.

"Dorinda! Dorinda, let me speak to you!"

She raised her eyes from the road and looked beyond the waving broomsedge to the topaz-coloured light on the western horizon. The longing to look in his face, to turn and rend him with her scorn, was as sharp as a blade; but some deep instinct told her that if she yielded to the impulse, the struggle was lost. To recognize his existence was to restore, in a measure, his power over her life. Only by keeping him outside her waking moments could she win freedom.

"Dorinda, you are hard. Dorinda———"

They were side by side now in the road. If he had reached out his hand, he could have touched her. If she had turned her head, she might have looked into his eyes. But she did not turn; she did not withdraw her gaze from the landscape; she did not relax in the weakest muscle from her attitude of unyielding disdain. Though he were to ride all the way home with her, she told herself, he could not force her to speak to him. No matter what he did, he could never make her speak to him or look at him again!

The sunken places in the road retarded him, and when he reached her side again, they were passing the burned cabin. For an instant, when they approached the fork, he hesitated, as if he were tempted to follow her still farther. Then, deciding abruptly, he wheeled about and alighted to open the red gate of Five Oaks.

"I'll see you again," he called back.

For a few minutes after he had disappeared, she sat rigidly erect, as if she had been frozen into her attitude of repulsion. Then, suddenly, she gave way; a shudder seized her limbs, and the reins slipped from her hands to the bottom of the buggy. She was like a person who has escaped some fearful calamity, and who has not realized the danger until it is over. When the trembling had passed, she stooped and picked up the reins. "It will be easier next time," she said, and a moment later, "I suppose I've got to get used to it. You can get used to anything if you have to." A dull misery stupefied her thoughts, and she was without clear perception of what the meeting had meant to her. "I can't understand why I suffer so," she pondered. "I can't understand how a person you despise can make you so unhappy."

As she drew nearer home, Dan quickened his pace, and the buggy rattled over the bridge and up the rocky slope to the stable. The glow had faded from the west, and the long white house glimmered through the twilight, which was settling like silver dust over the landscape. A banner of smoke drooped low over a single chimney. Beyond the roof the budding trees appeared as diaphanous as mist against the greenish-blue of the sky. In the window of the west wing a lamp was shining. So she had seen it on innumerable evenings in the past; so she would see it, if she lived, on innumerable evenings in the future.

Then, just as she was about to drive on to the stable, she observed that shadows were moving to and fro beyond the single lighted window. Though the outward aspect of the house was unchanged, there was, nevertheless, a subtle alteration in its spirit. For an instant, while she hesitated, there seemed to her an ominous message in these hurried shadows and this absence of noise. Her throat tightened, and she sprang from the buggy as the door opened and Rufus came out.

"He died a few minutes ago," he said.

A few minutes ago! "I'll never know now what he tried to tell me," she thought. "No matter how long I live, I shall never know."

10

After the last prayer, the earth was shovelled back into the hollow beneath the great pine in the graveyard, and the movement of the farm began again with scarcely a break in its monotony. Joshua Oakley had sacrificed his life to the land, and yet, or so it seemed to Dorinda, his death made as little difference as if a tree had fallen and rotted back into the soil. Even her own sorrow was a sense of pity rather than a personal grief.

When the neighbours had driven solemnly out of the gate, the family assembled in Mrs. Oakley's chamber and gazed through the window to the graveyard on the hill, as if they were waiting expectantly for the dead man to rise and return to his work. The only change would be, they acknowledged, that two hired labourers would grumble over a division of the toil which Joshua had performed alone and without a complaint. The farm had always belonged to Mrs. Oakley; but in order that her authority might be assured, Joshua had made a will a few months before his death and had left her the farm implements and the horses. Dissimilar as her parents had appeared to be, there was a bond between them which Dorinda felt without comprehending. This was the growth of habit, she supposed, or the tenacious clinging of happy memories which had survived the frost of experience. In his dumb way, Joshua had been proud of his wife, and Eudora had depended upon her husband for more substantial qualities than those of sentiment. He had been useful to her in the practical details of living, and she was feeling his loss as one feels the loss of a faculty. Here was another proof, Dorinda reflected, of the varied texture of life, another reminder of her folly in attempting to weave durable happiness out of a single thread of emotion.

"I don't see how we'll manage to get on without him," said Mrs. Oakley, who looked gaunt and bleached in the old mourning she had worn for her dead children.

"I reckon it means I'll have to stay on here," Rufus muttered in a tone of sullen rebellion. "I'll have to give up that job Tom Garlick promised me next winter in New York. It's darn luck, that's what I call it."

"Oh, no, you mustn't stay," Dorinda urged. "Ma and I can get on perfectly by ourselves. It won't make any difference if you go in the fall."

"You'd better take Dorinda's advice and get away, Rufus." Though Mrs. Oakley spoke in a quiet voice, her face had gone grey at the thought of losing Rufus also.

"Well, I'm afraid I can't help you now," said Josiah, glancing furtively at his wife, who had proved to be a termagant with generous impulses which were brief but explosive.

"Of course your Ma could always come to live with us," suggested Elvira, obeying the briefest of these impulses. "She'd find plenty to do looking after the chickens, and the children would keep her from being lonesome."

Mrs. Oakley's eyes filled with tears. The old hound, having outlived his master, lay at her feet, and stooping over she stroked his head with a trembling hand. "But what would become of the farm?" she asked in a voice that quavered. "I want to die on the farm where I was born."

"We'll stay here alone, Ma and I," Dorinda declared, with the stern integrity she had won from transgression. "The farm belongs to Ma, and she and I can take care of it. We don't need a man," she added crisply. "If I couldn't do better than the men about here, I'd be a mighty poor farmer."

Elvira breathed more freely, and the wrinkles vanished from Josiah's forehead. As for Rufus, he had lost interest in the discussion as soon as it was decided that he might leave the farm in the autumn.

"I'm sure none of us would want to take Ma against her will," Elvira said, relieved and conciliatory because her generosity had been wasted. "The place belongs to her anyway, so the rest of us haven't anything to say about what she does with it." With a habitual jerk, which had annoyed Dorinda the first moment she saw her, the girl adjusted the belt of her skirt and rested her hands on her rapidly spreading hips.

"You needn't worry about Ma," Dorinda rejoined firmly. "I am going to take care of her." Her one wish, she felt, was to get Elvira and Josiah out of the house. Even Rufus was less depressing. Rufus at least had good looks; but Josiah and Elvira existed in her mind only as appalling examples of inherent futility. While she looked at Josiah, it seemed to her that failure oozed out of the very pores of his skin. Though he worked from morning till night, he was hampered by a fumbling slowness which reminded Dorinda of the efforts of a half-witted person. Yet her father, in spite of his ignorance, had possessed an industry that was tireless, while her mother was afflicted by a veritable mania of energy. Was it a matter of circumstances, after all, not of heredity? Had the more active strain succumbed at last to the climatic inertia? Well, if the fight had narrowed down to one between herself and her surroundings, she was determined to conquer. Beneath her sombre brows her eyes looked out like caged bluebirds. She was wearing a black calico dress which had once belonged to Miss Seena Snead, and the mourning brought out vividly the dusk of her hair and the bright red of her lips. "There's no use talking to me. I've made up my mind," she said.

An hour later, when Josiah and Elvira had gone home, Dorinda helped her mother to take off her mourning and straighten the chamber in which Joshua had lain.

"It's the smell of mourning I can't stand," said the girl, while she folded the crape veil and laid it away in the bandbox. "Do you think I'll have to wear it?"

"It wouldn't be respectful not to," Mrs. Oakley replied, and she asked after a minute: "What do you want with those overalls of Rufus's that you took upstairs?"

Dorinda turned from the wardrobe and looked at her. "They are old ones I'm patching," she answered. "I am going to wear them when I'm milking. Those Jerseys have never been milked by a woman."

"I s'pose they'd get used to it."

"They might, but it's easier for me to wear overalls than to break them. You can't farm in skirts anyway."

"You ain't going to wear them on the farm, are you?"

"If I can farm better in them, I'm going to wear them."

Mrs. Oakley sighed. "Well, I hope nobody will see you."

"I don't care," Dorinda replied stubbornly. "I'm going to milk my cows my own way. I've got some common sense," she added sternly, "and I'm the only person, man or woman, in the county who has."

The old woman's face was as inanimate as a mask, but her eyes were fixed, with their look of prophetic doom, on the great pine in the graveyard. "I can't help thinking," she murmured, "how your father used to lie here day after day and look at that big pine. It seems as if that tree meant more to him than anything human."

Dorinda followed her gaze. "In a way it did," she said slowly, as if some inscrutable mystery were dissolving in a flood of surprise. "In a different way."

With a band of crape in her hands, Mrs. Oakley stared up at the harp-shaped boughs. "I reckon it's a heathenish way to think about things," she observed presently, "but I can't help feeling there's a heap of comfort in it."

When the room had been cleaned and the mourning pinned up again in newspapers, Dorinda begged her mother to rest before Rufus came back to supper.

"I couldn't, daughter, not with all I've got on my mind," Mrs. Oakley replied firmly. "I remember when the doctor tried to get your father to give up for a while, he'd shake his head and answer, 'Doctor, I don't know how to stop.' That's the trouble with me, I reckon. I don't know how to stop."

"If you choose to kill yourself, I don't see how I can prevent it." Dorinda's voice wavered with exasperation. If only her mother would listen to reason, she felt, both of their lives would be so much easier. But did mothers ever listen to reason? "I'm going to walk up to Poplar Spring and look at the woods you wrote me about," she added. "I hope we shan't have to sell them and put the money into the land."

"Your father was holding on to that timber to bury us with. There are all the funeral expenses to come."

"Yes, I know." Dorinda regarded her thoughtfully. "Poor Pa, it was all he had and he wanted to hold on to it. But, you see,"— her tone sharpened to the bitter edge of desperation—"I am depending upon my butter to bury us both, and who knows but your chickens may supply us with tombstones."

"I hope New York didn't turn you into a scoffer, Dorinda."

Dorinda laughed. "New York didn't get a chance, Ma. Pedlar's Mill had done it first."

"Well, there ain't anything too solemn for some folks to joke about. You ain't goin' out in Seena Snead's black dress, are you?"

"She's gone out of mourning, so she gave it to me."

"I'd think you'd hate to take charity."

There were times when it seemed to Dorinda that she could not breathe within the stark limitations of her mother's point of view. As she ran out of the room and the house, without heeding Mrs. Oakley's request that she should wear a hat at least on the day of the funeral, she asked herself if this aimless nagging was all that she could expect in the future. She was fond of her mother; but fondness, strangely enough, did not seem to make it easier for people to bear one another's tempers.

The path to Poplar Spring ran beside the eighteen-acre field, and she stopped amid the dusty fennel and ragweed to inspect the work of the last two days. The broomsedge had been partly cut down and burned, and the blackened ruins waited now for the final obliteration. "It will be hard work to get good grass here," she thought, "but if I keep turning cowpeas under, I may bring up the soil in time." In the pasture, beyond a rail fence, the grass was rank and high, for only Dan and Beersheba had grazed there for the last four or five years. The solitary cow, when they were fortunate as to own one, lived on the lawn or what was called "the home-field," where Mrs. Oakley milked in summer. Across the road she saw the scantily fenced west meadow, where her father had sown his winter wheat, and her eyes filled with tears as she gazed on the sprinkling of green over the earth. While she stood there she remembered the look on his face when he lay in his coffin; a look which was austere, inaccessible, with a reproachful wonder beneath its mask of solemnity, as if he were still asking life why it had crushed him. "Whatever I give, the farm will be always mine," she thought. "That was the way he felt. The farm isn't human and it won't make you suffer. Only human things break your heart." Everything appeared so simple when she regarded it through the film of sentiment that obscured

235

her judgment. Kinship with the land was filtered through her blood into her brain; and she knew that this transfigured instinct was blended of pity, memory, and passion. Dimly, she felt that only through this fresh emotion could she attain permanent liberation of spirit.

Moving away, she followed the path which threaded the scrub pines on the border of the broomsedge. Presently she distinguished the blur of Poplar Spring in the distance, and toward the east the acres of fair timber which had matured since her great-grandfather's death. In her new reverence for her father she shrank from cutting down the tall trees. "It would be slaughter," she said to herself. "I'll let the woods stand as long as I can."

Overhead, the pines were soughing in a light wind, and for a moment or two the sound of footsteps behind her was scarcely louder than the whispering trees. Then, with a start, she realized that she was followed, and glancing round, she saw Jason walking over the scarred field.

"I know you didn't want me at the funeral, Dorinda," he said, "but it was all I could do to show my respect for your father. He was one of the best men who ever lived."

Her breast quivered with pain, but she moved on without appearing to be aware of his presence.

"I was afraid you were angry because I came," he continued.

At this her pride was swallowed up in bitterness, and she stopped and looked back. "You had no right to come. You knew I did not want you there."

Without replying to her charge, he stared at her as if he were amazed by the change in her face. "This is the first time you've looked at me since you came home," he said. "You've treated me as if I were the dirt under your feet."

Her hand was on the slender bough of a pine, and stripping the needles from the branch, she flung them out on the wind with a passionate gesture. Over the chaos in her mind there darted the shadow of a regret. "If only I had killed him that night!"

"Even now, you won't let your eyes rest on me," he complained. "If you'd given me a chance, I'd have done anything you wanted. But you never gave me a chance. You never listened."

236

Her gaze, which had been fixed on the horizon beyond him, swept back to his face. "Your following me won't make me listen."

"If only you knew what I've suffered."

She was looking at him now with merciless eyes. For this thing she had ruined her life! Then, before the thought had left her mind, she realized that in his presence, with her eyes on his face, she was farther away from him than she had been in New York. Yesterday, he had had power over her senses; to-morrow, he might have power again over her memory; but at this instant, while they stood there, so close together that she could almost feel his breath on her face, her senses and her memory alike were delivered from the old torment of love.

"My nerve is going," he said weakly, attempting to soften her. "I've started drinking like Father."

Looking at him, she admitted that it was only her feeling for him, not the man himself, that had changed. Superficially, in spite of excessive drinking, he was as attractive as he had ever been; yet this appeal, which she had found so irresistible two years ago, failed now to awaken the faintest tremor in her heart. The contrast between his brown-black eyes and his red hair seemed to her artificial: there was something repellent to her in the gleam of his white teeth through his short red moustache. These were the physical details that had once affected her so deeply; these traits which she saw now, for the first time, in the spectral light of disenchantment.

"Can you never understand," she asked suddenly, "that I don't hate you because you mean to me—just nothing."

"You are sending me straight to the dogs."

She laughed. How theatrical men were! Beneath her ridicule, she felt the cruelty which gnaws like a worm at the heart of emotion in its decay.

"Why should I care?" she demanded.

"You mean you wouldn't care if I were to die a drunkard like my father?" His voice trembled, and she saw that he was wrestling with man's inability to believe that a woman's love can perish while his own still survives.

"No, I shouldn't care."

"You're hard, Dorinda, as hard as a stone."

Her smile was exultant. "Yes, I am hard. I'm through with soft things."

Turning her back on him, she walked rapidly away over the ploughed ground in the direction of the house. Oh, if the women who wanted love could only know the infinite relief of having love over!

11

On an afternoon in October, Dorinda stood under the harp-shaped pine in the graveyard and looked down on the farm.

The drift of autumn was in the air; the shadows from the west were growing longer; and in a little while Nimrod, the farm boy, would let down the bars by the watering-trough, and the seven Jersey cows would file sleepily across the road and the lawn to the cow-barn. At the first glimpse of Nimrod she would run down and slip into her overalls. Ever since the cows had come from Green Acres, she had milked them morning and evening, and she was wondering now how many more she could handle with only Fluvanna to help her. Only by doing the work herself and keeping a relentless eye on every detail, could she hope to succeed in the end. If she were once weak enough to compromise with the natural carelessness of the negroes, she knew that the pails and pans would not be properly scalded, and the milk would begin to lose its quality. Fluvanna was the superior of most ignorant white women; but even Fluvanna, though she was, as Dorinda said to herself, one in a thousand, would slight her work as soon as she was given authority over others. There were times when it seemed to Dorinda that this instinct to slight was indigenous to the soil of the South. In the last six months she had felt the temptation herself. There had been hours of weariness when it had seemed to her that it was better to be swift and casual than to be slow and thorough; but she had always suppressed the impulse before it was translated into outward negligence. Would her power of resistance survive, she wondered, or would it yield inevitably to the surrounding drought of energy?

Six months were gone now, and how hard she had worked! She thought of the mornings when she had risen before day, eaten a hurried breakfast by the crack of dawn, and milked the cows by the summer sunrise. From the moment the warm milk frothed into the pails until the creamy butter was patted into moulds and stamped with the name Old Farm beneath the device of a harp-shaped pine, there was not a minute detail of the work that was left to others. Even the scalding of the churns, the straining and skimming of the milk in the old-fashioned way without a separator, —all these simple tasks came under her watchful eyes. When the first supply of butter was sent off, she waited with nervous dread for the verdict. The price had seemed extravagant, for selling directly to her customer she had asked thirty cents a pound, while butter in Pedlar's store was never higher than ninepence in summer and a shilling in winter, measured in the old English terms which were still commonly used in Queen Elizabeth County.

"It seems a mighty high price," her mother had objected.

"I know, but Mrs. Faraday told me to ask more. She said the dairy would get a dollar a pound for the very best. Some people are always ready to pay a high price, and they value a thing more if they pay too much for it. I found out all I could about butter making in New York, and I'm sure nobody could have taken more trouble. It tasted like flowers."

"Well, perhaps—" Mrs. Oakley had sounded dubious. "We'll wait and see."

When the letter and check came together, Dorinda's spirits had soared on wings. The hotel and the dairy would take all that she could supply of that quality; and though she had known that her success was less fortuitous than appeared on the surface, she had not paused to inquire whether it was owing to influence or to accident. "If everything goes well, I'll have twenty-five cows by next fall," she said hopefully, "and Ebenezer and Mary Joe Green to help Fluvanna."

"You always jump so far ahead, Dorinda."

"I'm made that way. I can't help it. If I didn't live in the future, I couldn't stand things as they are."

Now, in the soft afternoon light, she stretched her arms over her head with a gesture of healthy fatigue. The aromatic scent of the pine was in her nostrils. In the sun-steeped meadows below there was the murmurous chanting of grasshoppers. At the hour she felt peaceful and pleasantly drowsy, and all her troubles were lost in the sensation of physical ease. She was thinner than ever; her muscles were hard and elastic; the colour of her skin was burned to a pale amber; and the curves of her rich mouth were firmer and less appealingly feminine. In a few years the work of the farm would probably coarsen her features; but at twenty-three she was still young enough to ripen to a maturer beauty. Though her hands were roughened by work and the nails were stained and broken, she wasted no regret upon the disfigurement of her body as long as her senses remained benumbed by toil. She slept now without dreaming. This alone seemed to her to be worth any sacrifice of external softness.

Her glance travelled over the corn-field, where the shocks were gathered in rows amid the stubble, and she reflected that the harvest had been better than usual. Then her eyes passed along the orchard path to the new cow-barn, and she watched the figure of William Fairlamb climbing down from the roof. An agreeable sense of possession stole into her mind, while she looked from the cow-barn to the back of the house, and saw her mother moving along the path from the porch. There were a hundred and fifty hens in the poultry yard now, and it seemed to Dorinda that the old woman's happiness had simmered down into an enjoyment of chickens. Though she still worshipped Rufus, he was only a disappointment and an increasing anxiety. Of late he had done no work on the farm; his days were spent in hunting with Ike Pryde or Adam Snead, and it was evident to Dorinda that he was beginning to drink too much bad whiskey. It would be a relief, she felt, when November came and he went away for the winter.

Turning her head, as she prepared to leave the graveyard, she glanced beyond the many-coloured autumn scene to the distant chimneys of Five Oaks. How far off was the time when the sight of those red chimneys against a blue or grey sky would not stab into her heart? Her love was dead; and her regret clung less to the thought that love had ended in disappointment than to the supreme tragedy that love ended at all. Nothing endured. Everything perished of its own inner decay. That, after all, was the gnawing worm at the heart of experience. If either her love or her hatred had lasted, she would have found less bitterness in the savour of life.

For the first few weeks after her meeting with Jason on the edge of the pines, she had been enveloped in profound peace. Then, gradually, it seemed to her that the farther she moved away from him in reality, the closer he approached to her hidden life. As the days went by, the freedom she had won in his presence wore off like the effects of an anodyne, and the bondage of the nerves and the senses began to tighten again. Never, since she had looked into his face and had told herself that she was indifferent, had she known complete disillusionment. The trouble was, she discovered, that instead of remembering him as she had last seen him, her imagination created images which her reason denied. Not only her pain, but the very memory of pain that had once been, could leave, she found, a physical soreness.

Beyond the fields and the road the sun was sinking lower, and the western sky was stained with the colour of autumn fruits. While she watched the clouds, Dorinda remembered the heart of a pomegranate that she had seen in a window in New York; and immediately she was swept by a longing for the sights and sounds of the city. "There's no use thinking of that now," she said to herself, as she left the brow of the hill and walked down the path through the orchard. "Like so many other things, it is only when you look back on it that you seem to want it. While I was in New York I was longing to be away. There comes Nimrod with the cows, and Fluvanna bringing the milk-pails."

On the back porch her mother was drying apples, for the apple crop had been good, and the cellar was already stored with russets and winesaps.

"We ought to have dried apples enough to last us till next year," Mrs. Oakley remarked, while she wiped the discoloured blade of the knife on her apron. "The whole time I was slicing these apples, I couldn't help thinking how partial your father was to dried fruit, and last fall there were hardly any apples fit to keep." Raising her hand to her eyes, she squinted in the direction from which her daughter had come. "I can't make out who that is running across the corn-field, but whoever it is, he's in a mighty big hurry."

Dorinda followed her gaze. "It's Rufus. He looks as if something were after him."

Mrs. Oakley's face was twisted into what was called her "neuralgic look." "He promised me to mend that churn before night," she said in a dissatisfied tone. "But I haven't laid eyes on him since dinner time. He goes too much in bad company. I haven't got a particle of use for Ike Pryde and those two Kittery boys over by Plumtree."

Dorinda nodded. "I'm glad he is going away. The sooner, the better."

"I reckon he has just recollected the churn." Mrs. Oakley's tone was without conviction, and she added presently, "He certainly does look scared, doesn't he?"

"I wonder what could have frightened him?" As the boy drew nearer, Dorinda saw that he was panting for breath and that his usually florid face was blanched to a leaden pallor. "What on earth has happened, Rufus?" she called sharply.

He waved angrily to her to be silent. His palmetto hat was in his hand, and when he reached the porch, he hurled it through the open door into the hall. Though his breath came in gasps as if he were stifling for air, he picked up a hammer from one of the benches, and without stopping to rest, bent over the broken churn at the side of the step.

"What on earth has happened, Rufus?" Dorinda asked again. She saw that her mother was trembling with apprehension, and the sight exasperated her against Rufus.

"You ought to have let me go away last spring," the boy replied in a truculent tone. He lifted the hammer above his head and, still wheezing from his race, drove a nail crookedly into the bottom of the churn. His hand trembled, and Dorinda noticed that the swinging blow fell unevenly.

"You haven't done anything you oughtn't to, have you, son?" his mother inquired shrilly.

Rufus turned his head and stared at her in moody silence. Though his handsome face wore his usual sulky frown, Dorinda suspected that his resentful manner was a veil that covered an inner disturbance. His dark eyes held a smouldering fire, as if fear were waiting to leap out at a sound, and the hand in which he clutched the hammer had never stopped shaking.

"Don't you let on I wasn't here, no matter who asks you," he said doggedly. "It wasn't my fault anyway. There isn't anybody coming, is there?"

243

"No, that's Nimrod bringing up the cows," Dorinda rejoined impatiently. "I must put on my overalls."

Whatever happened, the cows must be milked, she reflected as she entered the house. This morning and evening ritual of the farm had become as inexorable as law. Hearts might be broken, men might live or die, but the cows must be milked.

When she came back from the dairy, Rufus had disappeared, but her mother, who was preparing supper, beckoned her into the kitchen. "I haven't found out yet what's the matter," whispered the old woman. "He won't open his mouth, though I can see that he's terribly upset about something. I'm worried right sick."

"He's probably got into a quarrel with somebody. You know how overbearing he is."

"I reckon I spoiled him." Mrs. Oakley's lip trembled while she poured a little coffee into a cup and then poured it back again into the coffee-pot. "Your father used to tell me I made a difference because he was the youngest. I s'pose I oughtn't to have done it, but it's hard to see how I could have helped it. He was a mighty taking child, was Rufus."

"Where is he now?"

"Up in his room. I've called him to supper. He's loaded his gun again, but he didn't seem to want me to notice, and he's put it back in the corner behind the door."

"Oh, well, try not to worry about it, Ma. Some fool's play most likely. Can I help you get supper? I'll be straight back as soon as I've slipped out of these overalls. There's a lot of work for me afterwards in the dairy."

She ran upstairs to her room, and on the way down, as she passed Rufus's door, she called cheerfully, "Rufus, aren't you coming to supper?"

To her surprise, his door opened immediately, as if he had been hiding behind it, and he came out and followed her meekly downstairs into the kitchen. His excitement had apparently left him, but his healthy colour had not returned and his eyes looked strained and bloodshot. Bad whiskey, she thought, though she said as amiably as she could, "If I were you, I'd go to New York next week even if the job isn't ready."

244

He looked at her gratefully. "I was just thinking I'd better do that."

His manner was so conciliatory that it made her vaguely uneasy. Jason had been like that, she remembered, in the weeks before he had jilted her, and, unjustly or not, she had come to regard suavity in men with suspicion. It was on the tip of her tongue to ask Rufus if he had got into a scrape; but she decided, as she brought his supper to the table, that it was a situation which she had better ignore. No good had ever come, she reflected with the ripe wisdom of experience, of putting questions to a man. What men wished you to know, and occasionally what they did not wish you to know, they would divulge in their own good time. Her mother, she knew, had spent her life trying to make men over, and what had come of her efforts except more trouble and stiffer material to work on?

When she sat down at the table, she expected her mother to begin her usual interrogation; but the old woman allowed Rufus to finish his supper undisturbed. Even when the last cake was lifted from the gridiron, and Mrs. Oakley dropped into her chair behind the tin coffee-pot, she was still silent. The cords in her throat twitched and strained when she raised a cup to her lips, and after a vain effort to swallow, she pushed her plate away with the food untasted.

"Poor Ma," thought the girl, watching the drawn grey face, where the veins in the temples bulged in knots of pain, "can she never have peace?" A longing seized her to fold the spare frame in her young arms and speak comforting words; but the habit of reserve was like an iron mould from which she could not break away. Nothing but death was strong enough to shatter that inherited restraint and resolve it into tenderness. While words of affection struggled to her lips, all she said was, "You look worn out. Is your neuralgia worse?"

"No, it ain't worse. I've got a stabbing pain in my temple, that's all."

Rising from her chair, she began to mix cornbread and gravy for Rambler and Flossie. Though she tottered when she moved, she put aside Dorinda's offer of help. "I'm used to doing things," she said, without stopping for an instant. "You and Rufus had better go along about what you want to do."

The hound and the cat were at her skirts, and she had just put the tin plates down for them and taken up the empty dish, when there was a sound of wheels on the rocks outside, and Dorinda, who was watching Rufus, saw him turn a muddy grey, like the discoloured white-wash on the walls.

"Don't you let on that I was off this afternoon, Ma," he whispered hoarsely.

"I declare, Rufus, you talk as if you were crazy," snapped Mrs. Oakley, flinching from a dart of neuralgia. Though her tone was merely one of irritation, her hands trembled so violently that the china dish she was holding dropped to the floor and crashed into bits. "This china never was a particle of account!" she exclaimed, as she bent over to pick up the pieces.

"I wonder who it can be this time of night?" Dorinda said more lightly than she would have believed possible.

"Maybe I'd better go," Rufus jerked out.

"You sit right down, son," his mother retorted tartly.

Going into the hall, Dorinda opened the front door and stood waiting in the square of lamplight on the threshold. It was a dark night, for the moon had not yet risen, and all that she could distinguish was what appeared to be the single shape of a horse and buggy. Only when the vehicle had jogged up the slope among the trees, and the driver had alighted and ascended the steps of the porch, did she recognize the squat shape and flabby features of Amos Wigfall, the sheriff. She had known him at the store in his political capacity as the familiar of every voter; yet friendly as he had always appeared to be, she could not repress a feeling of apprehension while she held out her hand. People, especially farmers, she knew, did not venture out, except with good reason, on bad roads after dark.

"Why, it's you, Mr. Wigfall!" she exclaimed, with cheerful hospitality. "Ma, Mr. Wigfall is here. I hope you've got some supper for him." And all the time she was thinking, "I might have known Rufus had done something foolish. Poor Ma!"

The sheriff heaved his bulky figure into the house. "I ain't come to supper, Dorinda," he said heartily. "Don't you go and get yo' Ma upset. I don't reckon it's anything to worry about. I wouldn't have come if I could have helped it."

Still grasping the girl's hand, he stood blinking apologetically in the glare of the lamp. His face was so bloated and so unctuous that it might have been the living embodiment of the fee system upon which it had fattened. He was chewing tobacco as he spoke, and wheeling abruptly he spat a wad into the night before he followed Dorinda down the hall to the kitchen. "The fact is I've come about Rufus," he explained, adding, "I hope I ain't intrudin', mum," as he whipped off his old slouch hat with an air of gallantry which reminded Dorinda of the burlesque of some royal cavalier.

"Oh, no, you ain't intruding, Mr. Wigfall," Mrs. Oakley replied. "What was it you said about Rufus?"

"He said he was sure it wasn't anything to worry about," Dorinda hastened to explain. She did not glance at Rufus while she spoke, yet she was aware that he had risen and was scowling at their visitor.

"Wall, as between friends," the sheriff remarked ingratiatingly, "I hope thar ain't a particle of truth in the charge; but Peter Kittery was found dead over by Whistling Spring this evening, and Jacob has got it into his head that 'twas Rufus that shot him."

"It's a lie!" Rufus shouted furiously. "I never went near Whistling Spring this evening. Ma knows I was mending her churn for her from dinner till supper time."

"Wall, I'm downright glad of that, son," Mr. Wigfall returned, and he looked as if he meant it, fee or no fee. "Yo' Pa was a good friend to me when he got a chance, and I shouldn't like to see his son mixed up in a bad business. Jacob says you and Peter had a fuss over cards last night at the store. But if you ain't been near Whistling Spring," he concluded, with triumphant logic, "it stands to reason that you couldn't have done it. You jest let him come along with me, mum," he added after a pause, as he turned to Mrs. Oakley. "I'll take good care of him, and send him back to you as soon as the hearing is over to-morrow. Thar ain't no need for you to worry a mite."

"I never saw Peter after last night!" Rufus cried out in a storm of rage and terror. "I never went near Whistling Spring. Ma knows I was working over her old churn all the evening."

His words and his tone struck with a chill against Dorinda's heart. Why couldn't the boy be silent? Why was he obliged, through some obliquity of nature, invariably to appear as a braggart and a bully? While she stood there listening to his furious denial of guilt, she

247

was as positive that he had killed Peter Kittery as if she had been on the spot.

For a minute there was silence; then a new voice began to speak, a voice so faint and yet so shrill that it was like the far-off whistle of a train. At first the girl did not recognize her mother's tone, and she glanced quickly at the door with the idea that a stranger might have entered after the sheriff.

"It couldn't have been Rufus," the old woman said, with that whistling noise. "Rufus was here with me straight on from dinner time till supper. I had him mending my old churn because I didn't want to use one of Dorinda's new ones. Dorinda went off in the fields to watch the hands," she continued firmly, "but Rufus was right here with me the whole evening."

When she had finished speaking, she reached for a chair and sat down suddenly, as if her legs had failed her. Rufus broke into a nervous laugh which had an indecent sound, Dorinda thought, and Mr. Wigfall heaved a loud sigh of relief.

"Wall, you jest come over to-morrow and tell that to the magistrate," he said effusively. "I don't reckon there could be a better witness for anybody. Thar ain't nobody round Pedlar's Mill that would be likely to dispute yo' word." Slinging his arm, he gave Rufus a hearty slap on the back. "I'm sorry I've got to take you along with me, son, but I hope you won't bear me any grudge. It won't hurt you to spend a night away from yo' Ma, and my wife, she'll be glad to have you sample her buckwheat cakes. I hope you're having good luck with your chickens," he remarked to Mrs. Oakley as an afterthought. "My wife has been meaning to get over and look at yo' white Leghorns."

"Tell her I'll be real glad to see her whenever she can get over," Mrs. Oakley replied, as she made an effort to struggle to her feet. "Ain't you going to take any clean clothes to wear to-morrow, Rufus? That shirt looks right mussed."

Rufus shook his head. "No, I'm not. If they want me, they can take me as I am."

"Wall, he looks all right to me," the sheriff observed, with jovial mirth. "I'll expect you about noon," he said, as he shook hands. "Don't you lose a minute's sleep. Thar ain't nothing in the world for you to worry about."

Picking up the kerosene lamp from the table, Dorinda went out on the porch to light the way to the gate. "There's a bad place near the 'rockery,'" she warned him.

He had climbed heavily into the buggy, and Rufus was in the act of mounting between the wheels, when Mrs. Oakley came out of the house and thrust a parcel wrapped in newspaper into the boy's hand. "There's a clean collar and your comb," she said, drawing quickly back. "Be sure not to forget them in the morning."

12

Standing there on the porch, with the light from the lamp she held flaring out against the silver-black of the night sky, Dorinda watched the buggy crawling down the dangerous road to the gate. Something dark and cold had settled over her thoughts. She could not shake it off though she told herself that it was unreasonable for her to feel so despondent. As if despondency, she added, were the product of reason!

Mother love was a wonderful thing, she reflected, a wonderful and a ruinous thing! It was mother love that had helped to make Rufus the mortal failure he was, and it was mother love that was now accepting, as a sacrifice, the results of this failure. Mrs. Oakley was a pious and God-fearing woman, whose daily life was lived beneath the ominous shadow of the wrath to come; yet she had deliberately perjured herself in order that a worthless boy might escape the punishment which she knew he deserved.

"I'm not like that," Dorinda thought. "I couldn't have done it." At the bottom of her heart, in spite of her kinship to Rufus, there was an outraged sense, not so much of justice as of economy. The lie appeared to her less sinful than wasted. After all, why should not Rufus be held responsible for his own wickedness? She was shocked; she was unsympathetic; she was curiously exasperated. Her mother's attitude to Rufus impressed her as sentimental rather than unselfish; and she saw in this painful occurrence merely one of the first fruits of that long weakness. Since she had been brought so close to reality she had had less patience with evasive idealism. "I suppose I'm different from other women," she meditated. "I may have lost feeling, or else it was left out of me when I was born. Some women would have gone on loving Jason no matter how he treated them;

but I'm not made that way. There's something deep down in me that I value more than love or happiness or anything outside myself. It may be only pride, but it comes first of all."

The buggy had disappeared into the night, and lowering the lamp, she turned and entered the house. As she closed the door the mocking screech of an owl floated in, and she felt that the frost was slipping over the threshold. All the ancient superstitions of the country gathered in her mind. It was foolish, she knew, to let herself remember these things at such a time; but she had lost control of her imagination, which galloped ahead dragging her reason after it.

In the kitchen she found her mother bending over the dish-pan with her arms plunged in soapsuds.

"Come to bed, Ma. I'll finish the dishes."

To her surprise, Mrs. Oakley did not resist. The spirit of opposition was crushed out of her, and she tottered as she turned away to wipe her hands on a cup-towel.

"I reckon I'd better," she answered meekly. "I don't feel as if I could stand on my feet another minute."

Putting her strong young arm about her, Dorinda led her across the hall into her bedroom. While the girl struck a match and lighted the lamp on the table, she saw that her mother was shaking as if she had been stricken with palsy.

"I'll help you undress, Ma."

"I can manage everything but my shoes, daughter. My fingers are too swollen to unbutton them."

"Don't you worry. I'll put you to bed." As she turned down the bed and smoothed out the coarse sheets and the patchwork quilt, it seemed to Dorinda that the inanimate objects in the room had borrowed pathos from their human companions. All the stitches that had gone into this quilt, happy stitches, sad stitches, stitches that had ended in nothing! Her eyes filled with tears, and she looked quickly away. What was it in houses and furniture that made them come to life in hours of suspense and tear at the heartstrings?

Mrs. Oakley was undressing slowly, folding each worn, carefully mended garment before she placed it on a chair near the foot of the bed.

"Do you reckon they will do anything to Rufus?" she asked presently in a quavering voice.

She had released her hair from the tight coil at the back of her head, and it hung now, combed and plaited by Dorinda, in a thin grey braid on her shoulders. The childish arrangement gave a fantastic air to the shadow on the whitewashed wall.

"Not after what you said. Didn't you hear Mr. Wigfall tell you that he was taking him just for the night?"

Mrs. Oakley turned her head, and the shadow at her back turned with her. "Yes, I heard him. Well, if the Lord will give me strength to go through with it, I'll never ask for anything else."

"He'll be more likely to help you if you get some sleep and stop worrying. The Lord helps good sleepers." Though she spoke flippantly, she was frightened by the look in her mother's face.

"I don't feel as if I could close my eyes." Mrs. Oakley had climbed into bed, and was lying, straight and stiff as an effigy, under the quilt. "Don't you think it would be a comfort if we were to read a chapter in the Bible?"

Dorinda broke into a dry little laugh. "No, I don't. The only comforting thing I can imagine is to get my head on a pillow. I've got seven cows to milk by sunrise, and that is no easy job."

"Yes, you'd better go," her mother assented reluctantly, and she added with a sigh, "I can't help feeling that something dreadful is going to happen."

"You won't prevent it by lying awake. Don't get up in the morning until you're obliged to. I'll milk the cows before day and get Fluvanna to help about breakfast as soon as she comes. It's a long way to Queen Elizabeth Court-House, and we'll have to allow plenty of time for the horses. Do you want anything more?" She resisted an impulse to stoop and kiss the wrinkled cheek because she knew that the unusual exhibition of tenderness would embarrass them both. "Shall I put out the lamp for you?"

"No, I like a little light. You can see so many things in the dark after the fire goes out."

Dorinda moved away as noiselessly as she could; but she had barely crossed the hall before she heard a muffled sound in the room, and knew that her mother was out of bed and on her knees. "I can't do anything," thought the girl desperately. "It is going to kill her, and I can't do anything to prevent it." Every muscle in her body ached from the strain of the day while she washed the dishes and cleaned the kitchen for the next morning. She realized that she should have to do most of her farm work before sunrise, and she decided that, in case Fluvanna came late, it would be well to put out whatever she needed for breakfast. After that—well, even if Rufus had murdered somebody, she couldn't keep awake any longer.

In the morning, when she came back into the house after milking, she found that her mother was already in the kitchen, and that a pot of coffee was bubbling on the stove. Of course Fluvanna, on the day when she was particularly needed, had contrived to be late.

"I told you not to worry about breakfast, Ma," Dorinda said, provoked in spite of her pity.

"I know you did, but I couldn't lie in bed any longer. I was so afraid you might oversleep yourself and not wake me in time." She was the victim of a nervous apprehension lest they should be too late for the magistrate, and it was futile to attempt to reason her out of her folly. "You sit right down in your overalls and drink your coffee while it's hot," she continued, stirring restlessly. "I've got some fried eggs and bacon to keep up your strength."

"My strength is all right." Dorinda washed her hands and then came over to the table where breakfast was waiting for her. "The sun isn't up yet, and we can't start before day."

"Well, I wanted to be ready in plenty of time. You'll have to be away from the farm all day, won't you?"

"I don't know," Dorinda rejoined briskly. "Fluvanna and Nimrod will have to manage the best they can. I'm not going to worry about it. People can always be spared easier than they think they can."

Her animation, however, was wasted, for her mother was not following her. Mrs. Oakley had grown so restless that she could not sit still at the table, and she jumped up and ran to the stove or the safe whenever she could find an excuse. She wore the strained expression of a person who is listening for an expected sound and is afraid of missing it by a moment of inadvertence. Already, before lighting the stove, she had put on her Sunday dress of black alpaca, and had protected it in front by an apron of checked blue and white gingham. If she had had the courage, Dorinda suspected, she would have cooked breakfast in her widow's bonnet, with the streamer of rusty crape at her back.

"Is that somebody going along the road?" she inquired whenever Dorinda looked up from her plate.

"No, I don't hear anybody," the girl replied patiently. "Try to eat something, or you'll be sick."

Mrs. Oakley obediently lifted a bit of egg on her fork, and then put it down again before it had touched her lips. "I don't feel as if I could swallow a morsel."

"Drink a little coffee anyway," Dorinda pleaded.

Again the old woman made a futile effort to swallow. "I don't know what can be the matter with me," she said, "but my throat feels as if it were paralyzed."

"Well, I'll fix up a snack for you, and you can nibble at it on the way. Somebody will be sure to ask us to dinner. Now, I'll clear the table before I get ready."

But, after all, Dorinda was left at home for the day. Just as Nimrod, animated by misfortune, was leading Dan and Beersheba out to the wagon, a buggy drove briskly into the yard, and Nathan Pedlar alighted.

"I kind of thought you'd want a man with your Ma, Dorinda," he explained, "so I left Bob Shafer in charge of the store and came right over. Rufus spoke to me as he was going by with the sheriff last night, and I told him I'd take his Ma to the Court-House."

Though Dorinda was doubtful at first, Mrs. Oakley responded immediately. In spite of her protracted experience with masculine helplessness, she had not lost her confidence in the male as a strong prop in the hour of adversity. "I can't tell you how thankful I am to have you, Nathan," she replied eagerly. "Dorinda had just as well stay at home and look after the farm."

"Don't you think I'd better go too, Ma?" the girl asked, not without a tinge of exasperation in her tone. It seemed absurd to her that her mother should prefer to have Nathan Pedlar stand by her simply because he happened to be a man.

"I don't believe she'll need you, Dorinda," remarked Nathan, who, like Nimrod, was inspired by adversity. "But if you feel you'd like to come, I reckon we can all three squeeze into my buggy."

"There ain't a bit of use in your going," Mrs. Oakley insisted. "You just stay right here and take care of things."

"Well, I won't go." Dorinda gave way after a resistance that

254

was only half-hearted. "Take care of her, Nathan, and make her eat something before she gets there."

Running into the house, she wrapped two buttered rolls and boiled eggs in a red and white napkin, and put them into a little basket. Then she added a bottle of blackberry wine, and carried the basket out to the buggy, while Mrs. Oakley tied on her bonnet with trembling hands.

"Where's my bottle of camphor, Dorinda?"

"Here it is, Ma, in your reticule. Be sure and take a little blackberry wine if you feel faint." Not until she had watched the buggy drive through the gate and out on the road, where the sun was coming up in a ball of fire, did the girl understand what a relief it was not to go. "I believe she'd rather have Nathan," she decided, as she went upstairs to change into her old gingham dress, "because he doesn't know that she is not telling the truth."

When she thought of it afterwards, that day towered like a mountain in the cloudy background of her life. Alone on the farm, for the first time in her recollection, she felt forlorn and isolated. It was impossible for her to keep her mind fixed on her tasks. Restlessness, like an inarticulate longing, pricked at her nerves. When the morning work in the dairy was over, she wandered about the farm, directing the work in the fields, and stopping for a minute or two to talk with old Matthew Fairlamb, who was handing up the shingles to his son William on the roof of the new barn. At a little distance the old house of the overseer, which had been used as a tobacco-barn since her great-grandfather's death, was being cleaned and repaired for Jonas Walsh (one of the "poor Walshes") who had undertaken to work as a manager in return for a living and a share of the crops. After Rufus went, Mrs. Oakley insisted, a white man and his family would be required on the place, and though Dorinda preferred loneliness to such company, she found it less wearing to yield to her mother than to argue against her opinion. "Mrs. Walsh will be company for Ma, anyway," she said to herself. "Even if she is slatternly, they will still have chickens in common."

"Do you think Jonas will be useful?" she inquired of old Matthew, while she paused to watch the expert shingling of the roof.

Old Matthew made a dubious gesture, "Mebbe he will, an' mebbe he won't. I ain't prophesyin'."

"Well, he can shoot anyhow," William observed cynically, as he stooped down for the shingles his father held up. "He's got a gun and a coon dog."

"But I need him to work. How can you make a living out of the land unless you work it?"

Old Matthew chuckled. "The trouble with this here land is that tobaccy has worn it out. I ain't never seen the land yit that it wouldn't wear out if you gave it a chance. You take my advice, Dorindy, and don't have nothin' more to do with tobaccy. As long as you don't smoke and don't chaw, thar ain't no call for you to put up with it."

"I won't," Dorinda replied with determination. "All the tobacco-fields are giving way to cowpeas."

"I see you're making a new field alongside of the old one."

"Yes. I sowed sweet clover with lime, and turned the clover under when it was in bloom. I can't afford to do that again. It was an experiment, but it improved the land."

"You're right thar, honey. Put yo' heart in the land. The land is the only thing that will stay by you."

She smiled and passed on, stopping to say a few words to Mary Joe Green at the door of the hen-house. Though she was aware that her aimless movements accomplished nothing, she could not settle down to the steady work which was awaiting her. The sound of a wagon in the road shook her nerves into a quiver of fear, and she started whenever a bird flew overhead or an acorn dropped on the dead leaves at her feet. At dinner time she did not kindle a fire in the stove, but drank a glass of buttermilk and ate a "pone" of corn-bread while she stood on the front porch and looked at the road. One moment she wished that she had gone with her mother to the Court-House, and the next she was glad that she had waited at home. Whatever Rufus's fate might be, she felt that the mental strain would be the end of her mother. Even if Rufus were to go free, Mrs. Oakley's conscience would torment her to death.

As the day declined the place became insupportable to her, and leaving the house, she walked across the yard to the gate, with Rambler and Flossie trailing at her heels. The road under the honey-locust tree was strewn with oblong brown pods, as glossy as satin, and treading over them, she walked slowly past the bridge and up the shaded slope between the pasture and the band of Hoot Owl Woods. In the pasture she could see the Jerseys gathered by the stream under the willows, and now and then a silver tinkle of cowbells floated over the trumpet-vine on the fence.

It was a rich October afternoon, with a sky of burnished blue and an air of carnival in the wine-red and ashen-bronze of the woods. For an instant the brightness hurt her eyes, and when she opened them it seemed to her that the autumnal radiance fluttered like a blown shawl over the changeless structure of the landscape. Beneath the fugitive beauty the stern features of the country had not softened.

She walked on, still followed by Rambler and Flossie, beyond the woods to the fork of the road. Looking away from the gate of Five Oaks, she kept her eyes on the acres of broomsedge belonging to Honeycomb Farm. The stretch of road beyond the burned cabin was deserted, and the only sound was the monotonous droning of insects and the dropping of persimmons or acorns on the dead leaves under the trees. Far away, in the direction of Old Farm, the shocked corn on the hill was swimming in a rain of apricot-coloured lights. "If only it would last," she thought, "things would not be so hard to bear. But it is like happiness. Before you know that you have found it, it goes."

Turning away, because beauty was like a knife in her heart, she called Rambler back to her side. In the middle of the road, bathed in the apricot-coloured glow, Flossie was sitting, and farther on, she saw the figures of old Matthew and William Fairlamb on their way home from work. When they reached her they spoke without stopping.

"Good evening. We'll be over bright and early tomorrow."

"Good evening to you both. There won't be a killing frost to-night, will there?"

"Not enough to hurt. Thar ain't nothin' but flowers left out by this time, I reckon."

Old Matthew's cheeks were as red as winter apples, and his eyes twinkled like black haws in their sockets.

"Hee-hee! When thar ain't nothin' to hurt, we've no need to worry!"

As they trudged away, she turned and looked after them. She wanted to ask what they had heard of the shooting; but she resisted the impulse until they were too far away for her words to reach them. Standing there, while the two figures dwindled gradually into the blue distance, she was visited again by the feeling that the moment was significant, if only she could discover the meaning of it before it eluded her. Strange how often that sensation returned to her now! Everything at which she gazed; the frosted brown and yellow and wine-red of the landscape; the shocked corn against the sunset; the figures of the two men diminishing in the vague smear of the road; all these images were steeped in an illusion of mystery. "I've let myself get wrought up over nothing," she thought, with an endeavour to be reasonable.

By the time she came within sight of the house again the afterglow was paling, and a chill had crept through the thick shawl that she wore. Perhaps, in spite of old Matthew, there would be a heavy frost before morning, and she was glad to reflect that only the few summer flowers in her mother's rockery would be blighted. Smoke was rising from two of the chimneys, and she knew that Mary Joe had kindled fires in the kitchen and in her mother's chamber. Already Fluvanna would be well on with the milking. It was the first time Dorinda had trusted it to the girl and Nimrod, and she hoped that there would be nothing to find fault with when she went out to the barn.

Two hours later, when the milking and the straining were both over, she hurried out of the dairy at the noise of wheels in the darkness. As the buggy drew up to the steps, she saw that her mother was seated between Rufus and Nathan; and even before she caught the words they shouted, she understood that the boy had been discharged. It was what she had expected; yet after the assurance reached her, her anxiety was still as heavy as it had been all day. When her eyes fell on her mother's shrunken figure she realized that the old woman must have paid a fearful price for her son's freedom. "She looks bled," the girl thought bitterly. "She looks as if she would crumble to a handful of dust if you touched her." A hot anger against Rufus flamed in her heart. Then she saw that the boy was shaking with emotion, and her anger was smothered in pity. After all, who was to blame? Who was ever to blame in life?

"It's all right, Dorinda," Nathan said, as he helped Mrs. Oakley to the ground and up on the porch. "Your Ma held up splendidly, but it's been too much for her. She's worn clean out, I reckon."

"I wish you'd been there to see the way she did it," Rufus added. "Nobody said a word after she got through." Had he actually forgotten, Dorinda asked herself, that his mother had sworn to a lie in order to save him?

13

For the second time in her life Mrs. Oakley allowed herself to be put to bed without protest. She hung limp and cold when they placed her in a chair, and watched her children with vacant eyes while Rufus piled fresh logs on the fire and Dorinda brought bottles of hot water wrapped in her orange shawl. When the grey flannelette nightgown was slipped over her shoulders, the old woman spoke for the first time since she had entered the house.

"Dorinda, the Lord gave me strength."

"They have killed her," the girl thought resentfully; but she said only, "Now you must get to bed as quick as you can."

Mrs. Oakley stared up at her with eyes that were wind-swept in their bleakness. Her face looked flattened and drawn to one side, as if some tremendous pressure had just been removed. "I reckon I'd better," she answered listlessly.

"You must try to eat something. Fluvanna is making you some tea and toast."

"I ain't sick enough for tea."

"Then I'll make you a cream toddy. There's some nice cream I saved for you."

While Dorinda was speaking she leaned over the bed and wrapped the clammy feet in the orange shawl. "Can you feel the hot water bottles?" she asked. The feet that she warmed so carefully were as stiff already, she told herself in terror, as if they belonged to a corpse. Neither the hot water nor the blazing fire could put any warmth into the shivering body.

"Yes, I feel them, but I'm sort of numbed."

"Now I'll make the toddy. I've got some whiskey put away where Rufus couldn't find it. If Fluvanna brings your supper, try to eat the egg anyway."

"I'll try, but I feel as if I couldn't keep it down," Mrs. Oakley replied submissively.

Flames were leaping up the chimney, and the shadows had melted into the cheerful light. When Dorinda returned with the cream toddy, Mrs. Oakley drank it eagerly, and with the stimulant of the whiskey in her veins, she was able to sit up in bed and eat the supper Fluvanna had prepared. It was long after the coloured girl's hour for going home, but the excitement had braced her to self-sacrifice, and she had offered to stay on for the night. "I can make up a pallet jest as easy as not in yo' Ma's room," she said to Dorinda, "an' I'll fix Mr. Rufus' breakfast for him, so he can catch the train befo' day."

There were few negroes who did not develop character, either good or bad, in a crisis, Dorinda reflected a little later as she went out to the dairy. Though there was no need for her to visit the dairy, since Fluvanna and Nimrod had finished the work, she felt that she could not sleep soundly until she had inspected the milk. Was this merely what Rufus called "woman's fussiness," she wondered, or was it the kind of nervous mania that afflicted even the most successful farmer?

The brilliant autumn day had declined into a wan evening. From the dark fields the wind brought the trail of woodsmoke mingled with the effluvium of rotting leaves; and this scent invaded her thoughts like the odour of melancholy. Not even the frosty air or the fragrant breath of the cows in the barn could dispel the lethargy which had crept over her. "I'm tired out," she reasoned. "I've been going too hard the last six months, and I feel the strain as soon as I stop." Though she was saddened by the haunting pathos of life, she did not feel the intimate pang of grief. All that, it seemed to her, was over for ever. The power to pity was still hers, for compassion is a detached impulse, but she had lost beyond recall the gift of poignant emotion. Nothing had penetrated that dead region around her heart. Not her father's death, not her mother's illness—nothing. Drought had withered her, she told herself cynically, and the locust had eaten away the green of her spirit.

In the morning, Rufus went off on the early train, and Dorinda drew a breath of relief as she turned back to her work. The shock of the tragedy appeared to have cleared the boy's temper, and he

261

showed genuine distress when he parted from his mother. "I feel as if I'd never see her again," he said to Dorinda on the porch, while he was waiting for the farmer who had promised to stop for him on the way to the station.

Dorinda shook her head. Helplessness in the face of misery acted always as an irritant on her nerves. "You never can tell," she replied. "But remember all you have cost her and try to keep straight in the future."

"I swear I'll never give her another minute's worry," he responded, stuffing his handkerchief into his pocket.

Perhaps he meant it; but it seemed to Dorinda that his repentance, like his gift with tools, was too facile. "Whatever comes of this, it has been the death of Ma," she thought, as she went into the house.

When the day's churning was over, and she was in her mother's room, the new doctor from the Court-House arrived with his instruments and his medicine case. He was a brisk, very ugly young man, with an awkward raw-boned figure, and an honest face which was covered with unsightly freckles. As different from Jason as any man could well be! He had risen by sheer ability from the poorer class, and already, notwithstanding his plain appearance and uncompromising honesty, he had built up a better practice than the hereditary one of the Greylocks. For one thing, he insisted upon having his fees paid, and it was natural, Dorinda had discovered, to value advice more highly when it was not given away.

As the doctor sat down beside Mrs. Oakley's bed, she opened her eyes and looked at him without surprise and without welcome. Her bed was smooth and spotlessly clean; the best quilt of log-cabin design lay over her feet; and she was wearing a new nightgown which was buttoned closely about her neck. Without her clothes, she had the look, in spite of her ravaged face, of a very old child.

"I've never spent a day in bed in my life, doctor," she said, "except when my children were born."

"I know," he rejoined, with dry sympathy. "That is the trouble."

He did not waste words, but bent over immediately to begin his examination; and when it was over, he merely patted the old woman's shoulder before packing away his instruments.

"You'll have to stay in bed a while now," he said, as he stood up with his case in his hands. "I'll leave some medicine with your daughter; but it isn't medicine you need; it is rest."

Her groping gaze followed him with irrepressible weariness. "I don't know what will become of the chickens," she said. "I reckon everything will go to rack and ruin, but I can't help it. I've done all I could."

He turned on the threshold. "My dear Mrs. Oakley, you couldn't get up if you tried. Your strength has given out."

She smiled indifferently. All the nervous energy upon which she had lived for forty years was exhausted. There was nothing now but the machine which was rapidly running down. "Yes, I reckon I'm worn out," she responded, and turned her face to the wall.

Not until they had left the porch and crossed the trodden ragweed to where the buggy was waiting, did Dorinda summon the courage to ask a question.

"Is she seriously ill, doctor?"

At her words he stopped and looked straight into her eyes, a look as bare and keen as a blade. "She isn't ill at all in the strict sense of the word," he answered. "She told the truth when she said that she was worn out."

"Then she will never be up again?"

"One never knows. But I think this is the beginning of the end." He hesitated, and added regretfully, "I ought not to put it so bluntly."

She shook her head. "I'd rather know. Poor Ma! She is only sixty-two. It has come so suddenly."

"Suddenly." The word broke from him like an oath. "Why, the woman in there has been dying for twenty years!"

Her eyes were stony while she watched him mount into his buggy and turn the horse's head toward the gate. The wheels spun over the rocks and out into the road, as if they were revolving over the ice in her heart. Would nothing thaw the frozen lake that enveloped her being? Would she never again become living and human? The old sense of the hollowness of reality had revived. Though she knew it was her mother of whom they had been speaking, the words awoke only echoes in her thoughts. She longed with all her soul to suffer acutely; yet she could feel nothing within this colourless void in which she was imprisoned.

When the buggy had disappeared, she retraced her steps to the house and entered her mother's room with a smile on her lips.

"You'll have to rest now, Ma, no matter how you hate it."

At Dorinda's cheerful voice, the old woman turned over and looked at her daughter as if she were a stranger.

"I don't know how you'll manage," she answered; but her tone was perfunctory.

"Oh, we'll manage all right. Don't you worry. Just try to get well, Ma."

A change of expression rippled like a shadow over the grey features, and passed without leaving a trace. "I was afraid maybe the doctor didn't think I was sick enough to stay in bed. I know I ain't exactly sick, but I seem to have given way. I reckon Mary Joe can look after the chickens till I'm able to be up."

After this she fell into a doze from which she did not awaken until Dorinda brought her favourite dinner of jowl and turnip salad.

"The doctor says you must eat, Ma, or you'll never get back your strength."

"I know I ought to, daughter, but I feel as if something was choking me."

Day after day, month after month. Nothing else all through the autumn and winter.

Though Mrs. Oakley lived more than a year longer, she was never able again to leave her bed. For the greater part of the time she lay, silent and inert, in a state between waking and sleeping, unconcerned after all her fruitless endeavours. Rufus, she never asked for, and when his letters were read to her, she would smile vaguely and turn away as if she had ceased to be interested. Old Rambler spent his days on a mat at the side of her bed, and Flossie lay curled up on the patchwork quilt over her feet. If they were absent long, she would begin to move restlessly, and beg presently that they should be brought back. At the end, they were the only companions that she desired, for, as she said once, they "did not bother her with questions." The tragedy to Dorinda was not so much in her mother's slow dying as in her unconditional surrender to decay. For more than forty years she had fought her dauntless fight against the sordid actuality, and at the last she appeared to
264

become completely reconciled to her twin enemies, poverty and dirt. Nothing made any difference to her now, and because nothing made any difference to her, dying was the happiest part of her life.

"There ain't any use struggling," she said once, while Dorinda was cleaning her room, and after a long pause, "It doesn't seem just right that we have to be born. It ain't worth all the trouble we go through."

But there were other days when her inextinguishable energy would flare up in sparks, and she would insist upon sitting up in bed while the white Leghorns flocked by the window. Then she would recognize her favourite hens and call them by name; and once she had Romeo, the prize rooster, brought into her room, and kept him under her eyes, until he began to strut and behave indelicately, when she "shooed" him out in her old peremptory manner. Frequently, in the last few months, she asked to have Dan and Beersheba led to her window. Tears would come into her eyes while the long sad faces of the horses looked at her through the panes, and she would murmur plaintively, "There's a heap of understanding in animals. You'll never let those horses want, will you, daughter?"

"Never, Ma. In a few years, if nothing happens, I'll turn them out to pasture for the rest of their lives."

Mrs. Oakley would smile as if she had forgotten, and after a long silence, she would begin talking in an animated voice of her girlhood and her parents. As the weeks went by, all the years of her marriage and motherhood vanished from her memory, and her mind returned to her early youth when she was engaged to the young missionary. Her old tropical dream came back to her; in her sleep she would ramble on about palm trees and crocodiles and ebony babies. "I declare, it seems just as if I'd been there," she said one morning. "It's queer how much more real dreams can be than the things you're going through."

At the end of the year, in the middle of the night before she died, she awoke Dorinda, and talked for a long time about the heathen and the sacrifices that Presbyterian missionaries had made to bring them to Christ. "Your great-grandfather was a wonderful scholar," she said, "and I reckon that's where you get most of your sense. I s'pose missionaries have to be scholars. They need something

265

besides religion to fall back on in their old age." Never once did she allude to anything that had occurred since her marriage, and she appeared to have forgotten that she had ever known Joshua.

The next afternoon she died in her sleep while Nathan was sitting beside her bed. For a few minutes Dorinda broke down and wept, less from grief than from the knowledge that grief was expected of her; and Nathan, who was always at his best in the house of mourning, won her everlasting gratitude by his behaviour. She found herself depending upon him as if he had been some ideal elder brother such as she had never known. So naturally that fate seemed to have arranged it on purpose, he assumed authority over the household and the funeral. He thought of everything, and everybody deferred to him. Funerals were the only occasions when he had ever risen to dignity, and though he had sincerely liked Mrs. Oakley, the few days before her burial were among the pleasantest that he had ever spent in his life.

"I shall never forget how good you have been," Dorinda said, when it was over. "I don't know what I should have done without you." And though the words were spoken impulsively, as a matter of fact she never, in the future, forgot Nathan's kindness. It was a mark of her proud and self-sufficient nature that she could not forget either gratitude or resentment.

When he had driven away, she turned to Fluvanna, who was picking up bits of rusty crape from the floor of the porch.

"I really don't know what we should have done without him," she remarked over again.

"If you ax me, Miss Dorinda, he is one handy man at a funeral," answered Fluvanna, who relapsed into dialect on tragic or perilous occasions. "I was thinkin' right along how pleased yo' Ma would have been if she could have seen him, for she cert'n'y did like handy folks about her."

"Poor Ma, I wish she could have had the chickens a few years earlier," Dorinda sighed. "To think of the years she went without a cow."

"Well, she enjoyed 'em while she had 'em," Fluvanna responded fervently. "Have you thought yet what you're goin' to do, Miss Dorinda?"

"Yes, I've thought. The farm is mine. Ma left it to me, and I'm going to stay on as we are."

"Just you and me? Won't you get lonesome without some white folks?"

"After Jonas Walsh moves out of the overseer's house, I'll engage Martin Flower, who is a better farmer, and has a sensible wife. Mary Joe can take care of the chickens, and I'm going to hire her brother Ebenezer to help Nimrod with the cows. If everything goes well this winter, I'll be ready to start a real dairy in the spring. Then I'll need more hands, so we shan't be lonely."

"Naw'm, I don't reckon we'll get lonesome, not the way we work," Fluvanna agreed. "I ain' never seen no man work as hard as you do, Miss Dorinda. Yo' Ma told me befo' she passed away that you had stayin' power and she reckoned that you was the only one of the family that had. Sprightliness don't git you far, she said, unless you've got stayin' power enough to keep you after you git thar. Well, it's all your'n now, ain't it?" she inquired placidly, as Dorinda's eyes swept the horizon.

"Yes, it's all mine." Walking over to the edge of the porch, Dorinda looked across the vague, glimmering fields. Another autumn had gone. Another sunset like the heart of a pomegranate was fading out in the west. Again the wandering scents of wood smoke and rotting leaves came and went on the wind.

For an instant, the permanence of material things, the inexorable triumph of fact over emotion, appeared to be the only reality. These things had been ageless when her mother was young; they would be still ageless when she herself had become an old woman. Over the immutable landscape human lives drifted and vanished like shadows.

14

When she looked back on the years that followed her mother's death, Dorinda could remember nothing but work. Out of a fog of recollection there protruded bare outlines which she recognized as the milestones of her prosperity. She saw clearly the autumn she had turned the eighteen-acre field into pasture; the failure of her first experiment with ensilage; the building of the new dairy and cowbarns; the gradual increase of her seven cows into a herd. Certain dates stood out in her farm calendar. The year the blight had fallen on her corn-field and she had had to buy fodder from James Ellgood; the year she had first planted alfalfa; the year she had lost a number of her cows from contagious abortion; the year she had reclaimed the fields beyond Poplar Spring; the year her first prize bull had won three blue ribbons. With the slow return of fertility to the soil, she had passed, by an unconscious process, into mute acquiescence with the inevitable. The bitter irony of her point of view had shaded into a cheerful cynicism which formed a protective covering over her mind and heart. She had worked relentlessly through the years; but it was work that she had enjoyed, and above all it was work that had created anew the surroundings amid which she lived. In a changed form her mother's frustrated passion to redeem the world was finding concrete expression.

At thirty-three, the perspective of the last ten years was incredibly shortened. All the cold starry mornings when she had awakened before day and crept out to the barn by lantern light to attend to the milking, appeared to her now as a solitary frozen dawn. All the bleak winters, all the scorching summers, were a single day; all the evenings, when she had dreamed half asleep in the firelit dusk, were a single night. She could not separate these years into seasons.

In her long retrospect they were crystallized into one flawless pattern.

Through those ten years, while she struggled to free the farm from debt, she had scrimped and saved like a miser; and this habit of saving, she knew, would cling to her for the rest of her life. She went without butter; she drank only buttermilk, in order that she might keep nothing back from the market. Her clothes were patched and mended as long as they held together, and she had stopped going to church because her pride would not suffer her to appear there in overalls, or in the faded calico dresses she wore in the house. Though she was obliged to hire women to help her with the milking and in the dairy, she herself worked harder than any of them. Nothing, she told herself grimly, could elude her vigilance. In her passionate recoil from the thriftlessness of the poor, she had developed a nervous dread of indolence which reminded her of her mother. She went to bed, stupefied by fatigue, as soon as the last pound of butter was wrapped for the early train; yet she was up again before the break of day while the hands were still sleeping. And only Fluvanna, who lived in the house with her now, knew the hours she spent beside her lamp counting the pounds of butter and the number of eggs she had sent to market. If only she could save enough to pay off the mortgage and return the money she had borrowed from the Faradays, she felt that she should begin to breathe freely for the first time in her life.

And there was more than hard work in her struggle; there was unflagging enterprise as well. Her father had worked harder than she could ever do, toiling summer and winter, day and night, over the crops, which always failed because they were expected to thrive on so little. She remembered him perpetually hauling manure or shredding fodder, until he loomed in her memory as a titanic image of the labourer who labours without hope. "The truth is, I would rather have failed at the start than have gone on like that," she thought. "I was able to take risks because I was too unhappy to be afraid." Yes, she had had the courage of desperation, and that had saved her from failure. Without borrowed money, without the courage to borrow money, she could never have made the farm even a moderate success. This had required not only perseverance but audacity as well; and it had required audacity again to permeate the methodical science of farming with the spirit of adventure. Interest, excitement even, must be instilled into the heartless routine. The hours of work never varied. Chores were done by necessity, as in the old days without system, but by the stroke of the clock. Each milker had her own place, and milked always the same cows. After the first trial or two, Dorinda had yielded to the reluctance of the cow when her accustomed milker was changed. She had borrowed money again, "hiring money" they called it at Pedlar's Mill, to buy her first Jersey bull; but the daughters of that bull were still her best butter-making cows.

Gradually, as the years passed, her human associations narrowed down to Fluvanna's companionship and the Sunday afternoon visits of Nathan Pedlar and his children. The best years of her youth, while her beauty resisted hard work and sun and wind, were shared only with the coloured woman with whom she lived. She had prophesied long ago that Fluvanna would be a comfort to her, and the prophecy was completely fulfilled. The affection between the two women had outgrown the slender tie of mistress and maid, and had become as strong and elastic as the bond that holds relatives together. They knew each other's daily lives; they shared the one absorbing interest in the farm; they trusted each other without discretion and without reserve. Fluvanna respected and adored her mistress; and Dorinda, with an inherited feeling of condescension, was sincerely attached to her servant. Though Dorinda still guarded the reason of her flight to New York, she did this less from dread of Fluvanna's suspecting the truth than from secret terror of the enervating thought of the past. That was over and done with, and every instinct of her nature warned her to let dead bones lie buried. Sometimes on winter nights, when the snow was falling or the rain blowing in gusts beyond the window, the two women would sit for an hour, when work was over, in front of the log fire in Dorinda's room which had once been her mother's chamber. Then they would talk sympathetically of the cows and the hens, and occasionally they would speak of Fluvanna's love affairs and of Dorinda's years in the city. The coloured girl would ask eager questions in the improved grammar her mistress had taught her. "I don't see how you could bear to come back to this poky place. But, of course, when yo'

270

Pap died somebody had to be here to look after things. I don't reckon you'll ever go back, will you?"

"No, I shall never go back. I had enough of it when I was there."

"Wouldn't you rather look at the sights up there than at cows and chickens?"

Dorinda would shake her head thoughtfully. "Not if they are my cows and chickens."

In this reply, which was as invariable as a formula, she touched unerringly the keynote of her character. The farm belonged to her, and the knowledge aroused a fierce sense of possession. To protect, to lift up, rebuild and restore, these impulses formed the deepest obligation her nature could feel.

Though she talked frankly to Nathan about the farm and the debts which had once encumbered it, she had never given him her confidence as generously as she had bestowed it on Fluvanna. Kind as he had been, the fact that he was a man and a widower made an impalpable, and she told herself ridiculous, barrier between them. She had grown to depend upon him, but it was a practical dependence, as devoid of sentiment as her dependence upon the clock or the calendar. If he had dropped out of her life, she would have missed him about the barn and the stable; and it would have been difficult, she admitted, to manage the farm without his advice. There were the children, too, particularly the younger boy, who had been born with a clubfoot. The one human emotion left in Dorinda's heart, she sometimes thought, was her affection for Rose Emily's boy, John Abner.

If he had been her own son he could not have been closer to her; and his infirmity awakened the ardent compassion that love assumed in her strong and rather arrogant nature. Though he was barely fourteen, he was more congenial with her than any grown person at Pedlar's Mill. He devoured books as she used to do when she was a girl, and he was already developing into a capable farmer. Years ago she had given Nathan no peace until he had taken the child to town and had had an operation performed on his crippled foot; and when no improvement had resulted, she had insisted that he should have John Abner's shoes made from measurements. As a little girl, her mother had always said to her that she preferred lame ducks to well ones; and John Abner was the only lame duck that had ever come naturally into her life. Fortunately, he was a boy of deep, though reserved, affections, and he returned in his reticent way the tenderness Dorinda lavished upon him. Minnie May, who had grown into a plain girl of much character, had been jealous at first; but a little later, when she became engaged to be married, she was prudently reconciled to the difference Dorinda made in her life. The two other children, though they were both healthy and handsome, with a dash of Rose Emily's fire and spirit, were received as lightly and forgotten as quickly as warm days in winter or cool ones in summer. The girl Lena, who had just turned seventeen, was a pretty, vain, and flirtatious creature, with a head "as thick with beaux," Fluvanna observed, "as a brier patch with briers"; and the boy, Bertie, familiarly called "Bud," was earning a good salary in a wholesale grocery store in the city. It was pleasant to have Nathan and the children come over every week; but John Abner was the only one Dorinda missed when accident or bad weather kept them away. In the beginning they had visited her in the afternoons, and she had had nothing better to offer them than popcorn or roasted apples and chestnuts; but as the years passed and debts were paid, there was less need of rigid economy, and she had drifted into the habit of having the family with her at Sunday dinner. This had gradually become the one abundant meal of the week, and she and Fluvanna both looked forward to it with the keen anticipation of deferred appetite.

The work was so exacting and her nerves so blessedly benumbed by toil, that Dorinda seldom stopped to ask herself if she were satisfied with her lot. Had the question been put to her, she would probably have dismissed it with the retort that she "had no time to worry about things like that." On the surface her days were crowded with more or less interesting tasks; but in her buried life there were hours when the old discontent awoke with the autumn wind in the broomsedge. At such moments she would feel that life had cheated her, and she would long passionately for something bright and beautiful that she had missed. Not love again! No, never again the love that she had known! What she longed for was the something different, the something indestructibly desirable and satisfying. Then there would return the blind sense of a purpose in existence which had evaded her search. The encompassing dullness would melt like a cloud, and she would grasp a meaning beneath the deceptions and the cruelties of the past. But this feeling was as fugitive as all others, and when it vanished it left not the glorified horizon, but simply the long day's work to be done.

Years had passed now, and she had stopped thinking of Jason. Since she never left the farm, she was spared the accident of a meeting, and she had excluded him for so long from her consciousness that his memory had appeared to acquiesce in the banishment. For the first two or three years after her return, she had lived in dread of seeing him again in the flesh, or of having his image awake to life in her mind. She had been afraid to go to sleep, because in her dreams she was still defenseless against him; and after her love for him had died, her fear had remained embedded in hatred. But that had passed also, and she had ceased to remember him, except when Nathan or one of the labourers on the farm mentioned his name.

"Doctor Stout is taking all Jason's practice," Nathan said one day. "That comes, I reckon, of trying to please everybody."

"I thought drink was his ruin," Dorinda rejoined indifferently.

"Of course drink helped it along, though it began farther back with his being so pleasant that you couldn't believe what he said. At first folks liked it, but after a while they began to see through it. By the way, his wife has been acting kind of queer. They say she's got a screw loose somewhere in her brain."

"I know," was all that Dorinda answered, but she thought, "And I once wished I could be in her place!"

She remembered the way Geneva had slipped up behind her one afternoon in an old field where broomsedge was burning, and had talked in a rambling, excited manner about her marriage and how blissfully happy they both were. "Not that we shouldn't like a child," she had continued, with a grimace which had begun as a smile, "but we can't expect to have everything, and we are blissfully happy. Blissfully happy!" she had screamed out suddenly in her high, cracked voice. At the time Dorinda had been puzzled, but now she understood and was sorry. The staring face, with its greenish skin and too prominent eyes, framed in the beautiful flaxen hair, softened her heart. "At least Geneva was not to blame, yet she is the one who is punished most," she thought; and this seemed to her

273

another proof of the remorseless injustice of Destiny. "I suppose the Lord knew what was best for me," she said to herself in the pious idiom her mother had used; but, as the phrase soared in her mind, it was as empty as a balloon. When she remembered her girlhood now, she would think contemptuously, "How could I ever have had so little sense?" Were all girls as foolish, she wondered, or was she exceptional in her romantic ignorance of life?

Without warning, after not thinking of Jason for years, she dreamed of him one night. She dreamed of him, not as she knew that he was to-day, but as she had once believed him to be. For a moment, through the irresistible force of illusion, she was caught again, she was imprisoned in the agony of that old passion. In her dream she saw herself fleeing from some invisible pursuer through illimitable deserts of broomsedge. Though she dared not look back, she could hear the rush of footsteps behind her; she could almost feel the breath of the hunter on her neck. For minutes that were an eternity the flight endured. Then as she dropped to her knees, with her strength exhausted, she was caught up in the arms of the pursuer, and looking up, felt Jason's lips pressed to hers.

There was thunder in her ears when she awoke. Springing out of bed, she ran in her nightgown to the window and threw the shutters wide open. Outside, beneath a dappled sky, she saw the frosted November fields and the dark trees flung off sharply, like flying buttresses, between the hill and the horizon. The wind cut through her gown; far away in the moonlight an owl hooted. Gradually, while she stood shivering in the frosty air, the terror of her dream faded and ice froze again over her heart.

Through ten years of hard work and self-denial the firm, clear surface of her beauty remained unroughened. Then one October morning, Fluvanna, looking at her in the sunlight, exclaimed, "Miss Dorindy, you're too young to have crow's-feet!"

Crow's-feet! She turned with a start from the brood of white turkeys she was counting. Yes, she was too young, she was only thirty-three, but she was already beginning to break. Youth was going! Youth was going, the words echoed and reëchoed through the emptiness of the future. Week by week, month by month, year by year, youth was slipping away; and she had never known the completeness, the fulfilment, that she had expected of life. Even now, she could not tell herself, she did not know, what it was that she had missed. It was not love, nor was it motherhood. No, the need went deeper than nature. It lay so deep, so far down in her hidden life, that the roots of it were lost in the rich darkness. Though she felt these things vaguely, without thinking that she felt them, it seemed to her, standing there with her gaze on the brood of white turkeys, that all she had ever hoped for or believed in was eluding her grasp. In a little while, with happiness still undiscovered, she would be as wrinkled and grey as her mother. Only her mother's restless habit of work would remain to fill the vacancy of her days.

"I've been working too hard, Fluvanna," she said, "and what do I get out of it?"

"You oughtn't to let yo'self go, Miss Dorindy. There ain't any use in the world for you to slave and stint the way you do. You ought to go about mo' and begin to take notice."

Dorinda laughed. "You talk as if I were a widower."

"Naw'm, I ain't. No widower ever lived the way you do."

"It's true. I haven't bought a good dress or been anywhere for ten years."

"Thar ain't a particle of use in it. You'll be old and dried up soon enough. What's the use of being young and proud if you don't strut?"

Yes, Fluvanna was right. What was the use? She had made a success of her undertaking; but it was inadequate because there were no spectators of her triumph. She had kept so close to the farm that her neighbours knew her only as a dim figure against the horizon, a moving shape among corn-shocks and hay-ricks in the flat landscape, an image that vanished with these inanimate objects in the lengthening perspective. Even in the thin and isolated community in which she lived, she did not stand out, clearly projected, like James Ellgood; perhaps, for the simple reason, she told herself now, that she had drilled her energy down into the soil instead of training it upward.

"I believe you're right, Fluvanna," she said. "Now that we're out of debt and things are going fairly well, I ought to try to get something out of life while I'm still young."

After the turkeys were counted, she left Fluvanna to turn them out into the woods, and going into her bedroom, looked at herself in the mirror which had once belonged to her mother. While she

275

stared into the glass it seemed to her that another face was watching her beyond her reflection, a face that was drawn and pallid, with a corded neck and the famished eyes of a disappointed dreamer. Well, she would never become like that if she could prevent it. She would never let disappointment eat away the heart in her bosom.

She was still handsome. The grave oval of her face, the fine austerity of its modelling, would remain noble even after she became an old woman and the warm colour of the flesh was mottled and stained with yellow. It was true that lines were forming about her eyes; but the eyes themselves were as deeply blue as the autumn sky, and though her skin had coarsened in the last ten years, the dark red of her cheeks and lips was as vivid as ever. Her black hair was still abundant, though it had lost its gloss in the sunshine. In spite of hard work, or because of it, her tall, straight figure had kept the slender hips and the pointed breasts of a goddess. She did not look young for her age; the sunny bloom, like the down on a peach, had hardened to the glaze of maturity; but she had not lost the April charm of her expression. "For all I've ever had, I might as well have been born plain," she thought.

15

That afternoon she harnessed Molly, the new mare, to the buggy, and accompanied by Ranger, son of Rambler, drove over to Honeycomb Farm.

"I want a dress to wear to church," she said to Miss Seena, "something good that will last."

"Then you're going to church again? I must say it is time." Rawboned, wintry, rheumatic, the dressmaker was still an authority.

"The roads were so bad." To her surprise, Dorinda found herself becoming apologetic. "I couldn't take the teams out on Sundays, but I've bought a chestnut mare for my own use, and I'll begin going again."

"Well, I'm glad you ain't a confirmed backslider. What sort of material had you thought of?"

Dorinda reflected. "Something handsome. Silk—no, satin. That shines more."

"Why don't you order it out of a catalogue? My fingers have got so stiff I've had to give up sewin' the last few months. They put everything in catalogues now." Miss Seena selected one from the pile on the table and opened it as she spoke. "You'll want blue, I reckon. You were always partial to blue."

Dorinda frowned. "No, not blue. Any colour but blue."

"I thought you favoured it. Do you recollect the dress I bought to match yo' eyes one spring when you were a girl? My, but you did look well in it!"

"Isn't there any other colour worn?"

"Well, there's brown. The fashion books speak highly of brown this year. Black's real stylish too. With yo' bright complexion black ought to go mighty well. You'd better order this model. It is the newest style." She pointed to a picture which seemed to Dorinda to be the extreme of fashion. "Them box pleats and pointed basques is the latest thing. I reckon you'll have to get a new corset," she concluded sharply, looking the girl up and down. "These styles don't set well unless they're worn over a straight front."

"Then I'll get one." Dorinda was prepared for any discomfort. "And I need a coat—and a hat, a big one with a feather."

"You want a willow-plume. They're all the rage this season, and a long coat of seal plush. There're some handsome ones in the front of that catalogue. Seal plush is goin' to be mo' worn than fur, all the fashion books say."

After the choice was made and the letter written by the cramped fingers of the dressmaker, Dorinda drove home consoled by the discovery that crow's-feet make, after all, less difference than clothes in one's happiness. Strange how a little thing like a new dress could lift up one's spirits! Her changed mood persisted until she approached the fork of the road and saw a woman's figure against the dying flare of the sun. As she reached the spot, the woman came down into the middle of the road, and she recognized Geneva Greylock.

"I want to talk to you, Dorinda," Geneva began, with a trill of laughter. "Won't you stop and listen?"

She was wearing a thin summer dress, though the air was sharp, and round her waist she had tied a faded blue sash with streamers which blew out in the wind. Her face, in its masklike immobility, resembled the face of a dead woman. Only her gleaming flaxen hair was alive.

"I'm afraid it's too late," Dorinda replied as pleasantly as she could. "Supper will be waiting, and besides you ought not to be out in that dress. You will catch your death of cold."

Geneva shook her head, while that expressionless laughter trickled in a stream from her lips. "I'm not cold," she answered. "I'm so happy that I must talk to somebody. It is our wedding anniversary, and I'm obliged to tell somebody how blissfully happy we are. Jason went to sleep right after dinner, and he hasn't waked up yet, so I had to come out and find somebody to talk to. I've got a secret that nobody knows, not even Jason."

So it was the same thing over again! Her eyes looked as if they would leap out of her head, they were so staring and famished.

"I'll tell you what I'll do," Dorinda responded, her voice softened by pity. "If you'll get into the buggy, I'll drive you down to Gooseneck Creek. That will be halfway home." This was what marriage to Jason had brought, and yet there had been a time when she would have given her life to have been married to him for a single year.

"Oh, will you?" Geneva sprang up on the step and into the buggy. She was so thin that her bones seemed to rattle as she moved, and there were hollows in her chest and between her shoulder blades. "Then I can tell you my secret."

"I wouldn't if I were you. I've got to keep an eye on the road, so I can't talk."

For a few minutes Geneva rambled on in her strained voice as if she had not heard her. Then pausing, she asked abruptly, "Why did you never like me, Dorinda? I always wanted to be friends with you."

"I like you. I do like you."

Geneva shook her head. "You never liked me because you loved Jason. Jason jilted you." She broke into her cracked laugh again. "You don't know, but there are worse things than being jilted."

Anger flamed up in Dorinda's heart, but it died down before she allowed herself to reply. "I suppose there are," she said at last. "That was long ago, anyhow. So long that it doesn't matter what happened." Poor demented creature, she thought, how many months would it be before they put her away?

Suddenly Geneva leaned toward her and began to whisper so rapidly that Dorinda could scarcely follow her words. "If I tell you my secret, will you promise never to repeat it? When you hear it, you will know there are worse things than being jilted. I had a baby, and Jason killed it. He killed it as soon as it was born and buried it in the garden. He doesn't know that I saw him. He thinks that I was asleep, but I found the grave under the lilac bushes at the end of the garden path. Now, we are going to have another baby, and I'm afraid he will kill this one too. That's why I pretend to be so blissfully happy. Blissfully happy," she cried out in a high voice as she jumped over the wheel before the buggy came to a stop. Yes, they would probably have to send her away very soon. "I wish I had been kinder to her when I had the chance," Dorinda thought, as she turned the mare toward home.

The next Sunday afternoon she asked Nathan for news of Geneva. It was easy for her to speak of the Greylocks now since that dreadful encounter had obliterated even the memory of jealousy.

"Every six months or so she's taken like that," Nathan answered. "Then she goes clean out of her head; but they say it isn't as bad as the moping in between the attacks."

"Is there nothing that can be done?"

"Oh, they'll have to put her away, sooner or later. Her father has tried his best to get her to leave Jason, but she won't hear of it when she's in her right mind. Once he took her home while she was deranged and kept her in a room with barred windows. It didn't last, however, and as soon as she came to her senses, she insisted on going back to Jason. They lead a cat-and-dog life together, and when she is out of her head she runs about telling everybody that she had a child and he murdered it."

"Poor thing," said Dorinda. "She told me too."

"That's when she's crazy. As soon as she gets her senses again, you can't make her leave him."

For a few minutes Dorinda was silent. When she spoke it was to remark irrelevantly, "How little human beings know what is best for them."

"I didn't understand what you said, Dorinda."

"No matter. I was only thinking aloud."

It was a mellow October afternoon, and around them the fields were resting after a fair harvest. As far as she could see, east, north, west, the land belonged to her. Only toward the south there were the pale green willows of Gooseneck Creek, and beyond the feathery edge she saw the red chimneys of Five Oaks. But for those chimneys she would have felt that the whole horizon was hers!

"They say Five Oaks will come under the hammer before long." Nathan's gaze also was on the red smears in the sky. "It's mortgaged now for as much as it'll ever bring, and there's trouble about the taxes."

280

A wild idea shot into her mind. "I suppose it will bring a good deal?"

"If it is put up at a forced sale, it will probably go for a song. Nobody is buying land now. Amos Wigfall bought the old Haney place five years ago for a dollar an acre. Some day, if he looks out, it will be worth a hundred."

She looked at him with calculating eyes. "If I could buy Five Oaks, my farm would be as big as Green Acres."

His neighing laugh broke out. "Good Lord, Dorinda, what would you do with it?"

"I don't know what I'd do with it, but I want it. I'd give ten years of my life for the chance of owning Five Oaks before I die."

His laugh dropped to a chuckle. "Now, that's downright queer because I've been studying about bidding on it myself. It looks to me as if that would be the only way to save my money."

"Well, I'd rather you'd own it than anybody else," she said grudgingly. "But I'm going to the sale when it comes, and if I'm able to sell my prize bull, I'm going to bid against you. I've got almost five thousand dollars in bank."

"You'd better leave it there for the present. I wouldn't bid a cent on the place if it wasn't for the fact that I own most of it already. It's going to be hard to make anybody buy it. Just you wait and see."

"What will become of Jason?" she inquired abruptly.

Nathan looked dubious. "He'll go to work for James Ellgood, I reckon, or more likely drink himself out of the way. But he's been doing better of late, I hear. He was at church last Sunday in the Ellgood pew, looking all spruced up, as if he hadn't smelt whiskey for a month."

Her next words came quickly, as if she were afraid of drawing them back before they escaped. "Why didn't he ever go away after his father died?"

"He'd lost the wish, I reckon. Things happen like that sometimes. The old man hung on to him until all the sap was drained dry."

"His father died years ago."

"It must be going on nine years or so." He stopped to calculate as he did when he was adding up an account in the store. "Well, I reckon he'd used up all his energy in wishing to get away. When the chance came, he didn't have enough spirit left to take advantage of it." He sighed. "I've seen that happen I can't tell you how many times."

She looked away from him, and for a few minutes there was silence. Then he made a sound between a gasp and a chuckle, and turning to glance at him, she met an expression which she had never before seen in his face. Her nerves shivered into repulsion, while she drew farther away. Why were men so unaccountable? she asked herself in annoyance.

"I was just thinking," he stammered.

She regarded him with severity. After all, no one took Nathan seriously.

"I was just thinking," he began again, "that if you could make up your mind to marry me, we might throw the two farms into one."

"To marry you?" She stared at him incredulously. "Are you out of your head?"

He broke into an embarrassed laugh. "I reckon it sounds like that at first," he admitted, "but I hoped you might get used to the idea if you thought it over. It ain't as if I were a poor man. I'm about as well-to-do as anybody round Pedlar's Mill, if you leave out James Ellgood, and he's got a wife already, besides being too old. I ain't so young as you, I know; but I'm a long ways younger than James Ellgood. There ain't more than ten years' difference between us, and I think all the world of you. You might have things your own way just as you're doing now. I wouldn't want to interfere with you."

She was still gazing at him as if he were distraught. "I can't imagine," she replied sternly, "how you ever came to think of such a thing." It was absurd; it was incredible; and yet she supposed that even stranger things had happened! She had seen enough of the world to know that you took your husband, as Fluvanna observed, where you found him, and she was troubled by few illusions about marriage.

His face turned the colour of beet juice while he looked at her with humble, imploring eyes, like the eyes of young Ranger when they were training him. "I was just thinking how useful I could be
282

on the farm," he said apologetically. "You seemed so set on owning Five Oaks, and then you like to have the children about."

The incredulity faded from her face. "I do like to have the children about."

"Well, you know I'd never put myself in your way. You could have both the farms to manage just as you like. I'd buy Five Oaks whenever it was sold."

"Yes, the two farms could be thrown together—or farmed separately." Her mind was still working over Five Oaks, not over the question of marriage.

"Then couldn't you get used to the idea, Dorinda?"

His tone rather than his words awoke her with a start to his meaning. "The idea! You mean marriage? No, I couldn't do it. There's no use thinking about it."

His face scarcely changed, so little had he dared hope for her consent. "Well, I won't press you," he said after a minute, "but if the time ever comes——"

She shook her head emphatically. "The time will never come. Don't let that thought get into your head."

While she spoke her dispassionate gaze examined him, and she asked herself, with a tinge of amusement, why the idea of marrying him did not startle her more. He was ridiculous; he was uncouth; he was the last man on earth, she told herself firmly, who could ever have inspired her with the shadow of sentiment. Only after she had speculated upon these decisive objections did she begin to realize that absence of emotion was the only appeal any marriage could make to her. Her nerves or her senses would have revolted from the first hint of passion. The only marriage she could tolerate, she reflected grimly, was one which attempted no swift excursions into emotion, no flights beyond the logical barriers of the three dimensions.

"Of course, I'm not your equal," Nathan said abruptly. "You're a scholar like your great-grandfather, and you've read all his books. You know a lot of things I never heard of."

Dorinda laughed. "Much good books ever did me!" Much good indeed, she reflected. "There's no use thinking about it; I could never do it," she repeated in a tone of harsh finality, as she turned to walk homeward.

16

Two weeks later, one Saturday afternoon, Miss Seena brought over the new clothes; and Dorinda sat up until midnight, taking up the belt and letting down the hem of the black satin dress. When she put it on the next morning and listened to Fluvanna's admiring ejaculations, she remembered the day she had first worn the blue nun's veiling and the drive to church sitting beside Almira Pryde in the old carryall.

"You look like a queen, Miss Dorinda," Fluvanna exclaimed. "Thar ain't nothin'——"

"Anything, Fluvanna."

"There ain't anything that gives you such an air as one of them willow-plumes."

"Those, Fluvanna. Yes, it does look nice," Dorinda assented, after the correction. "I'm glad I got it black. It makes me look older, but there isn't anything so distinguished."

A few hours afterwards, while she walked slowly up the aisle in church, she felt rather than saw that the congregation, forgetting to stand up to sing, sat motionless and stared at her from the pews. For the first time in her life she tasted the intoxicating flavour of power. On the farm, success was translated into well-tilled acres or golden pounds of butter; but here, with these astonished eyes on her, she discovered that it contained a quality more satisfying than any material fact. What it measured was the difference between the past which Jason had ruined and the present which she had triumphantly built on the ruins he had left. In spite of everything that had happened, in spite of his betrayal of her faith and the black despair that had wiped love out of her heart, she, not he, was to-day the victor over life!

284

As she marched up the aisle, in her handsome, commonplace clothes, she might have been a contented rustic beauty whose first youth was slowly slipping away. A warm flush dyed her cheeks; her eyes were like blue stars beneath the projecting shadow of her eyebrows; she carried the willow-plume high above the dusky cloud of her hair; and the luxurious swish-swish of her satin skirt was as loud as the sound of wind in the grass. Not until she reached the pew where she used to sit between her father and mother, did she drop her eyes to the level of the congregation and discover that Jason was sitting with the Ellgoods under the high west window. She had not seen him face to face since the afternoon of her father's funeral, more than ten years ago, and he looked ages older, she thought, than she had remembered him. His skin had lost the clear red-brown of health and acquired a leathery texture. Though his hair was still red, there was a rusty edge where the light fell on it. His moustache, which was too long, drooped in bedraggled ends over his chin, as if he had fallen into the habit of chewing tobacco—he who had always been so fastidious! He was dressed neatly enough in his Sunday clothes; but sitting there in the broad band of sunlight, he reminded Dorinda of a tree when the sap has dried, with the brittle ashen-brown leaves still clinging to the boughs. Even his hands, which shook a little as they held the hymn-book open in front of his wife, were the hands of a man whose grasp had slackened. He was not yet forty, but life had already used him up and flung him aside.

Suddenly, he raised his eyes from the book and their glances met and crossed before they fell away again to the printed lines. In that instant, something passed between them which could never be uttered because it was profounder than speech. Resolute, imperious, her gaze swept him! While her eyes, as hard and cold as a frozen lake, gave back his reflection, she felt, with a shiver of terror, that the past had never died, that it existed eternally as a wave in the sea of her consciousness. Memory was there, flowing on, strong, silent, resistless, with no fresher tides of emotion to sweep over and engulf it in the flood of experience. In her whole life there had been only that one man. He had held her in his arms. He would remain always an inseparable part of her being. . . . Resentment struggled within her. All the strength of her spirit rebelled against the tyranny of the past, against the burden of a physical fact, which she dragged after her like a dead fish in a net. She saw him harshly as he was, and she despised herself because she had ever imagined him tenderly as he was not. As she opened her mouth to sing, it seemed to her that she was choked with the effluvium of the old despair. She shut her eyes while her voice rose with the hymn. Rain on the shingled roof; rain on the bare red earth; rain on the humped box-bush; rain on the bedraggled feathers of white turkeys. The face of the old man emerging from the blue light in the room, mottled, flabby, repellent. Memories like that. He meant nothing more to her now. Only the beauty that had turned into ugliness. Only the happiness of which she had been cheated. . . .

She was the last one to come out of church, and by the time she had spoken to the minister and a few of the older members who stopped to welcome her, the Ellgoods had driven away. She was glad that she did not see Jason again; for the sight of him, though it no longer stirred her heart, left that disagreeable pricking sensation in the nervous fibre of her body.

Nathan and the children were waiting for her at the gate of the churchyard, and she drove home with John Abner, while the others followed in Nathan's new surrey with the fringed top.

"You look good enough to eat, Dorinda," the boy said admiringly. "You ought to keep dressed up all the time."

She smiled down on him. "Much work I'd do on the farm! Ten years ago they almost turned me out of church because I milked in overalls; but they forgot that this morning when I went back wearing a willow-plume."

There was no one in the world who adored her as uncritically as did this boy with the clubfoot. He was a good boy, she knew, with a streak of morbid melancholy which was curiously attractive to her adventurous temperament. His face, with its bulging forehead and deep dark eyes, hiding stars of light in them like gleams at the bottom of a well, was an unusual one for a country boy, and made her wonder at times if there could be more in him than anyone suspected. In his childhood his clubfoot had been a torment to him, and for this reason he had kept away from the rough sports of other children.

"You'd rather farm than do anything else, wouldn't you, John Abner?" she asked abruptly.

"Except read. I'm glad winter is coming, so I can stay in the house and read."

"You wouldn't like to go to boarding school in the city?"

He shook his head, flinching as if from the cut of a whip. "Not with the other boys. I'd rather stay in the country with Father and you and the animals." His sympathetic understanding of animals was one of the strongest bonds between them. From his birth he had known what it was to suffer and endure.

"I hoped that the new kind of shoe would make it easier for you," she said presently. "Is it comfortable?"

"If it weren't so heavy. They are all heavy."

She sighed, for her heart was drooping with pity. John Abner had penetrated the armour of her arrogance in its one weak spot, which was her diffused maternal instinct. The longing to protect the helpless was still alive in her.

At home they found Fluvanna in a clean apron, with a blazing fire and a lavish Sunday dinner awaiting them. Roast duck with apple sauce, candied sweet potatoes, tomatoes stewed with brown sugar, and plum pudding, which was Nathan's favourite sweet. True, it was the one abundant meal of the week; but while she sat at the head of her table listening to the chatter of happy children, Dorinda remembered the frugal Sunday dinners of her mother and father, and her eyes smarted with tears. That, she had learned, was the hidden sting of success; it rubbed old sores with the salt of regret until they were raw again.

In the hall, after dinner, while Dorinda was fastening a worn blue cape over her satin dress, Nathan stood gazing thoughtfully up the staircase.

"Have you ever thought of putting a stove in the back hall, Dorinda?" he asked. "It would make a lot of difference in the comfort of the house, and it would help heat the bedrooms upstairs."

She turned and gazed at him, surprised at this fresh proof of his ingenuity. Yes, it was a good idea; she wondered why she had never thought of it herself. Indeed, since he had mentioned it, it seemed to her that it was what she had always intended to do.

"If only we could have had it in Ma's lifetime," she said. "It would have been such a help to her neuralgia."

"Yes, that's the trouble about getting comforts. We always remember that other people went without them. I've got the carpets now that Rose Emily wanted." After all, no one but Nathan had ever really understood her. With the thought she asked herself incredulously if understanding had anything whatever to do with love? Did people who loved ever understand? Wasn't the misunderstanding even a part of love's divine madness?

"Yes, I ought to have done it long ago," she murmured inattentively.

"I'll order one, if you want me to. There's a catalogue at the store, and I can get it at a discount. There are all sorts of contrivances for saving fuel, too, so it won't cost as much as you'd imagine. These new-fangled stoves give twice as much heat as an open fire, and don't burn one-fourth as much fuel. It's a close sort of heat. You wouldn't like it in your chamber, but it would be the very thing for this hall."

While they went out of doors together, she meditated upon the fact of his usefulness. He was always thinking of ways and means to be comfortable or economical before they occurred to her or to anyone else, and he had what he called a knack for mending anything that was broken. He was kind; he was honest in every fibre; he was neat in his appearance for a farmer; and he was, she reflected cynically, almost emasculate in his unselfishness. To be sure, he had habits which she disliked; but, as she told herself with dispassionate realism, one couldn't have everything. It never occurred to her that these habits might be broken by marriage, for she was wise enough to perceive that a man's habits are more firmly rooted than his emotions. What she felt was that in exchange for his helpfulness she might learn to tolerate the things to which she objected. What good ever came, she demanded impatiently, of trying to make any one over? Hadn't her mother tried for forty years to make her father stop chewing tobacco, and yet it was the last thing that he relinquished. No, she had few illusions remaining. Though she still told herself inflexibly that she could never make up her mind to marry Nathan, she felt, in spite of her will, that the insidious force of logic was gradually undermining her scruples. She had suffered too much from love in the past ever to walk again with open eyes into the furnace. Sex emotion, she repeated grimly, was as dead as a burned-out cinder in her heart. But respect she could still feel, and a marriage founded upon respect and expediency might offer an available refuge from loneliness. As she grew older, the thing she feared most was not death, not poverty even, but the lonely fireside.

She walked on, disheartened by indecision, and Nathan was obliged to repeat his question twice before she heard what he was saying.

"Have you thought over what I asked you, Dorinda?"

She shook her head. "There's no use thinking."

His only answer was a comical sigh, and after a long pause she repeated more sharply, "There's no use thinking about that."

Some hidden edge to her tone made him glance at her quickly. This was another moment when the keenness of Nathan's perceptions surprised her.

"You'd be just as free as you are now," he said discreetly but hopefully.

"I couldn't stand any love-making." Though the light bloomed on her lips and cheeks, her eyes darkened with memory.

He sighed again less hopefully. What a pity it was, she thought, that everything about him grew in the wrong way; his hair like moth-eaten fur, his flat clownish features; his long moustache which always reminded her of bleached grass. Well, even so, you couldn't have everything. If the outward man had been more attractive, the inward one, she acknowledged, would have been less humble; and when all was said and done, few virtues are more comfortable to live with than humility.

"It doesn't do any good to keep thinking of that," she reiterated firmly, but the firmness had oozed from her mind into her manner. The fact that she needed Nathan on the farm was driven home to her every day of her life. Without him, she would never become anything more than a farmer who was extraordinary chiefly in being a woman as well; and this provoking disadvantage was a continual annoyance. Her life, in spite of the companionship of Fluvanna, was an empty one, and as the shadow of middle age grew longer, she would become more and more solitary.

They had reached the high ground by the graveyard, and over Gooseneck Creek she saw the red chimneys of Five Oaks. At the sight a suffering thought awoke and throbbed in her brain.

"I'll never interfere with you, Dorinda," Nathan said in a husky tone.

She turned suddenly and looked into his eyes. "It doesn't do any good to keep thinking about it," she insisted in an expressionless voice as if she were reciting a phrase she had learned by heart.

17

The exact moment of her yielding was so vague that she could never remember it; but three weeks later they drove over to the Presbyterian church at Pedlar's Mill and were married. Until the evening before she had told no one but Fluvanna; and only the pastor's wife, a farmer or two, and Nathan's children, witnessed the marriage. As they stood together before the old minister, a shadowy fear fluttered into Dorinda's mind, and she longed to turn and run back to the safe loneliness of Old Farm. "Can it be possible," she asked herself, "that I am doing this thing?" She seemed to be standing apart as a spectator while she watched some other woman married to Nathan.

When it was over the few farmers came up to shake hands with her; but their manner was repressed and unnatural, and even the children had become bashful and constrained.

"Wall, you was wise to git it over," John Appleseed said. "I don't favour marryin' fur a woman as long as she's got a better means of provision; but it's fortunate we don't all harbour the same opinions."

He had attended with his idiot son, who was now a man of twenty-five, but still retained his fondness for a crowd or a noise. While she looked into his vacant face, Dorinda recalled Jason's ineffectual endeavours to enlighten the natives, and the lecture on farming that he had delivered to Nathan Pedlar and Billy Appleseed, the idiot. Poor Jason! After all, he had had his tragedy.

"Nobody wants to hear croaking at a wedding, John," William Fairlamb remarked genially.

"Oh, I don't mind him." Dorinda laughed, but the laugh went no deeper than her throat. Terror had seized her, the ancient panic quiver of the hunted, and her face wore a strained and absent look as if she were listening to some far-off music in the broomsedge. "How did I ever come to do such a thing?" a voice like a song was asking over and over.

On the drive home she could think of nothing to say. Her mind, which was usually crowded with ideas, had become as blank as a wall, and she sat gazing in silence over the head of the brisk young mare Nathan was driving. So small a thing as the fact that Nathan was holding the reins made her feel stiff and uncomfortable.

As they passed the old mill, Geneva Greylock came running out of the ruins and waved a blue scarf in the air. They could not see her face clearly; but there was a distraught intensity in the lines of her thin figure and in the violent gestures of her arms beneath the flying curves of blue silk, which wound about her like a ribbon of autumn sky.

"She's getting worse every day," Nathan said, glancing toward her as they spun past. "It won't be long now before they have to send her to the asylum. Last Sunday, when the minister was taking dinner with James Ellgood, Geneva went round the table and poured molasses into every soup-plate. When they asked her why she had done it, she said she was trying to make life sweeter."

"Poor thing," Dorinda sighed. "She was always ailing."

It was a brown afternoon in November, with a smoky sky and a strong, clean wind which rushed in a droning measure through the broomsedge. All the leaves had fallen and been swept in wind-drifts under the rail fences. The only animate shapes in the landscape were the buzzards flocking toward a dead sheep in the pasture.

"Did you tell the children to come straight over?" Nathan inquired presently.

"Yes, I've got their rooms ready. I had paper put on the walls instead of whitewash, and they look very nice. The new stove heats them comfortably."

"You mustn't let my children bother you, Dorinda."

"Oh, no. I'm glad to have them. They will be company for me. We can begin reading again at night."

The mare trotted briskly, and the edge of the wind felt like ice on Dorinda's face. "It's turning much colder," she said after a long pause.

"Yes, there'll be a hard frost to-night if it clears."

She turned away from him, lifting her gaze to the sky where broken clouds were driven rapidly toward the south. A sword of light was thrust suddenly through the greyness, and she said slowly, as if the words were of profound significance, "The wind seems to be changing." Always responsive to her surroundings, she told herself that the landscape looked as if it were running away from the wind. "Does it really look this way or is it only in my mind," she thought, as they went on past the fork. Of course, if she had to go over it again, she could never bring herself to be married; but since she had walked into the marriage with open eyes, all she could do now was to endeavour to make the best of her mistake. Nathan was a good man and—well, you couldn't have everything! Youth, with its troubled rapture and its unsatisfied craving, was well over. Green evening skies. The scent of wild grape. The flutter of the heart like a caged bird. Feet flying toward happiness. . . . Yes, he was a good man, and you couldn't have everything.

When she reached the farm she left Nathan to build up the fire in the hall stove, and ran upstairs to put the finishing touches to the bedrooms she had prepared for the children. Everything was in order. There was nothing that she could find to do; yet she lingered to straighten a picture or change the position of a chair until she heard wheels approaching. Then, after she ran downstairs and exchanged embarrassed greetings, she visited the hen-house and the barn before she went into the kitchen to help Fluvanna with supper. All the work of the farm, so heavy and engrossing on other days that it made her a slave to routine, was suspended like a clock after the hour has struck.

"Do you want me to make the hard sauce for the plum pudding, Fluvanna?"

"Naw, Miss Dorindy, there ain't nothin' on earth for you to bother yo' head with to-day. Miss Minnie May has made it, and she's helping me as much as I want. You sit right down in the parlour and wait till supper is ready. I don't see," she concluded in a fault-finding tone, "why anybody wanted to have a poky wedding like this. There ain't even a fiddle to make things lively."

Dorinda went out, but not into the parlour. As she passed through the hall she caught a glimpse of Nathan, in his new suit of grey tweed, sitting bolt upright in the best chair, while he slowly turned the leaves of the family Bible. No, she had always disliked the parlour, in spite of her great-grandfather's library which almost covered the walls. Would it be possible, she wondered, to turn the room into a more comfortable and cheerful place? Yet she shrank from making any definite change. Though she hated the furniture and the air of chill repose in which it had weathered the years, she could not banish the feeling that it was dedicated to the ancestral spirits of her family.

As she opened the back door, which admitted a gust of wind and a shower of brown leaves, she heard Nimrod laughing with Fluvanna in the kitchen. "Ef'n you ax me, it mought ez well be anybody's wedding ez hern. I lay she ain' never so much as smelt dat ar wedding-cake." Immediately, Fluvanna's more educated accents responded, "I declare I couldn't help feelin' all the time that I was baking a cake for a corpse."

"How in the world did I ever do it?" Dorinda asked herself for the hundredth time; and she pictured the years ahead as an interminable desert of time in which Nathan would sit like a visitor in the parlour and perpetually turn the leaves of the family Bible. Nothing but the first day that she had had young Ranger as an untrained puppy on her hands had ever seemed to her so endless. "I don't see how I'm going to stand it for the rest of my life," she thought. A different wedding-day from the one of which she had dreamed long ago! But then, as she had learned through hard experience, imagination is a creative principle and depends little upon the raw material of life. Nothing, she supposed, ever happened exactly as you hoped that it would.

Supper was a dreary affair. The children were restless and awkward, and even the wedding-cake, which Fluvanna had baked in secret, and over which she had lamented with Nimrod, was lumpy and heavy. Nathan endeavoured to enliven the meal by a few foolish jokes badly told, and when even Dorinda, who felt sorry for him, forgot to laugh, he stared at her with humble, sheepish eyes while he relapsed into silence. It was a relief when Bud, of Gargantuan appetite, refused a fifth slice of the indigestible cake, and the last piece was wrapped in a napkin and put away for Billy Appleseed.

"Are you going to have suppers like this every night?" Bud, the facetious, inquired, giving his stomach a comical pat.

For the first time a laugh unforced and unafraid broke from Dorinda and Nathan. After all, she concluded more hopefully, it was possible that the children might make the house brighter.

"I like it over here better than I do at home," John Abner said. "It's farther away."

"Farther away from what?" asked Nathan, who was trying to appear easy and flippant.

"Oh, I don't know. Farther away from school, I reckon."

"I wouldn't want to go back to the city if we could have plum pudding every night till Christmas," Bud persisted.

Dorinda shook her head. "Oh, you greedy boy!" she exclaimed, smiling. "When you are a little older you'll learn that you can't have everything."

When supper was over she put on her overalls and lighted her lantern, for the short November day was already closing in. She knew that the milkers were probably slighting their work, and it made her restless to think that the cows might not have been handled properly. The negroes were cheerful and willing workers, but ten years of patient discipline on her part had failed to overcome their natural preference for the easiest way.

"You ain't going out again, are you, Dorinda?" Nathan asked anxiously, while he watched her preparations.

"Yes, we had supper early so Fluvanna and Mary Joe could help with the milking, but I'd better go out and see what they are doing. There's a lot to do in the dairy and the darkeys are still a little afraid of the new machinery."

Nathan laughed good-humouredly. "I might as well help you. Dairy work is the sort that won't keep."

"No, it won't wait. The butter has to be packed for the early train."

"That means you'll be up before daybreak?"

She nodded impatiently. "Well, you're used to that. Don't you breakfast by candlelight in winter?"

"Yes, I'm used to it. I'll come out now and help."

"I don't want you. There's plenty of work for you in the fields, but I don't want you meddling in my dairy."

For the first time she understood what work had meant in her mother's life; the flight of the mind from thought into action. To have Nathan hanging round her in the dairy was the last thing, she said to herself, that she had anticipated in marriage.

"I didn't mean to interfere with you." He fell back into the house, and with a sigh of relief she fled out to the new cow-barn, where the last milkers still lingered and chatted over the wedding. As she passed into the heavy atmosphere and inhaled the pasture-scented breath of the cows, she felt that a soothing vapour had blown over her nerves.

"I declar, Miss Dorindy, you mought jes' ez well not be mah'ed at all," Nimrod remarked dolefully.

"Well, I won't let it interfere with my work. No man is going to do that."

Mary Joe bridled and giggled; for, being an engaging mulatto girl, she knew all that could be told of the interference of men. "Naw'm, dat dey ain't, nor breck yo' heart needer. Hit's a pity we ain't all ez strong-minded ez you is."

Dorinda laughed. "Break my heart? I should think not," she replied. And she meant what she said while she was saying it. One man had ruined her life; but no other man should interfere with it. She was encased in wounded pride as in defensive armour.

One of the other milkers, a big black woman named Saphira, smiled approvingly. "Hi! Dat's moughty sassy, Miss Dorindy," she exclaimed, "but hit ain't natur!"

After the milkers had gone home, Dorinda went into the dairy with Fluvanna and Mary Joe and worked until nearly midnight. Usually, she had finished by nine o'clock, at the latest, but to-night there were a dozen extra tasks for her willing hands to perform. As the hours went on she became so particular and so sharply critical that the two coloured women were driven to tears. "Ef'n you ax me, hit's a good thing she cyarn't git mah'd but oncet," muttered Mary Joe, as she was leaving.

At midnight, when there was nothing else that she could find to do and her limbs were aching from fatigue, Dorinda went back into the house and locked the hall door which Nathan had left unfastened. The lamp on the bracket by the staircase was flaring up, and she stopped to lower the wick, while Ranger rose from his bed on a mat by the door and sidled up to her.

"Is that you, Dorinda?" whispered a voice from beyond the bend in the staircase. "Do you work this late every night?" When she looked up, she saw Minnie May blinking down on her.

"No, not every night. We had put off the dairy work so that Fluvanna could go to the—" Her tongue stumbled over the word "wedding," so she said "church" instead.

Holding her red flannel wrapper together over her flat girlish breast, Minnie May stole noiselessly down the staircase. Her pale red hair hung in a tight pigtail down her back, and the wrinkles of premature middle age were visible in her young forehead. She was a girl who had, as Fluvanna tartly observed, "run to character instead of looks."

"I tried to wait up for you," she said, "but you were so long coming, and Pa wouldn't let me go out to the dairy. Mr. Garlick stopped by long enough to tell us about Geneva Greylock, and I thought you ought to know it. She threw herself into the old mill-pond this evening and was drowned."

"Drowned?" Dorinda's voice was colourless. "Why, she waved to us as we came by." While she spoke, it seemed to her that she could never stop seeing the blue scarf flying round the distraught figure with its violent gestures.

"I know. John Appleseed saw her, but he didn't tell anybody, and when they missed her they didn't know where to look. It was the Haneys' little boy who saw the blue scarf floating on the pond when he was playing by the mill-wheel. For months, they say, she had gone about telling everybody that Jason had murdered her baby; but, of course, it was just a delusion."

"Poor thing." Dorinda turned away and went over to the wood stove where the fire was quite dead. "There was something wrong with her. Even as a girl she was always moping." Out of the fog of weariness there drifted a vision of the red chimneys of Five Oaks. So, like an old wound that begins to ache, the memory of Jason was thrust back into her life.

"Haven't you been to sleep, Minnie May?"

"No, I was listening for you. You came in so softly I hardly heard you."

"Well, you'd better go to bed. We have breakfast at five o'clock."

"Oh, I don't mind. I wake early, and I'll get up and help you pack the butter."

As the girl went up the stairs, Dorinda opened the door of her room and stepped over the threshold. The fire had been freshly made up and a pleasant ruddiness suffused the large quaintly furnished chamber where her parents had lived and died. Nathan had tried to keep the room warm and to sit up for her; but overcome at last by the loneliness and the firelight, he had fallen asleep on the big couch by the hearth. Having removed only his coat, he lay stretched out on his back, snoring slightly, with his jaw drooping above his magenta tie and his glazed collar. His features wore the defenseless look which sleep brings to men and women alike, and she felt, with a pang of sympathy, that he was at her mercy because he cared while she was indifferent. She would be always, she realized, the stronger of the two; for it seemed to her one of the inconsistencies of human nature that strength should be measured by indifference rather than by love.

Picking up the old grey blanket from the foot of the bed, she spread it over him so gently that he did not stir in his sleep. The honesty she had felt in him from the beginning was the single attribute that survived in unconsciousness. If only she could remember his goodness and forget his absurdity, life would be so much easier.

Too tired to do more than let down her hair and slip into a wrapper, she dropped on the bed and drew the patchwork quilt up to her chin. As the firelight flickered over her face, she remembered the night when Rufus was arrested. Now, as then, she felt that the end of endurance was reached. "Even if I am married to Nathan and Geneva has drowned herself, I can't keep awake any longer."

18

Up by the barn John Appleseed's threshing machine was droning like a gigantic swarm of June beetles. After a rainy spring the sky had cleared with the beginning of summer, and as the weeks went on, the weather remained warm and dry for the wheat harvest.

Standing on the porch, with her curved palm screening her eyes, Dorinda watched for Nathan to leave the threshing and come home to dinner. All the morning Fluvanna had been baking wheaten bread for the white men and corn-pone for the coloured hands, who had their midday meal out under the locust trees at the back of the house. It was five years since the night of her wedding-day, when Nathan had fallen asleep by the fire, and never in those five years had she known a season of such bountiful crops.

As she watched there in the sunlight, she looked exactly what she was in reality, a handsome, still youthful woman of thirty-eight, who had been hardened but not embittered by experience. Her tall straight figure had thickened; there was a silver sheen on the hair over her temples, and lines had gathered in the russet glow of her skin. Repose, dignity, independence, these were the attributes with which she faced middle age, for the lines in her face were marks of character, not of emotion. She had long ago ceased to worry over wrinkles. Though she clung to youth, it was youth of the arteries and the spirit. Her happiness was independent, she felt, of the admiration of men, and her value as a human being was founded upon a durable, if an intangible, basis. Since she had proved that she could farm as well as a man there was less need for her to endeavour to fascinate as a woman. Yet, as she occasionally observed with surprise, in discouraging the sentimental advances of men, she had employed the most successful means of holding their interest. When all was said and done, was she not the only woman at Pedlar's Mill who did not stoop habitually to falsehood and subterfuge to gain her end?

Looking back from the secure place where she stood, she could afford to smile at the perturbation of spirit which had attended her wedding. Marriage had made, after all, little difference in the orderly precision of her days. She held the reins of her life too firmly grasped ever to relinquish them to another; and as she had foreseen on her wedding-night, she possessed an incalculable advantage in merely liking Nathan while he loved her. On her side at least marriage had begun where it so often ends happily, in charity of mind. Though she could not love, she had chosen the best substitute for love, which is tolerance.

After five years of marriage, Nathan was scarcely more than a superior hired man on the farm. Dorinda still smiled at his jokes; she still considered his appetite; she still spoke of him respectfully to the children as "your father"; but he had no part, he had never had any part, in her life. It was his misfortune, perhaps, that by demanding nothing, he existed as an individual through generosity alone. Yet humble as he was in the house, his repressions fell away from him as soon as he was out on the farm. The mechanical gesture of sowing or reaping released his spiritual stature from the restraints that crippled it in the flesh. Contact with the soil dissolved his humility, as alcohol dissolved the inhibitions which had made Rufus when he was sober colourless and ineffectual in comparison with Rufus when he was drunk. Farming was Nathan's solitary outlet, for he did not drink and he had observed scrupulously his promise not to encroach on Dorinda's freedom. He left her at liberty, as he often reminded her, to have things her own way, and nothing in his nature, except his habits, was strong enough to resist her. Though she had been able to break him of chewing tobacco in the house, he still drank his coffee from his saucer and sat with his feet on the railing of the porch. Yet he was an easy man, she reflected, to live with, and for a woman who was growing arrogant with prosperity, an easy man was essential. At thirty-eight her philosophy had crystallized into the axiom, "you can't have everything."

In the midst of the abandoned acres the broad cultivated fields were rich and smiling. Where the broomsedge had run wild a few years ago, the young corn was waving, or the ragged furrows of the harvest wheat were overflowing with feathery green. In the pasture, if she had looked from the front porch instead of from the back one, she would have seen the velvety flanks of the cattle standing knee-deep in grass. At her feet, a flock of white Leghorns, direct descendants of Romeo and Juliet, were scratching busily in the sheepmint.

Lifting her hand from her eyes, she brushed a lock of hair back from her forehead and glanced down at the blue and white gingham dress she had put on for dinner. Of late she had fallen into the habit of powdering her face with her pink flannel starch-bag and changing into a clean dress before dinner. Her life, she knew, was becoming simplified into an unbreakable chain of habits, a series of orderly actions at regular hours. Vaguely, she thought of herself as a happy woman; yet she was aware that this monotony of contentment had no relation to what she had called happiness in her youth. It was better perhaps; it was certainly as good; but it measured all the difference between youth and maturity. She was not old. At thirty-eight, she was still young; and there were moments in the spring when her tranquillity was shot through with arrows of flame. Her romantic ardour lay buried under the years, but she realized now and then that it was still living.

"Dar dey is!" exclaimed Nimrod behind her, and immediately afterwards she heard Fluvanna's voice inquiring if it "wasn't time to begin dishing up dinner?"

Across the fields the men were walking slowly, Nathan and John Appleseed a little ahead, the others straggling behind them, with John Abner limping alone at a distance. She would have recognized Nathan's loping walk as far off as she could distinguish his figure, and John Abner's limp never failed to awaken a sympathetic feeling in her bosom. Of the four children, he was the only one who had grown into her life. Minnie May was married and the unselfish mother of an anæmic tow-headed brood; Bud was working his way to the head of the wholesale grocery business; and Lena had developed into a pretty, vain, empty-headed girl, who had been engaged half a dozen times, but had always changed her mind before it was too late. She attracted men as naturally as honey attracts flies, and since she was troubled by neither religion nor morality, her stepmother's only hope was "to get her safely married before anything happened." For John Abner, Dorinda felt no anxiety beyond the maternal one which arose from his lameness and his delicate health. He had been a comfort to her ever since he had come to the farm; and yet, in spite of John Abner and the knowledge that she had married from fear of a solitary old age, she realized that she was still lonely. Evidently, whatever else marriage might prevent, it was not a remedy for isolation of spirit.

As Nathan reached the porch he fumbled in the pocket of his overalls and drew out a greasy paper.

"John Appleseed brought me this notice about Five Oaks," he said. "Jason has never paid his taxes, and the farm is to be sold on the tenth of August. I saw the notice at the store yesterday, but I didn't stop long enough to take it in." Though Nathan still owned the general store at Pedlar's Mill, he had placed a manager in charge of it a few years ago.

The tenth of August! It seemed a long time to wait. Though Dorinda had expected the sale for the last five years, she told herself that it seemed a long time to wait. There was not the slightest surprise for her in Nathan's announcement. She had known for months that neither the taxes nor the interest on the mortgage could be paid, and that the farm would soon be sold at public auction. But with the inherent perversity of human nature, she felt now that the bare statement of the foreclosure had startled her out of a sleep. When the men had gone to wash their hands at the well, she lingered on the porch and gazed over the harvested fields and the low curve of the hill in the direction of Five Oaks. Peace surrounded her; peace was within her mind and heart; yet the past clung to her like an odour and she could not brush it away.

"It looks mighty like we'll get Five Oaks at last," Nathan said that night when they were alone. "To save my soul I can't see why you're so set on it, but when a woman wants a thing as much as that, it looks as if Providence couldn't hold out against her."

"Is there any chance of James Ellgood bidding it in?" This had been her secret dread ever since she had heard of the sale. Suppose James Ellgood, who could go as high as he liked, should begin bidding against her!

"There ain't one chance in a million that Jim will lift a finger.

He's hated Jason ever since Geneva drowned herself—and before too."

"When he loses his farm, do you know what he will do? Jason Greylock, I mean."

"He'll still own that little old house in the woods across Whippernock River. Maybe he'll go down there to live. There ain't much land belonging to it, but he's given up farming anyway since he's taken to drink. The two things don't work together."

"He's his father all over again," Dorinda said, with a shiver of repulsion.

"Yes, it looks like it." Nathan's tone was more compassionate. "John Appleseed saw him a few days ago when he was over there with Tom Snead looking for a foxhound puppy he'd lost. The dirt would have given you a fit, Dorinda, he said. There was a slatternly-looking coloured wench getting dinner; but she had thrown all the vegetable peelings out into the yard, and the front hall was stacked with kindling wood."

"Did he see Jason?"

"Yes, he came out when he heard the noise and asked what they wanted. The old man is getting the best of him, John Appleseed said."

"And while his father was alive, he hated him so."

"Well, it's often like that, I reckon. Maybe he hated him all the more because he felt he was like him." Nathan shook his head as if he were dislodging a gnat. "I must say, for my part, I'd have picked the old man of the two. At least he wasn't white-livered."

White-livered! It seemed to Dorinda that the old man himself was speaking to her out of his grave. Even he, steeped in iniquity, had scorned Jason because he lacked the courage of his wickedness.

Not for years had she heard directly of the Greylocks, and while she listened she felt that the streak of cruelty in her own nature was slowly appeased.

"I wonder why he never went North again?" Nathan said, as he rose to undress. "I remember he told me once years ago that all he wanted was a quiet life. He didn't care a damn for the farm, he said, he'd always hated it."

Yes, it was true, he had always hated it. Through his whole life he had been tied by his own nature to the thing that he hated.

303

When the tenth of August came, Dorinda put on her best dress, a navy blue and white foulard which Leona Prince, the new dressmaker, had cut after the fashionable "Princesse style." She was waiting on the porch when Nathan, who had just removed his overalls, looked out of the window to ask if they were going to walk.

"No, let's have the surrey." For a reason which she did not stop to define she preferred the long way by the road to the short cut over the fields. "Lena wants to go with us."

Nathan whistled. "What on earth has she got up her sleeve now?"

If she had spoken the thought in her mind, Dorinda would have replied tartly, "She wants to go because she thinks men will be there"; but instead she answered simply, "Oh, she's always ready to go anywhere."

"Well, can't she walk? It ain't over a mile by the short cut."

"She's afraid of seed-ticks. Besides, she's putting on her flowered organdie."

"What on earth?" Nathan demanded a second time. Then, after a meditative pause, he added logically, "I reckon she's got her eye open for young Jim Ellgood, but she'll be disappointed."

Lena had recently turned her seductions in a new direction; and Dorinda was divided between pity for the victim, a nice boy of twenty, and the fervent hope that Lena might be safely, if not permanently, settled. To be sure, young Jim had given no sign as yet of responding to her energetic advances; but the girl had never failed when she had gone about her business in a whole-hearted fashion, and Dorinda remained optimistic though vaguely uneasy about the results. Of course her step-daughter was the last wife in the world for a farmer. Scheming, capricious, dangerously over-sexed, and underworked, she had revealed of late a chronic habit of dissimulation, and it was impossible to decide whether she was lying for diversion or speaking the truth from necessity. Yet none of these moral imperfections appeared to detract an iota from the advantage of a face like an infant Aphrodite, vacant but perfect as the inside of a shell. A deplorable waste of any good man's affection, thought Dorinda. However, she had ceased long ago to worry over what she could not prevent, and she had observed that the strongest desires are directed almost invariably toward the least desirable.

"I am not sure that it is young Jim," she said, firm but indefinite. "Anyhow, you'll have to hitch up the surrey. The weeds would tear that dress to pieces."

When she spoke in that tone, she knew that Nathan never waited to argue. "All right. I turned the horses out to graze, but I'll see if I can find them." He went off obediently enough, after protesting again that it wasn't a mile by the short cut through the woods. Though Nathan always gave in to her wishes, he seldom gave in without grumbling.

It took him a quarter of an hour of hard hunting to catch the horses; but by the time Lena was ready, he appeared at the door with the surrey.

"If you don't hurry up and come on, the sale will be over before we get there," he remarked in the casual tone of a man who is not interested in the result.

"Why, I thought we had plenty of time," Dorinda replied; but she hurred Lena down the steps and into the vehicle, in spite of the girl's complaint that the ruffles on her skirt would be ruined if she did not spread a robe over the seat. Not until they had started off at a brisk pace and were well on the road, did Dorinda's heart stop its rapid pulsation. Suppose her own stupid folly in withstanding Nathan should cost her the possession of Five Oaks!

19

Up the long shady slope; into the branch road by the fork; between the wastes of joepye-weed and life-everlasting; over the rotting bridge across Gooseneck Creek, where the dragon-flies swarmed above the partly dried stream; up the rutted track through last year's corn-stubble; and past the broken fences of the farm-yard to the group of indifferent farmers gathered on benches, chairs, and upturned cracker-boxes, under the fine old oaks. All through the drive something invisible was whipping her on, as if the memory of wet branches stung her face in the blue August weather. A question was beating unanswered at the back of her brain. Why, since she neither loved nor hated Jason, should she long so passionately to own the place where he lived? Was it merely that the possession of Five Oaks would complete her victory and his degradation? Or was it simply that feeling like hers never died, that it returned again and again, in some changed form, to the place where it had first taken root?

When she reached the lawn, Ezra Flower, the auctioneer, was intoning from the front porch to the gathering under the trees. He was a fat little man, with a beard which stood out like ruffled grey feathers and the impudent manner of a bedraggled sparrow. From his scolding tone, Dorinda inferred that the bidding had been faint-hearted. Nobody wanted land, for land was the one thing that everybody owned and could not give away. While Nathan drove on to the side of the house, Dorinda walked quickly over to a chair a farmer was relinquishing. Only after she had seated herself between John Appleseed and William Fairlamb, did she glance round and observe that Lena had not followed her, but had stopped among the younger men and boys who were sprawling over the grass. Already

306

the girl was rolling her eyes and giggling without modesty. Well, what did it matter? Dorinda had tried, she felt sincerely, to do her duty by Nathan and his children; but it was impossible for any stepmother to be responsible for the character of a girl who possessed none. A stern expression forced her lips together, and she looked away to the twitching figure of Ezra Flower.

Still the auctioneer droned on, eliciting now and then responses as curt as oaths. Presently she heard Nathan's dry cough and his slow emphatic voice rasping out the words, "Three thousand dollars!" The bidding was about to begin in earnest, she saw, and a chill sensation ran over her as she settled her flaring skirt in the rush-bottomed chair.

While she sat there, listening to the rise and fall of the bidding, she tried to keep her mind firmly fixed on the objects before her. Overhead, the sky was of larkspur blue. Far away in the glittering fields, she heard the shrill chorus of grasshoppers chiming in with the monotonous hum of the auctioneer's voice. In the nearer meadow clouds of golden pollen were drifting like swarms of devouring insects. Over the grass on the lawn a flock of white turkeys moved in a sedate procession.

Yes, what had happened had happened, she told herself, and was over. Her affair was not with the past; it was not with the future. The only thing that concerned her vitally was the moment in which she was living. Only by keeping her mind close to the immediate present could she prevent her thoughts from slipping back into the abyss. Even now there were hours when memory seemed to be dragging her into the past; and when this occurred, a sense of weakness, of futility, of distaste for living, would sweep over her like a malady. To look back, she knew, meant the frustration of effort. To go on, taking the moment as it came, surmounting the obstacles, one by one, as they confronted her; to lavish her vital energy on permanent, not fugitive, endeavours,—these were the resolves which had carried her triumphantly over the years.

"Six thousand dollars," sang the auctioneer. "Going—going—going for six thousand dollars. Only six thousand dollars. Will nobody bid more? Not a quarter of what it is worth. Will nobody bid more for this fine old farm? Going—going—what? Nobody bids more? Going—going—gone for six thousand dollars!"

She rose and went over to where Nathan stood surrounded by a few farmers, who were trying in vain to pretend that they did not think him a fool. "Should have thought you had as much land as you knew what to do with," John Appleseed was saying, as she approached. "What are you going to do with Five Oaks, now you've got it? Eat it, I reckon?"

"It ain't mine. I bid on it for my wife," Nathan replied stubbornly. "She was so set on it I couldn't hold out against her."

Yes, Nathan was a good man, there was no denying it. Feeling nearer to him than she had ever felt in her life, she moved over to his side and slipped her hand through his arm.

"Wall, she got it dirt-cheap," the auctioneer declared. "Dirt-cheap, if I do say so."

"I don't see what you want with two farms, ma'am," chuckled Mr. Kettledrum, the veterinarian. "It looks as if you was goin' to live on one an' let Nathan live by himself on the other."

Then the faint-hearted bidders mounted their horses or stepped into their buggies, while Ezra Flower invited the new owners into the house. "Come right in an' clinch the sale with Doctor Greylock. He's settin' right there now with the papers to draw up," he added persuasively, as Dorinda hung back.

Beckoning Lena to follow them, Dorinda went up the steps with Nathan and entered the hall. Only once before had she been inside the house; but every detail of the interior had bitten into her memory. She knew the bend in the staircase down which the old man had roamed with his whip at night. She had never forgotten the litter of dust in the corners; the guns and fishing-poles crowded behind the door; the collection of hats on the table and sofa; the empty whiskey-bottles arranged in a row by the wainscoting. Above all, she remembered the stale odour of degeneration, of mingled whiskey and tobacco, which saturated the walls. Eighteen years ago, and nothing, not even that odour, had changed! In those eighteen years she had spent her youth and had restored dead land to life; but this house in which Jason had lived was still sunk in immovable sloth and decay.

Ezra Flower passed, with his sprightly sparrow-like twitter, through the hall, and flung open the door of a room on the right— the room in which she had sat with the drunken old man while the

308

storm broke outside. Jason, she saw, was standing on the very spot in the rug where his father had stood that afternoon in November.

As she crossed the threshold, it seemed to her that the room shifted and came forward to meet her. She heard Nathan's voice saying meaningless words. Then Jason took her hand and dropped it so limply that it might have been a dead leaf.

"Won't you sit down?" he asked courteously, for he had evidently kept sober until the sale could be concluded. "So you've bought Five Oaks," he continued, as indifferently as if he were speaking of corn or wheat. "Well, it's never been any use to me, and I'm not sorry to get rid of it. But I don't see what you're going to do with it. Isn't one farm as much as you're able to manage?" As he finished, he pushed a decanter of whiskey in the direction of Nathan. "We might as well have a drink over it anyway."

Yes, nothing had altered. It might have been the same dust that lay in a film over the floor, the furniture and the walls. It might have been the same pile of old newspapers on the table. It might have been the same spot of grease on the table cover; the same rat-trap baited with a piece of greenish cheese in one corner; the same light falling obliquely through the speckled window-panes. She would not have been surprised, when she turned her head, to see the sheets of rain blowing out like a curtain over the hunched box-bush.

Jason laughed, and the sound had a sardonic merriment. She had never thought that he resembled the old man, and she told herself now, while she watched him, that it was only the bad light or a trick of memory which gave him the discouraged and desperate air of his father. In looking at him she seemed not to brush aside, but to gather together all the years that had gone. Why had she ever loved him? What was there in this one man that was different from all other men whom she had known? Once she had beheld him within a magic circle of wonder and delight, divided and set apart from the surrounding dullness of existence. Now the dullness had swept over him as the waste flows over the abandoned fields.

He leaned back in his chair, glancing from Nathan to Ezra Flower with morose and weary eyes. His face, which had been charming in youth, was now spiritless and inert. There were yellow blotches under his eyes; his eyelids were puffed and heavy; his

309

features were swollen and leaden in colour; and even his hair, which had once been so alive, was as sandy and brittle as straw. Yes, the broomsedge had grown over him.

For a minute she scarcely heard what they were saying; then the details of the sale were discussed, and she made an effort to follow the words. When, presently, Nathan asked her to sign a paper, she turned automatically and wrote her name in the place that Ezra Flower pointed out to her. As she laid down the pen, she saw that Jason was smiling, and for an instant a glimmer of his old bright charm shone in his expression. She wished that he had not smiled. Then, with the wish still in her mind, she saw that he was smiling, not at her, but at Lena. His heavy gaze turned to Lena as instinctively as the eyes turn to a flaring lamp in a darkened room. His look was not amorous, for drink, Dorinda knew, not sex, was his preoccupation; but, while she watched it, a sensation of physical nausea attacked her.

Rising from her chair, she stood waiting for Nathan to finish the discussion. It was agreed, she understood vaguely, that Jason should leave the farm the first day of October, and that Nathan should take over the better part of the furniture. "I'll be glad to get rid of it," Jason remarked agreeably enough, "and I hope that you will make more out of the farm than I ever did. All I can say is that it ruined me. If I had been hard-hearted about it instead of soft, I'd be a different man from the one I am to-day."

"Yes, you weren't cut out for a farmer," Nathan rejoined mildly, and he added with one of his untimely jests, "Now, if you'd been as thrifty as my wife, you'd have found a way to make two leaves of alfalfa grow where there wasn't even one blade of grass before."

At this, for the first time, Jason looked at her attentively, and she knew from his gaze that his interest in her was as casual as his interest in Nathan. With his look, she felt that the part of her that was sex withered and died; but something more ancient than sex came to her rescue, and this was the instinct of self-preservation which had made her resolve in her youth that no man should spoil her life. In the matter of sex, he had won; matched merely as human beings, as man to man, she knew that she was the stronger. Though she did not realize its significance, the moment was a crisis in her experience; for when it had passed she had discarded for ever the allurements of youth. She felt securely middle-aged, but it was the middle age of triumphant independence.

Jason's glance had wandered from her to Nathan, and she detected the flicker of ridicule in his smile. Anger seized her at the suspicion that he was mocking them, and with the anger a passionate loyalty to Nathan welled up in her heart. She saw Nathan as clearly as Jason saw him, but she saw also something fine and magnanimous in his character which Jason could never see because he was blind to nobility. "I don't care," she thought indignantly, "he is worth twenty of Jason." Obeying a protective impulse, she moved nearer to her husband and laid her hand on his arm. It was the second time that afternoon that she had drawn closer to him of her own accord.

"Well, I reckon we'd better be starting home," Nathan said, as he held out his hand in simple good will. "I hope you'll make out all right where you're going."

"All I ask is a quiet life," Jason repeated. Then, as they were leaving the room, his eyes roved back to Lena and clung to her face as if he hated to see the last of her. "Take good care of that daughter of yours," he advised. "She's the prettiest girl I ever saw in my life."

"Well, she ain't bad-looking," Nathan retorted with spirit, "but she can't hold a candle to the way her mother and Dorinda looked when they were her age."

Without touching Jason's hand again, Dorinda walked quickly down the hall and out of the house. Not until they were driving over Gooseneck Creek, did it occur to her that she had not opened her lips at Five Oaks.

"I hope you're satisfied, Dorinda," Nathan remarked, with hilarity.

"Yes, I'm satisfied."

"I fancied you looked kind of down in the mouth while we were in the room. You ain't changed your mind about wanting the farm, have you?"

"Oh, no, I haven't changed my mind."

"I'm glad of that. You never can tell about a woman. He seemed to think that Lena was good to look at."

Though she had believed that her anger was over, the embers

311

grew red and then grey again. Middle age as an attitude of mind might enjoy an immunity from peril, but it suffered, she found, from the disadvantages of an unstable equilibrium.

"I wonder if he has forgotten Geneva," she observed irrelevantly.

At the reminder of that tragic figure Nathan's hilarity died. "When a thing like that has happened to a man," he responded, "he doesn't usually keep the dry bones lying around to look at."

The sun was beginning to go down and the sandy stretch of road, where the shadow of the surrey glided ahead of them, glittered like silver. After the intense heat of the day the fitful breeze was as torrid as the air from an oven.

"John Abner promised he would drive me over to the ice-cream festival at the church," Lena said hopefully. There were pearly beads on her shell-like brow and Nathan's leathery face was streaming with perspiration.

"Poor John Abner! It is so hot and he will be tired!" protested Dorinda, though she was aware that any protest was futile, for Lena possessed the obstinacy peculiar to many weak-minded women.

"He needn't stay," retorted the girl. "Somebody will be sure to bring me home." She pressed her pink lips together and smiled with the secret wisdom of instinct.

As soon as they reached the house Dorinda slipped into her gingham dress and hurried out to the barn. Milking had already begun, but she knew that it would proceed with negligence if she were long absent. In summer, as in winter, they had supper after dark, and for a little while when the meal was over she liked to rest on the porch with Nathan and John Abner. To-night, John Abner was away with Lena, and when Dorinda came out into the air, she dropped, with a sigh of relief, into the hammock beneath the climbing rose Nathan had planted.

"I never felt anything like the heat," she said, "there's not a breath anywhere."

Nathan stirred in the darkness and removed his pipe from his mouth. "Yes, if it don't break soon, the drought will go hard with the crops."

"And with the dairy too. The ice melts so fast I can't keep the butter firm."

She leaned back, breathing in the scent of his pipe. The protective feeling, so closely akin to tenderness, which had awakened in her heart at Five Oaks, had not entirely vanished, and she felt nearer to her husband, sitting there in the moonlight of her thoughts, than she had felt since her marriage. Even that moment at Five Oaks when Jason had laughed at him had not brought him so close. She longed to tell him this because she knew how much the knowledge of it would mean to him; yet she could find no words delicate enough to convey this new sense of his importance in her life. The only words at her command were those that had struggled in her mind over at Five Oaks: "He is worth twenty of Jason," and these were not words that could be spoken aloud.

"There goes a shooting star!" Nathan exclaimed suddenly out of the stillness.

"And another," she added, after a brief silence.

"I wonder what becomes of them," he continued presently. "When you stop to think of it, it's odd what becomes of everything. It makes the universe seem like a scrap-heap."

She left the hammock and sat down on the step at his feet. "That reminds me of all the trash over at Five Oaks. What in the world can we do with it? Doesn't that screech owl sound as if he were close by us."

"Well, we'll have to put a manager on that farm, I reckon. We can't look after both farms and make anything of them. I never heard so many tree-frogs as we've had this summer. What with the locusts and the katydids you can't hear yourself talk. But it's right pleasant sitting here like this, ain't it?"

"Yes, it's pleasant." She tried to say something affectionate and gave up the effort. "I like to think that Five Oaks belongs to us." Her accent on the "us" was the best that she could do in the matter of sentiment; yet she was sure that he understood her mood and was touched by its gentleness.

They talked until late, planning changes in the old farm and improvements in the new one. It was an evening that she liked to remember as long as she lived. Whenever she looked back on it afterwards, it seemed to lie there like a fertile valley in the arid monotony of her life.

Part Third   # Life-everlasting

For the next few years ...

1

For the next few years she gave herself completely to Five Oaks. Only by giving herself completely, only by enriching the land with her abundant vitality, could she hope to restore the farm. Reclaiming the abandoned fields had become less a reasonable purpose than a devouring passion in her mind and heart. Old Farm was managed by Nathan now, and since he had let his own place to a thrifty German tenant, he had, as Dorinda frequently reminded him, "all the time in the world on his hands." The dairy work, which had prospered when three trains a day were run between Washington and the South, still remained under her supervision; but all the hours that she could spare were spent on the freshly ploughed acres of Five Oaks. Over these acres she toiled as resolutely as the pioneer must have toiled when he snatched a home from the wilderness. Though she had installed Martin Flower in the house, she had rejected Nathan's idea of letting the farm "on shares" to the tenant. This was the only disagreement she had ever had with Nathan, and he had yielded at last to the habit of command which had fastened upon her. As she grew older she clung to authority as imperiously as a king who refuses to abdicate. There were moments in these years when, arrested by some sudden check on her arrogance, she stopped to wonder if any man less confirmed in humility than Nathan could have stood her as a wife. But, immediately afterwards, she would reflect, with the faint bitterness which still flavoured her opinion of love, that if she had married another man, he might not have found her overbearing.

Though the gentleness of mood which had stolen over her that August evening had not entirely departed, it lingered above the bare reason of her mind as a tender flush might linger over the austere pattern of the landscape. After that evening she had drawn no nearer to her husband, yet she had felt no particular impulse to stand farther away. Their association had touched its highest point in the soft darkness of that night, and she knew that they could never again reach the peak of consciousness together. But the quiet friendliness of their intercourse was not disturbed by Dorinda's interest in Five Oaks; and when, after a longer pursuit and a fiercer capture than usual, Lena finally married young Jim Ellgood, the days at Old Farm assumed the aspect of bright serenity which passes so often for happiness. Though Dorinda was not happy in the old thrilling sense of the word, she drifted, as middle age wore on, into a philosophy of acquiescence. John Abner was still her favourite companion, and he shared her ardent interest in Five Oaks. In time, she hoped he would marry some girl whom she herself should select, and that they would live with their children at Old Farm. When she suggested this to Nathan, he chuckled under his breath.

"It wouldn't surprise me if he wanted his head when he comes to marrying," he observed.

"Of course you think I am high-handed," she rejoined.

"Well, it don't make any difference to me what you are. And as long as you can manage me," he added, "you needn't worry about not keeping your hand in."

"It's for your own good anyway," she retorted. "You're too easy-going with everybody."

"I know it, honey. I ain't complaining."

He was refilling his pipe from his shabby old pouch of tobacco, and while he prodded the bowl with his thumb, he lifted his eyes and looked at her with his sheepish smile.

"I heard 'em talking about Jason Greylock yesterday at the store," he said.

She made a gesture of aversion. "What did they say?"

"Not much that I can recollect. Only that he is too lazy to come for his mail. He has buried himself in that house in the woods across Whippernock River, and he sometimes lets a whole month go by without coming to the post office."

"Perhaps he hasn't any way of getting over."

"He's still got his horse and buggy. I doubt if he's really as poor as he makes out. He hires Aunt Mehaley Plumtree to cook for him
318

and look after the poultry. She comes every morning and stays till dark."

"To think of coming down to that after Five Oaks!"

"Well, the country goes against you when you ain't cut out for a farmer. Since the old man brought him back from the North, I reckon Jason has had a hard row to hoe."

"He wasn't obliged to stay here," she observed scornfully.

"No, but he was always too easy-going. A pleasant enough fellow when he was a boy; but soon ripe, soon rotten."

"Oh, I give it up." Dorinda was untying her apron while she answered. "He isn't worth all the time we've wasted talking about him."

"Good Lord, Dorinda! You haven't been sitting here ten minutes."

"Well, ten minutes will pick a bushel, as Ebenezer says. They are waiting for me over at Five Oaks."

This was the secret of her contentment, she knew, breathless activity. If she was satisfied with her life, it was only because she never stopped long enough in her work to imagine the kind of life she should have preferred. While her health was good and her energy unimpaired, she had no time for discontent. If she had looked for it, she sometimes told herself, she could have found sufficient cause for unhappiness; but she was careful not to look for it.

In these years there were brief periods when her old dreams awakened. Beauty that seemed too fugitive to be real was still more a torment than a delight to her. The moon rising over the harp-shaped pine; the shocked corn against the red sunsets of autumn; the mulberry-coloured twilights of winter;—while she watched these things the past would glow again with the fitful incandescence of memory. But the inner warmth died with the external beauty, and she dismissed the longing as weakness. "You know where that sort of thing leads you," she would tell herself sternly. "Three months of love, and you pay for it with all the rest of your life."

Looking round at other women, she could not see that they were better off in the matter of love than she was herself. Even the few who had married the men they had chosen had paid for it—or so it appeared to her—with a lifetime of physical drudgery or emotional disappointment. She supposed they had compensations that she

319

could not discover—otherwise how could they have borne with their lives?—but there was not one among them with whom she would have changed places. Those who had been most deeply in love appeared to her to have become most bitterly disenchanted.

"I've a lot to be thankful for," she would repeat, while she went out to struggle against the scrub pine or broomsedge.

At Five Oaks, during those first seasons, she converted her repressed energy into the work of destruction. She would watch the reclaiming of the waste places, the burning of the broomsedge, the grubbing up of the pine and the sassafras, as if the fire and smoke were clearing her life of its illusions. Her nightmare dream of ploughing under the thistles was translated into the actual event. Perhaps, as the years went by, the reality would follow the dream into oblivion. At thirty, she had looked forward to forty, as the time of her release from vain expectation; but when forty came, she pushed the horizon of her freedom still farther away. "Perhaps at fifty I shall be rid of it for ever," she thought.

The winter had begun with a heavy snowstorm in December, and the week before Christmas Nathan went to bed with a cold which left him with an abscess in one of his teeth. There was no dental surgeon nearer than Richmond, and Doctor Stout had advised him to go to the city and have the tooth out as quickly as possible. "You won't have a minute's peace until you do," the doctor added decisively.

That was weeks ago, for Nathan had deferred the evil day until the twentieth of January when he was required as a witness in a lawsuit Bob Ellgood was bringing against the railroad. "As long as I've got to go to Richmond anyway, I might as well wait and kill two birds with one stone," he said.

A few days before the case was called his toothache began again with violence, and for two nights he had walked the floor in agony.

"You will be so thankful afterwards that it is over!" Dorinda assured him encouragingly.

She was busily seeding raisins for a plum pudding, and she paused long enough in her task to glance out of the window and shake her head. Though her forty-second birthday had just gone, the wintry flush in her cheeks and the imperious carriage of her head still created, at a little distance, the aspect of youth. There was a white lock on her forehead; but the premature greyness appeared theatrical rather than elderly above the intense blue of her eyes. "You look as good to me as you ever did," Nathan had said to her on her birthday.

As she turned from the window and put down the bowl of raisins, a frown wrinkled her forehead. "I wonder if it will ever stop snowing?" she said.

For days the weather had been bitterly cold, and the bare country had frozen under a leaden sky. Then at sunset the evening before a red fire had streamed over the rim of the horizon, and in the night snow had begun to fall. When Dorinda had gone out to the barn at five o'clock, she had found the landscape covered with a white blanket and deep drifts at the corners of the house and on the north side of the well and the woodpile. The blackness had been so thick that she had been obliged to walk in the flitting circle of light her lantern had cast on the ground. She had already sent off the butter to meet the five o'clock train to Washington; but Nimrod had overslept himself, and Nathan had hurried to the cabin to wake him, while John Abner had harnessed the horses to the wagon. Even then the coloured boy had had to take his breakfast with him and eat it at the station. If the train had been delayed, the butter would not have reached Washington until the day was well advanced.

All the morning and afternoon the flakes were driven in the high wind. Though Dorinda could see only a few feet in front of her, she knew that the dim fleecy shapes huddled on the lawn were not sheep but lilac bushes and flower-beds. The animals and the birds had long ago fled to shelter. As soon as the snow stopped falling the crows would begin flying over the fields; but now the world appeared as deserted as if it were the dawn of creation. In the kitchen, where she stayed when she was not obliged to be in the dairy, there was an ashen light which gave everything, even the shining pots and pans, an air of surprise. Fluvanna, who was stirring the mixture for the plum pudding, sat as close to the stove as she could push her chair, and shivered beneath her shawl of knitted grey wool.

"Well, I reckon I'll be glad to get it over," Nathan said in a mournful voice. "I've stood it about as long as I can."

He had dropped disconsolately into a chair by the table, and sat with his hands hanging helplessly between his knees. His face was tied up in a white silk handkerchief which Dorinda had given him at Christmas, and while she looked at him with sympathy, she could not repress a smile at the comical figure he made. Like a sick sheep! That was the way he always looked when anything hurt him. He was a good man; she was sincerely attached to him; but there was no use denying that he looked like a sick sheep.

"Nimrod can drive you over with the butter in the morning," she rejoined. "Then you can have your tooth pulled before you have to go to court."

Afterwards, when she recalled this conversation, the ashen light of the kitchen flooded her mind. A small thing like that to decide all one's future! Yet it seemed to her that it was always the little things, not the big ones, that influenced destiny; the fortuitous occurrence instead of the memorable occasion. The incident of his going was apparently as trivial as her meeting with Jason in the road, as the failure of her aim when the gun had gone off, as the particular place and moment when she had fallen down in Fifth Avenue. These accidents had changed utterly the course of her life. Yet none of them could she have foreseen and prevented; and only once, she felt, in that hospital in New York, had the accident or the device of fortune been in her favour.

"Yes, I'll do it," Nathan repeated firmly. "Ebenezer or Nimrod can meet the evening train. That ought to get me home in time for supper."

"If this keeps up," Dorinda observed, "everything will be late."

In the morning, as she had foreseen, everything was an hour later than usual. "The train is obliged to be behindhand," she thought, "so it won't really matter." Though it was still snowing, the wind had dropped and the stainless white lay like swan's-down over the country. All that Dorinda could see was the world within the moving circle of the lantern; but imagination swept beyond to the desolate beauty of the scene. "I'd like to go over with you," she said, when they had finished breakfast, "only the roads will be so heavy I oughtn't to add anything on the horses."

"It will be pretty hard driving," Nathan returned. "I hope I shan't take cold in my tooth."

"Oh, I can wrap up your face in a shawl, and I've got out that old sheepskin Pa used to use. You couldn't suffer more than you

322

did last night. Doctor Stout says the trouble isn't from cold but from infection."

He shook his head dolefully. "No, I couldn't stand another night as bad as that. The train will be warm anyhow, and even the drive won't be much worse than the barn was this morning. Jim Ellgood has his barn heated. I wonder if it wouldn't be a good idea for us to heat ours next year. Milking ain't much fun when your hands are frost-bitten."

"Yes, it would be a good idea," she conceded inattentively, while she brought a pencil and a piece of paper and made a list of the things she wished him to buy in town. "You may hear something about the war in Europe," she added, in the hope of diverting his mind from the pain in his tooth. Nathan was the only man at Pedlar's Mill who had taken the trouble to study the battles in France, and even Dorinda, though she made no comment, thought he was going too far when he brought home an immense new map of Europe and spent his evenings following the march of the German Army. Already he had prophesied that we should be drawn into the war before it was over; but like his other prophecies, this one was too far-sighted to be heeded by his neighbours.

When it was time for him to start, and Nimrod had brought the wagon to the door, she wrapped Nathan's face in her grey woollen scarf and tied the ends in a knot at the back of his head. "You can get somebody to undo you at the station."

He smiled ruefully. "No, I don't reckon I'd better get on the train tied up like this. I must look funny."

"It doesn't matter how you look," she responded; but she could not keep back a laugh.

As the wagon ploughed through the snow, she stood there, with her shawl wrapped tightly over her bosom and the lantern held out into the blackness before dawn. The air was alive with a multitude of whirling flakes, which descended swiftly and sped off into the space beyond the glimmer of her lantern. After the wagon had disappeared the silence was so profound that she could almost hear the breathless flight of the snow-flakes from the veiled immensity of the sky. By the glow of the lantern she could just distinguish the ghostly images of trees rising abruptly out of the shrouded stillness of the landscape. While she lingered there it seemed to her that the earth and air and her own being were purified and exalted into some frigid zone of the spirit. Humanity, with its irksome responsibilities and its unprofitable desires, dropped away from her; but when she turned and entered the house, it was waiting in the ashen light to retard her endeavours.

2

In the kitchen John Abner was lingering over his breakfast, and Fluvanna was frying bacon and eggs, while she complained of the weather in a cheerful voice.

"Are the cows all right?" Dorinda inquired of her stepson. Until the storm was over, the cows must be kept up, and John Abner, who was a diligent farmer, had been out to feed and water them.

"Yes, but it's rough on them. It's still as black as pitch, but the sooner we get the milking over the better. The hands are always late on a morning like this."

Dorinda glanced at the tin clock on the shelf. "It isn't five o'clock yet. We'll start as soon as you finish breakfast whether the other milkers have come or not. The cows can't wait on the storm."

"It's a pity Father had to go to town to-day."

"It may be fortunate that something decided him. The doctor said he wouldn't be any better until he had that tooth out. He walked the floor all night with whiskey in his mouth."

The smile that came into Dorinda's eyes when she looked at her stepson made her face appear girlish, in spite of its roughened skin and the lines which were deeper in winter. "I see the lanterns outside now," she added. "The women must be on the way to the milking." Wrapping her shawl over her head, she took down a coat of raccoon skins, which was hanging behind the door, and slipped her arms into the shapeless sleeves. Then going out on the back porch, she felt under a snowladen bench for the overshoes she had left there last evening. Dawn was still far away, and in the opaque darkness she could see the lanterns crawling like frozen glowworms through the whirling snow, which was blown and scattered in the glimmering circles of light.

In one of the long low buildings where the milk cows were sheltered, she found a few grotesquely arrayed milkers. From the beginning she had employed only women milkers, inspired by a firm, though illogical, belief in their superior neatness. Yet she had supplemented faith with incessant admonition, and this was, perhaps, the reason that the women wore this morning neat caps and aprons above a motley of borrowed or invented raiment. When she entered, stepping carefully over the mixture of snow and manure on the threshold, they greeted her with grumbling complaints of the weather; but before the work was well started they had thawed in the contagious warmth of her personality, and were chattering like a flock of blackbirds in a cherry tree. Since it is the law of African nature to expand in the sunshine, she was particular never to wear a dismal face over her work.

For the first minute, while she hung the lantern on the nail over her head, she felt that the meadow-scented breath of the cows was woven into an impalpable vision of summer. Though she shivered outwardly in the harsh glare of light, a window in her mind opened suddenly, and she saw Jason coming toward her through the yellow-green of August evenings. As with her mother's missionary dream, these visitations of the past depended less upon her mood, she had discovered, than upon some fugitive quality in time or place which evoked them from the shadows of memory. Concealing a shiver of distaste, she turned away and bent over a milk-pail.

"Your fingers are stiff, Jessie, let me try her a moment."

Hours later, when light had come and the work of the dairy was over for the morning, she went back into the house, and the ashen light went with her over the threshold. Fluvanna was busy with dinner, and a pointer puppy named Pat was fast asleep by the stove. Young Ranger, the son of old Ranger, lay on a mat by the door, and though many Flossies had passed away, there was always a grey and white cat bearing the name to get under one's feet between the stove and the cupboard. The room, Dorinda told herself, was more cheerful than it had ever been. She remembered that her mother could never afford curtains for the windows, and that Fluvanna had laughed at her when she had bought barred muslin and edged it with ruffles. "Good Lord, Miss Dorinda, who ever heard tell!" the girl exclaimed. Yet, in the end, the curtains, with other innovations, had become a part of the established order of living. Why was it so difficult, she wondered, to bring people to accept either a new idea or a new object? Nathan was the only man at Pedlar's Mill who lived in the future, and Nathan had always been ridiculed by his neighbours. The telephone, the modern churn, and the separator, what a protracted battle he had fought for each of these labour-saving inventions! He was talking now of the time when they would have an electric plant on the farm and all the cows would be milked and the cream separated by electricity. Was this only the fancy of a visionary, or, like so many of Nathan's imaginary devices, would it come true in the end?

At twelve o'clock John Abner came in for dinner, and, after a hurried meal, went out to help clear away the snow from the out-buildings. As there was no immediate work to be done, Dorinda sat down before the fire in her bedroom and turning to her work-basket, slipped her darning-egg into one of Nathan's socks. She disliked darning, and because she disliked it she never permitted herself to neglect it. Her passionate revolt from the inertia of the land had permeated the simplest details of living. The qualities with which she had triumphed over the abandoned fields were the virtues of the pioneers who had triumphed over life.

The room was quiet except for the crackling of the flames and the brushing of an old pear tree against the window. In the warmth of the firelight the glimpse of the snow-covered country produced a sensation of physical comfort, which stole over her like the Sabbath peace for which her mother had yearned. Lifting her eyes from her darning, she glanced over the long wainscoted room, where the only changes were the comforts that Nathan had added. The thick carpet, the soft blankets, the easy chair in which she was rocking,— if only her mother had lived long enough to enjoy these things! Then the thought came to her that, if her parents had been denied material gifts, they had possessed a spiritual luxury which she herself had never attained. She had inherited, she realized, the religious habit of mind without the religious heart; for the instinct of piety had worn too thin to cover the generations. Conviction! That, at least, they had never surrendered. The glow of religious certitude had never faded for them into the pallor of moral necessity. For them, the hard, round words in her great-grandfather's books were not as hollow as globes. Her gaze travelled slowly over the rows of discoloured bindings in the bookcases, and she remembered the rainy days in her childhood when, having exhausted the lighter treasures of adventure, she had ploughed desperately in the dry and stubborn acres of theology. After all, was the mental harvest as barren as she had believed? Firmness of purpose, independence of character, courage of living, these attributes, if they were not hers by inheritance, she had gleaned from those heavy furrows of her great-grandfather's sowing. "Once a Presbyterian, always a Presbyterian," her mother had said when she was dying.

As the afternoon wore on she grew restless from inaction, and the ruddy firelight, which had been so pleasant after the cold morning, became oppressive. Putting her work-basket aside, she went out into the hall and opened the back door, where Ebenezer, with a comforter of crimson wool tied over his head and ears, was shovelling the snow-drifts away from the angle of the porch. At a distance other men were digging out the paths to the barn, and the narrow flagged walk to the dairy was already hollowed into a gully between high white banks.

Ebenezer, a big, very black negro, with an infinite capacity for rest and the mournful gaze of an evangelist, wielded his shovel vigorously at the sound of the opening door, while he hummed in a bass voice which was like the drone of a tremendous beehive. He was subject to intervals of dreaminess when he would stop work for ten minutes at a time; but the only attention Dorinda had bestowed on his slackness was a mild wonder if he could be thinking.

"Try to get that snow away before dark, Ebenezer," she said, "and tell Nimrod he must start earlier than usual to meet the evening train."

Turning back into the empty hall, she was surprised to find that she had begun to miss Nathan. It was the first time since her marriage that he had spent a whole day away from the farm, and she realized that she should be glad to have him in the house again. The discovery was so unexpected that it startled her into gravity, and passing the kitchen, where she saw Fluvanna poking wood into the open door of the stove, she walked slowly into her room and stood looking about her as if a fresh light had fallen across her surroundings. Yes, incredible as it was, she really missed Nathan!

Though she had never loved him, after nine years of marriage she still liked him with a strong and durable liking. It was a tribute, she realized, to her husband's character that this negative attachment should have remained superior to the universal law of diminishing returns. No woman, she told herself, could have lived for nine years with so good a man as Nathan and not have grown fond of him. She recognized his disadvantages as clearly as ever; yet recognizing them made little difference in her affection. She liked him because, in spite of his unattractiveness, he possessed a moral integrity which she respected and a magnanimity which she admired. He had accepted her austerity of demeanour as philosophically as he accepted a bad season; and to love but to refrain from the demands of love, was the surest way he could have taken to win her ungrudging esteem.

When she went out to remind Nimrod that he must start earlier to meet the six o'clock train, the snow was light and feathery on the surface, and the air was growing gradually milder. At sunset the sky was shattered by a spear of sunshine which pierced the wall of clouds in the west. Between that golden lance and the solitary roof under which she stood swept the monotonous fields of snow.

"If it clears, there'll be a good moon to-night," she thought.

When the milking hour came she yielded to the persuasions of John Abner and did not go out to the barn. "It is time you learned that nobody is indispensable," he said, half sternly, half jestingly. "There are mighty few jobs that a full-grown man can't do as well as a woman, and loafing round a cow-barn in wintertime isn't one of them."

"The negroes get so careless," she urged, "if they aren't watched."

He was standing in front of the fire, and while he held out his stout boots, one by one, to the flames, the snow in the creases of the leather melted and ran down on the hearth. The smell of country life in winter—a mingled odour of leather, manure, harness oil, tobacco, and burning leaves—was diffused by the heat and floated out with a puff of smoke from the chimney. His features, seen in profile against the firelight, reminded her of Jason. John Abner was not really like him, she knew; but there were traits in every man, tricks of expression, of gesture, of movement, which brought Jason to life again in her thoughts. Twenty-two years ago she had known

329

him! Twenty-two years filled to overflowing with dominant interests; and yet she could see his face as distinctly as she had seen it that first morning in the russet glow of the broomsedge. Dust now, she told herself, nothing more. Her memories of him were no better than deserted wasps' nests; but these dry and brittle ruins still clung there amid the cobwebs, in some obscure corner of her mind, and she could not brush them away. Neither regret nor sentiment had preserved them, and yet they had outlasted both sentiment and regret.

With a start of exasperation, she tore her mind from the past and glanced down at John Abner's clubfoot. "Are those boots comfortable?" she asked gently.

"Oh, they do as well as any," he replied irritably. Though any reference to his deformity annoyed him, there were times when she felt obliged to allude to it as a factor in his career. For good or ill, that clubfoot, like the mark of Jason in her life, had been his destiny. With his unusual gifts and without the sensitive shrinking from crowds which his lameness had developed into a disease, he might have achieved success in any profession that he had chosen. "You stay by the fire," he added, "while I take a turn at the bossing."

She nodded. "Very well, I'll be in the dairy when you are ready for me."

"I'll manage the whole business if you'll let me."

"But I shan't let you." She was smiling as she answered, and she perceived from his face that he was big enough to respect her for her inflexible purpose. While authority was still hers she would cling to it as stubbornly as she had toiled to attain it.

He went out laughing, and she dropped back in her chair to wait until the hour came for her work in the dairy. John Abner was right, of course. One of the exasperating things about men, she reflected, was that they were so often right. It was perfectly true that she could not stay young for ever, and at forty-two, after twenty years of arduous toil, she ought to think of the future and take the beginning of the hill more gradually. Though she was as strong, as vital, as young, in her arteries at least, as she had ever been, she could not, she realized, defend herself from the inevitable wearing down of the years. Her eyes wandered to the mirror in the bureau which had belonged to her mother, and it seemed to her that, sitting there in the ruddy firelight, the magic of youth enveloped her again with a springtime freshness. Her eyes looked so young in the dimness that they bathed her greying hair, her weather-beaten skin, and her tall, strong figure, which was becoming a little dry, a trifle inelastic, in the celestial blueness of a May morning.

"I wonder if it is because I've missed everything I really wanted that I cannot grow old?" she asked herself with a start.

It was seven o'clock when she returned from the dairy, and John Abner was already in the kitchen demanding his supper.

"The train is certain to be hours late," he said. "There's no use waiting any longer for Father."

"Yes, we might as well have supper. I can cook something for him when he comes."

"I saw Mr. Garlick going over a few minutes ago. His daughter, Molly, went down yesterday with young Mrs. Ellgood to a concert. Mrs. Ellgood has always been crazy about music. Did you ever hear her play on the violin?"

"No, I never went anywhere even before I was married. I'm glad she's coming up with your father. He always liked her in spite of the fact that she despises the country."

When supper was over, and John Abner had eaten with an amazing appetite, they went back into her bedroom and sat down to wait before the fire. Though she had never been what Nathan called "an easy talker," she could always find something to say to her stepson; and they talked now, not only of the farm, the spring planting, the new tractor-plough they had ordered, but of books and distant countries and the absurd illustrations in the Lives of the Missionaries, which John Abner was reading for the fourth time.

"Alfalfa has been the making of Five Oaks," Dorinda said. "It's a shame Pa never knew of it."

"I wonder if Doctor Greylock ever comes back to his farm. If he does, he must be sorry he lost it."

"Well, he ruined the place, he and his father before him. It was no better than waste land when we bought it."

John Abner bent over to caress the head of the pointer. "I can't blame anybody for wanting to quit," he said. "There's a lot to be said for those missionary chaps. They were the real adventurers, I sometimes think."

He rose from his chair and shook himself. "Why, it's almost ten o'clock. There's no use staying up any longer. If we've got to wake before five, it is time we were both asleep."

"I believe I hear the buggy now." Dorinda bent her ear listening. "Isn't that a noise on the bridge? Or is it only another branch cracking?"

"You can't hear wheels in this snow. But I'll go out and take a look round. There's a fine moon coming up."

When he had unbarred the front door, she slipped into her raccoon coat and overshoes, and flung her knitted shawl over her head. After a minute or two, she saw John Abner's figure moving among the shrouded trees to the gate, and descending the steps as carefully as she could, she followed slowly in the direction he had taken. By the time she was midway down the walk, he had disappeared up the frozen road. Except for the lighted house at her back she might have been alone in a stainless world before the creation of life. A cold white moon was shedding a silver lustre over the landscape, which appeared as transparent as glass against the impenetrable horizon. Even the house, when she glanced round at it, might have been only a shadow, so unreal, so visionary, it looked in the unearthly light of the snow. While she lingered there it seemed to her that the movement of the air, the earth, and the stars, was suspended. Substance and shadow melted into each other and into the vastness of space. Not a track blurred the ground, not a cloud trembled in the sky, not a murmur of life broke the stillness.

Presently, as she drew nearer the gate, a moving shape flitted in from the trees by the road, and John Abner called to her that the buggy was in sight. "I'll wait and bed down the mare," he said. "Nimrod will be pretty hungry, I reckon, and he won't look after her properly."

"Well, I'll go right in and fix supper for both of them."

Without waiting for the vehicle, she hurried into the house and replenished the fire in the stove. Then, while she broke the eggs and put on water to boil for coffee, she told herself that Nathan's coffee habit was as incurable as a taste for whiskey. The wood had caught and the fire was burning well when John Abner appeared suddenly in the doorway. He looked sleepy and a trifle disturbed.

"That wasn't Father after all," he said. "They told Nimrod there wasn't any use waiting longer. He was shaking with cold, so I sent him to bed. As soon as I've made the mare comfortable, I'll come and tell you all about it."

"I was just scrambling some eggs. I wish you'd eat them. I hate to waste things."

"All right. I'll be back in a jiffy."

He ran out as quickly as his lameness would permit, and she arranged the supper on the table. After all, if Nathan wasn't coming home to-night, John Abner might as well eat the eggs she had scrambled. There was no sense in wasting good food.

After attending to the mare the boy came in and began walking up and down the floor of the kitchen. He did not sit down at the table, though Dorinda was bringing the steaming skillet from the stove. "It's a nuisance all the wires are down," he said presently.

"Yes, but for that we might telephone."

"The telegraph wires have fallen too. Nimrod said they didn't know much more at the store than we do."

"Well, you'd better sit down and eat this while it's hot. It doesn't do any good to worry about things."

"One of the coloured men, Elisha Moody, told Nimrod he would be coming home in an hour, and he would stop and tell us the news. Mr. Garlick is going to wait at the station until his daughter comes."

"The news?" she asked vaguely. For the first time the idea occurred to her that John Abner was holding back what he had heard. "Doesn't Nimrod know when the train is expected?"

"Nobody knows. The wires are broken, but the train from Washington went down and came up again with news of a wreck down the road. I don't know whether it is Father's train or another, Nimrod was all mixed up about it. He couldn't tell me anything except that something had happened. The thing that impressed Nimrod most was that all the freight men carried axes. He kept repeating that over and over."

"Axes?" Dorinda's mind had stopped working. She stood there in the middle of the kitchen floor, with the coffee-pot in her hand, and repeated the word as if it were strange to her. Behind her the fire crackled, and the pots of rose-geraniums she had brought away from the window-sill stood in an orderly row on the brick hearth.

"I suppose they had to cut the coaches away from the track," replied John Abner indefinitely. "Elisha will tell us more when he stops by. He's got more sense than Nimrod, who was scared out of his wits."

"I would have given him some supper. Why didn't he come in?"

"He said his wife was waiting for him and he wanted to get to his cabin."

Dorinda poured out the coffee and carried the pot back to the stove. "I'm afraid your father will catch his death of cold," she said anxiously, "and with that tooth out!"

She was fortified by a serene confidence in Nathan's ability to take care of himself. The only uneasiness she felt was on account of the abscess. With all his good judgment, when it came to toothache he was no braver than a child.

John Abner seemed glad to get the hot coffee. "You might as well keep some for Elisha," he suggested. "It's almost time he was coming and I know he'll be thankful for something hot."

Though he ate and drank as if he were hungry, there was a worried look in his face, and he kept turning his head in the direction of the road.

"I don't suppose it's anything really serious," Dorinda remarked reassuringly. "If it had been, we should certainly have heard it sooner."

Dropping into a chair beside him, she raised a cup of coffee and drank it slowly in sips. Presently, notwithstanding her effort to minimize the cause for alarm, she became aware that anxiety was stealing over her as if it emanated from her surroundings. She felt it first in the creeping sensation which ran like spiders over her flesh; then in an almost imperceptible twitching of her muscles; and at last in a delicate vibration of her nerves, as if a message were passing over electric wires in her body. Then, suddenly, the fear mounted to her brain, and she found herself listening like John Abner for the crunching of wheels in the snow.

"Do you hear anybody, John Abner?"

"A branch snapped, that was all. I'll make up the fire in your chamber. It's more comfortable in there."

After he had gone into the bedroom, she fed the two dogs and the cat before she washed the dishes and placed the coffee where
334

it would keep hot for Elisha. As she was leaving the kitchen she noticed the rose-geraniums and moved the pots farther away from the heat. "If we are going to keep up the fire, it will be too warm for them there," she thought.

3

The log fire was blazing in her bedroom, and John Abner stood before the window which looked on the gate and the road.

"The panes are so frosted you can't see your hand before you," he said, as she entered.

Standing there beside him, she gazed through the leafless boughs of the lilac bushes. "No, even the moonlight doesn't help you," she answered. "It must be bitterly cold in the road. I hope the mare got warm again."

"Yes, I covered her up. Nimrod had some whiskey and he was going to make a hot toddy." John Abner shivered in the icy draught that crept in through the loose window-sashes. "Hadn't you better lie down?" he asked, turning back to the fire. "It won't be long now."

She shook her head. "That coffee will keep me awake. Lie down on the couch, and I'll listen for Elisha. I drew up the shades, so he will know we haven't gone to bed."

For a few minutes he resisted her, his eyes blinking in the firelight while he struggled to bite back a yawn. Then he gave up and flung himself down on the big soft couch. "It would take something stronger than coffee to keep me awake to-night," he said. "If I drop off, will you wake me?"

"If there is any news. But you will hear Elisha when he comes."

He laughed drowsily. "I believe I could sleep straight through Judgment Day."

Taking the quilt from the bed, she covered him carefully from head to foot. As she tucked him in, she remembered her wedding-night when she had found Nathan asleep on the couch in front of the fire. "If he hadn't been like that, I couldn't have stood him," she thought.

Sinking into the easiest chair by the flames, she picked up the sock she had partly darned in the afternoon. Then, observing that the lamp was shining in John Abner's face, she lowered the wick and folding the sock, replaced it in her work-basket. The chair creaked gently as she rocked, and fearing the noise might disturb him, she sat motionless, with her eyes on the hickory logs and her foot touching the neck of the pointer.

While she sat there she recalled, with one of the irresponsible flashes of memory which revived only when she was inactive, the afternoon when she had waited in the dripping woods to see Jason drive home with Geneva. She was a girl then; now she was a woman and middle-aged; yet there was an intolerable quality in all suspense which made it alike. Compared to those moments, this waiting was as the dead to the living agony. "Suppose I had married Jason and he was on that train, could I sit here like this?" she asked herself. "Suppose I had married Jason instead of Nathan, would marriage have been different?"

Then, because the question was useless and she had no room for useless things in her practical mind, she put it sternly away from her, and rising, slipped into her coat and went out of the house. Closing the door softly, she passed out on the porch and down the frozen steps to the lawn. The snow was slippery in thin places, and she knew that Elisha would try to keep to the road where the deep drifts were less dangerous. Advancing cautiously, she moved in the direction of the gate, but she had gone only a few steps when she saw Elisha's old spring-wagon rolling over the bridge. Quickening her steps dangerously, she ran over the slippery ground.

"I've kept some hot coffee for you, Uncle Elisha. Can't you come into the kitchen and get something to eat?"

"Naw'm, I reckon I'd better be gittin' erlong home. My ole grey mare, she's had jes' about enuff er dis yeah wedder, en she's kinder hankerin' fur de stable."

"We can keep her here. There's plenty of room in the stable, and you can spend the night with Ebenezer."

"Thanky, Miss Dorindy, bofe un us sutney would be glad uv er spell er res'. My son Jasper, he's on dat ar train dat's done been stalled down de track, an' I'se gwine out agin about'n sunup."

"Have they heard anything yet?" asked Dorinda, while the wagon crawled over the snags of roots in the direction of the stable.

Elisha shook his muffled head. "Dey don' know nuttin', Miss Dorindy, dat's de Gospel trufe, dey don' know nuttin' 'tall. Dar's a train done come down f'om de Norf, en hit's gwine on wid whatevah dey could git abo'd hit. Hi! Dey's got axes erlong, en I 'low dar ain' nary a one un um dat kin handle an axe like my Jasper."

"I'm afraid it's a bad wreck," Dorinda said uneasily.

"Yas'm, dar's a wreck somewhar, sho' 'nuff, but dey don' know nuttin' out dar at de station. All de wires is down, ev'y las' one un um, en dar ain' nobody done come erlong back dat went down de road. Ef'n you'll lemme res' de night heah, me en de mare'll go out agin befo' sunup."

"There's all the room in the world, Uncle Elisha. Wait, and I'll give you a lantern to take to the stable." She went indoors and returned in a few minutes with a light swinging from her hand. "As soon as you've attended to your mare, come in and I'll have something for you to eat."

As she passed her bedroom on the way to the kitchen she saw that John Abner was still sleeping, and she did not stop to arouse him. Why should she disturb his slumber when there was nothing definite that she could tell him? Instead, she hastened about her preparations for Elisha's supper, and by the time the old negro came in from bedding the mare, the bacon and eggs were on the table. Withdrawing to a safe distance from the stove, he thawed his frost-bitten hands and feet, while his grizzled head emerged like some gigantic caterpillar from the chrysalis of shawls he had wound about him.

"Were there many people at the station?" she inquired presently.

"Naw'm, hit was too fur fur mos' folks. Marse John Garlick, he wuz spendin' de night in de sto', en so was Marse Jim Ellgood. Young Marse Bob en his wife wuz bofe un um on de train."

"Well, make a good supper. Then you can go up to Ebenezer's. I saw smoke coming out of his chimney, so it will be warm there."

Because she knew that he would enjoy his supper more if he were permitted to eat it alone, she went back to the fire in her bedroom
338

where John Abner was still sleeping. She watched there in the silence until she heard Elisha exclaim, "Good night, Miss Dorindy!" and go out, shutting the back door behind him. Then she locked up the house, and after lowering the wick of the hall lamp, touched John Abner on the shoulder.

"You'd better go to bed. In a little while you will have to be up again."

He opened his eyes and sat up, blinking at the firelight. "I could have slept on into next week."

"Well, don't wake up. Go straight upstairs."

"Did Elisha ever come?"

"Yes, he put his mare in the stable and went up to spend the night with Ebenezer."

"What did he tell you?"

"Only that they haven't found out anything definite at the station. You know how cut off everything is when the wires are down. Mr. Garlick and James Ellgood are both waiting out there all night."

"Then it was Father's train. It must have been a bad wreck."

"I'm afraid so. This suspense is so baffling. Anything in the world might happen, and we shouldn't know of it until the next day."

Her face was pale and drawn, and while she spoke, she shivered, not from cold but from anxiety. She saw John Abner glance quickly toward the front window and she knew that he, like herself, was feeling all the terror of primitive isolation. How did people stand it when they were actually cut off by the desert or the frozen North from communication with their kind?

"You know now what it must have been like in the old days before we had the telegraph and the telephone," she said. "Pedlar's Mill was scarcely more than a stopping place in the wilderness, and my mother would be shut in for days without a sign from the outer world."

"I never thought of it before," said John Abner, "but it must have been pretty rough on her. The roads were no better than frozen bogs, so she couldn't get anywhere if she wanted to."

"That was why she got her mania for work. The winter loneliness, she said, was more than she could endure without losing her mind. She had to move about to make company for herself. There were

339

weeks at a time, she told me once, when the roads were so bad that nobody went by, not even Mr. Garlick, or an occasional negro. During the war the trains stopped running on this branch road, and afterwards there were only two trains passing a day."

"I suppose it was always better on the other side of the railroad."

"They're nearer the highway, of course, though that was bad enough when Ma was first married. Over here the roads were never mended unless a few of the farmers agreed to give so much labour, either of slaves or free negroes. Then, after the contract was made, something invariably got in the way and it fell through. Somebody died or fell ill or lost all his crops. You know how indisposed tenant farmers are to doing their share of work."

"And there wasn't even a store at Pedlar's Mill until Father started one?"

"Nothing but the mill. That was there as far back as anybody could remember, and there was always a Pedlar for a miller. The farmers from this side took corn there to be ground, and sometimes they would trade it for sugar or molasses. But the only store was far up at the Court-House. People bought their winter supplies when they went to town to sell tobacco. All the tobacco money went for coffee and sugar and clothes. That was why Pa raised a crop every year to the end of his life."

John Abner rose and stretched himself. "Well, I'm precious glad I live in the days of the telephone and the telegraph, with the hope of owning an automobile when they get cheaper." Going over to the window, he held his hand over his eyes and peered out. "You can't see a thing but snow. We might as well be dead and buried under it. Shall I take the butter over in the morning?"

"No, I'd like to go myself. You'd better stay and look after the milking." How inexorable were the trivial necessities of the farm! Anxieties might come and go, but the milking would not wait upon life or death. Not until John Abner had gone upstairs did she perceive that she had been talking, as her mother would have said, "to make company for herself." "I've almost lost my taste for books," she thought, "and I used to be such a hungry reader."

After putting a fresh log on the fire, she flung herself on the bed, without undressing, and lay perfectly still while a nervous tremor, like the suspension of a drawn breath, crept over her. Toward daybreak, when the crashing of a dead branch on one of the locust trees sounded as if it had fallen on the roof, she realized that she was straining every sense for the noise of an approaching vehicle in the road. Then, rising hurriedly, she threw open the window and leaned out into the night. Nothing there. Only the lacquered darkness and the moon turning to a faint yellow-green over the fields of snow!

At four o'clock she went into the kitchen and began preparations for breakfast. When the coffee was ground, the water poured over it in the coffee-pot, and the batterbread mixed and put into the baking dish, she returned to her room and finished her dressing. By the time John Abner came down to go out to the cow-barn, she was waiting with her hat on and a pile of sheepskin rugs at her feet.

"I suppose we might as well send the butter out. Fluvanna has it ready," she said, watching him while he lighted his lantern from the lamp on the breakfast table. "If the trains have begun running again, they will expect it in Washington."

"It won't hurt anyway to take it along. I'll tell Nimrod to hitch up."

They both spoke as if the wreck had been merely a temporary inconvenience which was over. Vaguely, there swam through Dorinda's mind the image of her mother cooking breakfast in her best dress before she went to the Court-House. The old woman had worn the same expression of desperate hopefulness that Dorinda felt now spreading like a mask of beeswax over her own features. Already, though it was still dark, the life of the farm was stirring. As John Abner went out, she saw the stars of lanterns swinging away into the night, and when he returned to breakfast, Fluvanna was in the kitchen busily frying bacon and eggs. Before they had finished the meal, Nimrod appeared to say that the wagon was waiting, and rising hastily Dorinda slipped on her raccoon-skin coat.

"We'd better start," she said. "Give Uncle Elisha his breakfast, and tell him we will bring Jasper back with us. Keep the kettle on, so you can make coffee for Mr. Nathan as soon as he gets here."

Hurrying out, she climbed into the heavy wagon, and they started carefully down the slippery grade to the road. As they turned out of the gate, the wheels slid over the embedded rocks to the frozen ruts in the snow. Only a circle of road immediately in front of them was visible, and while the wagon rolled on, this spot of ground ap-

341

peared to travel with them, never changing and never lingering in its passage. Into this illuminated circle tiny tracks of birds drifted and vanished like magic signs.

Presently, as they drew nearer Pedlar's Mill, a glimmer, so faint that it was scarcely more than a ripple on the surface of black waters, quivered in the darkness around them. With this ripple, a formless transparency floated up in the east, as a luminous mist swims up before an approaching candle. Out of this brightness, the landscape dawned in fragments, like dissolving views of the Arctic Circle. The sky was muffled overhead, but just as they reached the station a pale glow suffused the clouds beyond the ruined mill on the horizon.

"If the train was on time, it must have gone by an hour ago," Dorinda said, but she knew that there was no chance of its having gone by.

"Hit's gwineter thaw, sho' 'nuff, befo' sundown," Nimrod rejoined, speaking for the first time since they started.

"Yes, it's getting milder."

At that hour, in the bitter dawn, the station looked lonelier and more forsaken than ever. Hemmed in by the level sea of ice, the old warehouse and platform were flung there like dead driftwood. Even the red streak in the sky made the winter desolation appear more desolate.

At first she could distinguish no moving figures; but when they came nearer, she saw a small group of men gathered round an object which she had mistaken in the distance for one of the deserted freight cars.

Now she saw that this object was a train of a single coach, with an engine attached, and that the men were moving dark masses from the car to crude stretchers laid out on the snow.

"The trains are running again," Dorinda said hoarsely. "They must have got the track cleared."

"I hope dey's gwineter teck dis yeah budder," Nimrod returned. "Git up heah, hosses! We ain' got no mo' time to poke."

A chill passed down Dorinda's spine; but she was unaware of the cause that produced it, and her mind was vacant of thought. Then, while the wagon jolted up the slope, some empty words
342

darted into her consciousness. "Something has happened. I feel that something has happened."

"Do you see anybody that you know, Nimrod?"

"Naw'm, I cyarn see nobody." Then he added excitedly, "But dar's somebody a-comin'. Ain' he ole Marse Jim Ellgood?"

The horses stopped by the fence and began nuzzling the snow, while Nimrod dropped the reins and jumped down to lift out the butter. Standing up in the wagon, Dorinda beat her chilled hands together. Her limbs felt stiff with cold, and for a moment they refused to obey her will. Then recovering control of herself, she stepped down from the wagon and followed Nimrod in the direction of the store. Immediately, she was aware of a bustle about the track, and she thought, "How much human beings are like turkeys!" The group of men had separated as she approached, and two figures came forward to meet her across the snow. One was a stranger; the other, though it took her an instant to recognize him, was Bob Ellgood. "Why, he looks like an old man," she said to herself. "He looks as old as his father." The ruddy, masterful features were scorched and smoke-stained, and the curling fair hair was burned to the colour of singed broomsedge. Even his eyes looked burned, and one of his hands was rolled in a bandage.

She stopped abruptly and stood motionless. Though she was without definite fear, an obscure dread was beating against the wall of her consciousness. "Something has happened. Something has happened. Something has happened." Her mind seemed to have no relation to herself, to her feelings, to her beliefs, to her affections. It was only an empty shed, and the darkness of this shed was filled suddenly with the sound of swallows fluttering.

When Bob Ellgood reached her, he held out his unbandaged hand. "Father and I were just going over to your place, Mrs. Pedlar," he said. "We wanted to be the first to see you. We wanted you to hear of Nathan from us——"

"Then he is dead," she said quietly. It had never seemed possible to her that Nathan could die. He had not mattered enough for that. But now he was dead.

"He died a hero," a stranger, whom she had never seen before, said earnestly.

"Yes, he died a hero," Bob Ellgood snatched the words away from the other. "That is what we wish you to know and to feel as long as you live. He gave his life for others. He had got free, without a scratch, and he went back into the wreck. The train had gone over the embankment. It was burning and women were screaming. He went down because he was strong. He went down and he never came back."

"God! Those shrieks!" exclaimed the strange man. "I'll hear them all my life. As long as I live, I'll never stop hearing them."

"He got free?" she repeated stupidly.

"But he went back. He got an axe from somebody, and he went back because he was strong. He was cutting the car away to get a woman out. He did get her out——" He broke off and added hastily, "When we found him, he was quite dead. . . ."

Dorinda stared at him vacantly, seeing nothing but his blackened features and the scorched place on his head. "Will they bring him to the farm?" she asked.

"If you wish it." Bob's voice was shaken. "But we feel that we should like him to rest in the churchyard."

Silently, scarcely knowing what he asked, she assented. So Nathan had forced people to take him seriously, even though he had to die before they would do it. Was it worth it? she wondered. Would it have pleased him if he had known?

"May I go to the church? Have they taken him there?"

She saw that Bob hesitated before he answered. "I hope you won't see him," he replied after a minute. "We believe he was killed instantly, but——" He broke off and then went on desperately, "If you will go home and leave the arrangements to us, we promise you that everything shall be as he would have wished. We should like him to have the funeral of a hero."

"The funeral of a hero!" she echoed. She did not know, she could not imagine what kind of funeral that would be; but she felt intuitively that Nathan would have liked it, and that she had no right to deny him the funeral that he would have liked.

Without replying in words, she bent her head and turned back to the wagon, where a completely demoralized Nimrod awaited her. A stunned sensation held her emotions imprisoned, and a few minutes later, as she drove homeward, it occurred to her that she was

344

proving unequal again to one of the supreme occasions of her life. Emotionally, would she always prove unequal to the demands of life? She was not feeling what she knew that she ought to feel; she was not feeling what she knew that they expected of her. Her stern judgment told her that she was a hypocrite; but it was hypocrisy against which she was inert and helpless. Though she was overwhelmed by the general tragedy, she was without a keen sense of widowhood. Something within her soul, that thin clear flame which was herself, remained unshaken by her loss, as it had remained unshaken by every tragedy but one in her life. She was leaving Nathan, with regret but not with grief, to his belated popularity. How could she begrudge him in death the thing that he had wanted most when he was alive? Yes, beholding him as she did with compassion but without pretense, she knew that he would have enjoyed the funeral of a hero.

4

Waking in the blackness before dawn, she heard John Abner come downstairs and stop in the hall to light his lantern.

"I ought to go out to the milking," she thought, and then more slowly, "I can't believe that Nathan is dead."

Would the idea ever grow familiar to her? Could she ever live with the fact, acknowledged and yet unregarded, as she had lived with the fact of her marriage? "There never was a better man in the world," she said aloud. Here on the farm she found herself missing him with the first vague sense of loss. The insensibility which had protected her at the station disappeared when her mind dwelt on his good qualities,—his kindness, his charity, his broad tolerance of her prejudices. She knew that she should miss him more and more in all the details of the farm, and that she should begin to sorrow for him as soon as she had time to realize that she had lost him for ever. Yesterday was a void in her mind. When she thought of the long day after her return from the station, she could remember only the incredible tenderness of John Abner, and the visit in the afternoon from James Ellgood, who had told her that the news of the wreck had just travelled as far as the farms beyond Whippernock River, and that the absent minister was returning at midnight.

On this, the second day after Nathan's death, the primitive ceremonies of the funeral began. The earliest and one of the most depressing signs of mourning was the loud demoralization of the negroes, who rose to the funeral as fish to bait, and became immediately incapable of any work except lamenting the dead. As long as there was hope left in tragedy, they were able to brace themselves to Herculean exertions; but superstition enslaved them as soon as death entered the house. The cows, of course, had to be milked;

but with the exception of the milking and the necessary feeding of the stock, the place was like an abandoned farm until the burial was over. Though Nathan's charred body remained at Pedlar's Mill, the pall of mourning extended to Old Farm. John Abner had even suggested sending a telegram to the hotel and the dairy in Washington and letting the milk spoil; but the thought of all the good cream that would be thrown away was too much for Dorinda's economical instincts, and she had checked the impulse with the reminder that Nathan had hated a waste. Yes, he had hated a waste, it is true, but he had also loved a funeral. She remembered her mother's death, and the completeness, the perfection, of his arrangements.

"Am I too hard?" Dorinda asked herself. "Ought I not to see that everything gets so upset? After all, as Fluvanna says, a person does not die but once." The small ironic demon of her sagacity concluded, in spite of her will: "It is a good thing, or there wouldn't be any room left for life."

Breakfast was no sooner over than she was engulfed in a continuous deluge of sympathy. She was up in the attic with Fluvanna, going over the black things which had been left from the mourning of her parents, when the coloured woman glanced out of the dormer-window and gasped breathlessly. "Thar they are, Miss Dorinda. You hurry up and get into that black bombazine befo' they catch you out of mournin'."

She held up a dingy dress which had once belonged to Mrs. Oakley, and Dorinda slipped into it with the feeling that she was preparing for her own coffin. As she was about to go down to meet her callers, Fluvanna unfolded and shook out before her the crape veil which had been worn by two generations of widows. Her grandmother had bought it in more affluent circumstances, and after her death, for she had been one of the perpetual widows of the South, it had lain packed away in camphor until Mrs. Oakley was ready for it. Now it was Dorinda's turn, and a shiver went through her heart as she inhaled the rusty smell of bereavement.

"You'll have to get a new veil after the burial," Fluvanna observed, "but I reckon you can make out with this crape until that is over. It has turned real brown, but there won't many people notice it in church."

Putting the proffered veil aside, Dorinda hastened downstairs,

347

after reminding Fluvanna that she must make coffee in case the visitors expected something to eat.

"If only they would leave the dignity and take away the sordidness of death," she thought.

At the foot of the staircase, Miss Seena Snead was waiting for her with a black serge dress that she had borrowed from one of the neighbours.

"What in the world have you got on, Dorinda?" she asked, while the tears brimmed over her kind old eyes. "I declare it looks as if it was made befo' the Flood. I no sooner heard of po' Nathan's death than I began to study about where I could find a good black dress for you to wear to the funeral. I wasn't a bit surprised that Nathan turned out to be such a hero. I always knew there was a lot mo' in him than some folks suspected. Then, while I was in the midst of trying to recollect who had died last year, young Mrs. John Garlick drove into our yard with this dress and a widow's bonnet in her arms. She told me she's stoutened so she couldn't make the dress meet on her, and she'd be obliged if you'd do her the favour to wear it. The bonnet she sent along because it's a widow's bonnet anyway, and she can't wear it herself until she loses John. That makes her sort of superstitious about keepin' it put away as if she were saving it for a purpose. John bought it for her in New York when she lost her mother. Wasn't that like a man all over again, to go and buy his wife a bonnet with a widow's ruche when her mother died?"

"I'm much obliged to her," Dorinda replied stiffly, taking the bonnet out of the bandbox.

"It'll be real becomin' to you," Miss Seena exclaimed consolingly. Though her tears were still streaming for Nathan, her imagination had already envisaged Dorinda as a widow in weeds. "It makes you look mo' strikin' than colours. There ain't nothin' you can wear so conspicuous as crape, my po' Ma used to say."

Dorinda put on the dress and stood straight and still in the middle of her bedroom floor while the dressmaker let down the hem and took a pleat in the belt. "I've never seen anybody keep her figger so well as you've done," remarked Miss Seena. "It's stayin' out of doors an' movin' about so much, I reckon. My Ma used to say that when you get on in life, you have to choose between keepin' yo' face

348

or yo' figger; but it looks as if you had managed to preserve both of 'em mighty well. You get sort of chapped and weather-beaten in the wintertime, an' the lines show mo' than they ought to, but that high colour keeps 'em from bein' too marked. You're forty now, ain't you, Dorinda?"

"Forty-two. It's hard sometimes for me to believe it."

"Well, you're the hard kind that don't wear away soon. Look at Geneva Ellgood, poor thing. She broke almost as quick as she grew."

Dorinda sighed. "She needed love too much ever to find it," and she thought, "The surest way of winning love is to look as if you didn't need it."

"Everybody knew that it was Jim Ellgood that made Jason marry her, and folks about here were mighty mad with him for throwing you over. It was that mo' than drink that ruined his practice because people didn't want a man to doctor them who hadn't behaved honourable. He began to go downhill right after that, and he and Geneva lived like cat and dog befo' she drowned herself. Jason is about as bad off now as she was, tho' men don't ever seem to get the craze that they're goin' to have a baby. But he's got a screw loose, or he wouldn't live way back yonder in the woods, with no-body but an old coloured woman to look after him." She was kneeling on the floor pinning up Dorinda's skirt, with the help of the red pincushion, shaped like a tomato, which she wore fastened to the bosom of her dress. "It was fortunate for you that Geneva got him," she concluded, "and that you waited and took Nathan instead. You must find a heap of comfort in feeling that you're the widow of a hero."

The widow of a hero! Already Nathan's spirit, disencumbered of the gross impediment of the flesh, was an influence to be reckoned with. Alive, he had been negligible, but once safely dead, he had acquired a tremendous advantage.

"I believe I'll drop if I have to stand a minute longer," Dorinda said in a fainting voice.

Miss Seena was immediately solicitous. "Poor child, I reckon the shock must have unnerved you. You lie right down, and I'll have this dress ready befo' the minister gets here."

At last the dressmaker stopped talking and settled down to her work, and in the afternoon, when the Ellgoods came with the

349

minister to tell Dorinda of the arrangements for the funeral, she received them in the black serge dress with a bit of crape at her throat. A fire was burning in the parlour beneath the two black basalt urns on the mantelpiece and the speckled engraving on the wall above. While she was still shaking hands with the Ellgoods, a stream of people, led by Minnie May and Bud, poured into the hall. Minnie May had brought her six children with her, and the smaller ones immediately began to play with their dolls behind the rosewood sofa in the corner, while the eldest boy fingered the books which ran halfway up the walls on three sides of the room.

"Don't you think I ought to make them stop?" Minnie May asked presently. "They'd be more at home, anyway, in the kitchen where Fluvanna is making gingerbread for them."

"Tell Fluvanna not to forget to bring in some blackberry wine and cake," Dorinda whispered in reply.

Before she had spoken to her first visitors, the parlour was crowded; and John Abner was obliged to bring chairs from the spare room. "To think of my having to wear a bonnet with a widow's ruche!" Dorinda found herself thinking, while she was condoled with in husky accents by the old minister. "If they'd go away and let me have time to think, I might feel; but I can't feel anything as long as they're all talking to me." Though most of the faces were familiar to her, and some of them she had passed in the road ever since her childhood, there were several persons whom she did not seem to remember. These, she discovered presently, were strangers who had been on the wrecked train with Nathan. Two of them he had rescued from the burning cars at the cost of his life.

Bad as the roads were, only the tenant farmers who lived beyond Whippernock River had been prevented from coming. The bridge had been damaged by the storm, and the thawing ice had made the shallow stream unfordable. Old Mr. Kettledrum, who had given up his practice and become "the mail rider" for the new rural delivery, had been almost swept away when he had tried to cross at the ford. Even Willow Creek was so high that the log bridge had been torn to pieces by the flood. Yet neither flood nor snow had held the neighbouring farmers at home. White and black, rich and poor, they had turned out to visit the widow of a hero in her affliction. Even Mr. Kettledrum had sent word that, undaunted by his narrow

350

escape from drowning, he had driven round the circuit in order to bring Dorinda the morning papers.

"To think that all this should be about Nathan," Dorinda said to herself, while she sat there with the newspaper James Ellgood had given her in her lap.

> "HERO ON WRECKED TRAIN GIVES HIS LIFE FOR OTHERS
> DESCENDANT OF FIRST MILLER OF PEDLAR'S MILL DIES AFTER SAVING WOMEN AND CHILDREN. MONUMENT TO BE ERECTED IN CHURCHYARD AT PEDLAR'S MILL."

After this there was a list of contributions for the monument, beginning with one thousand dollars, which had been subscribed by an anonymous stranger from the North.

Yes, dreadful as it was, she couldn't get over the feeling that there was something unreal and theatrical in the event. She might have been on the stage at a school festival, listening to all these people declaiming selections from Shakespeare. Nathan's heroism sounded to her as unnatural as the way things happened in Shakespeare. She felt ashamed of herself. Had she failed Nathan in his death because she could not recognize him in what she thought of vaguely as his heroic part? Well, ashamed or not, she simply could not take it in. If you could once take it in, she said to herself stupidly, the whole of life would be different; yet, for the moment, she was too stunned, too confused, to credit the incredible. The tragedy appeared too magnificent to be true.

The minister was an old man. He had known Dorinda's mother when they were both young; he had known Nathan when he was a child; and he wheezed now with distress when he talked of him. His face was as grey and inflexible as a rock, Dorinda thought, though his voice reminded her of a purling brook. Over his bulging forehead his limp white hair hung in loose strands which curled at the ends. She had not seen him for years outside the pulpit, and it embarrassed her that he should stand on a level with her and wipe his eyes on the shreds of a silk handkerchief. While he rambled on, she looked beyond him and saw all those persons, some of whom were unknown to her, moving about the parlour, which was as sacred to her as a tombstone. They were whispering, too, among themselves, and she knew that they were speaking of Nathan in the sanctimonious tone which they had consecrated to missionaries who had died at their posts or to distinguished generals of the Confederacy. She observed John Abner go out to help put up the horses, and glancing out of the window, she saw Fluvanna coming from the hen-house with a bunch of fowls in her hands. With her usual foresight, the girl, who had kept her head better than the other negroes, was preparing supper for the multitude.

The old minister had finished once, but he was beginning again in a florid oratorical style. How long would he go on, she wondered, and would it be like this at the funeral? There was much to be said, she conceded, for the Episcopal service which circumscribed the rhetoric of clergymen. When at last he sat down, wiping his glasses, in the cushioned rocking-chair close to the fire, Bob Ellgood stood up and explained the funeral arrangements as if he wished her to understand that they were to be worthy of Nathan. This was Wednesday, and the public funeral, the funeral of a hero, would be held at three o'clock on Friday afternoon. Then he handed her a list of the pall-bearers, many of them merely "honorary," Dorinda perceived, and among them there were several names that she did not know.

"They were on the wrecked train," Bob replied to her question, "and wish to pay this last mark of respect." These were the men, he told her, who had started the list of contributions. "It is our idea to build a monument by public subscription," he concluded, "over his grave in the churchyard. Then future generations will remember his heroism."

"Poor Nathan," she thought, while her eyes filled with tears. "If only he could hear what they are saying." There had never been a monument erected by public subscription at Pedlar's Mill, and she could not help thinking how pleased Nathan would have been if he could have taken an active part in the plan. Well, some people had to wait until they were dead to get the things that would have made them happy while they were living.

As soon as Bob Ellgood stopped speaking, a general droning began in the room, and she grasped, after an instant of confusion, that everybody was trying to tell her of some boyish act of generosity which was still remembered. These recollections, beginning with a single anecdote related in the cracked voice of the minister, gathered fulness of tone as they multiplied, until the room resounded with a chorus of praise. Was it possible that Nathan had done all these noble things and that she had never heard of them? Was it possible that so many persons had seen the greatness of his nature, and yet the community in which he lived had continued to treat him as more or less of a clown? Over and over, she heard the emphatic refrain, "I always thought there was a heap more in Nathan Pedlar than people made out."

Sitting there in the midst of the belated appreciation, it seemed to Dorinda that the shape of an idea emerged gradually out of the fog of words. All his life Nathan had been misunderstood. Though she was unaware of the exact moment when the apotheosis occurred, she realized presently that she had witnessed the transformation of a human being into a legend. After to-day, it was impossible that she should ever think of Nathan as unromantically as she thought of him while he was alive. Death had not only ennobled, it had superbly exalted him. In this chant of praise there was no reminder of his insignificance. Could it be that she alone had failed to recognize the beauty of his character beneath his inappropriate surface? Had she alone misunderstood and belittled him in her mind? Her heart swelled until it seemed to her that she was choking. When she remembered her husband now, it was the inward, not the outward, man that she recalled.

"I reckon he warn't mo' than eight years old when he took that whipping for stealing old man Haney's cherries rather than tell on Sandy Moody's little boy Sam," Ezra Flower, the auctioneer, was reciting. "I can see the way he stood up and took the lashing without a whimper, and the other boys teasing him and calling him a clown on account of his broken nose. Yes, ma'am, I always knew thar was a heap mo' in Nathan Pedlar than most folks made out."

The warm room, the firelight, the humming voices, faded into a mist. Beyond the window-panes, which flamed with a reflected glow, Dorinda saw the white fields and against the fields there flickered a vision of the room in which she was sitting. Out of this vision, the prayer of the minister stole over her like some soporific influence. An inescapable power of suggestion, as intense yet as diffused as firelight, was reassembling her thoughts of the past. "Yes, there was more in Nathan than anybody ever suspected," she found herself repeating.

With one of those sudden changes that come in Virginia, the day of Nathan's funeral brought a foretaste of spring. The snow had melted so rapidly that the roads were flowing like brooks, and Whippernock River, with its damaged bridge, was still impassable. But an April languor was in the air, and the sky over the wintry fields was as soft as clouds of blue and white hyacinths. Though a number of farmers who lived beyond Whippernock River had been unable to come to the funeral, people had arrived by train from the city and in every vehicle that could roll on wheels from the near side of the railroad. The little church was crowded to suffocation while the minister read his short text and preached his long sermon on the beauty of self-sacrifice. When the last hymn was sung with gasps of emotional tension, and the congregation flocked out into the churchyard, with Nathan in his flower-banked coffin and Dorinda hidden in her widow's weeds, a wave of grief spread like a contagious affliction over the throng. With her head reverently bowed, Dorinda tried to attend only to the words of the minister, to see only the open grave at her feet, with the piles of red clay surrounding the oblong hole. Yet her senses, according to their deplorable habit in a crisis, became extraordinarily alive, and every trivial detail of the scene glittered within her mind. She saw the blanched and harrowed face of the minister, who prayed with closed eyes and violent gestures as if he were wrestling with God; she saw the nodding black plumes of Miss Texanna Snead, and remembered that Nathan had once called her "a plumed hearse"; she saw the gaping mouths of the children, whom their mothers, in the excitement of the occasion, had neglected to wash; she saw even the predatory brood of chickens which had invaded the graveyard and was scratching upon the graves. The ground at her feet was heaped with flowers, and among the floral crosses and wreaths and pillows, she observed the design of a railway engine made of red and white carnations, and tried to recall the names on the card. Long after she had forgotten every word of the prayer, she could still see that preposterous floral engine and smell the strong scent of fading carnations.

354

Standing there beside the open grave, recollections blew in and out of her mind like chaff in the wind. Her first sermon. The old minister praying with eyes so tightly shut that they looked like slits made by a penknife. The way her feet could not reach the floor. Peppermints in a paper bag to keep her quiet. Her mother smelling of soap and camphor. Missionaries in the front pew. The saving of black babies. The way she had yawned and stretched. Nathan was there then, a big boy who sang, with a voice as shrill as a grasshopper, in the choir. Rose Emily too. How pretty she was. Then Rose Emily as she lay dying with the happy light in her eyes and the flush in her cheeks. Twenty-two years ago! Well, she had done her best by Rose Emily's children.

Afterwards, when she drove home with John Abner, she found that, though they had buried the actual Nathan in the churchyard, the legendary Nathan of prayer and sermon still accompanied them.

"I wish Father could have heard what they said of him," John Abner remarked, with detached reverence, as he might have spoken of one of the public characters in the Bible. "It would please him to know what they thought of him after he was gone."

"Perhaps he does know," Dorinda responded.

For a few moments they talked of this; of the way death so often makes you understand people better than life; of the sermon and the flowers, and the general mourning.

"Did you see Jacob Moody there?" asked John Abner presently. "He used to work for Father before we moved to Old Farm, and Jacob told me he swam Whippernock River to come to the funeral."

Dorinda wiped her eyes. "Things like that would have touched Nathan. I never saw any one get on better with the coloured people. It was because he was so just, I suppose."

"Those were Jacob's very words. 'Mr. Nathan was the justest white man I ever saw,' he said. Put back that heavy veil, Dorinda. It is enough to smother you. There now. That's better. Your face looks like the moon when it comes out of a cloud."

Dorinda smiled. "Even that old German who has just moved into the Haney place was there. I wonder what he thinks now of Germany? We shan't hear anything about the war after this. I used to tell your father he couldn't have felt more strongly if it had been fought at Old Farm."

"I was beginning to get interested myself," John Abner returned. "I'll try to follow it on the map just as he did in the evenings. Well, it will be over before next winter, I reckon."

"And all that waste so unnecessary!" Dorinda exclaimed.

They were turning in at the gate by the bridge. Straight ahead, she saw the house, with the smoke flying like banners from the chimneys. On the hill beyond, the big pine was dark against the blue and white of the sky.

5

Although Dorinda would have been astonished had she discovered it, the years after Nathan's death were the richest and happiest of her life. They were years of relentless endeavour, for a world war was fought and won with the help of the farmers; but they were years which rushed over her like weathered leaves in a storm. To the end, the war came no nearer to her than a battle in history. There was none of the flame-like vividness that suffused her mother's memories of the starving years and the burning houses of the Confederacy. Only when she saw victory in terms of crops, not battles, could she feel that she was part of it.

In the beginning the Germans had seemed less a mortal enemy than an evil spirit at large, and she had fought them as her great-grandfather might have fought a heresy or a pestilence. That men should destroy one another appeared to her less incredible than that they should deliberately destroy the resources which made life endurable. That they should destroy in a day, in an hour, the materials which she was sacrificing her youth to provide! At night, lying in bed with limbs that ached so she could not sleep, and a mind that was a blank from exhaustion, she would hear the rotation of crops drumming deliriously in her thoughts. Potatoes. Corn. Wheat. Cowpeas. Clover. Alfalfa. And back again. Alfalfa. Cowpeas. Potatoes. Corn. Wheat. Clover. That was all the seasons meant to her, one after one. Her youth was going, she knew; but youth had brought so little that age could take away, why should she regret it? The hair on her temples had turned from grey to white; her skin, beneath its warm flush, was creased with lines and roughened from exposure; but her eyes were still bright and clear, though the caged look had gone out of them.

What she felt most, as the struggle went on, was the failure of elasticity. The tyranny of detail was more exacting, and she rebounded less quickly from disappointment. Notwithstanding what Doctor Faraday had called her "superb constitution," her health began to cause her uneasiness. "The war has done this," she thought, "and if it has cost me my youth, imagine what it has cost the men who are fighting." It was a necessary folly, she supposed, but it was a folly against which she rebelled. Had humanity been trying unwisely to hurry evolution, and had the crust of civilization proved too thin to restrain the outbreak of volcanic impulses? Her two years with Doctor Faraday had accustomed her to the biological interpretation of history. "And the worst thing about the war," she concluded grimly, "is not the fighting. It is not even the murder and plunder of the weaker. The worst thing about it is the number of people, both men and women, who enjoy it, who embark upon it as upon a colossal adventure."

If John Abner had gone to France, the war would have come closer to her; but John Abner was tied by his clubfoot to the farm. The crowning humiliation of his life came, she knew, when he watched the other boys from Pedlar's Mill start off for the training camp. Her pity for him was stronger than her relief that she could keep him, and she wished with all her heart that he could have gone. "You will be more useful on the farm," she said consolingly, as they turned away; but he only shook his head and stared mutely after the receding train. What John Abner desired, she saw, was not usefulness but glory.

Of the boys they saw go, a few were killed; but they were boys whom she knew only by sight. Two of Josiah's sons went, and one died of influenza after he had been decorated three times; but this boy had lived away so long that she did not feel close to him. Bob Ellgood's second son returned a nervous wreck from shell shock, and whenever Dorinda saw him on the porch at Green Acres, trying to make baskets of straw, she would feel that her heart was melting in pity. But even then the war did not actually touch her. Her nearest approach to the fighting was when Fluvanna's son Jubal died in a French hospital, and she was obliged to read the letter aloud because Fluvanna was too distressed to spell out the words. Dorinda had known Jubal from his babyhood. He had grown up on the farm, and she had taught him to read. The day the news came the two women worked until they were ready to drop from exhaustion. Work had always been Dorinda's salvation. It was saving her now from the war as it had once saved her from the memory of Jason.

With the return of peace, she had hoped that the daily life on the farm would slip back into orderly grooves; but before the end of the first year she discovered that the demoralization of peace was more difficult to combat than the madness of war. There was no longer an ecstatic patriotism to inspire one to fabulous exploits. The world that had been organized for destruction appeared to her to become as completely disorganized for folly. Even at Pedlar's Mill there were ripples of the general disintegration. What was left now, she demanded moodily, of that hysterical war rapture, except an aversion from work and the high cost of everything? The excessive wages paid for unskilled labour were ruinous to the farmer; for the field-hands who had earned six dollars a day from the Government were not satisfied to drive a plough for the small sum that had enabled her to reclaim the abandoned meadows of Five Oaks. One by one, she watched the fields of the tenant farmers drop back into broomsedge and sassafras. She was using two tractor-ploughs on the farm; but the roads were almost impassable again because none of the negroes could be persuaded to work on them. Even when she employed men to repair the strip of corduroy road between the bridge and the fork, it was impossible to keep the bad places firm enough for any car heavier than a Ford to travel over them. Yet these years, which she had believed would mean the end of her prosperity, passed over her also and were gone.

After all, the men farmers had suffered more. James Ellgood allowed his outlying fields to run to waste again because he could not find labourers to till them. Old John Appleseed gave up his market garden after he had lost all his vegetables one spring when he was ill and there was nobody to gather them. It was in such a difficulty that Dorinda was aided by a gift she had never depended on in the past, and this was her faculty for "getting on," as she would have called it, with the negroes. Unlike James Ellgood, who was inclined to truculence, she had preserved her mother's friendly relations with the established coloured families at Pedlar's Mill. When the scarcity of labour came, the clan of Moodys provided the field-workers that she required. The Moodys, the Plumtrees, and the Greens, were scattered on thrifty little farms from the settlement of Plumtree to the land beyond Whippernock River; yet, one and all, they were attached by ties of kindred to the descendants of Aunt Mehitable. In a winter of frozen roads and a disastrous epidemic of influenza, the relatives of Aunt Mehitable, who had died long ago, sent pleading messages to Dorinda, and she gave generously of the peach brandy and blackberry cordial she had inherited from her mother. There was scarcely a cabin that the pestilence did not enter, and wherever it passed, Dorinda followed on Snowbird, her big white horse with the flowing mane and the plaited tail which had never been docked. That was a ghastly winter. From November to March the landscape wore the spectral and distraught aspect of one of the engravings after Doré in her mother's Bible. Doctor Stout was still in France, and there was no physician but Jason Greylock at Pedlar's Mill. Dorinda met him sometimes going or returning on horseback from a desperate case; but he appeared either not to recognize her or to have forgotten her name. People said that he was still a good doctor when he had his senses about him. The pity was that he was often too drunk to know what he was doing. He looked an old man, for his skin was drawn and wrinkled, the pouches under his eyes were inflamed with purple, and there were clusters of congested veins in his cheeks.

One afternoon, when the epidemic was at its worst, she rode up to the door of one of the humbler cabins and met him coming away.

"You ought not to go in there," he said shortly, for he was sober at last. "Two children have just died of pneumonia, and the others are ill. They are the worst cases I've seen."

Mounted on her white horse, like some mature Joan of Arc, she glanced down on him. Her face was expressionless but for its usual look of dauntless fortitude. She was thinking, "At last I shall have to speak to him, and it makes no difference to me whether I speak to him or not." It was a quarter of a century since she had driven home with him that February afternoon. A quarter of a century, and she had not forgotten! Well, when you have only the solitude to distract you, your memory is obliged to be long!

"I am not afraid," she replied in level tones, after she had dismounted and tethered Snowbird to the branch of a tree. "Are you?"

While he could wrap himself in his professional manner, it occurred to her that he was not without dignity. Even though there were only the rags of it left, he was less at her mercy than he would have been in the character of a remembered lover. For an instant it seemed to her that he waited for her question to sink in. Then he answered with the sound of a laugh that had been bitten back.

"I? No. What have I to fear?"

Her smile was as sharp as a blade. "There is always something, isn't there, even if it is only the memory of fear?"

"You think, then, that I was always a coward?" Yes, he was sober enough now, restrained by those shreds of professional responsibility which was the only responsibility he had ever acknowledged.

She laughed. "I stopped thinking of you twenty-five years ago."

"I know." He looked as if he were impressed by her words. "You took the best man, after all. There was more in Nathan than anybody realized."

"Every one says that now."

"Well, it's true even if every one says it. You married a good man."

It was her hour of triumph; and though it was her hour of triumph, she knew that, like everything else in her life, it had come too late. A quarter of a century outlasts expectancy. The old pang was dead now, and with it the old bitterness. It made no difference any longer. Nothing that he could say or do would make any difference. She had outlived both love and hatred. She had outlived every emotion toward him except disgust. That last scene at Five Oaks returned to her, and her lips twisted with aversion. "Yes, I married a hero," she rejoined, and she added to herself, "If only Nathan could hear me!"

"You made your life in spite of me. I'm glad of that."

She laughed again. How little men knew of women! Even Nathan, who had loved her, had never seen her as she was. "Yes, I made my life in spite of you."

"It was too much, I suppose, to expect you to understand how I failed. I never ran after women. That wasn't my weakness. I never wanted to do any of the things I did. I never wanted to throw you over. I never wanted to marry Geneva. I never wanted to ruin

361

either of your lives. I never wanted to stay in this God-forsaken solitude. I never wanted to let drink get a hold on me. I did not want to do a single one of these things; but I did them, every one. And you will never understand how that could be."

She shook her head. "It doesn't matter now. It isn't worth thinking about."

"All the same I wish you could understand that I was not the kind of man to do the things that I did. I was a different sort of fellow entirely. But what I was never seemed strong enough to withstand the pull of what I was not. Of course, you'll never see that. You'll just go on thinking I was born rotten inside. Perhaps you're right. I don't know. I can't work it out."

She looked through him and beyond him to the brown solitude of the winter fields. The sunken roads were swimming in melted snow; the bushes were like soaked rags; the trees were dripping with a fluid moisture which was heavier than rain. From the sodden ground a vapour steamed up and floated like a miasma on the motionless air.

"Men like you ought to have been sent to the war," she said.

"They wouldn't take me. I was too old, and besides I've got the drink habit."

"And you blame somebody else for that, I suppose?"

"No, I don't blame anybody. I don't blame anybody for anything. Least of all myself. It was the way things turned out. Strange as it may seem to you, I always did the best that I could. If Father had died sooner, it might have been different. But everything happened too late. The broomsedge grew over me before I could get away."

Exultation flared up and then died down to ashes. "You ruined Five Oaks, and I saved it," she said.

"Yes, you have done well with the farm." Twenty-five years of toil and self-denial, and in the end only: "You have done well with the farm!"

"That shows what you can do even with poor land when you put your heart into it," he added.

"Not the heart, but the head," she retorted sharply, as she went past him into the cabin.

6

When the spring came and the epidemic was over, she had won the loyal friendship of the poorer tenant farmers and the negro landowners; but her energy and her resilience were less than they had ever been in her life.

Machinery could not work alone, and even tractor-ploughs were obliged to be guided. She had installed an electric plant, and whenever it was possible, she had replaced hand labour by electricity. In the beginning she had dreaded the cost, but it was not long before she realized that the mysterious agency had been her safest investment. The separator in the dairy was run by electricity. With the touch of a button the skimmed milk was carried by pipes to the calf-yard or the hog-pen. Pumping, washing, churning, cooling the air in summer and warming it in winter, all these back-breaking tasks were entrusted to the invisible power which possessed the energy of human labour without the nerves that too often impeded it, and made it so uncertain a force.

"What would Pa say if he could see so many cows milked by machinery?" she asked John Abner, after the first experiment with electricity in the cow-barn.

"Do you think it will help much in milking?"

"In the end it may. The young cows don't mind it, but you'll never get the old ones to put up with it."

"Then until the young ones have turned into the old ones, we'll have to take whatever milkers we can find. Cows must be milked twice a day, and no darkey wants to work more than three times a week."

"They're still living on their war wages. If I ran this farm the way men manage the Government, we'd be over head and ears in debt. Perhaps," she suggested hopefully, "when the negroes have spent all they've saved up, they'll begin to feel like working."

John Abner grinned. "Perhaps. But it takes a long time to starve a darkey."

"Well, I'll see what Fluvanna can do about it," Dorinda retorted. She did not smile at his jest because the problem, she felt, was a serious one. The negro, who was by temperament a happiness-hunter, could pursue the small game of amusement, she was aware, with an unflagging pace. Without labourers, the farms she had reclaimed with incalculable effort would sink again into waste land. "Yes, I'll see what Fluvanna can do," she repeated.

In the end, it was Fluvanna who, with the assistance of the patriarchs among the Moodys, the Greens, and the Plumtrees, drove the inveterate pleasure-seekers back to the plough. Looking at the coloured woman, generous, brisk, smiling, with her plump brown cheeks and her bright slanting eyes, Dorinda would ask herself how she could have managed the farm without Fluvanna. "Heaven knows what I should have done if I had not had a pleasant disposition about me," she said. In return for Fluvanna's sunny sympathy and her cheerful alacrity, which never faltered, Dorinda had discreetly overlooked an occasional slackening of industry.

Though the years were hard ones, she was more contented than she had ever been. The restless expectancy had ceased, and with it the indefinite longing which had awakened with the scent of spring rains on the grass, or the sound of the autumn wind in the broom-sedge. Even the vision of something different in the future, that illusion of approaching happiness which she had believed as indestructible as hope itself, had dissolved as the glimmer of swamp fires dissolves in the twilight. She knew now that life would never be different. Experience, like love, would always be inadequate to the living soul. What the imperfect actuality was to-day, it would be to-morrow and the day after; but there was rest now, not disquietude, in the knowledge. The strain and the hard work of the war had tired her nerves, and she looked forward to the ample leisure of the time when she could expect nothing. Since Nathan's death she had lost the feeling that life had cheated her. It was true that she had missed love; but at the first stir of regret she would shake her head and remind herself that "you couldn't have everything," and that, after all, it was something to have married a hero. Nathan's victorious death had filled the aching void in her heart. Where the human being had failed her, the heroic legend had satisfied.

As she grew older, it seemed to her that men as husbands and lovers were scarcely less inadequate than love. Only men as heroes, dedicated to the service of an ideal, were worthy, she felt, of the injudicious sentiments women lavished upon them. At twenty, seeking happiness, she had been more unhappy, she told herself, than other women; but at fifty, she knew that she was far happier. The difference was that at twenty her happiness had depended upon love, and at fifty it depended upon nothing but herself and the land. To the land, she had given her mind and heart with the abandonment that she had found disastrous in any human relation. "I may have missed something, but I've gained more," she thought, "and what I've gained nobody can take away from me."

Without John Abner, who was much to her, though not so much as she had once believed he would be, and the indispensable memory of Nathan to fall back upon, she sometimes wondered what her middle years would have brought to her. John Abner, it is true, was subject to moods, and recently he had been warped by a disappointment in love; but even if he was not always easy to live with, she knew that, in his eccentric fashion, he was attached to her. With Nathan, it was different. In the years that had passed since his death, he had provided her with the single verity which is essential to the happiness of a woman no longer young, and that is a romantic background for her life. The power of mental suggestion, which is stronger than all other influences in the world of emotion, had cultivated around her this picturesque myth of Nathan. No one spoke to her now of his ugliness, his crudeness, his reputation as a laughing-stock; but whenever she went to church, she beheld the imposing monument which public sentiment had placed over his grave. Every soldier who went from Pedlar's Mill was reminded by fire-breathing orators that the heroes of war must be worthy of the hero of peace. Every appeal from the Red Cross in the county bore his name as an ornament. As time went on this legend, which had sprung from simple goodness, gathered a patina of tradition as a tombstone gathers moss. Yes, it was something, Dorinda assured her rebellious heart, to have been married to a hero.

In these years she might have married again; but a distaste for physical love, more than the rigid necessity of her lot, kept her a widow. When, a year after his wife's death, Bob Ellgood began, according to the custom of the country, to motor over to Old Farm on Sunday, she was at first flattered, then disturbed, and at last frankly provoked. Walking through the pasture with him one afternoon in April, she reflected, not without chagrin, that this also was one of the blessings that had come at the wrong time. "Thirty years ago, before I knew Jason, I could have loved him," she thought; and she remembered the Sunday mornings in church when she had gazed longingly at his profile and had asked herself, "Can he be the right one, after all?" She had wanted him then with some sudden cobweb of fancy, which had been spun by an insatiable hunger for life. If he had turned to her at that moment, she would have loved him instead of Jason, and the future, which was now the past, would have been different. But he had not wanted her then; he had first to make a disappointing marriage, and by the time he had discovered his mistake, it was too late to begin over again. Well, that was the way things happened in life!

"Why won't you marry me, Dorinda?" he asked, wheeling abruptly round from the pasture bars.

Startled, she cast about for a reason which might appear plausible to his masculine vanity. Was there a reason? Had she any reason behind her resolve, or was aversion as physical a process as first love? Once he had been handsome, a young blond giant, and now he was coarsened and beefy, with a neck like a bull's and a rapidly spreading girth. There was a purple flush in his face and puckers of flesh between his collar and his slightly receding chin. This, also, was the way things happened, she knew. Yet, after a moment's compassionate regard, she discerned that he wore his unalluring age as easily as he had once worn his engaging youth. He appeared unaware even that it might be a disadvantage in courtship.

"Suppose I looked like that?" she said to herself, and then, "Perhaps women are more fastidious than they used to be, but men have not yet found it out. Or is it simply because I am independent

366

and don't have to marry for support that I can pick and refuse?"

"Have you decided why you won't marry me?" he inquired presently.

He was smiling at her, and it seemed to her—or was it only her imagination?—that a gleam, like the star in the eyes of her prize bull, flickered and went out in his glance. His face was so close to her that for an instant she believed he was going to kiss her. Not that look! something cried in her heart. Oh, never that look again!

"I can't tell," she answered, walking on again. "There isn't any reason. I've finished with all that."

He was undismayed. "I'll keep on. I'm not in a hurry." Actually at fifty-five, he was not in a hurry.

"It isn't any use," she replied as firmly as she could. "It isn't the least use in the world."

"Well, I'll keep on anyway."

In the end, though she had spoken with decision, she had failed to convince him. That had been two years ago, and he still came in his big car every Sunday afternoon. But as he had warned her, he was not in a hurry, and his courtship was as deliberate as his general habit of body.

Although it seemed to her that she had grown wiser with the years, she had never entirely abandoned her futile effort to find a meaning in life. Hours had come and gone when she had felt that there was no permanent design beneath the fragile tissue of experience; but the moral fibre that had stiffened the necks of martyrs lay deeply embedded in her character if not in her opinions. She was saved from the aridness of infidelity by that robust common sense which had preserved her from the sloppiness of indiscriminate belief. After all, it was not religion; it was not philosophy; it was nothing outside her own being that had delivered her from evil. The vein of iron which had supported her through adversity was merely the instinct older than herself, stronger than circumstances, deeper than the shifting surface of emotion; the instinct that had said, "I will not be broken." Though the words of the covenant had altered, the ancient mettle still infused its spirit.

There were winter nights, in front of her sinking fire, when she would live over the romantic folly and the thwarted aims of her youth. Then, through what appeared to be an endless vista, she would survey the irreconcilable difference between character and conduct. In her own life she could trace no logical connection between being and behaviour, between the thing that she was in herself and the things she had done. She thought of herself as a good woman (there were few better ones, she would have said honestly) yet in her girlhood she had been betrayed by love and saved by the simplest accident from murder. Surely these were both flagrant transgressions according to every code of morality! They were acts, she knew, which she would have condemned in another; but in her memory they appeared as inevitable as the rest of her conduct, and she could not unravel them from the frayed warp-and-woof of the past. And she saw now that the strong impulses which had once wrecked her happiness were the forces that had enabled her to rebuild her life out of the ruins. The reckless courage that had started her on the dubious enterprise of her life had hardened at last into the fortitude with which she had triumphed over the unprofitable end of her adventure. Good and bad, right and wrong, they were all tangled together. "How can I tell," she could ask, "what I should have done if I had not been myself?"

7

Riding slowly down the road from Five Oaks to Gooseneck Creek, Dorinda watched the few sheep browsing among the lengthening shadows of the October afternoon. Beyond them the life-everlasting broke in silver waves against the dim blue horizon. Over the whole landscape, with its flat meadows, its low rounded hill in the east, its crawling rust-coloured roads, hung a faint, hazy drift, as inaudible as the dying quiver of insects. Passing at a walk on her white horse against the rich autumn sunset, she reached the log bridge at the creek and kept on toward the fork of the road. She had taken the longer way home in order that she might inspect the new gate which William Fairlamb had finished. Round her, as evanescent as the last flare of day, there was this quivering haze, which was half dreamlike and half the tremor of perishing things. Nature drifting into rest; flowers drifting into dust; grasshoppers drifting into death; faint sunshine drifting into darkness. And in her own mind shadowy images or impressions drifting into thoughts.

It was five years now since the war had ended, and in those years she had recovered both her inward confidence and her outward prosperity. The misfortunes that had threatened the two farms had passed over her like wild geese. Even the labour question had been lessened, if not solved, by the application of electricity and gasoline. She had made a name that was not unknown among the farmers of the state; she had reclaimed two unproductive farms from the clutch of broomsedge and sassafras. In shallow soil, where her father had ploughed only six inches deep, she was now raising rich and abundant crops. Her dairy, she knew, was as well managed, her butter as good, as any that could be found in the country. The products of her dairy, with the name Old Farm stamped under the device of the harp-shaped pine, were bringing the highest prices in the market. She could smile now, with her butter selling in the Washington dairy at a dollar a pound, over the timidity with which she had modestly asked thirty cents in the beginning. By that subtle combination of prudence and imprudence which she called character, she had turned disappointment into contentment and failure into success.

Riding there in the silver gleams which flashed up from the life-everlasting, she appeared, after the hard years, to have ripened into the last mellowness of maturity. Though her figure in the shirtwaist and knickerbockers of brown corduroy was no longer youthful, it was still shapely. The texture of her skin was rough and hard like the rind of winter fruit, but the dark red had not faded, and her eyes beneath the whitened hair were still as blue as a jay bird's wing. Though she did not look young for her fifty years, she looked as if the years had been victorious ones.

As she opened the new gate, and passing through, turned to close it behind her, she heard the sound of approaching wheels, and saw the piebald horse and peculiar gig of Mr. Kettledrum ascending from the dip in the road. When he reached her they stopped to speak, after the manner of the country, and the old "mail rider," who was just returning on his circuit of twenty-six miles, described, with sprightliness, the condition of the roads over which he had travelled.

"Three big trees blew down on the Whippernock road the other night," he said, "and I reckon they'll lie thar until they rot if the farmers down that way don't cut them up for logs to burn. The Government sent an inspector down last week and he rode over my circuit along with me." A note of pride crept into his quavering voice. "He told me he'd never seen any worse roads in the whole course of his recollection. No, ma'am, not in the whole course of his recollection."

"I hope he'll do something about them. After all, the Government is responsible for the rural delivery."

Mr. Kettledrum shook his head. "I ain't lookin' for nothin' to be done, at least not in my time. It don't look as if the Government can afford to inspect and improve too, particularly when they're inspectin' the roads where mostly Democrats travel. But it was a

370

real comfort to know he thought it was the worst mail road he'd ever laid eyes on in the whole course of his recollection."

"I've been trying to get some of the negroes to mend this bad place before winter. The only way is for the farmers to keep their own roads in repair. The state started to improve the road between Pedlar's Mill and Turkey Station, and all it did was to cut down every last one of the trees. There isn't a patch of shade left there."

"That's true. I know it, ma'am," assented Mr. Kettledrum, who liked to talk of the road, as a man likes to talk of an affliction. "Don't I travel that road between ten and two o'clock on hot August days?" Then his face saddened to the look of stoical resignation with which men survey the misfortunes of others. "When I come along thar this mornin' they was bringin' Jason Greylock away from his house in the woods, and I stopped for a word with him. He was too weak to speak out loud, but he made a sign to say that he knew me. If thar ever was a wasted life, I reckon it was Jason's, though he started out with such promise. Bad blood, bad blood, and nothin' to counteract the taint of it."

"Where were they taking him?" Dorinda inquired indifferently; and turning, she glanced over the autumn fields to the red chimneys of Five Oaks. The house was occupied now by Martin Flower, the manager, and smoke was rising in a slender column from the roof.

Mr. Kettledrum cleared his throat. "I thought perhaps they'd sent word to you. Mr. Wigfall told me they was comin' over to ask if you could make a place for Jason at Five Oaks. They seemed to think you owed him a lodgin' on the farm considerin' you bought it so cheap and made so much money out of it."

A flush of anger stained Dorinda's forehead and her eyes burned. "I owe him nothing," she answered. "The place was sold at public auction after he had let it run to seed, and my husband bought it fairly for what he bid. If I did well, it is because I toiled like a field-hand to restore what the Greylocks had ruined." She broke off with a gasp, as if she had been running away from herself. The old "mail rider," she saw after a moment, stared at her in surprise.

"Yas'm, I'm sorry I spoke, ma'am," he replied mildly. "You've earned the right to whatever you have, that thar ain't no disputin'. I was just thinkin' as I come along what a pleasant surprise it would be to your Pa if he could come back an' see all those barns and dairy-houses, to say nothin' of that fine windmill an' electric plant.''

Dorinda sighed. "Poor Pa. My only regret is that he couldn't share in the prosperity. He worked harder than I did, but he never saw any results. It has taken me thirty years." Yes, she was fifty now, and it had taken her thirty years.

"You've kept the old house just as it was in his day. Wall, I favour a shingled roof, myself, even if it does burn quicker when it ketches fire. But thar's something unfeeling to me about one of these here slate roofs. They ain't friendly to swallows, an' I like to see swallows flyin' over my head at sunset."

"Yes, a slate roof is almost as ugly as a tin one." She regarded him steadily for a minute while she bent over to stroke Snowbird's neck. The light struck her face obliquely through the fiery branch of a black-gum tree, and if Mr. Kettledrum had been gifted with imagination, he would have seen the look of something winged yet caged flutter into her blue eyes.

"What is the matter with Doctor Greylock?" she asked.

In Mr. Kettledrum, who was wafted off on waves of agreeable retrospection, the sudden question produced mental confusion. He was past the sportive period when one can think without effort of two things at the same time. "Eh, ma'am?" he rejoined, cupping one gnarled hand over his ear.

"I asked you what was the matter with Doctor Greylock?"

"Oh, Doctor Greylock! Thar's no disputin', ma'am, that you owe him nothin' in the matter of Five Oaks."

"I haven't seen him for five years," she said with deliberate slowness. "I thought he was still living in that house by Whippernock River."

"So he was till this morning; that's what they told me. But it seems they've heard nothing of him since Aunt Mehaley Plumtree stopped doin' for him six months ago because he told her he didn't have the money to pay her wages. He'd put everything he had, which was mighty little, I reckon, in some wild-cat scheme of oil wells in Mexico, and they'd either burst or leaked, if they ever was thar in the beginnin', which I doubt. Everybody knows he never paid his taxes, but that thar little old place in the backwoods wasn't worth a cent, so nobody troubled about tryin' to collect 'em. Anyhow, he had to do for himself ever since Aunt Mehaley left him,

372

an' he's been gittin' sicker an' sicker with consumption all the time. When Ike Pryde was over that way squirrel huntin' yesterday, he stopped in thar an' found Jason out of his head, without a bite to eat in the house. The whole place, hen-house and all, Ike said, was as bare as the pa'm of his hand. Wall, he ran home an' got his wife to come over, and she did the best she could till they could lay hands on the sheriff. Jason had just kept alive on whiskey and some persimmons he'd managed to pick up from the ground. He must have been that way for weeks."

The colour had ebbed from Dorinda's cheeks and she looked as if she had withered. There was no distress in her mind, only a cloud of horror through which she could not see clearly. She lifted her hand and drew it across her eyes, brushing away the mist that obscured them. There was nothing there. Nothing but the drooping shadows over the road, the shocked corn against the sunset, the blur of scarlet and gold and wine-colour in the woods. There was no horror in these things; yet while she looked at them they became alive and struck out at her like a serpent.

"I have no sympathy to waste on him," she said harshly, and then, "Won't James Ellgood take care of him?"

Mr. Kettledrum shook his head, vaguely apologetic. "Not James. He hates him like poison. Maybe thar's something in the notion that Jason drove his wife crazy. I ain't takin' sides. But like most soft-hearted men James is like a rock when he gets set against a thing. Thar wa'n't no place for Jason to go but the poorhouse. The old women thar can look after him when he needs it."

"Well, you can't blame James Ellgood," Dorinda replied. "As far as I can see nobody owes Jason Greylock anything but trouble."

She was determined not to make excuses for him simply because he was dying. Everybody died sooner or later, and the vein of posthumous sentiment was not, she told herself sharply now, her affliction. Nothing was altered in the past because Jason had drunk himself into the poorhouse or the grave. Nothing was altered, she repeated, and yet she could not see the past any longer because of the present. Neither love nor hate but the poorhouse was the reality.

"It is a hard thing to have to die in the poorhouse," she said.

"So 'tis, ma'am," assented Mr. Kettledrum, who had stinted

373

himself all his life in the hope of attaining an honourable old age. "But he's light-headed most of the time and don't know it. Anyhow," he continued astutely, "it ain't so hard on him as it would be on a man who had lived more respectable. He wasted mo' on drink, I reckon, than it would cost to bury him decently."

"That's the dreadful part of it. It would be easier to help a man you didn't despise." She rode on a few paces and then turned back to the side of the gig. "If you see Mr. Wigfall at the station, tell him I'll give him what he needs for Doctor Greylock, but I cannot have him at Five Oaks."

"I'll tell him," Mr. Kettledrum rejoined, and he added impulsively for one of his unhurried observations, "You carry yo' years well, if you don't mind my remarkin' on it."

She smiled. "That's because I never think of them. Most women want their youth back again; but I wouldn't have mine at any price. The worst years of my life are behind me, and my best ones ahead."

"You look it," the old man agreed, and then, without reason, he sighed. "Ah, I recollect you thirty years ago, when they used to say you had a face like a May mornin'. Not that you ain't a fine figure of a woman now; but as we old men get on in years, our thoughts turn backward and we like to dwell on young things. Thirty years ago you looked as if sugar wouldn't melt in yo' mouth."

He drove on regretfully, while Dorinda, on Snowbird, trotted homeward. The light on the shocked corn was so faint that it waned to a shadow while she looked at it. A flock of wild geese curved like blown smoke in the afterglow. Immersed in this twilight as in the sadness of memory, she gazed at the autumn scene, with the small gold leaves on the locust trees, the windmill beyond the house, and the flickering of firelight in the west wing. A prosperous farm to-day, a casual observer would have remarked; but to Dorinda, who never forgot, the whole place wore the look of wistful brooding which she remembered whenever she thought of her father.

Her exultation over Jason's ruinous end had diminished now into an impersonal pity. She had longed to punish him for his treachery; she had hated him for years, until she had discovered that hatred is energy wasted; but in all her past dreams of retribution, she had never once thought of the poorhouse. Even as a question of justice, it seemed to her that the poorhouse was excessive. That terror of

374

indigence which is inherent in self-respecting poverty was deeply bred in her nature, and she knew that her humbler neighbours were haunted by fear of charity as one is haunted by fear of smallpox in a pestilence. Yes, whatever he deserved, the poorhouse was too much. Though the horror of his fate did not lessen the wrong he had done, by some curious alchemy of imagination it reduced the sum of human passions to insignificance. What did anything invisible matter at the gate of the poorhouse?

Though her first impulse, derived from Presbyterian theology, was to regard his downfall as a belated example of Divine vengeance, her invincible common sense reminded her that Divine vengeance is seldom so logical in its judgments. No, he had not ended in the poorhouse because he had betrayed her. On the contrary, she saw that he had betrayed her because of that intrinsic weakness in his nature which would have brought him to disaster even if he had walked in the path of exemplary virtue. "His betrayal of me was merely an incident," she thought. "Drink was an incident. If he had been stronger, he might have done all these things and yet have escaped punishment." For it was not sin that was punished in this world or the next; it was failure. Good failure or bad failure, it made no difference, for nature abhorred both. "Poor Jason," she said to herself, with contemptuous pity. "He was neither good enough nor bad enough, that was the trouble."

8

As she stepped on the porch, the door opened and John Abner came out, accompanied by Amos Wigfall and one of the tenant farmers, Samuel Larch, who lived on the far side of Pedlar's Mill. John Abner looked morose, but this had become his habitual expression since he had been crossed in love, and she was less disturbed by it than she was by the anxious suavity on the face of the sheriff.

"I was admirin' yo' improvements," Mr. Wigfall remarked. "Thar's been a heap of changes since the old days when yo' Pa an' Ma lived here."

She met his wandering glance and held it firmly. "I saw Mr. Kettledrum and he gave me your message."

The sheriff's flabby face stiffened. "My message, ma'am?"

"About Doctor Greylock. I cannot have him at Five Oaks. He has no claim on me." Hesitating an instant, she repeated slowly, weighing each separate syllable, "He has no claim on me, but I will pay you whatever you need to keep him out of the poorhouse."

Mr. Wigfall uttered an obsequious noise which might have been either a bray or a cough. "I don't reckon thar's a mo' charitable-minded lady in the county, ma'am. It ain't often that you refuse to help an' when you do, you're likely to have a good reason."

"Well, I'm ready to help Doctor Greylock," Dorinda rejoined impatiently, "but there's no sense in the notion that I owe him something because he ruined Five Oaks and I saved it."

"Naw'm, thar cert'n'y ain't no sense in that," Mr. Wigfall conceded with suspicious alacrity.

"He thinks we might let him live in one of the unused wings," John Abner explained. "Of course that will mean we'll have to provide for him too, and as you say he hasn't really the shadow of a claim on us. Poor devil!"

"The idea has got about that he's dangerous from drink," said Mr. Wigfall, "and thar wouldn't nobody take him in, pay or no pay. The choice was between the county gaol an' the poorhouse, an' considerin' everything the poorhouse seemed mo' hospitable. Doctor Stout can look after him thar, and a bunch of female paupers can take turns at the nursing."

"If he's still out of his head, you can hardly expect Martin Flower to want him at Five Oaks," John Abner suggested.

"Oh, he's come to himself now," Samuel Larch rejoined before the sheriff could reply. "I was the first to git to him after Ike Pryde brought word, an' when I first clapped eyes on him he was clean out of his senses. But even then he was as weak as a baby an' he couldn't have lifted a finger against you. Soon as he had a few swallows of soup and a little brandy, he began to pick up, an' by the time he'd been fed regular he could talk like himself again. Doctor Stout thinks he'll hang on a few months longer if he gets plenty of milk an' fresh eggs."

"Well, I imagine he isn't likely to get them in the poorhouse," John Abner observed, with his sarcastic smile.

"Of course there isn't the slightest reason why we should help him," Dorinda insisted, as if the deprecating sheriff had started an argument. After a moment's silence she added in a sharper tone, "But you can't possibly let him die in the poorhouse."

Mr. Wigfall, who had occupied a position of authority long enough to feel uncomfortable when he was displaced, shuffled his feet in the rocky path while he fingered uneasily the brim of his hat. "Naw'm," he replied with as much dignity as he could command, and a few minutes later, he repeated in a louder voice, "Naw'm."

Dorinda looked over his head at John Abner.

"It isn't human," she began, and, correcting herself, continued more deliberately: "It isn't Christian to let a man die in the poorhouse because he has lost all he had."

The two men nodded vacantly, and only John Abner appeared unimpressed by her piety.

"Naw'm, it cert'n'y ain't Christian," Mr. Wigfall agreed, with a promptness that was disconcerting.

"He can't possibly be looked after there," Dorinda resumed, as if she had not been interrupted.

"Naw'm, he can't be looked after thar."

For an instant she hesitated. Though she understood that her decision was a vital one, she felt as remote and impersonal to it as if it were one of those historic battles in France, which cost so much and yet were so far away. It even occurred to her, as it had occurred so often during the war, that men were never happy except when they were making trouble. Of course Jason could not be left in the poorhouse. Having acknowledged this much, she, to whom efficiency had become a second nature, was irritated because these slow-witted country officials appeared helpless to move in the matter.

"There isn't any call to worry Martin Flower's wife," she said. "She's ailing, anyway, and it would put her out to have a sick man, even if he were sober, in the house. You'll have to bring him here until you can make some other arrangement. It is true," she repeated harshly, "that he hasn't the shadow of a claim on us; but we have plenty of milk and eggs, and for a few weeks he may have the spare room on the first floor."

Mr. Wigfall gasped before he could articulate. Though he had prayed fervently to have the burden of an extra pauper, especially a pauper who had known better days and acquired the habit of drink, removed from his shoulders, he had never imagined, from his acquaintance with the leisurely methods of Providence, that his prayer would be so speedily answered. While he stared at Dorinda, his mute relief was as obvious as if he had uttered it at the top of his voice.

"He's glad to wash his hands of him," she thought, and then: "Who wouldn't be?"

"I don't reckon anybody will dispute yo' charity, Mrs. Pedlar," Samuel Larch was wheezing out. "Thar ain't nobody stands any higher to-day in this here community than you do. You're hard on the surface, as my wife says, but you're human enough when you're whittled down to the core."

Dorinda smiled, but her eyes were tired and wrinkles showed in her ruddy skin. If they knew! If only they knew! she reflected; and she wondered if many other reputations were founded like hers upon a flattering ignorance of fact.

378

"Tell your wife it is hard things that wear well," she responded. "After all, somebody has to bear the burden, and I am better able to do it than any of the rest of you, except perhaps," she concluded indifferently, "James Ellgood."

"Yas'm. I'm downright glad you take that sensible view of it," the sheriff replied, as soon as he was capable of speaking. "Everybody about here knows that when they come to you, they'll get justice."

Justice! That was Nathan's favourite word, she remembered. She could hear him saying as plainly as if he were present, "Any man has a right, Dorinda, to demand justice." Strange how often Nathan's words, which she had scarcely heeded when he was alive, returned to her in moments of difficulty or indecision. Only in the last few years had she begun to realize her mental dependence upon Nathan.

"I reckon we can manage to get him over here to-morrow evening," Samuel Larch was saying. "Thar ain't no call for you to send all the way to the poorhouse. Maybe Reuben Fain will let us have that auto-wagon of his."

"Oh, I'll come for him in the big car in the morning," Dorinda replied. "It isn't my way to do things by halves."

The sheriff nodded. "Naw'm, it ain't yo' way to do things by halves," he echoed thankfully.

After the two men were out of sight, she turned apologetically to John Abner. Although he said little, for he was never a great talker, she had observed that his face wore a look of severe disapprobation.

"There wasn't anything else to do, was there, John Abner?" she asked, in the deferential tone she reserved for a crisis. It was not often that Dorinda deferred, and on the rare occasions when she did so, she was able to administer a more piquant flattery than the naturally clinging woman has at her command.

"It looks to me as if they were letting you down," John Abner rejoined moodily; but his face cleared under her persuasion. After all, what he liked best was to be treated as an authority not only on farming, but on human nature as well. The fact that he had lived as a recluse, and knew nothing whatever of life, did not interfere with the sincerity of his claim to profound wisdom. Men were so

379

immature, she found herself thinking; and they were never so immature as when they strutted most with importance. Since the
emotional disaster of her youth, she had been incapable of either
loving or hating without a caustic reservation; and she felt that the
hidden flaw in her relations with men was her inability to treat a
delusion of superiority as if it were a moral principle. This was a
small indulgence, she imagined, to a woman who loved passionately;
but to one who had safely finished with love and attained the calm
judgment of the disillusioned, it was an indulgence which might
prove to be particularly irksome.

Slipping her arm through John Abner's, she walked with him
into the house. "Well, of course, in a way you're right; but after all,
even if they are imposing on us, we couldn't very well refuse to do
anything."

Though the two farms would go to John Abner at her death,
there were moments when, notwithstanding his affection for her,
she suspected uncomfortably that he would like complete authority
while she was living. Not that he was ever disagreeable or ungenerous about the way she managed him. He was, she knew, honestly
devoted to her, and he admired her without the pity that had always
tempered her admiration for him. But he shared, she told herself,
with all males who were not milksops, the masculine instinct to
domineer over the opposite sex.

"Well, if it's anybody's business, it's James Ellgood's," he protested.

She raised her straight grey eyebrows with a quizzical smile.
"All the same you can hardly blame James Ellgood for not making
it his business. Nothing will ever let him forget that Jason drove
Geneva out of her mind."

"Well, perhaps he did, but there was no law to punish him."

"That's what James Ellgood feels, of course, and I suppose he
is right. If it were simply a question of punishment——"

"You mean it's more than that?"

"Well, isn't it?" She had learned that she could always win him
to her point of view by disguising a naked fact in the paraphernalia
of philosophy. "From our side, I suppose it's one of humanity."
Though she despised sophistry as heartily as she despised indirect-
380

ness, she could bend both to her purpose when it was a matter of compulsion.

"If you mean that our humanity is more important than his punishment?" he returned in a mollified tone.

"Yes, I do mean that. You have said it so often yourself." That would finish his opposition, she knew, and without his opposition, life on the farm would be easier for the next two or three weeks.

"Won't it make a lot of trouble?" he inquired.

She frowned. "I'm afraid it will. Of course, if he gets better, he can move over to Five Oaks, and anyway the authorities ought to make some kind of provision for him. We can't be expected to take over the poor-farm." Her tone was suddenly bitter with memory; but she concluded hastily: "In the meantime, I'll warm the spare room and get it ready. If the doctor says he must have fresh air, we can move his bed out on the back porch."

John Abner looked resentful. "I'm sorry for the poor devil, of course, even if he did drive his wife crazy; but I don't see the sense in turning the place upside down for somebody who hasn't the slightest claim on you. He isn't even a poor relation."

"He isn't anybody's poor relation, that's the trouble."

"I'm not so sure." John Abner could be brutally candid at times. "There are a lot of Idabella's mulatto children still hanging about Five Oaks."

She shivered with disgust. "What the law doesn't acknowledge, I suppose it doesn't bother about."

"Well, it isn't any business of mine," John Abner said, after deliberation. "If you choose to bring him here, of course you have the right. But I hope you aren't going to wear yourself out waiting on him. You've got no moderation in such things. After Snowbird's sickness last winter, you didn't look like yourself."

She shook her head. "I'd do much more for Snowbird. But I shan't wait on him. I'll get Fluvanna's sister, Mirandy. She's an old woman, and a good hand with sick people, even if she hasn't any sense in the dairy." As she finished, she heard a voice in her mind asking distinctly, "Why am I doing this? Why should I take the trouble?" And there wasn't any answer. Even when she dragged her mind for an excuse or even an idea, she could not unearth one.

She had stopped loving Jason thirty years ago; she had stopped hating him at an indefinite period; she had stopped even remembering that he was alive; yet she could not, without doing violence to her own nature, let him die in the poorhouse. After all, it was not her feeling or lack of feeling for him, it was the poorhouse and her horror of the poorhouse that decided his fate.

"I'll have to go with you," John Abner was saying. "You can't manage it by yourself."

"No. I'd rather have you. If we start right after dinner, that ought to bring us back before the milking is over. The road is rough, I'm afraid. We'll have to take some pillows in the back of the car."

"If he's bad off, perhaps Doctor Stout won't let him come," John Abner suggested hopefully.

"Well, we'll stop at the doctor's house on the way. That's why I want to start early."

That night, after the last of the day's work was over, they sat in front of Dorinda's fire and talked as they used to talk when John Abner was a boy and had not been warped by disappointment. Their thoughts were in the future, not in the past, and Dorinda's visions were coloured by the optimism which she had won more from perseverance than from any convincing lesson of experience. Because of the very defects of his qualities, John Abner suited her. It was true that his companionship had its imperfections; but she would not have exchanged his sullen reticence for the golden fluency of the new minister at Pedlar's Mill. Her stepson's personality was attractive to her, for he gave an impression of inexhaustible strength in reserve; and in the matter of disposition he influenced her less as an example than as a warning, which, after all, she reflected, was the kind of influence she needed.

"When all is said, we are as contented as we could expect to be," she remarked, when he rose to go upstairs. "If you don't marry, we'll have a pleasant old age by the fireside."

He laughed shortly, for he was in one of his gentler moods. There was a charm, she thought, in his long thin features, his sallow skin with bluish shadows about the mouth, his squinting eyes, and his straight black hair which fell in stringy locks over his forehead.

"You may marry again yourself," he said abruptly. "You aren't
382

as handsome as you used to be, but you're still better-looking than anybody about here."

She shook her head obstinately. "With white hair and wrinkles!"

"Well, there's more than white hair and wrinkles. I don't know what it is, but it's there," he answered, as he turned away and went out of the room.

In the morning she awoke with a feeling of despondency. Dread had come over her while she slept, and she felt it dragging at her memory after she had opened her eyes. Why had she yielded to that erratic impulse the evening before? Why had she allowed those two men to impose on her? "It is because I am a woman," she thought. "If I were a man, they would never have dared." Yes, John Abner was right (here was another instance of how right he so often was) and the county authorities had taken advantage of her weakness. "Well, I've let myself in for it now, and I'll have to go through with it," she said aloud, as she got out of bed and began dressing.

At breakfast, while she tried to eat and could not because of the lump in her throat, she reminded herself of her mother on the day of her journey to the Court-House. "All I need is a crape veil and a handkerchief scented with camphor," she said, with a laugh.

"What are you talking about, Dorinda?" John Abner asked, with a frown.

"I was thinking of my mother. Poor Ma! She'd be living now if she hadn't worried so."

"Well, she'd be nearly a hundred, I reckon. And don't you begin worrying. Are you out of temper because you let those men put something over on you?"

"I don't know. It seems different this morning. I can't see why I did it."

"I heard the men talking about it in the barn. Somebody, the sheriff, I reckon, had told Martin Flower, and he said you'd bitten off more than you could chew."

Dorinda flushed angrily. "When I want Martin Flower's interference, I'll ask for it."

Already a message had gone to Mirandy, and the old negress was waiting outside for directions when breakfast was over. The floor and the woodwork of the spare room must be scrubbed; the

383

bed thoroughly aired before it was made up; a fire kindled in the big fireplace; and the red-bordered towels, which her mother had reserved for the visiting elder, must be hung on the towel-rack. Last of all, Mirandy must remember to keep a kettle boiling day and night on the brass footman.

"I wonder why I am doing all this?" Dorinda asked herself. Was it, as she believed, from impersonal compassion? Or was it because her first lover, merely because he had been the first, was impressed eternally on the unconscious cells of her being? "No, I'm not doing it for Jason," she answered. "Even if I had never loved him, I couldn't let the man who had owned Five Oaks die in the poorhouse."

"Before we bring him here," John Abner said, "you'd better warn Aunt Mirandy that consumption is catching." He shook his head with a sardonic smile. "I'm afraid he's going to be a nuisance; but I believe you would have done the same thing if it had been smallpox."

She looked at him with inscrutable eyes. "I was never afraid of taking things."

"But you don't even like Jason Greylock."

"Like him? Who could? What has that to do with the poorhouse?"

A look of rare tenderness, for he was not often tender, came into John Abner's eyes while he squinted at her over the table. "Well, you're a big woman, Dorinda, even if you're trying at times. There's an extra dimension in you somewhere."

Though praise from John Abner was one of the things that pleased her most, she was incapable, she knew, of draining the sweetness of the moment before it escaped her. When happiness came to her she had always the feeling that she was too dull or too slow to realize it completely until it was over, when she responded to the memory as she had never responded to the actual occurrence.

"You're very good to me, John Abner," she answered. Her words were insufficient, but the habit of reticence was, as usual, too strong for her.

For hours she went about her work with the thoroughness that she exacted of herself on days of mental disturbance. Not until the car was waiting at the door, and Fluvanna was hastening out with robes and pillows, did Dorinda turn aside from her ordinary activities, and go into the room she had selected for Jason. Yes, everything was in order. The floor and walls were clean; the windows had been closed after an airing; and the fire burned brightly on the sunken stones in the fireplace. Even the big iron kettle steamed away on the footman. There was soap in the soap-dish on the washstand; an abundance of soft warm blankets covered the bed; on the candle-stand stood a blue thermos bottle, and her mother's Bible lay beside it, with the purple book-marker she had embroidered marking a favourite text. "It ought to seem pleasant," she thought, "after the poorhouse."

Outside, she found John Abner at the wheel of the car and Fluvanna arranging the pillows on the back seat.

"Would you like to drive, Dorinda?"

"No, but I'll sit in front with you. When we come back, one of us will have to sit with him, and I'd rather it would be you."

9

They talked little on the long drive. John Abner was intent on the wheel, and Dorinda held her cape closely about her, and gazed straight ahead at the twisted road and the hazy brightness of the October landscape. A veil of glittering dust drifted up from the meadows of life-everlasting; in the underbrush by the fences, sumach and sassafras made splashes of crimson and wine-colour; farther away, the changing woods were tossed in broken masses against the cloudless arch of the sky.

As they approached the Court-House, the country was less thinly settled, and throngs of barefooted children ran beside the car and offered bunches of prince's feather and cockscomb. In some of the fields men were ploughing, and among them Dorinda observed the phlegmatic faces of Swedes or Germans. As the car sped by, they stopped in their ploughing or cutting, and turned to stare curiously like slow-witted animals. Over all was the blue haze of October and the drifting silver pollen of life-everlasting.

At Doctor Stout's, a new green and white cottage near the road, which looked as trivial as a butterfly on the edge of the autumnal solitude, they were told that the doctor had already gone to the poorhouse.

"He was that upset he couldn't sleep last night," said Mrs. Stout, a pretty, plump, deep-bosomed woman, in a pink and white gingham dress and a starched apron. "It seemed to prey on him to think of Doctor Greylock, who used to have the best practice around here, dying up yonder in the poorhouse. He was so promising, too, they say, when he came back, and his people owned that big place over near Pedlar's Mill. Drink was his ruin, I reckon, and that made it so hard, for everybody was afraid to take in a man that was out of his head. I couldn't have had him here on account of the children and measles just broken out yesterday. But there ought to be some way of caring for sick and crazy people without sending them to the poorhouse. And now with all the poorhouses going, there soon won't be any place for them but the gaol." She was a voluble person, but at last the flow of words stopped, and they drove on between dusty borders of sassafras.

"Is it true that Doctor Stout was born in a poorhouse?" Dorinda asked presently.

"Nobody knows. It doesn't surprise me to hear that he was."

"And now Jason is dying in one. Is that the result of character or merely accident, I wonder?"

"Of both probably," John Abner rejoined. "I've read of too many decent human beings going on the rocks to believe the fable that virtue alone will get you anywhere, unless it is to the poorhouse instead of the gaol."

"There it must be now," Dorinda exclaimed, pointing to the right of the road. "Do we turn in over that ditch?"

"It seems to be the only way. Hey! Get out of the road there!" shouted John Abner to a skulking black and tan foxhound.

Withdrawn from the road, behind the fallen planks which had once made a fence, the poorhouse sprawled there, in the midst of the life-everlasting, like the sun-bleached skeleton of an animal which buzzards had picked clean of flesh. The walls and roof were covered with whitewash; there was whitewash on the smooth, round stones that bordered the path to the door; and the few starved cedar trees in the yard were whitewashed to the thin foliage at their tops. At one side, a few coarse garments were fluttering from clothes-lines, and several decrepit paupers were spreading wet things on the bushes that grew by the back porch.

Like other relics of an abruptly changing era, the county poorhouse possessed both the advantages and the disadvantages of desuetude. The seven aged paupers and the one indigent young mother who now accepted its charity were neglected, it is true, but they were neglected in freedom. Where there was no system there was less room for interference. If the coarse clothes were thin, they were as varied as the tempers or the inclinations of the paupers. Though the fare was mean, the complaints over it were bountiful. It is hard to be a pauper; it is particularly hard to be an aged pauper; but if these nine inmates (including the week-old infant) could have chosen between liberty and fraternity, they would probably have preferred the scant food and the rough clothes to the neat livery of dependence. Dorinda, however, perceived none of the varied blessings attendant upon orderless destitution. All she saw was the ramshackle building and the whitewashed cedars, which reminded her vaguely of missionary stories of the fences of dry bones surrounding the huts of Ethiopian kings. "It looks as bare as the palm of my hand," she said aloud.

The doctor's Ford car was standing in front of the door, with one wheel in a mud-hole and one in a pile of trash; and when they stopped, an old woman, who was hanging the wash to dry on the bushes, put down the wet clothes and came over to meet them. She was so old that her skin was like bark; her mouth was closed as tight as a nut-cracker over her toothless gums; and her small red eyes flickered between eyelids which looked as if they had worn away. As she mumbled at them, she wiped her steaming wet hands on her skirt.

"You ain't got any sweet stuff, is you, honey?" she whined, until the doctor appeared at the door and beckoned them round the corner of the house where the sunshine was falling. As usual he looked brisk, kind, incurably sanguine.

"There is no longer any question. These county poorhouses must go," he said, as they followed the beaten track which wound by the side of the building. "It costs the county not a cent under two thousand dollars a year to keep this place open for these eight inmates. It would be cheaper in the end to board them at the City Home where there is some system about the way things are managed." Then he lowered his voice, which had been high and peremptory, as if he wished to be overheard. "We brought Doctor Greylock here because he couldn't be left alone, and none of the negroes would go near him. There's a scare about him, though he's perfectly harmless. A little out of his head now and then, but too weak to hurt anybody even if he tried."

"Is he delirious now?"

"No, he's in his senses this morning, and quiet—you'll find him as quiet as you could wish. Is there anybody to look after him at Five Oaks?"

"We're not taking him to Five Oaks. There's no place for him there. But I've got a nurse for him, Aunt Mirandy Moody. She knows how to take care of the sick, and I believe she can manage him."

"Oh, anybody can manage him now," Doctor Stout said reassuringly.

A tremor of weakness passed over Dorinda. She felt that her knees and elbows were shaking, and there was a meaningless noise in her ears. Was it Jason of whom they were speaking? No, it was not Jason, for it seemed to her that Jason had died long ago, so long ago that she couldn't remember him. She was standing by the wall of the poorhouse, and an obscure pauper, somebody who could be "easily managed," was dying within. She dropped her eyelids to shut out the brown cloud, as thick as the smoke of burning leaves, which rolled up from the meadows. When she opened her eyes again the sunshine on the whitewashed wall dazzled her. If only she had known! If only she could have looked ahead to this moment! Those summer evenings thirty years ago, and this autumn day beside the wall of the poorhouse! The whitewashed cedars, the sunken road, the flat fields, the ridged earth where labourers moved slowly, and over all the glittering dust of life-everlasting.

"He ought to drink as much milk as he can," Doctor Stout was saying in his professional voice. "And eggs when he will take them. Every two hours he should have nourishment in some form, and an eggnog with whiskey three or four times a day. You can't expect him to do without whiskey. I've got a bottle for you to take back with you. He may need some on the way if he seems to be losing strength."

She nodded. "I learned a little when I was a girl in a doctor's office in New York; but everything has changed since the war. You'll come over to-morrow?"

"I'll drop in whenever I am called that way. If he gets much worse, you can telephone me. I feel that he has a professional claim on me."

The weakness had gone now. She felt courageous and full of

389

vitality, as if the rich blood had surged up through her veins. With the return of strength, her self-reliance, her calm efficiency, revived. She was facing the present now, not the past, and she faced it imperiously.

"You think he is able to be moved?" she asked.

"Even if it is a risk,"—he met her gaze candidly,—"wouldn't anything be better than to die in this place?"

She acquiesced by a gesture. Then, threading her way between the stunted rose-bushes, she spoke in a smothered voice, "Is he ready to go with us?"

"He is waiting on the back porch. It's sunny there."

"The car is open, you know, but John Abner is putting up the top."

"Fresh air won't hurt him. You've plenty of rugs, I suppose, and he'll need pillows."

"I've thought of that. You can fix the back seat like a bed. Of course we shall drive very slowly." Glancing up at the sun, she concluded in her capable manner: "It's time we were starting. John Abner and I both have work to do on the farm."

Doctor Stout bent an admiring gaze on her, and she knew from his look that he was thinking, "Sensible woman. No damned mushiness about her." Aloud, he said, "He is ready to go. You'll find that he doesn't say much. When a man has touched the bottom of things, there isn't much talk left in him. But I think he'll be glad to get away."

"Well, I'll see what I can do." Stepping in front of him, she turned the sharp angle of the wall and saw Jason lying on a shuck mattress in the sunshine. Beneath his head there was a pile of cotton bags stuffed with feathers and tied at the ends. Several patchwork quilts were spread over him, and one of the old women was covering his feet as Dorinda approached. His eyes were closed, and if he heard her footsteps on the ground, he made no sign. A chain of shadows cast by the drying clothes on the line fell over him, and these intangible fetters seemed to her the only bond linking him to existence. While she looked down on him, all connection between him and the man she had once loved was severed as completely as the chain of shadows when the wind moved the clothes-line.

He lay straight and stiff under the quilts, and above the variegated pattern his features protruded, shrivelled, inanimate, expressionless, like the face of a mummy that would crumble to dust at a touch. His eyes beneath his closed lids were sunk in hollows from which the yellow stains spilled over on his bluish cheeks. The chin under the short stubble of beard was thrust out as if it would pierce the withered skin. It was not the face of Jason Greylock. What she looked on was merely a blank collection of features from which poverty and illness had drained all human intelligence. Turning away, she saw through a mist the doddering old woman who was fussing about the mattress and the decrepit manager who was too ancient and incompetent for more serious employment.

"They've come for you. We'll get you away," Doctor Stout said in his cheerful tones which rang with an artificial resonance. Then he turned to Dorinda. "The stimulant is wearing off. He'll need something stronger before he is able to start."

At the words, Jason opened his eyes and looked straight up at the sky. "I am thirsty," he said, while his hand made an empty clawlike gesture. If he were aware of their figures, she realized that they meant nothing to him. He had withdrawn from the external world into the darkness of some labyrinth where physical sensations were the only realities. While she watched him it came over her with a shock that the last thing to die in a human being is not thought, is not even spirit, but sensation.

One of the old women, who appeared to be in authority, brought a glass of blue milk, and taking a flask from his pocket the doctor added a measure of whiskey. Then lifting Jason's head, he held the glass to his lips.

Suddenly, it seemed to Dorinda that her impressions of the actual scene dissolved and slipped like quicksilver from her mind. She ceased to look, ceased to think, overcome by an emotion which was not grief, though it was the very essence of sadness. Closing her eyes, she waited for some sound or touch that would restore the fading glow of her reason. Why was she here? Where was it leading her? What was the meaning of it all?

She heard a strangled voice gasp, "You're hurting me," and looking round she saw that the doctor and John Abner were carrying Jason to the car.

"You'll feel better presently," the doctor said soothingly. "I'll give you something for the pain."

Like an automaton, she followed them; like an automaton, she stepped into the car and took her place by Jason's side on the back seat. She had intended to drive home, but she knew that she was incapable of controlling the big car. "Some one had better be back here with him," the doctor had insisted, and she had obeyed his directions in silence. "I've put the whiskey under the rug. Give him an eggnog as soon as you put him to bed."

The car started slowly, and they had driven for some miles before she found sufficient courage to turn and look at the figure beside her. Dazed by the sedative, he was staring straight in front of him, oblivious of the autumn sunshine, oblivious of the uninteresting country, oblivious of her presence, lost beyond reach in that dark labyrinth of sensation. His face was the face of one who had come to the edge of the world and looked over. It expressed not pain, not despair even, but nothingness. A grey woollen comforter was tied over his head, and his features appeared to have fallen away beneath the mummy-like covering. He was neither young nor old, she saw; he was over and done with, a thing with which time had finished. And he was a stranger to her! She had never loved him; she had never known him until to-day. The weight on her heart was so heavy that it was suffocating her. Again she thought: "Why am I here? What is the meaning of it all?" Again she felt as she had felt at her father's death: "The pathos of life is worse than the tragedy."

They drove on in silence; but it was a silence that reverberated like thunder in her brain. Nothing and everything was over. Ahead of her the road sank between the autumn fields and the brilliant patches of woods. The blue haze swam before her in the direction of the river. They passed the same ragged white and black children, who held up the same withered flowers. The same labourers were at work in the fields, bent in the same gestures of ploughing. As they went by a house set far back from the road, with a little crooked path leading up to a white wicket-gate, she imagined herself walking up the path and through the wicket-gate into another life.

John Abner looked back. "Am I going too fast? He coughs as if he were choking."

She turned to Jason and replaced a pillow which had slipped from under his head. His boots, with lumps of red clay still clinging to them, were stretched out stiffly on the pile of rugs. And those worn boots with the earth on the soles seemed to her so poignantly moving that her eyes filled with tears. His cough stopped, and she spoke to him in a raised voice as if he were at a distance, "Are you suffering now?"

If he heard her, he made no response. It seemed to her while she looked at him that he was in reality at a distance, that everything but the shell of physical pain in which he was imprisoned had already perished. She wondered if he remembered her, or if her image had dropped from him, with other material objects, in that blind wilderness. From his apathy, she might have been no more to him than one of the old women in the poorhouse. A shiver ran over her, as if she had been touched by a dead hand. Youth, beauty, victory, revenge,—what did any of these things signify before the inevitable triumph of time?

Yes, time had revenged her. If she had stood still, if she had not lifted a finger to help, time would still have revenged her; for time, she saw, always revenges one. She thought of the hot agony of that other October afternoon. Of the patter of rain on the roof. Of the smell of wet grass underfoot. Of the sodden sky. Of the branches whipping her face.

They passed the station, where a train had just gone by; they passed the old Haney place, where the new German tenant was ploughing; they passed Honeycomb Farm and the fork of the road, where the burned cabin and the blasted oak used to be. The new gate stood there now, and beyond it, there was the sandy road through the meadows of joepye-weed and life-everlasting. Against the sky, she could still see unchanged the chimneys of Five Oaks. Then they spun easily down the wooded slope, crawled over the patch of corduroy road, and, turning in at the bridge, rolled up to the front porch of Old Farm.

"Well, we got him here," John Abner said, with a breath of relief.

As they helped Jason to alight, it seemed to Dorinda that his bones were crumbling beneath her touch. If she had awakened to

393

find that the whole afternoon had been a nightmare, she would have felt no surprise. Even the quiet house, with its air of patient expectancy, startled her by its strangeness.

Mirandy, a big, strong, compassionate old negress, who was born for a nurse but had missed her vocation until she was too old to profit by it, came out to help, and among them they carried Jason into the spare room and put him to bed. His clothes were so soiled and ragged that John Abner went upstairs and brought down some woollen things of his own. A fire blazed in the cavernous fireplace. Ripples of light and shadow danced over the yellow walls. The whole room smelt of burning logs and of the branches of pine on the mantelpiece. Warmth, peace, comfort, enfolded them as they entered.

When they had undressed Jason and covered him up warmly, Dorinda brought the eggnog, and Mirandy slipped her arm under the pillow and raised his head while he drank it. The tormented look had gone from his face. About his mouth the outline of a smile flickered.

"It feels good," he said, and closed his eyes as the glass was taken away.

"You'll eat some supper?"

"Yes, I'll eat some supper."

"You're not in pain now?"

"No, I'm not in pain now."

He spoke in a dazed way, like a child that is repeating words it does not understand. Had he forgotten that he had known her? Or had he reached the depths from which all memories appear as frail as the bloom on a tree? She did not know. She would never know probably. She had lost even the wish to know. Whether he had loved her or not made no difference. It made no difference whether or not he remembered. In that instant beside the poorhouse wall, the old Jason had been submerged and lost in this new Jason who was a stranger. Not in thirty years but in a single minute, she had lost him. Stripped of associations, stripped of sentiment, this new Jason was protected only by the intolerable pathos of life. How futile, how unnecessary, it had all been,—her love, her suffering, her bitterness.

He opened his eyes and looked at her.

"This isn't Five Oaks?"

"No, it is Old Farm."

"Old Farm? That is the Oakley place. Am I going to stay here?"

"Until you are better."

"Until I am better," he repeated.

"Are you comfortable now?"

He closed his eyes again. "Yes, it feels good."

"In a little while I'll give you some veronal and you will sleep."

A change passed over his face and he sighed, "I'd like to sleep."

She drew back and turned to go out of the room. Yes, the connection between youth and middle age was broken for ever.

10

In the night she heard him coughing, and slipping into her flannel wrapper, she went into the kitchen and beat up an egg with milk and brandy. When she took it into his room, he appeared feverish and asked for veronal. "But the brandy will undo it," he added mechanically. His face was flushed and when she touched his hand it was burning. "Is it near day?" he inquired.

"No, it is only one o'clock. I thought you were sleeping."

"I was, but I wake up this way. I've done it every night for months."

She gave him veronal, and then raised his head while he sipped the eggnog. "An owl has been hooting so loud I thought it was at the window," he said, looking up at her over the rim of the glass.

"It's up in the big pine. You've been dreaming."

The fire had burned down to a few embers, which flickered out when she tried to stir them to life. A dim light from the screened lamp on the floor behind the chintz-covered chair left the bed and his uncovered face in shadow.

"Do you feel better?" she asked, as she was turning away.

"Yes, I feel better." His eyes followed her from the shadow with a glance of mute interrogation.

"I'll put this stick by your bed." She went out into the hall and came back with one of John Abner's hickory sticks. "If you want anything or feel nervous, knock on the wall. I am a light sleeper, and Mirandy is in the room off the kitchen."

She waited, but he did not answer. Had he understood her, or was he incapable of grasping the meaning of sounds? It was like the inconsistency of life, she thought, that he, who once had been so voluble, should have become almost inarticulate at the end. She

396

knew that he was trying to give as little trouble as possible, yet he seemed unable to put his wish into words.

Before going out, she made one last effort with the embers, but the wood she threw into the fireplace did not catch. When she went over to the bed again, Jason was lying with closed eyes. "He doesn't look as if he could last much longer," she thought dispassionately.

The still October days drifted by, hazy, mellow, declining into the rich light of the sunsets. With the dry weather and sufficient food after starvation, Jason appeared to improve. The old wheel-chair which had once belonged to Rose Emily was brought down from the attic, and he sat out, muffled in rugs, on bright afternoons. He liked his meals, though he never asked for them. Sometimes, after a hard spell of coughing, he would say, "How long is it before I have my eggnog?"; yet he never attempted to hasten the hour. Twice, after a severe hæmorrhage, they believed he was dying, but he recovered and was wheeled out again on the lawn. Day after day, he sat there in the sunshine, passive, silent, wrapped in a curious remoteness which was like the armour of an inscrutable reserve. Yet it was not reserve, she felt instinctively. It was something thinner, vaguer, something as impalpable as a shadow. It was, she realized suddenly one day, an emptiness of spirit. He was silent because there was nothing left in him to be uttered. He was remote because he had lost all connection with his surroundings, with events, with the material structure of living. Through the autumn days he would sit there, propped on pillows, in his wheel-chair between the half-bared lilac bushes and the "rockery," where Mrs. Oakley had planted portulaca over an old stump. His head would sink down into the rugs, and his unseeing eyes would gaze up the road to the starry fields of the life-everlasting. Behind him there was the porch and the long grey roof where swallows were wheeling. From the locust trees by the wings a rain of small yellow leaves fell slowly and steadily in the windless air, turning once as they left the stem, and drifting down to the flagged walk and the borders of sheepmint and wire-grass. His figure, bowed under the rugs, seemed to her to become merely another object in the land-scape. He was as inanimate as the fields or the trees; and yet he made the solitude more lonely and the autumn dreaminess more pensive. His features had the scarred and seared look that is left in

397

the faces of men who had fought their way out of a forest fire. Only the look that Jason wore now had passed from struggle into defeat. He appeared to be waiting, without fear and without hope, for whatever might happen. "I've seen so many people die," she thought, and then, "In fifty years many people must die."

She had come home this afternoon a little earlier than usual, and, still in riding breeches, she stood by the porch and looked down on the inert figure in the wheel-chair. Jason's eyes were open, but she could not tell whether he saw her or not. The mask of his features was as blank as if an indestructible glaze were spread over his face; and he stared straight before him, searching the road and the distant fields of life-everlasting for something that was not there. Though his helplessness was his only hold on her, she felt that it had become too poignant for her to bear. If only he would speak! If only he would complain! If only he would say what he was seeking! In the faint sunshine, beneath the ceaseless rain of leaves, he gathered a deeper meaning, a fresher significance. A glamour of sadness enveloped him. For an instant the memory of the Jason she had first known flickered over him like a vanishing ray of sunlight. As the gleam faded, she felt that he was passing with it into some unearthly medium where she could not follow. It was, she told herself, only the endless riddle of mortality, renewed again and yet again in each human being. It was the old baffling sense of a secret meaning in the universe, of a reality beneath the actuality, of a deep profounder than the deeps of experience. The reserve of even one human being was impenetrable; the reserve of every human being was impenetrable. Of what was he thinking? she wondered, and knew that she could never discover. Had he loved her in the past, or had his desire for her been merely a hunger? Would he have been faithful to her if stronger forces had not swept him away? Which was the accident, his love or his faithlessness? When it was over, had she dropped out of his life, or had she continued to exist as a permanent influence? Was he better or worse than she had believed him to be? She had never known, and now she could never know. The truth would always elude her. She could never wring his secret from this empty shell which was as unfathomable as the sea. She felt that the mystery was killing her, and she knew that it was a mystery which could never be solved.

398

She tried to ask, "How much did I mean in your life?" and found herself reciting, parrot-like, "Do you feel any pain?"

He shook his head, without looking at her. His gaze was still on the road where it dipped at the bridge and travelled upward into the dreamy distance.

"Are you ready for your eggnog?" The effort to make her voice sound light and natural brought tears to her eyes.

At last she had touched him. The quiver of appetite stole over his face, and he turned his eyes, which were dark with pain, away from the road. "Is it almost time?" This was what he lived for now, an egg with milk and whiskey every four hours.

"It must be nearly. I'll go and see." As she still lingered, the quiver on his face deepened into a look of impatience, and he repeated eagerly, "You will go and see?"

"In a minute. Has the doctor been here?"

"Nobody has been here. A few people went by in the road, but they did not stop."

"Something must have prevented the doctor. He will come to-morrow."

"It makes no difference. I am a doctor."

A thought occurred to her while she watched him. "Would you rather be at Five Oaks? It might be managed."

He shook his head. "It doesn't matter. You are good to me here. I don't know why." He broke off with a rough, grating cough which sounded like the blows of a hammer. A few minutes afterwards, when the spell of coughing was over, he repeated, so mechanically that the words seemed to reach no deeper than his lips, "I don't know why."

He had not said as much as this since she had brought him to Old Farm, and while she listened a piercing light flashed into her mind, as if a lantern had been turned without warning on a dark road. In this light, all the hidden cells of her memory were illuminated. Things she had forgotten; things she had only dimly perceived when they were present; swift impulses; unacknowledged desires; flitting impressions like the shadow of a bird on still water,—all these indefinite longings started out vividly from the penumbra of darkness. As this circle of light widened, she saw Jason as she had first seen him more than thirty years ago, on that morning in winter.

399

She saw his dark red hair, his brown-black eyes, his gay and charming smile with its indiscriminate friendliness. Time appeared to stand still at that instant. Beyond this enkindled vision there was only the fall of the locust leaves, spinning like golden coins which grew dull and tarnished as soon as they reached the ground. Then, as suddenly as it had come, the vision faded and the light flickered out. There remained this stranger, huddled beneath the rugs in the wheel-chair, and around him the melancholy stillness of the October afternoon.

"People have to be kind to each other sometimes," she answered.

His brief animation had passed. He seemed to have forgotten his words as soon as he had uttered them. The blank despair was in his eyes again as he fixed them on the empty road, searching— searching. His face, so scarred and burned out by an inner fire, wore a lost and abstracted look, as if he were listening for some sound at a distance.

"I'll bring the eggnog in a minute," she added hastily, and went into the house. She felt embarrassed by her rugged health, and by her firm and energetic figure when she contrasted it with his diminished frame. Yet her pity, she knew, could make no impression on vacancy.

As the weeks passed, she grew to look for his chair when she returned from work in the fields. There was no eagerness, no anxiety even. There was merely the wonder if she should still find him in the pale afternoon sunshine, watching the road for something that never came. If he had been absent, she would scarcely have missed him; yet, in a way, his wheel-chair made the lawn, or the fireside on wet days, more homelike. He was a poor thing, she felt, to look forward to, but at least he was dependent upon her compassion.

Then one afternoon in November, when she returned, riding her white horse through the flame and dusk of the sunset, she saw that the wheel-chair was not in its accustomed place between the porch and the "rockery." When she had dismounted at the stable door and watched the bedding down of Snowbird, she walked slowly back to the house. Even before she met Mirandy running to look for her, she knew that Jason was dead.

"He 'uz settin' out dar de hull evelin'," began Mirandy, who being old still spoke the vivid dialect of her ancestors. "He sot out

400

dar jes' lak he's done day in an' day out w'ile I wuz gittin' thoo wid de ironin'. Den w'en de time come fuh his eggnog, I beat it up jes' ez light, en tuck it out dar ter de cheer, en dar he wuz layin' back, stone daid, wid de blood all ovah de rugs en de grass. He died jes' ez quick ez ef'n he ain' nevah ketched on ter w'at wuz gwineter happen. 'Fo' de Laws, hit wa'n't my fault, Miss Dorindy. I 'uz jes' gittin' erlong thoo wid de ironin', lak you done tole me."

"No, it wasn't your fault, Mirandy. Have you telephoned for the doctor?"

"Yas'm, Fluvanna, she done phone fuh 'im right straight away. We is done laid 'im out on de baid. You'd 'low jes' ter look at 'im dat hit wuz a moughty pleasant surprise ter find out dat he wuz sholy daid."

Turning away from her, Dorinda went into the spare room, where the fire was out, and in deference to one of Aunt Mehitable's superstitions, Mirandy had draped white sheets over the furniture and the pictures. The windows were wide open. In the graveyard on the curve of the hill, she could see the great pine towering against the evening sky. A stray sheep was bleating somewhere in the meadow, and it seemed to her that the sound filled the universe.

So at last he was dead. He was dead, and she could never know whether or not he remembered. She could never know how much or how little she had meant in his life. And more tragic than the mystery that surrounded him at the end, was the fact that neither the mystery nor his end made any difference. The passion that had ruined her life thirty years ago was nothing, was less than nothing, to her to-day. She was not glad that he was dead. She was not sorry that he had died alone.

Turning back the end of the sheet, she looked down on his face. Despair had passed out of it. The scarred and burned look of his features had faded into serenity. Death had wiped out the marks of the years, and had restored, for an instant, the bright illusion of youth. He wore, as he lay there with closed eyes, an expression that was noble and generous, as if he had been arrested in some magnanimous gesture. This was what death could do to one. He had wasted his life, he had destroyed her youth; yet, in a few hours, death had thrown over him an aspect of magnanimity.

She was standing there when John Abner came in from milking

401

and joined her. "Poor devil," he said. "I suppose it's the best thing
that could have happened."

"Yes, it's the best thing."

"Is there anybody we'd better get a message to?"

"No one I can remember. He had lost all his friends."

"Has the doctor been here?"

"Not yet, but Fluvanna telephoned for him."

"Then we might as well have the funeral to-morrow. There is
no reason to postpone it. He's been dying for months."

Yes, he had been dying for months; yet, she realized now, his
death had come to her with a shock. Though the moment had been
approaching so long, she felt that it had taken her by surprise, that
she had not had sufficient time to prepare.

"Of course, it isn't as if we could be expected to feel it," John
Abner said, reasonably enough, and she repeated vacantly:

"No, of course it isn't."

11

The next afternoon, standing beneath an inclement sky in the overgrown graveyard at Five Oaks, she wondered how, even after thirty years, she could have become so insensible.

There had been rain in the night, and the weather was raw and wintry, with a savage wind which prowled at a distance in the fields and woods. Over the graveyard, where the sunken graves were almost obliterated by periwinkle, the dead leaves were piled in sodden drifts which gave like moss underfoot. The paling fence had rotted away, and white turkeys were scratching in the weeds that edged the enclosure. Dampness floated down in a grey vapour from the boughs of the trees. When the new minister opened his mouth to speak his breath clung like frost to his drooping moustache. Yet, bad as the day was, either compassion or curiosity had drawn the nearer farmers and their families to Five Oaks, and a little gathering of men and women who remembered the Greylocks in their prosperity watched the lowering of Jason's body into the earth. In the freshly ploughed field beyond, Mirandy and Fluvanna stood among an inquisitive crowd of white and coloured children.

More than thirty years ago. More than thirty years of effort and self-sacrifice—for what? Was there an unfulfilled purpose, or was it only another delusion of life? The moaning wind plunged down on the dead leaves and drove them in eddying gusts over the fields, over the road, and into the open grave. It seemed to her that the sound of the autumn wind, now rising, now sinking, now almost dying away, was sweeping her also into the grave at her feet. She had no control over her memories; she had no control over her thoughts. They stirred and scattered, as aimless, as inanimate, as the dead leaves on the ground. Memories that had outlived emotions, as empty as withered husks, were released from their hidden graves, and tossed wildly to and fro in her mind. Little things that she had forgotten. Little things that mean nothing when they happen and break the heart when they are remembered. She felt no sorrow for Jason. He was nothing to her; he had always been nothing; yet her lost youth was everything. What she mourned was not the love that she had had and lost, but the love that she had never had. Impressions drifted through her thoughts, vague, swift, meaningless, without form or substance. . . .

Out of this whirling chaos in her mind, Jason's face emerged like the face of a marionette. Then dissolving as quickly as it had formed, it reappeared as the face of Nathan, and vanished again to assume the features of Richard Burch, of Bob Ellgood, and of every man she had ever known closely or remotely in her life. They meant nothing. They had no significance, these dissolving faces; yet as thick and fast as dead leaves they whirled and danced there, disappearing and reassembling in the vacancy of her thoughts. Faces. Ghosts. Dreams. Regrets. Old vibrations that were incomplete. Unconscious impulses which had never quivered into being. All the things that she might have known and had never known in her life.

The minister's voice ceased at last. Since he had never seen Jason he had trusted, perhaps imprudently, to his imagination, and Dorinda wondered how he could have found so much to say of a life that was so empty. She bent her head in prayer, and a few minutes afterwards, she heard the thud of earth falling from the spade to the coffin. The red clay fell in lumps, dark, firm, heavy, smelling of autumn. It fell without breaking or scattering, and it fell with the sound of inevitableness, of finality. For an eternity, she heard the thuds on the coffin. Then the voice of the minister rose again in the benediction, and she watched, as in a trance, John Abner bring the two flat stones from the edge of the ploughed field and place them at the head and foot of the grave.

She turned away, and became aware presently that the clergyman had followed her and was speaking. "It is a sad occasion, Mrs. Pedlar," he said, and coughed because her blank face startled the end of his remark out of his mind. "A sad occasion," he repeated, stammering.

404

"All funerals are sad occasions," she responded, and then asked: "Will you come to the house for a cup of coffee?"

She hoped he would refuse, and he did refuse after a brief hesitation. He had a sick call to make near by, and already the day was closing in. While he held her hand he spoke with unction of her generosity. Wherever he went, he said, he heard of her good works. This, he realized, was a concrete example of her many virtues, and he reminded her hopefully that the greatest of these is charity.

Then he went off in his Ford car, and Dorinda stood where he had left her and stared after him as if she were rooted there in the damp periwinkle.

"The wind is cutting. Come away," John Abner urged, taking her arm. "Funerals are always depressing, but you did what you could." It was true. She had done what she could, and she realized that this, also, would not make any difference.

She walked away very slowly because she found that her knees were stiff when she attempted to move. It was while she was treading on the spongy earth at the edge of the ploughed field that she saw life crumble like a mountain of cinders and roll over her. She was suffocated, she was buried alive beneath an emptiness, a negation of effort, beside which the vital tragedy of her youth appeared almost happiness. Not pain, not disappointment, but the futility of all things was crushing her spirit. She knew now the passive despair of maturity which made her past suffering seem enviable to her when she looked back on it after thirty years. Youth can never know the worst, she understood, because the worst that one can know is the end of expectancy.

Smothered in this mountain of cinders, she walked to the old buggy and stepped between the wheels to the front seat. A minute later they drove past the barn where she would have killed Jason if her hand had not wavered. Past the house where she had felt her heart crouching in animal terror before the evil old man. Through the woods where the wet boughs had stung her face. Rain. Rain. The sound of rain beating into her memory. Rain on the shingled roof, pattering like the bare feet of children. Rain on the hunched box-bush and the white turkeys. Rain on the sandy road. Rain on the fork of the road, on the crushed leaves smelling of autumn.

405

Everything was before her then. There is no finality when one is young. Though they had been unendurable while she had passed through them, those years of her youth were edged now with a flame of regret. She felt that she would give all the future if she could live over the past again and live it differently. How small a thing her life appeared when she looked back on it through the narrow vista of time! It was too late now, she knew, for her youth was gone. Yet because it was too late and her youth was gone, she felt that the only thing that made life worth living was the love that she had never known and the happiness that she had missed.

When she reached the house she went to her room in silence, and sank on a couch in front of the fire as if she were sinking out of existence. Fluvanna, finding her there a little later, helped to undress her and went to tell John Abner that she was ill enough to have the doctor summoned. Hearing her from the hall, Dorinda did not take the trouble to contradict. The doctor did not matter. Illness did not matter. Nothing mattered but the things of which life had cheated her.

Lying there in the shadowy firelight of the room, she heard the wind wailing about the corners of the house and rustling in the old chimneys. She saw the crooked shape of a bough etched on the window-panes, and she listened for the soft thud of the branches beneath the sobbing violence of the storm. Though the room was bright and warm, a chill was striking through her flesh to the marrow of her bones. Shivering by the fire, she drew the blankets close to her chin.

The door opened and John Abner came in. "Can't you eat any supper, Dorinda?"

Behind him, in the glare of lamplight, she saw Fluvanna with a tray in her hands. The blue and white china and the Rebekah-at-the-well tea-pot lunged toward her.

"No, I can't eat a mouthful." Then changing her mind, she sat up on the couch and asked for tea. When they poured it out for her, she drank three cups.

"You got a chill, Dorinda. It was raw and wet out there."

"Yes, I got a chill," she replied; but it was the chill of despair she meant.

"The wind is rising. We are going to have a bad storm. I suppose I'd better go out again and take a look."

After he had gone, she lay there still shivering beneath the blankets, with her eyes on the low white ceiling, where the firelight made shimmering patterns. Outside, the wind grew louder. She heard it now at a distance, howling like a pack of wolves in the meadow. She heard it whistling round the eaves of the house and whining at the sills of the doors. All night the gusts shook the roof and the chimneys, and all night she lay there staring up at the wavering shadows of the flames.

And the youth that she had never had, the youth that might have been hers and was not, came back, in delusive mockery, to torment her. It was as if the sardonic powers of life assumed, before they vanished for ever, all the enchanting shapes of her dreams. She remembered the past, not as she had found it, but as she had once imagined that it might be. She saw Jason, not as she had seen him yesterday or last year, but as he was when she had first loved him. Though she tried to think of him as broken, ruined, and repellent, through some perversity of recollection, he returned to her in the radiance of that old summer. He returned to her young, ardent, with the glow of happiness in his eyes and the smile of his youth, that smile of mystery and pathos, on his lips. In that hour of memory the work of thirty years was nothing. Time was nothing. Reality was nothing. Success, achievement, victory over fate, all these things were nothing beside that imperishable illusion. Love was the only thing that made life desirable, and love was irrevocably lost to her.

Toward morning she fell asleep, and when she awoke at dawn the wind had lulled and a crystal light was flooding the room. Within herself also the storm was over. Life had washed over her while she slept, and she was caught again in the tide of material things. Rising from the couch, she bathed and dressed and went out of doors into the clear flame of the sunrise.

Around her the earth smelt of dawn. After the stormy night the day was breaking, crisp, fair, windless, with the frost of a mirage on the distant horizon. The trees were bare overhead. Bronze, yellow, crimson and wine-colour, the wet leaves strewed the flagged walk and the grass. Against the eastern sky the boughs of the harp-shaped pine were emblazoned in gold.

Turning slowly, she moved down the walk to the gate, where, far up the road, she could see the white fire of the life-everlasting. The storm and the hag-ridden dreams of the night were over, and the land which she had forgotten was waiting to take her back to its heart. Endurance. Fortitude. The spirit of the land was flowing into her, and her own spirit, strengthened and refreshed, was flowing out again toward life. This was the permanent self, she knew. This was what remained to her after the years had taken their bloom. She would find happiness again. Not the happiness for which she had once longed, but the serenity of mind which is above the conflict of frustrated desires. Old regrets might awaken again, but as the years went on, they would come rarely and they would grow weaker. "Put your heart in the land," old Matthew had said to her. "The land is the only thing that will stay by you." Yes, the land would stay by her. Her eyes wandered from far horizon to horizon. Again she felt the quickening of that sympathy which was deeper than all other emotions of her heart, which love had overcome only for an hour and life had been powerless to conquer in the end,—the living communion with the earth under her feet. While the soil endured, while the seasons bloomed and dropped, while the ancient, beneficent ritual of sowing and reaping moved in the fields, she knew that she could never despair of contentment.

Strange, how her courage had revived with the sun! She saw now, as she had seen in the night, that life is never what one dreamed, that it is seldom what one desired; yet for the vital spirit and the eager mind, the future will always hold the search for buried treasure and the possibilities of high adventure. Though in a measure destiny had defeated her, for it had given her none of the gifts she had asked of it, still her failure was one of those defeats, she realized, which are victories. At middle age, she faced the future without romantic glamour, but she faced it with integrity of vision. The best of life, she told herself with clear-eyed wisdom, was ahead of her. She saw other autumns like this one, hazy, bountiful in harvests, mellowing through the blue sheen of air into the red afterglow of winter; she saw the coral-tinted buds of the spring opening into the profusion of summer; and she saw the rim of the harvest moon shining orange-yellow through the boughs of the harp-shaped pine. Though she remembered the time when loveliness was like a sword in her heart, she knew now that where beauty exists the understanding soul can never remain desolate.

A call came from the house, and turning at the gate, she went back to meet John Abner, who was limping toward her over the dead leaves in the walk. His long black shadow ran ahead of him, and while he approached her, he looked as if he were pursuing some transparent image of himself.

"You are yourself again," he said, as he reached her. "Last night I was disturbed about you. I was afraid you'd got a bad chill."

"It went in the night. The storm wore on my nerves, but it was over by morning." Then before he could reply, she added impulsively, "Bear with my fancies now, John Abner. When I am gone, both farms will be yours."

"Mine?" John Abner laughed as he looked at her. "Why, you may marry again. They are saying at Pedlar's Mill that you may have Bob Ellgood for the lifting of a finger."

Dorinda smiled, and her smile was pensive, ironic, and infinitely wise. "Oh, I've finished with all that," she rejoined. "I am thankful to have finished with all that."

American Century Series

GENERAL EDITOR, LOUIS M. HACKER

Dean of General Studies, Columbia University

Published by

 SAGAMORE PRESS INC.

50 Rockefeller Plaza, New York 20, N. Y.